The European Union and Southeastern Europe

Troubled Waters Ahead?

P.I.E. Peter Lang

Bruxelles · Bern · Berlin · Frankfurt am Main · New York · Oxford · Wien

András INOTAI

The European Union and Southeastern Europe

Troubled Waters Ahead?

"College of Europe Studies"
No. 7

The author gratefully acknowledge the financial support by
Friedrich Ebert Foundation (Budapest)
and the College of Europe (Bruges)

1 avenue Maurice, B-1050 Brussels, Belgium
www.peterlang.com; info@peterlang.com

ISSN 1780-9665
ISBN 978-90-5201-071-7
D/2007/5678/40

Bibliographic information published by "Die Deutsche Bibliothek"
"Die Deutsche Bibliothek" lists this publication in the "Deutsche Nationalbibliografie"; detailed bibliographic data is available on the Internet at <http://dnb.ddb.de>.

Contents

List of Tables

Introduction

At the end of 2005 relations between the European Union (EU) and Southeastern Europe (SEE) reached a turning point, marking 2006-2007 as a critical period of development. Previous conceptions of politics in this region must be reconciled with an assessment of the current situation, as new challenges will have a decisive impact. They will influence the future of Southeastern Europe as well as the future of European integration, a point that has not been stressed in previous studies.

The new situation requires new analytical approaches and an updated strategy in order to incorporate the following developments:

- The enlargement of the EU to Central and Eastern Europe in 2004 has generated an ambiguous situation in SEE. On the one hand, it obviously increased the benign pressure on all countries to speed up their internal reforms and adjust to EU norms in order to become members of the enlarged and further expanding Union in the foreseeable future. On the other hand, it has made clear that the region is lagging behind. This could have the effect of increasing the level of disappointment, or at least the indifference, in some parts of society, meaning that the catching up process may be delayed substantially or even rendered impossible. In any event, it will certainly be painful and costly.
- The 2007 EU membership of Bulgaria and Romania (two countries generally considered as the most successful in the region) as well as accession negotiations with Croatia are likely to deepen divisions within the region. Certainly, the already substantial economic gap may widen further, at least for the short- to medium-term. Moreover, some countries (and failed states) fear that they may be excluded from European integration.
- Parallel to the aforementioned developments, the strategy of the gradual enlargement of the EU, based on clear principles and conditionalities, is at a decisive stage. The Western Balkans seems to have reached a breaking point despite its apparent stabilization. Although immediate security risks are not high, conflicts remain that have been artificially hidden in recent years. These latent pressures could easily transform into real security dangers. A number of problems that were swept under the carpet by international agree-

ments during emergency situations did not disappear, nor could they be "absorbed" by imposed political solutions.

- 2006 was a year of far-ranging political decisions for the region. First, there was the May 21 referendum on the future status of the union between Serbia and Montenegro, which resulted in the independence of Montenegro. Second, negotiations began in February on the future status of Kosovo. Much more significant than the consequences of Montenegro's independence, Kosovo's future status will have a crucial though highly uncertain impact on all countries involved in the process. Third, Bosnia-Herzegovina had to come to a new constitutional arrangement with a much more stability-anchored framework, thus replacing the outdated Dayton constitution based on an immediate cease-fire. In contrast to these factors, the October decision on the date of accession of Bulgaria and Romania to the EU, a fundamentally important issue for both countries, seems to be a "minor" element. It was, however, extremely important both for domestic stability and as a clear message to the entire region.
- At this critical turning point in history, the EU has to deal with a large number of equally important issues, among them addressing the challenge of globalization, identifying community-level priorities, and encouraging state-level reforms. The global role of European integration is certainly dependent on what will happen in SEE, considered by many politicians as the real "backyard" of Europe. However, nobody would argue that greater competitiveness, the more effective use of resources, or the simplification and speeding up of the decision-making process are less important issues in shaping the future of the EU. Consequently, numerous relevant factors have to be taken into account once a coherent strategy is designed for SEE in general and for the Western Balkans in particular.
- Finally, the Balkans is not only a part of Europe, but also an important region in terms of global politics. Far beyond European efforts, the future of this region will be influenced by the attitude and basic strategic interests of the United States, which used to have a crucial stake in shaping the short-term security framework in this war-ridden and ethnically hostile part of Europe during the late 1990s. As a melting pot of "cultural globalization", forward-looking European approaches have to consider the growing influence of other players with different traditions, values and religions as well.

This study, commissioned by the Budapest Office of the Friedrich-Ebert-Foundation, is based on several background documents. In 2005 the

Institute for World Economics prepared a paper dealing with the current economic issues of the countries belonging to the SEE region, with special attention to their institutionalized relationship with the EU. As a continuation of this study, the current monograph, while making use of several findings of the previous study, started from another position. In order to assess the effectiveness of the current EU approaches to the region and to call attention to potentially critical developments in the future, it focused on those issues that are of strategic importance in the short or medium-term. Thus, more or less uniformly structured studies on seven countries (including Albania, Bosnia-Herzegovina, Bulgaria, Croatia, Macedonia, Romania and Serbia-Montenegro) have been prepared using a specially developed "questionnaire". The current document makes extensive use of the main findings of these country studies. The authors of the respective country surveys have been included in the literature review. In addition, the most recent international scholarly literature was consulted, as well as information available on the Internet. Also, basic materials from the European Commission and the Stability Pact were included, in particular the latter as the author of this study had the honour to be co-chairman of the Working Table 2 (on economic, trade, energy and infrastructure issues) of the Stability Pact in 2004 and 2005.

Although it has a clear economic focus, this study has an interdisciplinary character. Most of the developments in the SEE region cannot be understood just by using an exclusively economic approach. Moreover, all policy analyses and recommendations have to take into account the non-economic preconditions, realities and consequences of economic decisions.

Due to its nature, the study has several other specific features. First, it is strategy-oriented, due both to the nature of the discussed topics and to the necessity of a long-term and sustainable policy framework to be elaborated by the EU in cooperation with the respective countries. Second, following from the previous feature, its future-orientedness has to be underlined. Although a description of both the traditions and the current situation received substantial coverage in the study, the general analytic framework is clearly directed towards the future of the region in general and future EU policies in particular. This approach explains why such a large number of potentially critical issues have been included in the survey. These range from matters dealing with regional cooperation in migration to ethnic issues. Furthermore, the longer-term impact of the war will be considered, in addition to the (forceful) adjustment to EU norms. Third, its critical character has to be stressed, since most developments in the area are subject to an in-depth survey containing several points of investigation. Included in this method are, of course, EU policies towards the SEE region in general, and towards individual countries in particular. Fourth, the study is placed in a comparative context. Indeed, individual countries of the region are compared on several levels, as the predominant EU approach follows the same benchmark method. In addition, in some issues other levels of comparison of the SEE with Central and Eastern Europe seemed to be appropriate, both in the context of socio-economic transformation and preparations for and expectations of EU membership. The fifth and final point is that the analysis takes into account the global framework for SEE: it is not only a geographic area of Europe or an institutionally linked region to the EU (albeit on qualitatively different levels), but it is also part of the global balance of power, particularly in regards to international terrorism and crime. Moreover, it represents a very special and, in the European context, probably the most specific "melting pot" of different values, religions, mentalities and ways of life.

This study is structured as follows. Chapter I describes and analyzes the development and the current state of the EU's official relations with the individual SEE countries in a comparative context. Chapter II focuses on the economic development of the respective Balkan countries, based on their macroeconomic performance, economic legislation, and the main factors that may affect the sustainability of positive trends in the years to come. Key development issues with a substantial impact on EU policy-making, be they of an economic, social, or mentality-related nature, are addressed in Chapter III. Chapter IV deals with non-EU international actors (both small and large) that have qualitative influence on the future of the region and, as a result, also on the future of the EU's policies towards the Balkans. In light of current developments, a fundamental and critical analysis will be offered in Chapter V on the overall experience of the SEE countries regarding their adjustment to the EU norms and conditionalities, not only in economic and institutional terms but also in social and mental terms. Chapter VI offers a sweeping evaluation of EU policies, dilemmas and emerging goals, including the impact of developments in the geographic map of the Western Balkans on the future of European integration. On this complex basis, policy recommendations will be formulated. Chapter VII contains fundamental conclusions.

The study contains a relatively large number of tables. Most have been incorporated into the basic document, while others have been placed in the Appendix section (additional statistical tables, graphs and maps).

Work on the present study started in late 2005 and early 2006. Before the final draft was concluded, several new developments in the SEE region needed to be taken into account. They include the accession preparations for the EU membership of Bulgaria and Romania, the ongoing negotiations with Croatia, negotiations on SAA with other Western

Balkan countries, the independence of Montenegro, negotiations on the future status of Kosovo, and the planned institutional pattern to be applied in Bosnia-Herzegovina in 2007. The assessment of the adjustment process of the region and the evaluation of chances and risks of the further enlargement of the EU towards SEE in general, and towards the Western Balkans in particular, have been based on a detailed analysis of all known factors and anticipated developments.

* * * * *

Hereby, the author would like to thank colleagues at the Institute for World Economics, Budapest and the Economic Policy Institute, Sofia for their continuous and valuable support, not only by writing the respective country studies but also by providing additional information on specific topics. Needless to say, the author of the final study is fully responsible for the contents, analysis, findings and policy recommendations, as well as the structure of the document. Also the support given by the Library and the technical staff of the Institute for World Economics is appreciated. Last but not least, and on behalf of the entire research team, the author would like to thank the Friedrich Ebert Foundation and the College of Europe, Bruges, for the financial support of the study.

CHAPTER I

Institutional Relations between the EU and Southeastern Europe

I.1. Short Historical Overview

I.1.1. Brussels' institutionalized relations with Southeastern Europe (excluding Albania) date back to the mid-1970s and were a natural consequence of transferring trade policy competences from member states to the community level. Two parallel approaches were used. On the one hand, as an autonomous measure, Bulgaria and Romania were considered as less developed countries and became incorporated into Brussels' General System of Preferences (GSP) framework that promised to offer better market access to commodities exported by countries belonging to this system. On the other hand, Brussels offered trade agreements to all Central and Southeastern European countries that should have replaced previous member-country level bilateral agreements, in exchange for establishing diplomatic relations with the European Economic Community (EEC). This way, however, remained closed for all members of the "socialist integration" (CMEA or Comecon), due to a fear of serious and very negative repercussions in their relations with the dominant military, political, ideological and economic power of the region: the Soviet Union. The only country that could make use of this offer was, in fact, Yugoslavia that had a relatively large room to manoeuver due to its independent status in military and external political terms. Evidently, the contents of the trade agreement at that time[1] cannot be compared to the association agreements offered after 1990 and widely used by all countries of the region. Even less, there were neither direct nor indirect linkages with eventual future membership.

---

1 The agreement did not foresee free trade but just gradual liberalization in a ten-year period. Important export products qualified as sensitive (textiles, clothing, iron and steel and, most importantly, agricultural goods) were excluded from the liberalization scheme. Limited financial assistance was agreed on and access to favourable credits of the European Investment Bank (EIB) was opened. Also, the status of Yugoslav guest workers in the EU was regulated. In turn, the agreement did not contain any sections on institutionalised flow of Yugoslav guest workers to Western Europe in the future.

In 1980, and certainly not independent from the death of Tito and the concerns about emerging uncertainties related to the future of Yugoslavia, Brussels has upgraded the previous document to a trade and cooperation agreement. The really surprising element was not the contents (in fact, it did not differ substantially from the previous pact), but the speed at which the new document was prepared and signed, after several years of failed Yugoslav efforts to upgrade relations. From the very beginning of the Western European integration, but particularly following the transfer of previous nation-state competences to Brussels, trade policy has constantly been used as one, and probably the most important, policy instrument of the EU to influence external developments in general, and the domestic politics and attitudes of selected countries, in particular. Somewhat better terms of economic cooperation were offered in the hope that the EU might be helpful in contributing to the sustainability of peace and order in a Yugoslavia already showing the first signs of disintegration in the 1980s.

Another country that could sign a trade agreement in 1980 was Romania. This step, being part of Ceausescu's "independent" foreign policy was considered in Brussels as a breakthrough in the integration's relations with Central and Eastern Europe. However, it had not been followed by any other country, and the agreement largely failed to fulfil Brussels' expectations. Romania, eager to eliminate its high foreign debt within a few years and irrespective of the huge damage to the domestic economic development and the society, created an artificial trade surplus stemming from forced exports and heavy restrictions on imports. In addition, Ceausescu's domestic policies, the oppression of any economic or social initiative, the unprecedented personal cult developed by and around the "conducatur", as well as the organized and state-level management of "human trafficking", *i.e.*, the selling of Germans living in Romania for money to the Federal Republic of Germany, have created growing distaste and disappointment in Brussels and the EU's national capitals. As a result, the agreement was suspended by Brussels.

I.1.2. Yugoslavia's special institutionalized relations with the EU were rapidly undermined in the late 1980s and early 1990s by three developments. First: in the summer of 1988, Brussels and Moscow were finally able to sign a joint declaration on mutual diplomatic recognition (the so-called Luxembourg declaration), which immediately opened the way to bilateral trade, and a year later, to trade and cooperation agreements between Brussels and the individual Central and Eastern European countries. In about three years' time all countries of the region have reached the same level of institutional relations with the EU that, for almost two decades, used to be the privilege of Yugoslavia.[2] Second: the unprecedented systemic change in Central and Eastern Europe has eliminated Yugoslavia's "special status" practically within a few months. Even more, the lack of such developments in Yugoslavia has suddenly put the "Western Balkans" into a dispreferred status. Third: the disintegration of Yugoslavia, parallel to the first and promising signs of political and democratic consolidation in Central Europe (Czechoslovakia, Hungary and Poland), has created a completely new situation in which the main politics-driven (conditionality-based) objective and key elements of traditional trade policy became completely useless. If the European Union was not prepared for the systemic change in Central and Eastern Europe, it was even less equipped to provide strategic answer(s) to the unprecedented developments in former Yugoslavia. The disintegration of the federal state into independent republics immediately generated nation-state and not community-level answers and soon led to the diplomatic recognition of such sovereign states as Slovenia and Croatia.[3]

I.1.3. While EU diplomacy became paralyzed in the Western Balkans (excluding Slovenia) for several years, substantial upgrading of relations with Central and Eastern Europe started from the early stage of transformation. Between 1991 and 1995, association agreements were signed with all countries and the prospect of full membership became a realistic objective after the Madrid summit of the European Council in December 1995. Based on the recommendations of the Commission in its first truly strategic paper on enlargement (Agenda 2000) that was published in 1997, official negotiations on membership were proposed with five Central and Eastern European countries (plus Cyprus). This group, consisting of Estonia, Poland, the Czech Republic, Hungary and Slovenia has already included one previous republic of Yugoslavia. In the second step, in December 1999, the way to start similar negotiations became opened for another six countries, including Bulgaria and Romania. The latest in this new geographic and political situation, a strategy towards the "Western Balkans" became inevitable. First, Southeastern Europe was already split into different categories of countries, with Slovenia already making progress in negotiations, with Bulgaria and Romania at the starting point of official talks on accession and the remaining new or artificially created states without any meaningful relations to the EU. Second, the wars among various ex-Yugoslav countries were ended with substantial international intermediation and,

2 And of the German Democratic Republic due to the special character of intra-German trade from the very date of signing the Rome Treaty in 1957.

3 According to some observers, the "premature" recognition of Croatia by Germany has contributed to the open hostilities and real war between Croatia and Serbia.

no less importantly, with NATO's military intervention against Serbia. The EU was challenged by several high priority issues: how to create sustainable stability in the region; how to support democratic development and, in most cases, nation-building in the new countries; and how and at what level to include the Western Balkans (Croatia, Serbia-Montenegro, Bosnia-Herzegovina, Macedonia, Kosovo and also Albania) into the institutionalized framework of European integration. Moreover, Brussels had to define its role and identify the key strategic elements of its "regional" approach in the context of international players, since a number of actors, led by the United States and the United Nations on the political level and by international financial institutions (led by The World Bank and the IMF) on the economic level, were already present in the post-war (and pre-reconstruction) period in the Western Balkans.

This task became ever more urgent due to the open contradiction between the decisive economic role of the EU in the region and its low-profile political presence. Before the dramatic events, the EU was the most important trading partner of Yugoslavia. In addition, a large number of joint ventures had been established and inter-firm links were well developed (particularly with small- and medium-sized companies in Slovenia, but also in Croatia and in Serbia). Several hundred thousand Yugoslav citizens were employed in Western Europe, an important source for economic and social modernization both through remittances of part of their income earned and through bringing back to their home country technological and managerial skills, business practices and social values. No less importantly, Yugoslavia enjoyed high popularity as a country of international tourism, particularly in the summer period along the Adriatic coast. Finally, over a long period, the country pursued a much more relaxed (open) cultural policy than all other Soviet-dominated countries of Central and Eastern Europe. Even though all contacts with the EU and its member countries heavily suffered in the war-ridden 1990s, the basic pattern of economic relations ("dependence") did not change. On the contrary, as a result of the economic transformation, by the beginning of official accession negotiations, Bulgaria and Romania were also turning to the EU as their principal trading partner.

A large part of the total population of about 55 million of the analyzed region had been closely connected with the EU. EU countries are not only natural destinations of their export trade (in the case of the Western Balkans certainly dramatically shrunk) and not less natural origin of their imports. During and after the hostilities and military operations, Western Europe proved to be the primary region attracting and hosting migrants and refugees. Financial integration includes substantial EU transfers, personal remittances and some foreign direct investments (the latter much more directed to Bulgaria and Romania than to the Western Balkans). Moreover, several Balkan countries use the euro either as their own national currency or as a parallel currency, or as the anchor currency of monetary stabilization and a relevant instrument for confidence-building in the international business community. Finally, high potentials can be identified in various service sectors (mainly in tourism) and in the upgrading of the transit role this region used to play for decades in the flow of commodities (and people) between Western Europe and the Middle East (mainly Turkey). One can add that the EU had been present for decades in the Balkans, since Greece had become a full-fledged member of the Community in 1981, a quarter century ago.

However, strong economic and financial "dependence" on the EU does not automatically mean the sharing of the same political and social values (Gligorov, 2002). According to international experience, economic integration can, but will not necessarily, lead to higher levels of convergence in non-economic fields. Sometimes there is a time lag only between economic and socio-political convergence. In turn, in other cases such a convergence does not take place at all, or, even worse, economic integration itself may lead to unsustainable conditions. Therefore, the basic dilemmas of an adequate EU strategy towards the region have to be complemented by the above considerations as well.

I.2. The New Institutional Framework

The EU approved its "regional approach" in order to redesign its relationships with all SEE countries constituting the former Yugoslavia in 1996. The background to this decision was the lifting of UN Security Council sanctions originating from the Dayton peace agreement. Dayton was designed to end a war, but not to build a sustainable new stability framework, either on the regional or the nation-state levels. This "deficiency" was clear to EU policy makers from the very beginning. However, in order to launch a new and target-oriented approach, more barriers had to be eliminated. Therefore, a year later, in April 1997, the General Affairs Council of the EU underlined that full cooperation with the International Criminal Tribunal[4] for the former Yugoslavia was an

[4] The International Criminal Tribunal for the former Yugoslavia (ICTY) was established by Security Council resolution 827. It was passed in May 1993 in the face of grave violations of international humanitarian law that had been committed on the territory of the former Yugoslavia since 1991. The ICTY's mission includes four objectives: (a) to bring to justice persons allegedly responsible for serious violations of humanitarian law, (b) to render justice to the victims, (c) to deter further crimes, and

integral part of the EU's conditionality for Western Balkan countries. A comprehensive strategic approach was prepared only in 1999, after ending the war in Kosovo and NATO's military activities.

The key role is played by the European Commission in implementing EU policy towards the countries of SEE. In this context, its main tasks are the following:

- contributing to the design of EU policy toward the region,
- implementing EU assistance for the region,
- developing assessment reports for the EU member states on progress made by each country of SEE towards EU integration, and
- negotiating contractual agreements on behalf of the EU.

The Bulgarian and Romanian road to EU membership was paved by association agreements similar to those signed with the new member states during the 1990s. Following the successful termination of negotiations in late 2004, both countries could sign the Accession Treaty in April 2005, with membership scheduled for 2007.

All other SEE countries (Albania, Bosnia-Herzegovina, Croatia, Macedonia,[5] Romania and Serbia-Montenegro, as well as Kosovo under UNMIK control for the time being) had to follow a different path, with more stages and a larger number of conditionalities towards potential membership in a not clearly defined future. The situation has not been made more transparent by different international controls in some parts of the Western Balkans and by overlapping international and EU-managed programmes. Concerning the first, Bosnia-Herzegovina is "managed" by EU authorities, while the control over Kosovo is maintained by the United Nations (UNMIK) and NATO (Kfor). As regards the second issue, in 1999, following the Kosovo war, the international community formulated its strategic instruments, principles and objectives for the Western Balkan region. The five key issues comprise regionality, conditionality, separation of agendas, the European perspective and "standards before status". Out of the five topics, one, regionality, became the fundamental objective of the Stability Pact created in 1999 as a result of international cooperation mainly between the EU, the leading industrial countries (G-8), the OECD (and its member countries), and international financial institutions.

(d) to contribute to the restoration of peace by promoting reconciliation among people and states on the territory of former Yugoslavia (Amato, 2005).

5 In the EU's political vocabulary, the official name of the country is (still) Former Yugoslav Republic of Macedonia (FYROM). In turn, in 2004, the United States acknowledged "Macedonia" as the official name of the country. Following the growing trend in professional literature and international practice, this study will use the term "Macedonia".

Parallel with the Stability Pact, and to a large extent overtaking the other objectives, a genuine EU programme was announced at the same time, essentially based on the criteria of conditionality and European perspective. This itinerary starts with the Stabilization and Association Process (SAP) and may lead to a Stabilization and Association Agreement (SAA) and to the application for membership and the starting of accession negotiations. In 2003, the European Council held in Thessaloniki decided to offer membership perspective to all Western Balkan countries provided they fulfil the necessary preconditions for accession.

I.2.1. Stabilization and Association Process

Originally perceived as a fundamental element of the EU's Common Foreign and Security Policy, through which the EU can finally start playing a qualitatively different political role at least in crisis-ridden parts of the continent, the SAP was officially inaugurated in November 2000 in Zagreb. In fact, it became an instrument to implement EU policies in the Western Balkans in order to support the region's stabilization and economic recovery. Three basic instruments were developed: (a) bilateral preferential trade regimes in the form of automatic trade measures, (b) the CARDS financial programme to fund selected projects, and (c) the signing of Stabilization and Association Agreements after meeting different conditions. Two special features have to be underlined. First and mainly due to the growing pressure of the Western Balkan countries, the EU had to link this approach to potential membership already in 2000, at the summit of the European Council in Feira, Portugal.[6] Second, a number of partly old, partly new conditions (or eligibility criteria) concerning "European values, principles and standards" have been introduced on the way from SAP to SAA, such as respect for international law, the rule of law, democratic principles, human and minority rights, the establishment of a free market economy, regional cooperation, etc. In the framework of the SAP, the contracting parties commit themselves to formal association with the EU within a certain transitional period, including gradual trade liberalization leading to free trade and implementing convenient reforms in order to incorporate EU standards into their national legislation.

Although this policy instrument is in operation, its functioning cannot be qualified as perfect, particularly if we try to measure its performance with expectations and fears on both sides. On the EU side, the rather traditional approach prevailed that, based on the successful domestic adjustment and pre-accession process experienced in the new

---

[6] Most of the experts include this element in 2003 only, when the Thessaloniki summit explicitly offered the "European perspective" to SAP countries.

member states, this "success story" can be repeated in the Western Balkans. In several cases, basic differences have not been taken into account or were believed to be irrelevant on the way to European integration (even without a clear road map and a date). This "deficiency" appeared as a concern on the side of the Western Balkan countries. However, there were two more immediate concerns based on practical experience. First, the regional context of the EU approach could hardly be implemented, since the SAP turned out more an instrument of differentiation than of "homogenization". It was clear from the very beginning of the process that some countries would be able to adjust more rapidly or would face a lower number and quality of conditionalities. This would definitely split the region into countries with different speeds and sometimes with ungainly competition. Also, some countries did not observe the general rules of not applying for membership before a certain institutional level had been reached. The situation became even worse when the EU itself ignored some of the own rules that were previously set and considered the overall guiding principles of the Balkan adjustment process. Moreover, unclear or too pliant EU principles have increased doubts about the objectivity of some reports and assessments published by EU organs. Second, the "European perspective" in the indefinite future could not convince the countries that the SAP would be the direct way to membership. More and more conditionalities and technical stages within the implementation process were rightly feared and some of them already became manifest. Regular reports, the necessity of feasibility studies, delays in the negotiation process, renewed approvals to enter a new period of institutionalized relations on the EU side intensified such concerns.

In effect, the SAP has the following stages: (a) pre-negotiation period, (b) starting of bilateral negotiations with an agenda of clear conditionalities to be fulfilled before finishing the given stage, (c) feasibility study consisting of two actions, namely commissioning the study (mandate given by the European Commission) and publishing its results after finishing the evaluation, with a substantial time gap (calculated in years and not in months) between the two actions, and not automatically with a positive conclusion, (d) in case of positive assessment, negotiations on SAA, (e) the signing of SAA, (f) the ratification process of SAA, (g) putting the SAA into force symbolizing a higher level relationship but still far away from membership and with no explicit qualification to start accession negotiations (again, in the undetermined future).

Table I.1
Status of institutionalized relations between the EU and the Western Balkan countries, with respect to the road from SAP to SAA

Country	Status	Date
Albania	SAP negotiations SAA negotiations ended SAA signed	January 31, 2003 February 18, 2006 June 12, 2006
Bosnia-Herzegovina	Feasibility study approved SAA negotiations started SAA to be signed (pending on policy reform)	November 18, 2003 November 21, 2005 2007?
Croatia	SAA signed SAA ratified SAA in force	September 07, 2001 December 10, 2004 February 01, 2005
Macedonia	SAA ratified SAA in force	January 12, 2004 April 01, 2004
Serbia	SAA negotiations relaunched	June 13, 2007
Montenegro	SAA negotiations started Technical part of SAA completed SAA initialled	September 26, 2006 December 01, 2006 March 15, 2007
Kosovo	Not part of the negotiation process	-----

(a) after secession from Serbia in May 2006, SAA negotiations based on Montenegro's new status have been initiated.

Source: Frattini (2005), Altmann (2005), Novák (2005), Commission country reports in 2006 and press information.

Measured against this agenda, the current situation is the following. Five countries have started the SAP negotiations, while Kosovo, due to its special status until now, was not involved into this process. However, it also benefits from various instruments of the SAP, such as financial assistance through the CARDS programme or trade concessions. Out of the five SAP countries, three of them could conclude the process and sign SAA: Croatia, Macedonia and most recently, and at the surprise of many observers, Albania.[7] After a protracted and repeatedly extended period of SAP-level talks,[8] Serbia-Montenegro could open negotiations

7 The conclusion of negotiations on SAA in February 2006 and the signing of the respective documents in June 2006 was surprising, for Albania did not demonstrate the necessary determination in addressing and implementing the priority issues identified by the EU in various monitoring reports (such as electoral reform, the war against organized crime and corruption).

8 The feasibility study should have been started already in the autumn of 2003. However, with reference to lacking cooperation of Serbia-Montenegro with the ICTY

on an SAA in early November 2005. Two weeks later, the Council provided the Commission with the mandate to negotiate SAA with Bosnia-Herzegovina, as well. Negotiations with Belgrade were frozen in early May 2006, due to the non-identification and non-delivery of the war criminal Ratko Mladic to the Hague tribunal. After more than one year, still without delivering Mladic, SAA negotiations were resumed, certainly not independent from the unfolding settlement of the status of Kosovo and the well-known hard position of Belgrade on this issue. Negotiations with Bosnia-Herzegovina, believed to be finished before the end of 2006 are still pending, due to the lack of necessary police reforms. Following independence, Montenegro started SAA negotiations in the autumn of 2006 and could make substantial progress within a half year. However, the SAA status could not yet be reached. (For a summary see Table I.1.)

There are some conclusions to be drawn both from developments in the last years and the current situation. First, the EU-driven process indicates not only different levels of the negotiation procedure but also the different time period required of each country to proceed from one sub-stage to another sub-stage. Second, initial (inherited) advantages or disadvantages could not always be considered as lasting features, so that there is room for differentiation (or harmonization) within the timeframe of the rather complicated multi-stage process. Third, EU policies tried to acknowledge some progress in all cases, provided the basic political conditions were considered fulfilled. Although negotiations have been carried out on the bilateral level, the regional impact of further institutional progress has always been carefully assessed in order to avoid too big disruptions produced by the EU. Fourth, despite this EU effort, Western Balkan countries experienced big disruptions due to their individual efforts, partly based on different levels of adjustment to the EU, but also based on specific (and not always objective) criteria, including their geopolitical situation, strategic importance, subjective attitudes, etc. Finally, and probably most importantly, EU positions expressed in the upgrading of bilateral institutional relations have always taken into account the evolving political agenda and its potential impact on the stability of the region. Even if nobody is ready to make an official statement on the issue, the recent upgrading of almost all countries in late 2005 and early 2006 (starting accession negotiations with Croatia, the Commission's proposal to grant candidate status to Macedonia, which means that official negotiations on accession may start in the near future, SAA with Albania, the already mentioned advances registered in

in The Hague, the process remained frozen for almost a year. The feasibility study got green light in September 2004 and was finished in April 2005 – with a positive conclusion (Reuter, 2005b).

the case of Serbia-Montenegro and Bosnia-Herzegovina) has to be seen in the general and dynamic context of the anticipated and foreseeable, however largely incalculable, developments in the Balkans. In this light, the membership of Bulgaria and Romania and, more importantly, possible geographic and geopolitical changes in the Western Balkans can be mentioned (the approaching and unavoidable decisions on the future of the state union between Serbia and Montenegro, as well as the future status of Kosovo or the evolving new system in Bosnia-Herzegovina).

I.2.2. Stabilization and Association Agreements (SAA)

This is a higher stage of institutionalized cooperation between the EU and the Western Balkan countries and is based on the successful fulfilment of the SAP conditions. The latter mainly include political issues and basic elements of establishing a democratic system, as a precondition of working and sustainable relations with the EU. According to Brussels, the SAA, to a large extent following the construction of the traditional association agreements (Europe agreements) with Central and Eastern European countries almost 15 years ago, can only promise success, if the SAP-related political preconditions have been met.

While the SAA is rather similar to the Europe Agreements, it contains some additional elements. First, unlike the Europe Agreements signed with Poland, Czechoslovakia and Hungary in December 1991,[9] it contains the EU's commitment to future membership. Thus, a linkage has been created between association and full membership, even if the terms are not clarified. There is no reference in the contract as to what is the exact relationship between association, implementation of the SAA and the possibility of membership. Both the timeframe (roadmap) and the fulfilment of additional criteria remain unclear, and the situation is best characterized by labelling SAA countries as "potential candidates" (and not candidates, as it happened in the case of CEE countries, Michalopoulos, 2001). Second, regional cooperation, including the signing and implementation of bilateral free trade agreements became a precondition for successful enforcement of the SAA. This formed part of the Europe Agreements as well, but has not been included into the well-known Copenhagen criteria Central and Eastern European countries had to cope with in the pre-accession period. Third, and a less helpful instrument, trade concessions granted by the EU are restrictive concerning the rules of origin which definitely limits the scope of exports on the one hand, and the potential of regional cooperation, on

---

9 As a unilateral approach, these countries added their own view to the preamble of the Europe Agreements, according to which they (but not Brussels) considered the agreement as a stepping stone towards later full membership.

the other. Once all bilateral free trade agreements in the region are in place, the regional cumulation may become the rule replacing the current framework.

In all other aspects, the SAA seems to be a copy of the Europe Agreements. Its main elements, taken from the bilateral SAA with Croatia, are:

- It is an agreement of two parts. Trade policy and other community level issues are in the competence of the EU (with ratification by the European Parliament), while other chapters of the SAA have to be ratified by each of the member countries. The two-track approach makes it possible that vital trade instruments enter into force relatively soon, while the ratification process of the full-fledged agreement may require (much) more time.
- Political dialogue determined by the Council for Stabilization and Association. Its competences comprise all questions that the contracting parties want to discuss.
- Development of economic and trade relations with the aim of creating a free trade area as a result of asymmetric trade liberalization. The EU dismantles trade barriers quicker than the associated countries and abolishes all quantitative restrictions at the moment of signing the agreement, with the exception of some agricultural products. Generally, the liberalization process on the EU side takes 2 to 5 years, while Croatia has to abolish all trade barriers within a period of 6 years, and Macedonia in 10 years.
- Regulation of the flow of manpower, services, capital and the establishment of business according to the *acquis communautaire*. Workers who are citizens of the associated country and are already employed in the EU enjoy non-discrimination in all aspects of labour law and social benefits. Also, their spouses or children are allowed to work as long as the contract for the given person is valid. EU citizens will have the same rights in the Western Balkan countries. Both sides grant national treatment for the establishment of enterprises, except for some activities (*e.g.*, transportation). The associated country is permitted to protect some of its activities during a three-year period in case of "serious difficulties". Transborder services have to be liberalized as a result of a four-year gradual process. Within this period, the associated country has to incorporate EU rules in its national legislation.
- Harmonization of legislation, implementation of competition rules.
- Judiciary and home affairs: special attention is devoted to the independence of the courts and the improvement of their efficiency as well as the education of lawyers. Another part of this chapter deals with problems concerning the movement of people, visa require-

ments, border control, prevention of illegal migration and re-admission of illegal immigrants residing in another country. In this context, the EU will provide technical and administrative assistance.

- Financial cooperation within the CARDS programme (more in detail later in this chapter).
- The core element of the institutional framework aimed at supervising the SAA is the Council for Stabilization and Association, a joint institution composed of the EU Council and the governments of the associated country. The Council is assisted in its work by a Committee on Stabilization and Association, also composed of representatives of the EU, the European Commission and the associated country. Finally, a Parliamentary Committee for Stabilization and Association serves as a forum for meetings between European parliamentarians and their counterparts in the associated country.

I.2.3. Beyond the SAA

The SAA is generally considered as the gateway towards full membership. As the practice of the new member states shows, the entering into force of the full-fledged Europe agreement was immediately used by individual countries to submit their application for membership in Brussels. A few weeks after the date the Europe agreement was in place, in the spring of 1994 Hungary[10] and Poland applied for membership. The first Western Balkan country having SAA was Macedonia. Although the document entered into force only in April 2004, the official application arrived in Brussels already one month earlier. Croatia was even more "audacious" when it submitted its application request already in February 2003, or two years (!) before the SAA started to operate and even one year before it was ratified.

The official request for membership is followed by the "avis", or a detailed questionnaire prepared by the European Commission on all areas of political, economic and social activities of the country, with special regard to the respective community-level policies and other accession criteria (*e.g.* the "enhanced" Copenhagen patterns). This process may last a year or more, ending with the recommendation of the Commission to the Council whether or not to start accession negotiations. In the case of Croatia, the Commission published its positive assessment in April 2004 (still almost a year before the already ratified SAA came into force), while the equally positive answer on Macedonia was obtained only in November 2005.

---

[10] This step was also motivated by domestic political reasons, namely the first democratic general elections in the spring of 1994.

On the basis of this decision, the road is practically clear to official negotiations. However, the Council may still object to the opinion of the Commission,[11] and it is the Council that has to fix the starting date for negotiations. From the moment of the Council's decision, the associated country can be legitimately considered as a "candidate" country. Croatia reached this stage in June 2004, and was invited to start negotiations nine months later, in March 2005. However, it turned out that Zagreb still failed to comply with one important precondition, namely the identification and extradition of an alleged war criminal, general Gotovina. As a result, negotiations were postponed and could only start in early October with the screening process (together with Turkey), once the practical cooperation of the Croatian authorities with the Hague Tribunal was verified (two months later Gotovina was arrested and delivered to the ICTY). One of the interesting features that can hardly prove the uniformity of EU policies was that cooperation with the tribunal has been a precondition for Serbia-Montenegro to start moving even from the baseline scenario (lacking any kind of institutionalized relations) towards the first level of the pyramid, namely the conclusion of an SAP. Of course, there were other elements too, separating Croatia from Serbia, that were taken into account, but just one of the most fundamental preconditions was applied in a double-standard.

Macedonia's way to official negotiations still requires one important decision. The European Council has approved the Commission's positive recommendation and gave candidate status to Macedonia in December 2005. However, in contrast to the CEE countries and other previous candidates, the starting date of the negotiations has not been defined until today. (Well-informed circles put the starting of official talks by the end of 2006, however, the country is still waiting for the date.)

All other countries of the Western Balkans are still on the other side of the "EU wall". It is uncertain whether they will follow the Croatian and Macedonian example of combining the signing (and, even more, the ratification) of the SAA with immediate application for membership. Certainly, similar to the situation in the Western Balkan candidate countries, their political and economic situation as well as the expectation (sometimes turning into increasing intolerance or disappointment) would make such steps likely. In turn, the growing enlargement fatigue of some key member countries and increasing inward-looking attitudes of EU politicians can become an important consideration in trying not to overstretch the enlargement capacity of the EU at the given moment. Albania, a country with signed SAA, can provide an interesting example

[11] There has never been such a case in the enlargement history of the EU. In turn, there has been one case in which the Commission's negative opinion was overruled by the Council, and Greece could start accession negotiations in 1977-1978.

in the near future (even if the ratification process may last for about two years).

Table I.2
Position of SEE countries in the pyramid of "institutionalized" relations of the EU

Country	Full membership	Accession negotiations started	Before accession negotiations	SAA signed	SAA before signing	SAA negotiations started	No institutionalized framework
Greece	1981						
Slovenia	2004						
Bulgaria	2007						
Romania	2007						
Croatia	2010?	2005					
Turkey	After 2015?	2005					
Macedonia	After 2012?		X				
Albania	Before 2015?			X			
Bosnia-Herzegovina	Before 2015?				X		
Serbia	Before 2015?					X	
Montenegro	Before 2015?				X		
Kosovo	?						X

Source: own compilation and estimates based on information by the European Commission and expert opinions.

Looking at the EU-related map of the whole of Southeastern Europe, a highly diverging pattern emerges. It expresses substantially different "institutional" realities that hardly support the EU in developing adequate, coherent, reliable and confidence-building Balkan policies across the individual countries. Greece had been a member since 1981, while Slovenia became a full member in 2004. Bulgaria and Romania, with signed (and partly in the last minute ratified) accession treaties, became members in 2007. Croatia, along with Turkey, started official negotiations, while Macedonia is waiting for this moment. Albania signed SAA, while Serbia-Montenegro and Bosnia-Herzegovina started SAA talks. Montenegro is preparing to open SAA-related negotiations, while Kosovo's place in the institutional pyramid of the international network of Brussels will remain open until decision on the future status will have been taken. The current situation and future developments are illustrated in Table I.2.

I.2.4. The Stability Pact (SP)

Although the EU is the generally acknowledged anchor of stabilization and economic development in the Balkans, it is by far not the only actor in the region. The international community is represented in this area by a large number of organizations, initiatives and instruments. The role of the United Nations, the NATO and the OSCE, although important in some specific fields, do not form the central focus of this study. When necessary, reference will be made to their activities – mainly in cooperation or in cases contrasting with EU policies and endeavours – in the respective chapters. Also, specific attitudes, goals and means of key international players in the region will be discussed in Chapter IV.

However, special mention has to be made of an international initiative dating back to June 1999, when the Stability Pact emerged as a basic forum for the future stability of Southeastern Europe during the Cologne International Convention. With the participation of a number of countries and international economic and financial organizations, the Stability Pact set its main objective to prepare and enforce bilateral and multilateral treaties and intra-state agreements in order to overcome the region's conflicts as well as political and economic deficits, partly deeply rooted in centuries or decades of "common" history. While the EU tried to achieve the same objective through different levels of bilateral institutionalized relations linked to various conditionalities, the wider international framework emphasized the primary importance of creating the basis for genuine cross-region cooperation. On the surface, the first could be described as a classic top-down approach by imposing rules of the game on a group of countries, while the second could be considered as a grass-root (bottom to top) initiative. However, both the construction and the experience with the operation of the SP indicate that it did not miss the same top-bottom inclination from its very birth. To a large extent, it was due to the financial sources and stability-related ideas of the SP that were provided by the international community, including, obviously, also the EU.

Target countries included Albania, Bosnia-Herzegovina, Bulgaria, Croatia, Macedonia, Moldova, Romania and Serbia-Montenegro. One can see that, based on the institutionalized approach of the EU, the group does not fully cover the EU "map". It included two countries with clear accession agenda and, in fact, with membership in 2007, one country in the negotiation stage, but also Moldova, which does not belong to the potential candidates.[12]

Participants in the SP include the European Commission, all EU member countries, all countries of Southeastern Europe (including Turkey), as well as the United States, Japan, Canada, Russia, Norway and Switzerland. Furthermore, other international political and economic organizations are represented, such as the United Nations, NATO, OSCE, the UN's Agency for Refugees, as well as financial institutions such as The World Bank, OECD, IMF, EBRD, respectively. Finally, regional economic organizations such as, among others, the Organization for Economic Cooperation in the Black Sea Region, the Central European Initiative, Initiative for Cooperation in South-Eastern Europe, South-East-Europe Co-operation Process are completing the wide range of actors.

The SP, with a small secretariat in Brussels, is not a new international organization, nor does it have its own financial resources. Its main task is to help identify and coordinate stabilization, modernization and cooperation programmes of the member countries. It wants to bring together players on different levels, such as the international organizations, governments in SEE and non-governmental and local actors, agencies and the business community.

SP activities are developed in three main forums, called "Tables". One deals with human rights and refugee issues, while the second is devoted to economic reconstruction and cooperation. The third focuses on security matters and justice and internal affairs. From the point of view of the current study, the second table requires a brief discussion. Its activities include regional trade issues, capital movements, financial topics, as well as infrastructural development. Alongside with EU conditionalities, although not necessarily sufficiently coordinated, one of the SP's main objective was to convince the eight member countries of the importance – not only in political, but foremost in economic terms – of creating a free trade area in the Balkans. As a result, 28 bilateral free trade agreements were signed and were expected to enter into force in 2006. In this case, as of 2007, the bilateral treaties could almost automatically be converted into a multilateral free trade scheme. Another achievement was the identification of major regional infrastructure projects, partly in order to eliminate damages caused by the wars, partly to carry out new developments fostering regional trade and cooperation. Special attention has to be paid to the multi-annual effort to create a

12 Accordingly, while Bulgaria and Romania until membership, as well as all Western Balkan countries and Turkey belong to the Enlargement DG in Brussels, Moldova's place is in the Neighbourhood DG.

common market for energy, the basic document of which was signed by the end of 2005.

Despite the evidently active role of the SP in the region, it has a number of shortcomings that has given rise to criticism from many sides. Some analysts criticize the "unconditionality" of the organization. In fact, member countries have only been required to commit themselves to the idea of developing regional economic relations. Member countries produce lists of projects, but mostly without own financial commitment. Money and technical support are expected from international players. Moreover, the SP's objectives were designed for the short term, which is understandable when looking at the disastrous situation of the whole region, both in general economic terms and, more importantly, concerning the state of physical infrastructure. Certainly, long-term objectives, like the EU's promise of future membership for instance, have not been formulated (Altmann, 2005). Another criticism emerges from the contrasting goals of SP and SAP. While the first, through its limited instruments and financial capabilities, tries to overcome huge economic, political and mental differences and focuses on regional cooperation, the latter may generate larger divisions across countries, for – as we have already demonstrated – the individual members are not able or willing to take the same policy measures at the same time (or, as usual, the consequences of the same measures differ) (Van Meurs-Yannis, 2002). Additionally, the SP's problem inherent from its inception is mentioned, namely it has too many players and too many agents. It is very difficult to design and implement clear and successful policies in such a framework. No less importantly, SP's relation to the process of enlargement, namely the role to be played by a multilateral body in the strictly bilateral process of EU enlargement, is not clear (Gligorov, 2002). Still, in principle, the two organizations could support each other, since the EU has a regional approach to SEE but does not have a clear-cut regional policy. Under ideal conditions, the latter could be contributed by the SP. Finally, other experts miss the strategic orientation of the SP. They acknowledge its positive role in short-term stabilization, but fail to understand that the key problem of SEE is how the whole region could be gradually brought into the mainstream of European civilization, which is much more than just a task and result of economic development (Mintchev, 2001). In this context, bringing these countries closer to the EU needs an integration strategy far beyond imposing EU rules on the target countries or even offering them (opaque) membership perspective. One personal critical remark should be added here. The effectiveness of SP-driven policies in general, and that of trade policy instruments, in particular, is further diluted by the fact that EU membership (or free trade already achieved or to be achieved in the near future) may have a detrimental impact on regional trade if no adequate measures are taken. Looking at the coming accession of Bulgaria and Romania, two key countries in regional trade, such measures should be in place not following accession but well before it, in order to preserve the achievements, however modest, of regional cooperation. In addition, several SP countries are participants in various regional and trade-related initiatives.[13] Despite the rather limited positive impact of such a membership, there is no sign of their giving up this position before membership in the EU, when trade policy competences have to be immediately and fully transferred to Brussels, and other special arrangements cancelled (except those incorporated into the overall economic network of Brussels).

After several years of activities, the Stability Pact is entering a phase of transition. Responsibilities will be shifted to the region by early 2008 in the framework of a new regional structure. In the future, regional actors have to become the driving force of the South East European Cooperation Programme (SEECP). A secretary general position will be created and filled by a person from the region. Moreover, a Regional Cooperation Council will be proposed that will engage non-EU players. Sound coordination between the European Commission, the World Bank, the European Investment Bank, the EBRD and other institutions should ensure further and intensified focus of the international community on the SEE region (Rehn, 2006).

* * * * *

In summary, the institutional network of the EU and the international organizations (by far not all of them have been presented here, being more of a political and military nature) allows us to draw the following conclusions:

1. The EU is the leading, although not always unquestionable, actor in regional stabilization, cooperation and adjustment to the norms of the European integration.
2. There are multiple interrelations (interaction) between the EU and other international organizations. However, these contacts cannot develop their favourable input, since they lack the necessary co-operation, or official contacts are on a low level of EU priorities in the region. In contrast, sometimes different strategic ap-

13 According to a paper on different regional initiatives, in 2002 all countries of the SP participated in 4 to 6 cooperation schemes. Five out of the six regional organizations (CEFTA was an exception in focussing only on trade and agriculture) identified 10 to 18 different priorities to be addressed in the activities of the given organization (Lopandic, 2002).

proaches and the implementation of different policy instruments mutually reduce the effectiveness of these activities.

3. Finally, the lack of genuine, bottom-up regional initiatives is evident, although not really surprising. The only such effort, the Process of Co-operation in SEE, which started as a unique forum for multilateral dialogue in the region did not exert any meaningful impact on regional stabilization and development. In fact, it remained a non-player in the "basket" of many other initiatives. The paralysis of the regional efforts can easily be explained by the events of the last 15 years. More importantly, this inertia has its fundamental roots in centuries past.[14] The obvious policy-taker status of the SEE countries *vis-à-vis* the not less obvious policy-maker, the EU, provides further explanation. However, one has to take into account that the lack of own initiatives does not necessarily mean that the gap can easily be filled by imported and (at least partly) imposed policies, values and expectations. While genuine bottom-up processes could be gradually harmonized with external conditions and could enhance the absorption capacity of the given region or country, their lack can easily turn negative. In such a case, external pressure and rules will be blamed for the domestic and regional inertia – a highly dangerous development that could hardly be considered a factor of sustainable regional stability.

I.2.5. Financial Support

SEE became a beneficiary of substantial financial support by the international community between 1991 and 2005. During this period, the composition of contributors, the main objectives and forms of the support, as well as the timeframe of different programmes were rather varied. The EU proved to be by far the largest contributor, although not the only one, and in some specific cases as part of multinational programmes.

The activities started in the early 1990s with humanitarian aid (ECHO) provided to countries affected by the war (Bosnia-Herzegovina,

[14] Countries belonging to a less "unfortunate" region in the last fifteen years, were similarly unable to give birth to a genuine regional cooperation. Each Central European country looked to Brussels and made its regional cooperation fully dependent on external factors. At least in the last 500 years, the chance for economic and socio-political modernization of Central and, much more, of Southeastern Europe was a question of foreign elements and not the outcome of a genuine region-based strategy.

Macedonia, Serbia-Montenegro including Kosovo).[15] Its main objective was to provide food aid, health care and emergency support to hundreds of thousands of refugees (from shelters to educational facilities). ECHO had to return to Macedonia in 1999, following the Kosovo war, when again several hundred thousand refugees from Kosovo crossed the Serbian-Macedonian border.

A major undertaking, also in the international framework, was proposed by the EU after the Dayton agreement (November 1995) to rebuild the Western Balkans. The project foresaw free aid in the amount of USD 5 bn for a four-year period between 1996 and 1999. The EU's contribution amounted to USD 1 bn allocated in the PHARE for humanitarian aid and reconstruction (OBNOVA). In addition, EU member countries offered substantial help of about Euro 1.8 bn.

Following 2000, the international community (EU, non-EU states and international financial institutions) has been offering an annual amount of Euro 6.5 bn to SEE, including Bulgaria, Romania and Moldova. The support given to the Western Balkans reached its peak of Euro 3.9 bn in 2002 (Calic, 2005). This sum incorporates not only aid or official EU provisions but also the credits given by international organizations, such as the IMF,[16] the World Bank and, not least, the European Investment Bank (EIB).

Apart from the above mentioned financial programmes, the most important contribution came from the EU budget, mainly under two headings: pre-accession aid and the newly created CARDS (Community Assistance for Reconstruction, Development and Stabilization) project. According to EU rules, countries that were given the green light to start official negotiations on accession, the pre-accession budget was made available. Other countries remain in the framework of CARDS. On the basis of this differentiation, two groups were created. Bulgaria and Romania, the two acceding countries benefited from the pre-accession money from the very beginning of its establishment within the financial framework from 2000 to 2006. In turn, Albania, Bosnia-Herzegovina, Macedonia, Serbia-Montenegro and Kosovo belonged under the umbrella of CARDS. Croatia represents an in-between situation, since, as a country that started negotiations, it is already included in the pre-accession financial framework, however, it was also entitled to benefit from CARDS provisions until the end of 2006 (when CARDS will be

---

15 According to national sources, Macedonia received Euro 36.5 mn between 1992 and 2001, while Serbia-Montenegro (mainly due to Kosovo) registered an amount of Euro 670 mn starting 1991.

16 Several countries of SEE have valid agreements with the IMF. The EU contributed to some IMF-led stabilization programmes (*e.g.* Serbia-Montenegro).

finished). Macedonia, still fully in the CARDS framework, is expected to become the beneficiary of the pre-accession fund in the near future, once official negotiations start.

Moreover, all countries of SEE have access to special community programmes, including education and training (*e.g.* TEMPUS), culture, research, energy, environment, civil society, etc.

CARDS money is listed in the EU budget under the heading of "external relations". For the period between 2000 and 2006, Euro 5.13 bn was allocated for the SAP countries (excluding Bulgaria and Romania, as well as Croatia for the years 2005 and 2006, since they receive money from the pre-accession fund under a different heading). More than half of the money was made available to Serbia-Montenegro (including Kosovo), while the other members of the region generally got a much more modest amount. Taking into account the items not divided by countries, such as regional assistance, macro-financial support and other objectives, the proportions may have been even more distorted. Evidently, following the wars, particularly the consequences of NATO's military intervention, Serbia-Montenegro needed the biggest support in order to rebuild some of the vital infrastructure networks (roads, bridges, energy supply). It is no less important to note that the figures reveal a decreasing trend in transfers: the original sum assigned for 2000 was halved by 2006 (taking into account the statistical effect of Croatia's abandoning of the CARDS framework). Country-related figures can be found in Table I.3.

CARDS money is available for a large number of activities, from infrastructure through easing refugee problems to institution building and police cooperation. About one-third is dedicated to economic and social development (agriculture, trade, local initiatives, etc.). Another one-quarter finances physical infrastructure (transportation and energy). 14% is dedicated to justice and home affairs, 12% to stabilization of democratic institutions (including refugee politics), 10% to the establishment of adequate institutions and 5% to the environment and natural resources. The priorities in using the money differ widely from country to country, based on specific needs. For instance, in the first three years of the programme, Serbia used almost 60% of the money for rebuilding war-ridden infrastructure. Only 3% of the money available for Albania was spent for the same purpose, and none by Croatia.[17] The general experience is that CARDS was very helpful in financing investments in

[17] Between 2001 and 2004 Croatia received CARDS funds in the value of Euro 262 mn. Almost 30% of the money was spent on democratic stabilization, another 27% on economic and social development, 23% on reforming the judiciary and police, 16% on administrative capacity building and 5% on environment and natural resources (Lakatos, *Croatia country study*, 2005, pp. 16-17).

infrastructure, energy and housing, while the programme has not yet shown convincing results in institution building or justice and home affairs. Evidently, investments in the latter sectors generate positive effects in a longer term, keeping in mind the difficulties created by the wars and ethnic hostilities in these countries.

Table I.3
CARDS Programme allocation for 2000-2006 (Euro mn)

Country	2000	2001	2002	2003	2004	2005	2006	Total
Albania	33.4	37.5	44.9	46.5	63.5	44.2	45.5	315.5
Bosnia-Herzegovina	90.3	105.2	71.9	63.0	72.0	49.4	51.0	502.8
Croatia	16.8	60.0	59.0	62.0	81.0	(a)	(a)	278.8
Macedonia	13.0	56.2	41.5	43.5	59.0	45.0	40.0	298.2
Serbia-Montenegro (b)	650.5	385.5	351.6	324.3	307.9	282.5	245.5	2,547.8
Interim Civilian Administrations	10.0	24.5	33.0	32.0	35.0	36.0	35.0	205.5
Regional	20.2	20.0	43.5	31.5	23.0	47.9	42.0	228.1
Other (c)	141.5	118.0	11.0	17.0	22.5	19.7	19.8	349.5
Macro-financial assistance (d)	70.0	120.0	100.0	15.0	16.0	33.0	50.0	404.0
Total	*1045.7*	*926.9*	*756.4*	*634.8*	*679.9*	*557.7*	*528.8*	*5,130.2*
Croatia: pre-accession 2005-2006						105.0	140.0	245.0
Total (including Croatia) 2005-2006						*662.7*	*668.8*	*5,375.2*

General remarks: • figures for 2006 are purely for information purposes and correspond to the multi-annual indicative programming (MIP).

• figures include assistance from PHARE and OBNOVA where relevant in 2000, and from CARDS 2001 and onwards.

• 2005 budget implementation: re-use of recoveries from 2004-2005, *i.e.* above-budget allocation 2005: Euro 6 mn for Macedonia, Euro 7.5 mn for regional programme.

(a) see pre-accession fund for 2005 and 2006.

(b) includes the Republic of Serbia, the Republic of Montenegro and the province Kosovo, currently under UN administration. About 40% of the total amount (more than Euro 1,000 mn) was allocated to Kosovo. Amounts for Serbia in 2002-2003 include assistance from Regional Programme for Integrated Border Management destined for the whole of FRY/Serbia-Montenegro. In 2004, Euro 8 mn for that purpose is shown under the regional programme.

(c) Until 2001: Humanitarian aid, specific measures, rapid intervention operations, EIDHR and GFSP. From 2002: administrative costs and the Western Balkan's contribution to the European Training Foundation.

(d) For 2000-2002: disbursement and not commitments.

Source: European Commission, http://www.europa.eu.int/comm/enlargement/cards/financial_en.htm.

CARDS money has been distributed through three different mechanisms in the Western Balkans. In Albania, Bosnia-Herzegovina and Croatia the Delegation of the European Commission is authorized to perform this task. In turn, money for Serbia-Montenegro and Macedonia is managed by the European Agency of Reconstruction (EAR). Finally, funds in support of regional projects are distributed from Brussels, through EuropeAid. Interestingly, the share of the money effectively used differs considerably not only from country to country, but according to the disbursing institution as well. The fact that EAR enjoys a higher level of autonomy in drafting and implementing projects while the respective Delegations always have to face more bureaucratic procedures has clearly shaped the "success rate" of spending. By the end of 2003, almost 80% of the money managed by EAR could be disbursed, while the same figure for Delegation-led programmes reached 45% only (Calic, 2005 and http://europa.eu.int/comm/europeaid/evaluation/programme/cardsrep. htm). However, other factors influenced the efficiency of using CARDS funds as well. Bosnia-Herzegovina and Croatia share the same distribution mechanism, however, they differ significantly in their absorption rate of money (74% for Bosnia and 31% only for Croatia and 29% for Albania). Also, in EAR-managed programmes, Montenegro (86%), Kosovo (83%) or Serbia (82%) proved much more successful than Macedonia (52%).

In order to improve the absorption capacity, several Western Balkan countries have started to upgrade their institution-building process. This effort has become particularly manifest in the case of Croatia, where not only CARDS-related institutions were developed but serious steps have been undertaken in order to receive and efficiently use the pre-accession funds opened up for the country recently.

The efficiency rate of using EU funds cannot be correctly assessed without taking into consideration the priorities and mechanisms of different programmes. For instance, money offered by some countries with a less bureaucratic mechanism than that of Brussels can be obtained easier. However, in most cases, these funds are tied to priorities of the donor country, and the beneficiaries do not have a chance to influence the priority-setting process. In this context, the difference between US funds and the EU CARDS programme is striking, since the latter is based on the real needs of the Western Balkan countries.

Beyond slower than desired procedures, some other deficiencies of the CARDS programme should be mentioned. First, the original goal of spending 10% of the money on regional projects failed since between 2002 and 2004 only about 5% of the available funds financed regional activities. Second, the financial needs of individual countries are increasing in line with their economic development and adjustment to the EU.

In contrast to growing needs of successful modernization, CARDS annual commitments have been decreasing from the very beginning of starting the programme. Instead of bringing Western Balkan countries closer to the EU, both in income terms and in effective development and adjustment performance, the diminishing financial support may become a major barrier to further progress in the coming years. The "economics of aid" is best illustrated in developments in Kosovo. It includes a front-loaded approach at the moment of settling the crisis, with decreasing amounts in the succeeding years. No less importantly, the structure of foreign aid supports the immediate needs of reconstruction more than the sustainability of the recovery process (RIINVEST, 2005).[18]

Moreover, the current approach does not help less advanced countries to catch up. Just the opposite is likely to happen, namely that, contrary to basic EU objectives, regional discrepancies will keep growing. It should be mentioned here that this "construction failure" is clearly manifest in the different amounts available to countries that are part of the CARDS, participate in pre-accession programmes or enjoy EU funds as full members. For instance, Bulgaria, as a beneficiary of the pre-accession fund, got a *per capita* support of Euro 45, while this sum amounted to Euro 25 on average in the SAP countries, and reached only Euro 15 in the case of Croatia. (These figures can hardly be compared with the annual net financial support of less developed member countries such as Greece or Portugal that used to have several bn Euro a year. Also, Hungary as a new member country expects to get in the coming financial period of 2007 to 2013 an average annual amount of Euro 3 bn.) Third, EU resources, although declining in the SAP countries, have become more important for the beneficiaries, since other international financial support dropped even more drastically. Therefore, the EU has to reconsider its financial strategy towards the region, since it is going to remain its outstanding external anchor and supporter.

Until 2007, Bulgaria and Romania, and now Croatia as well, have been beneficiaries of the pre-accession funds. This money consists of three parts, namely the traditional PHARE programme primarily for institution-building and legislative approximation; SAPARD for agriculture and rural development; and ISPA to finance infrastructural and

[18] In the starting year of 1999, 77% of total aid was directed to humanitarian purposes, followed by reconstruction and institution building in the next period until 2004. However, the total spending has been sharply decreasing after 2001, just at a time when short-term stabilization would have badly needed longer-term supportive elements in order to sustain initial results. For a summary table see Appendix Table I.2.5/1.

environmental projects in line with the requirements of the EU structural fund. Pre-accession funds help prepare the accession countries for the challenges of full membership and for the best possible utilization of new channels of financing following accession.

As a comparison to the pre-accession funds made available to Croatia and amounting to Euro 245 mn for two years, Romania, with a four times larger population used to get Euro 1.2-1.3 bn for a comparable two-year period, or five to six times more than Croatia in the first two years of its membership in the pre-accession framework.

This situation dramatically changed with the membership of Bulgaria and Romania. According to preliminary figures, the two new member countries would be entitled to Euro 15.4 bn for a three-year period from 2007 to the end of 2009. Bulgaria is expected to receive about Euro 6.4 bn (or more than Euro 2.1 bn on an annual basis), while Romania's development will be supported by a sum of Euro 9 bn (Euro 3 bn on annual average). A breakdown according to the main objectives is contained in Appendix Table I.2.5/2. Based on EU rules, both countries get access to this money once they will have joined the EU. Any delay in the original membership date of 2007 would have substantially downgraded their financial support, for they would have remained in the category of candidate countries financed from a different and much more modest envelope of the EU budget. Still, unlike the new members of 2004, Bulgaria and Romania only have a financial framework until the end of 2009, when the budget will be revised and modified according to eventual new priorities (including the costs of further enlargements).

Western Balkan countries will also be affected by the new financial framework in several aspects. First, all previous financial instruments (PHARE, SAPARD, ISPA, CARDS and pre-accession funds available for Turkey) will be combined within a new package called Instrument of Pre-Accession Assistance (IPA). Second, the previous role played by the European Agency for Reconstruction (EAR) will be taken over by the Commission. Third, all Western Balkan countries, irrespective of their current EU-related status, will be placed into the same IPA framework. Thus, Croatia and Turkey will have to share the financial support with Macedonia, Albania, Bosnia-Herzegovina, Montenegro, Serbia and Kosovo. Fourth, financial allocation will be based on a three-year "rolling planning", in harmony with the basic EU rule of using funds during a three-year period (the well-known n+2 principle). This approach has two important objectives. On the one hand, it makes longer-term planning and project implementation possible. On the other hand, it is considered a powerful instrument of conditionality, since, at any moment of the given period, Brussels can freeze or curtail its financial support to any country that does not fulfil its commitments or acts against basic

European values and rules. The amount available for IPA is Euro 11.5 bn for the seven-year period (or more than Euro 1.6 bn at a yearly average)[19]. Thus, it is substantially higher than the overall sum of Euro 679 mn available for the year 2006. However, it will still remain considerably less than the potential transfers member countries are or will be entitled to. (For comparison: even taking into account the "phasing-in" character of the beneficiary position, as of 2007 Bulgaria and Romania will have access to two and four times higher amounts, respectively, than the total sum of EU financial support to the Western Balkans in 2006.)

19 In June 2007, the Commission approved the three-year (2007-2009) strategy of financial support to be provided to the three candidate countries (Turkey, Croatia and Macedonia) and the five potential candidates of the Western Balkans (Albania, Bosnia-Herzegovina, Kosovo, Montenegro and Serbia). According to this document, the above mentioned countries get Euro 3.962 mn. Turkey will get the largest amount of transfers (Euro 1.6 bn), followed by Croatia (Euro 439 mn) and Macedonia (Euro 210 mn). The national envelopes of other Western Balkan countries contain Euro 1.7 bn altogether for the three-year period.

CHAPTER II

Basic Features of Macroeconomic Performance in Regional Comparison

Achievements, Barriers, Policy Dilemmas and Tasks

Southeastern Europe, as defined in our study, occupies a territory of 614,000 km² (larger than the largest EU member country, France) and has a total population of 55 mn, similar to that of France, Italy or the United Kingdom, respectively. Despite the "geographic community", the region consists of countries with different geographic, economic and partly historical features. Some of the basic characteristics are contained in Table II.1.

Table II.1
Land, population and economic size of the SEE countries

Country	Total area Thousand km²	Population mn (2002)	GDP (2002) in current USD bn	GNI *per capita* (2002) in USD(a)
Albania	28.8	3.2	4.8	1,380
Bosnia-Herzegovina	51.1	4.1	5.2	1,270
Bulgaria	110.9	8.0	15.6	1,790
Croatia	56.5	4.4	22.4	4,640
Macedonia	25.7	2.1	3.7	1,700
Romania	238.4	22.4	44.5	1,850
Serbia-Montenegro	102.2	10.7	15.7	1,400
of which: Serbia	77.3	8.0		
Kosovo	10.9	2.1		
Montenegro	14.0	0.6	.	.
Total SEE	613.6	54.9	111.9	.

(a) Figures calculated at purchasing parity power (PPP rates) would be substantially higher for all countries. Also, differences between Croatia and Bulgaria and Romania, respectively, would be much smaller.

Source: World Development Indicators, 2003.

Chapter II focuses on key economic indicators of the region in general, and of individual countries, in particular. A fundamental macroeconomic survey represents the starting point of a multi-level analysis of economic and socio-political developments and the identification of policy dilemmas. The chapter is structured in the following way. First, an overall picture on the current macroeconomic situation of the SEE countries will be provided. Statistical time series are important in order to be aware of the long road and difficulties these countries had been facing over the last decade and a half. In the next section, comparison will be made with the CEE countries with the purpose of highlighting basic differences (and, sometimes, similarities), with other transforming economies, already members of the EU and well ahead on the way in transformation and socio-economic modernization. This assessment will be followed by identifying the basic barriers to sustainable development and catching up both to the level of the CEE and the EU-25 countries. Next, a short section looks at the key economic actors of transformation that may partly explain the different performance levels, the size and quality of barriers and the longer-term sustainability of favourable developments. This section leads to the major longer-term economic policy dilemmas that can be identified, despite unquestionable results of the last years. Finally, the fundamental tasks will be addressed that have to be tackled in order to solve (part of) the current uncertainties and ensure at least a medium-term sustainability of the initiated growth pattern.

II.1. Current Macroeconomic Situation

II.1.1. As a clear sign of economic consolidation in the last years, all SEE countries could return to high growth rates. In the context of the positive trends, however, some remarks have to be made. First, as it will be demonstrated later, the factors underlying favourable growth rates are partly different from country to country and explain more short term revival than medium- and longer-term sustainability. Second, economic recovery has to be seen in comparison with the last years of the pre-transformation period. In fact, as a consequence of dramatic decline in output after 1990, recovery started on a rather low level. Thus, high growth rates emerge on the basis of a substantially reduced level of output, in many countries with still large gap between the level of current performance and that of the pre-transformation years. Obviously, economic decline in SEE can be attributed to the general phenomenon in all transformation countries, described as a "transformation crisis". However, in SEE other factors played a relevant role in the negative spiral of economic growth as well. First and foremost the consequences of the Balkan wars, including armed conflicts between various ex-Yugoslav republics, serious ethnic clashes and the NATO intervention, have to be highlighted. In addition, for several reasons, economic restructuring started later than in most CEE countries and remained ambiguous in its aims and policy measures and not even exempt from the eventual risk of returning to the past. While Bulgaria and Romania seem to have overcome this "hesitant" period, economic policy-making in the WB countries is far from clear and transparent.

Table II.2
Real GDP growth in the SEE countries (annual rates in %)

Country	1990-1995 average	1996-2000 average	2001	2002	2003	2004	2005	2006 preliminary
Albania	-2.3	5.8	7.0	2.9	5.7	6.2	5.3	5.0
Bosnia-Herzegovina	.	24.4	4.5	3.7	3.2	6.0	5.5	5.0
Bulgaria	-3.6	-0.7	4.1	4.9	4.5	5.7	5.5	5.5
Croatia	-5.9	3.4	4.4	5.2	4.3	3.8	4.3	3.8
Romania	-2.5	-1.2	5.7	5.1	5.2	8.4	4.1	5.0
Serbia-Montenegro(a)	-11.4	0.7	5.3	3.8	2.1			
- Serbia						9.3	6.8	
- Montenegro						3.7	4.1	
Macedonia	-5.6	3.0	-4.5	0.9	2.8	4.1	3.6	4.0
SEE average	-4.4	0.4	4.9	4.7	4.5	7.1	4.5	4.8

(a) excluding Kosovo since 1999.

Note: comparing official macroeconomic figures of different international economic organizations (United Nations, OECD, EBRD, IMF, World Bank, etc.), sometimes relevant differences can be found. For an interesting comparison see EBRD (2006, p. 19). Moreover, neither national statistics contribute to a higher level of transparency. In this and the next tables we have relied on figures published by the Economic Commission for Europe of the United Nations. Concerning 2005 estimates and 2006 forecasts, the EBRD Transition Report (2006a) was also consulted.

Source: Economic Commission for Europe (2005b), EBRD (2006a) and national statistics.

The coexistence of old mechanisms and new efforts are shaping the general picture not only in the economy, but in the social and mental spheres alike. As a further difference, various economic policies needed different instruments and were linked differently to the new factors of economic growth, such as privatization, liberalization and cooperation with international direct capital. No wonder that different policies generated different performance levels (and most probably different degrees of sustainability as well) across the countries of the region, and further tended to widen the division within the Balkans. (Table II.2)[1]

With some exceptions, the negative figures all through the 1990s call attention to a "lost decade" due to several developments mentioned above. However, return to positive growth rates can be observed in all countries starting 2001. Without going into detailed analysis at the moment, concerning the main driving forces of growth, some observations have to be made. First, growth rates are encouraging, but, with the exception of some countries in certain years, they don't exceed the last decade's growth record of some CEE economies on a higher level of development. Second, the Baltic countries, sharing a deep crisis with SEE in the first half of the 1990s, reveal sustainable and higher growth rates than most SEE countries. Third, growth rates cannot be considered "stabilized" in various countries, since they are exposed to domestic and external influences, with a high level of volatility. This phenomenon was widely observed in the second half of the 1990s mainly in Albania, Macedonia and Serbia-Montenegro. Fourth, this volatility cannot be directly linked to changes in the "business cycle" in the European Union. While CEE economies develop rather strongly in comparison with the EU growth rate (and particularly that of Germany), such a correlation cannot be observed in the WB countries. This can be explained partly by the special forces of growth in the first years of transformation and rebuilding from the war (domestic demand plays a more important role), but also partly by a lower level of openness to the outside world and the low level of trade with the EU (both in terms of volume and as a share of the GDP). Fifth, growth rates in the first half of this decade show substantial cross-country differences. While Romania and Bulgaria seem to have fostered a high-growth path, the macroeconomic performance of Bosnia and Macedonia is modest and future growth rates in Serbia are still not free from uncertainties and negative surprises. Sixth, despite positive growth rates in the last five years, four out of the seven countries, namely Bulgaria, Croatia, Macedonia and Serbia-Montenegro did not reach their pre-transformation level by 2005, while Romania returned to the 1989 GDP level in 2004. Evidently, the situation is substantially different in Bulgaria and Croatia on the one hand, and in Macedonia, and particularly, in

---

1 Different comparisons exist. Figures may substantially differ by using different starting years. Already by changing the year of comparison from 1989 to 1990, the general picture may be modified, since 1989 was already a year with negative growth in some countries. Therefore, utmost caution is needed in such exercises. For instance, the widely publicized fact that Poland was the first CEE country that could reach the pre-transformation GDP level, well ahead the Czech Republic or Hungary, is based on the fact that the Polish economy was already declining in the 1980s. Therefore, its level of comparison was much lower than that of other CEE countries. Based on 1980 figures, we would come to substantially different ranking and relative performance indicators.

Serbia-Montenegro, on the other. Bosnia's performance cannot be evaluated, since there are no figures available for the first half of the 1990s. Most probably, the GDP level is still far behind that achieved in the last years of the Yugoslav Federation. Thus, the only exception is Albania, where the GDP exceeded the 1989 level by 38% in 2005. This, however, is due to the most radical transformation from a textbook orthodox and closed economy towards a more liberal one (Table II.3).

Table II.3
Real GDP levels in 2004 and 2005, compared to 1989, the last year of the pre-transformation period (in %)

Year	AL	B-H	BG	CR	MD	RO	SM	SEE
2004/1989 (a)	30.1	229.9(c)	-8.0	-5.3	-16.5	0.8	-48.3	-6.5
2005/1989 (b)	138	.	94	98	88	104	58	97

(a) based on the difference from 100, as benchmark indicator (for GDP in 1989). Negative signs indicate lower output than in 1989.

(b) based on 100% GDP level in 1989 and relative figures for 2005. Lower than 100% means still lower GDP than in 1989.

(c) 1995 = 100

Source: for (a) Economic Commission for Europe (2005b) and for (b) EBRD (2006a).

GDP decline in *per capita* terms was less dramatic since most countries had to register a huge outflow of people, either due to war and ethnic cleansing (in the Western Balkans), or to serious economic difficulties stemming from the transformation process (in Bulgaria and Romania). The only country with rapid population growth was Albania, resulting in a much lower GDP *per capita* growth rate than indicated by the 30% overall GDP growth over 15 years.

Still, the income gap *vis-à-vis* the EU-25 remains enormous. In 2004, and at purchasing power parity (PPP), Romania reached 32% of the EU-25 average, while Bulgaria's figure was about 30%. Croatia, the relatively most developed SEE country accounted for 46% of the average, similar to Poland but substantially behind that of Slovenia, the Czech Republic, Hungary or even Slovakia. Other Western Balkan countries showed a *per capita* GDP of one-fourth to one-fifth of the EU-25 average, with Albania bringing up the rear (Hunya, 2005, p. 55). Calculations based on official exchange rates reveal an even larger income gap.[2]

II.1.2. GDP growth was driven in the region by varying gross industrial production. Between 2000 and 2004 Bulgaria's industrial perform-

[2] In this comparison, the WB countries, excluding Croatia, range between 4 (Kosovo) and 9% (Sertbia-Montenegro and Macedonia) of the EU-25 average (Altmann, 2005, p. 202).

ance was excellent (a cumulative growth of 46%), while other SEE countries performed less favourably, with Macedonia even showing declining industrial output in the observed period. Also, in comparison with CEE countries, industrial output remained modest (Table II.4).

On the SEE level, GDP growth was not driven by industrial output but by other factors. With the exception of Bulgaria, and an "equilibrium situation" in Croatia, growth rates of industrial output remained below GDP growth rates in the period between 2000 and 2004. This sharply contrasts with the decade-long performance features of CEE, where industrial output substantially outpaced GDP growth rates and proved the most important factor of sustainable and high growth. It is not difficult to find interdependence between industrial performance, cooperation with foreign capital and outward orientation of production in small national economies.

Table II.4
GDP and gross industrial production (cumulative growth rates between 2000 and 2004, 2000 = 100)

Country	GDP	Gross industrial production
Albania	123.2	115.4
Bosnia-Herzegovina	116.3	130.6
Bulgaria	120.5	146.0
Croatia	118.9	120.6
Macedonia	101.9	94.0
Romania	126.6	122.7
Serbia without Montenegro	120.5	105.9
SEE-7	122.7	116.2
CEE-5 (a)	.	124.2
CEE-8 (b)	114.6	125.6
EU-15	106.7	101.2

(a) Czech Republic, Hungary, Poland, Slovenia and Slovakia.

(b) CEE-5 and Estonia, Latvia, Lithuania.

Source: Economic Commission for Europe (2005a), WIIW database. Similarly, the above figures indicate that, except for Bulgaria and to some extent Romania and Croatia, industrial productivity growth remained sluggish, very much in contrast to CEE countries where it became one of the most important driving forces of enhanced production and higher GDP growth. Most probably, substantial productivity reserves exist but their exploitation requires adequate economic policies, including the speeding up of privatization and a greater openness to the international business community.

II.1.3. Different industrial performance is closely linked to the development of gross fixed capital formation. For Albania and Bosnia-

Herzegovina comparable figures are not available. However, there is a strong correlation between rapid industrial output and double-digit growth rates of gross fixed capital formation in Bulgaria and, to a lesser extent, in Romania and in Croatia. In turn, Serbian and Macedonian statistics reveal negative rates in several years (Table II.5).

Table II.5
Gross fixed capital formation in selected SEE countries (annual growth rates in %)

Country	1999	2000	2001	2002	2003	2004	2000-2004 cumulative
Bulgaria	20.8	15.4	23.3	8.5	13.9	12.0	170.7
Croatia	-3.9	-3.8	7.1	12.0	16.8	4.4	146.3
Macedonia	-1.4	-3.2	-8.6	17.6	1.1		
Romania	-4.8	5.5	10.1	8.2	9.1	10.1	143.2
Serbia-Montenegro(a)		13.3	-4.1	-0.8			

(a) Gross fixed investment.

Source: Economic Commission for Europe (2005a), Hunya (2005).

II.1.4. One of the most serious problems of the SEE countries is the high to extremely high level of unemployment. In a separate chapter this issue will be discussed in more detail. Right now only the basic facts will be addressed that cannot be ignored in a comprehensive macroeconomic survey. With the exception of Romania, official unemployment rates are double-digit, showing the highest figures in Bosnia and Macedonia. The next subgroup consists of Serbia-Montenegro, while Bulgaria and Croatia form another group. Another feature of the labour market is the persistently high level of unemployment, except in Bulgaria where the official rate is rapidly declining, but still above 10% (at the end of 2004). Moreover, high unemployment levels are accompanied by low levels of participation rate (between 50 and 56%). In addition, official statistics do not cover the full reality for two reasons. First, there is a widespread hidden unemployment that is not registered (vice versa, there is also employment outside the official labour market). Second, unemployment figures do not say anything about future trends, since they can be features of an economy before or after fundamental structural changes. In the first case, sooner or later an even higher unemployment rate can be expected, while the second situation promises declining unemployment in the coming years (see the clear difference between Croatia, Serbia, and most probably, Romania, for the first, and Bulgaria for the second case). (Table II.6)

Table II.6
Select basic unemployment figures for SEE countries

Country	Unemployment rate		Change		Participation rate 2004
	2000	2004	2004/1989	2004/2000	
Albania	16.8	14.4	-31.8	+2.4	.
Bosnia-Herzegovina	39.4	44.9	-58.1	-5.4	.
Bulgaria	17.9	12.2	-54.6	+5.7	49.7
Croatia	22.3	18.5	-43.1	+3.8	50.5
Macedonia	45.1	44.6	-53.1	+0.6	52.2
Romania	10.5	6.2	-47.3	+4.3	54.8
Serbia-Montenegro	26.6	28.0	-43.6	-1.4	56.0

Source: Economic Commission for Europe (2005a), Hunya (2005), Novák (2005).

II.1.5. Economic restructuring, sustainable growth and positive impact on the labour market are closely linked to the privatization policies of SEE countries. For different reasons, privatization started in this region later than in CEE countries and, in many cases, remained half-hearted, with a number of serious barriers partly inherited from the past (ex-Yugoslav model of self-management of enterprises), partly created by widespread social and political opposition or at least hesitation. According to EBRD figures, the share of the private sector in GDP was between 40% (in Serbia-Montenegro) and 75% (in Albania). The weighted average of SEE reached 61% in 2002, while comparable figures for the 8 new Central European and Baltic EU members stood at 76% (Table II.7).

Table II.7
Private sector share in GDP (2002)

AL	BH	BG	CR	MD	RO	SM	SEE	CEB(a)	CIS(b)
75	45	70	60	60	65	40	60.9	76.4	66.6

(a) Eight Central European and Baltic countries.

(b) Commonwealth of Independent States.

Source: Falcetti-Sanfey-Taci (2003).

Most recent country data offer a more positive picture, since privatization has been speeded up in some countries. By 2004, the share of the private economy reached 50% in the GDP of Bosnia. However, its role in total employment remained limited (36%). At the same time, it has to be considered that strengthening the private sector in economic development is a two-way street. It is not sufficient to privatize large-scale state-owned companies, but one has to create favourable conditions for the bottom-up emergence of new micro-, small- and medium-sized private enterprises (SMEs) as well. In 2000, the total number of SMEs in the SEE region amounted to 750,000 out of which more than 600,000 were micro firms. In the Czech Republic alone, there were at the same time almost 880,000 SMEs (of which 830,000 belonged to the category of micro companies). In another comparison, the number of SMEs per 1000 inhabitants reached 85 in the Czech Republic, 46 in Poland, but only 8 in Serbia-Montenegro and about 14 in Croatia, Macedonia and Romania each. The only exception was Bulgaria, with an indicator of 28 (similar to Hungary). (In detail see: Falcetti-Sanfey-Taci, 2003.)

II.1.6. For understandable reasons and advised by international financial institutions, in the first years of the belated transformation process, all countries gave priority to anti-inflationary policies. In the first half of the 1990s all countries experienced extremely high inflation rates, due to the liberalization of previously frozen (centrally dictated) prices and, in the Western Balkans, to the huge inflationary impact of civil wars. Annual consumer price increase reached astronomic magnitudes in Bosnia (833 times in 1992 and another 327 times in 1993). In Croatia, the highest annual inflation rate was registered in 1993, with a 15 fold price increase (similar to Macedonia one year earlier), while the Bulgarian inflation rate reached its peak level in 1997 with a more than 10 fold increase. For many years, and with a returning character, inflation rates stayed on a three-digit scale in Romania.

In this situation, all SEE countries considered their economic policy priority to combat inflation. In fact, annual inflation rates could be substantially curbed, but policy instruments and anti-inflationary achievements diverged. After successful financial reforms in the second half of the 1990s, five countries could stabilize price development and reached sustainable, low, one-digit inflation rates (Albania, Bosnia-Herzegovina, Bulgaria, Croatia and Macedonia). In turn, and despite undeniable success, inflation rates in Romania (until 2004) and Serbia still remained in the low double-digit category. (Statistical figures are contained in Table II.8.)

Table II.8
Annual consumer price changes in the SEE countries (in %)

Country	Highest inflation	1998-2000 average	2001	2002	2003	2004	2005	2006 preliminary
Albania	226 (1992)	7.0	3.1	5.3	2.5	3.0	2.4	3.0
Bosnia-Herzegovina	83,328 (1992)	2.6	1.8	0.9	0.2	-0.7	2.9	2.5
Bulgaria	1,058 (1997)	10.5	7.4	5.8	2.3	6.1	5.0	3.5 (7.9) (c)
Croatia	1,486 (1993)	5.0	3.7	1.7	1.8	2.1	3.3	3.0 (4.5) (c)
Macedonia	1,511 (1992)	1.9	5.2	2.3	1.1	-0.4	0.5	2.0
Romania	256 (1993)	50.2	34.5	22.5	15.4	11.9	9.0	7.5
Serbia-Montenegro	90.5 (1996) (a)	50.7	90.4	19.3	9.6			
- Serbia						11.4	16.2	11.4
- Montenegro						4.3	3.0	3.2(d)
SEE-7	81.2 (1997) (a)	26.4	30.1	16.2	10.6	9.5	5.5	5.1
EU-8 (b)	66.6 (1990)	8.6	5.9	2.7	2.0	4.2	3.3	2.8

(a) figures not available for the period 1990 to 1994.

(b) CEE and Baltic countries that joined the EU in 2004.

(c) large differences between various international and national statistics.

(d) figures forecast by different official and expert sources fluctuated between 2.9 and 3.5%.

Source: Economic Commission for Europe (2005a), Novák (2005), KOPINT (2005), EBRD (2006a) and national statistics.

II.1.7. As part of the anti-inflationary policies, in recent years all countries carried out successful fiscal adjustment. Initially, high deficits became controlled overwhelmingly in the framework of IMF-initiated and -supervised economic policies. The central budget deficits seem to be manageable, while some countries have a balanced budget, and Bulgaria even registers a surplus. Albania and Croatia have general government deficits at only above 4.5% of the GDP. Macedonia was able to bring down deficit from over 6% in 2001 to 1% in 2004. The overall positive picture of combating inflation and reducing budget deficits has, however, been accompanied by a number of negative side effects, such as delayed investments in physical and human infrastructure, high level of unemployment, depressed wages and pensions, low level of living standard, high or further growing regional differences within the individual countries, and, last but not least, the neglected area of enhancing competitiveness and generating structural changes in the real economy.

II.1.8. The economic and social response to the unavoidable negative consequences of IMF-driven and quick fiscal adjustment can be identified in the rapid growth and the high share of the informal economy in total economic activities. Based on different studies on several aspects of the informal economy, the Economic Commission for Europe distinguishes three types of such activities. "Underground production" comprises legal economic activities that remain hidden for reasons of tax evasion. "Informal activities" are also legal and characterized by low level of organization, typically based on unofficial relationships. Finally, "illegal activities" that are banned by law, are included in the definition (Economic Commission for Europe, 2005a).

Table II.9
Share of the informal sector in SEE, 2000-2004 (in % of GDP)

Country	ECE national accounts method	ECE currency demand and DYMIMIC method (a)	EBRD estimate 000-2002
Albania	28	35	33.4
Bosnia-Herzegovina	53	37	34.1
Bulgaria	22	38	36.9
Croatia	7	35	33.4
Macedonia	14	36	45.1
Romania	21	37	34.4
Serbia-Montenegro	35	39	29.1
Memorandum items:			
Czech Republic	9	20	19.1
Hungary	18	26	25.1
Poland	14	29	27.6
Slovakia	15	20	18.9
OECD average	.	16	18.0

(a) Dynamic multiple-indicators multiple-cause model consisting of two parts: first linking unobserved variables to observed indicators (monetary transactions, participation rates, official working hours, etc.) and second, specifying causal relationship between the size of unobserved economy and its causes (taxation level, degree of regulation, tax morality, etc.).

Source: Economic Commission for Europe (2005a), Falcetti-Sanfey-Taci (2003).

It is a common feature of all transforming economies that the informal sector plays a substantial role in the generation of GDP. As a result of growing structural inflexibilities in recent years, nor do developed OECD countries represent an exception to this general trend. Differences appear, however, in the size of such activities. In Western Europe, the informal sector produces about 18% of the GDP, similar to the figures calculated for the Czech Republic or Slovakia (19% each). This share is higher in Poland and Hungary (28 and 25%, respectively). However, they cannot be compared with 33 to 45% measured in most of the SEE countries.[3]

Table II.10
Foreign trade of the SEE countries (in USD bn)

Country	Exports 2004	Exports 2001-2004	Imports 2004	Imports 2001-2004	Balance 2001-2004	Coverage export/import in % 2001-2004 cumulative
Albania	0.6	1.7	2.3	6.9	-5.2	24.6
Bosnia-Herzegovina	1.8	5.2	5.9	17.7	-12.5	29.4
Bulgaria	9.9	28.3	14.4	40.4	-12.1	70.0
Croatia	8.0	23.8	16.6	50.7	-26.9	46.9
Macedonia	1.7	5.5	2.9	9.3	-3.8	59.1
Romania	23.5	66.3	32.7	90.1	-23.8	73.6
Serbia-Montenegro	3.7	10.6	11.1	29.7	-19.1	35.7
Memorandum items:						
Czech Republic	68.5	189.0	69.4	198.2	-9.2	95.4
Hungary	54.8	162.6	59.2	178.2	-15.6	91.2
Slovakia	27.5	76.5	29.4	83.2	-6.7	91.9
Slovenia	15.8	48.1	17.2	52.0	-3.9	92.5
SEE-7	49.2	141.4	85.9	244.8	-103.4	57.8
CEE-5	241.4	681.7	264.8	774.8	-93.1	88.0
Baltic-3	19.2	54.7	27.7	79.8	-25.1	68.5

Source: Economic Commission for Europe (2005a) and own calculations.

II.1.9. Another negative impact of the austerity policies can be detected in the overall picture of the external sector that is the key area of competitive performance. All SEE countries register high trade and current account deficits. Although in recent years some countries show tendencies of increasing exports, sometimes even higher export growth rates than those of imports, the trade deficit has not stopped growing. Despite some initially favourable signs, exports remain low in comparison to CEE countries. The total exports of the seven SEE countries in 2004 amounted to USD 49 bn, of which almost 50% was represented by Romania and another 20% by Bulgaria. Only Hungary's exports reached almost USD 55 bn in the same year. In contrast, imports were at the level

[3] Unofficial estimates result in even higher figures in some ex-Soviet republics (68% in Georgia and 61% in Azerbaijan).

of USD 86 bn, or 75% higher than exports. The average coverage ratio of the region was 57%. In the CEE countries, except for Poland, this coverage figure fluctuated between 92 and 99% in 2004. Detailed figures are given in Table II.10.

Cumulative figures covering a four-year period exacerbate the trends reflected in 2004 statistical data. On a four-year basis, the SEE countries can be classified in different groups. For some of them, exports amount to 25 to 35% of imports (Albania, Bosnia-Herzegovina, Serbia-Montenegro). The trade imbalance is less serious but substantial in Croatia and Macedonia. Only Bulgaria and Romania can be considered relatively large exporters with a less serious cumulative trade deficit. Concerning the share of imports covered by exports, these two EU accession countries show figures similar to the Baltics (and also partly to Poland).

II.1.10. The partial compensation of the huge trade deficit is expected to come from the revenues of the service sector (mainly tourism in some countries, as in Croatia and Bulgaria), by remittances of citizens working abroad (a widespread phenomenon to be discussed later in detail), and by international financial resources. The share of foreign direct investment, an important factor of the balance-of-payments position is modest to minimal, except in Bulgaria, Romania and partly Croatia. This is another substantial difference in the main factors of current account in the CEE countries.

The growing importance of non-trade revenues notwithstanding, current accounts regularly reveal high deficits, particularly in Bosnia-Herzegovina and Serbia-Montenegro. The deficits of Bulgaria and Romania can be financed if the countries sustain high growth rates, rapid export expansion, growing tourism revenues and, not less importantly, constant inflow of foreign direct investments. In the following tables overall figures of the current account situation as well as the main components of the current account will be presented (Tables II.11 and II.12).

Table II.11
Current account of the SEE countries
(in % of GDP, negative sign indicates deficit)

Country	2002	2003	2004	2005	2006 forecast
Albania	-8.5	-6.7	-4.4	-5.0	-4.0
Bosnia-Herzegovina	-22.2	-24.5	-20.9	-22.5	-18.8
Bulgaria	-5.6	-9.2	-4.8	-5.6	-6.5
Croatia	-8.6	-6.9	-4.9	-6.3	-4.5
Macedonia	-9.5	-3.3	-7.7	-1.4	-6.3
Romania	-3.4	-6.0	-8.4	-8.7	-7.4
Serbia (a)	-13.5	-9.2	-12.6	-9.5	-13.0
Montenegro (a)	-12.6	-7.4	-7.8	-12.2	-5.0
Memorandum items:					
Czech Republic		-6.3	-4.8	-5.3	-2.1
Hungary		-8.8	-8.6	-6.1	-7.7
Poland		-2.2	-4.2	-1.4	-1.7
Slovakia		-0.8	-3.6	-8.6	-4.0
Slovenia		-0.4	-2.7	-2.0	-0.6
CEE-5 average		-4.0	-4.8	-4.7	-3.0

(a) Serbia and Montenegro have separate, independent central banks and, therefore, separate trade and current account statistics, as well as balance-of-payments figures.

Source: WIIW database, Holzner (2005).

The above figures indicate that all SEE countries run substantial trade deficits. This can be the result of successful modernization when – during a certain period – imported inputs are necessary to revive and restructure domestic production and create sizeable export capacities. This may be the case for Bulgaria and Romania, but hardly for any other country. In the latter situation we are dealing with highly import-dependent economies that possess a weak export basis. Therefore, the financing of the trade deficit will remain the task of revenues in the non-trade sector. The service balance can contribute to covering part of the trade deficit mainly due to high revenues from tourism, particularly in Croatia, but probably also in Montenegro and, increasingly, in Bulgaria. However, in recent years, the lion's share of financing turned out to be financial transfers, mainly to the WB countries, except for Croatia. Almost one-fourth of Bosnia's GDP is represented by such flows, but this item accounted for about 15% of the GDP of Albania, Macedonia and Serbia as well. One of the key uncertainties is to what extent such financial transfers will remain in place in the coming period.

Table II.12
Main components of the current account balance
(in % of GDP, negative signs indicate deficits)

Country	Year	Balance on goods	Balance on services	Balance on incomes	Balance on transfers
Albania	2002	-23.9	-0.1	2.6	12.9
	2003	-21.9	-1.4	2.8	13.7
	2004	-19.6	-0.6	2.2	13.6
Bosnia-Herzegovina	2002	-59.2	3.3	9.1	24.6
	2003	-58.4	3.7	7.5	22.7
	2004	-55.4	4.5	5.4	22.2
Bulgaria	2002	-10.2	2.9	-1.7	3.4
	2003	-12.5	3.0	-3.2	3.5
	2004	-14.0	3.7	-1.8	4.6
Croatia	2002	-24.6	13.6	-2.4	4.8
	2003	-27.3	19.8	-4.2	4.9
	2004	-24.3	17.7	-2.2	4.3
Macedonia	2002	-21.3	-0.6	-0.8	13.2
	2003	-18.4	-0.1	-0.7	15.9
	2004	-20.9	-0.8	-0.7	14.7
Romania	2002	-5.7	0.0	-1.0	3.3
	2003	-7.8	0.1	-2.4	4.0
	2004	-9.0	-0.4	-2.3	4.2
Serbia (a)	2002	-24.7	1.9	-0.7	10.0
	2003	-24.2	1.5	-1.1	12.1
	2004	-31.7	1.8	-1.0	15.3
Montenegro (a)	2002	-32.7	7.6	5.8	6.7
	2003	-25.1	7.8	6.9	3.2
	2004	-28.1	9.1	6.8	2.9

(a) see Table II.10.

Source: WIIW Database, Holzner (2005).

II.1.11. Despite current account deficits, gross external debt still seems to be manageable for most countries, since it stands at relatively low levels. Moreover, it has not increased in recent years. However, two potential dangers have to be pointed out. Both the size of the external debt as expressed in the GDP of the given countries and the rapid increase of external indebtedness recently can be observed in the case of Croatia and Montenegro. Another important element of financial stability is the stock of foreign reserves at the respective Central Banks. Basic figures have been incorporated into Table II.13.

Table II.13
Foreign financial position of the SEE countries
(end of period, in % of GDP, Euro-based calculations)

Country	Gross External Debt			National Bank Reserves		
	2002	2003	2004	2002	2003	2004
Albania	22.0	20.6	19.8	15.9	15.0	15.4
Bosnia-Herzegovina	36.8	32.7	30.7	21.2	22.6	26.6
Bulgaria	65.1	60.2	63.0	13.1	14.4	17.0
Croatia	62.2	77.6	82.1	23.3	25.7	23.3
Macedonia	37.7	34.5	33.4	17.3	17.5	15.4
Romania	30.9	31.3	30.7	12.1	12.6	18.4
Serbia (a)	71.2	64.7	57.9	13.7	16.3	16.8
Montenegro (a)	.	65.7	80.4	.	.	.

(a) for note see Table II.10.

Source: WIIW database, Hunya (2005).

II.1.12. In their stabilization policies, the SEE countries opted for different exchange rate policies. Some of them had a certain manoeuvering room in choosing the supposedly best policy, some others, however, facing a serious financial crisis, had to accept the currency board solution as the only option in order to regain the confidence of the international financial community in general and that of potential investors, in particular.

Bulgaria and Bosnia-Herzegovina have introduced currency boards and fixed their national currency first to the DM, later to the Euro. In addition, in Bosnia the Euro appeared as parallel legal tender. Macedonia has a strict peg to the Euro. Montenegro and Kosovo do not have their own currencies but use the Euro instead. Other countries have some flexibility in the development of the value of the national currencies *vis-à-vis* the Euro (and other major currencies), although floating is allowed within a rather narrow margin only. In this context, Croatia's system seems to be the most rigid, while Serbia recently loosened the margins somewhat and let the dinar float within broader bands (crawling peg system). Romania only decided to move from a crawling peg system towards free, or at least, freer floating.[4] The shorter and longer term economic impact of the chosen currency regime will be analyzed in the forthcoming parts of this chapter.

4 Several studies deal with the exchange rate regimes of the SEE countries. For a detailed description see Gligorov (2005) and Crespo-Cuaresma-Fidrmuc-Silgoner (2005).

II.1.13. Achievements in macroeconomic consolidation are reflected in the most recent country ratings provided by influential international agencies. Although none of the SEE countries reaches the highest category (different stages of "A"), but all of them have reached the encouraging investment-rating ("B"). Moreover, all of them indicate a stable rating or positive outlook for upgrading in the near future.

Table II.14
SEE country rating by leading international agencies (status as of 2006)

Country	Fitch ICBA	Moody's	Standard and Poors
Albania	.	.	.
Bosnia-Herzegovina	.	BR (RUR)	.
Bulgaria	BBB (stable)	Baa3 (stable)	BBB (positive)
Croatia	BBB- (stable)	Baa3 (stable)	BBB (stable)
Macedonia	BB (positive)	.	BB+ (stable)
Romania	BBB- (stable)	Ba1 (positive)	BBB- (stable)
Serbia-Montenegro	BB- (stable)	.	BB- (positive) (a) BB (positive) (b)

(a) for Serbia.

(b) for Montenegro.

Source: OECD (2006).

II.2. Basic Differences in Comparison to CEE Countries

II.2.1. The analysis of key macroeconomic indicators and developments has demonstrated a number of differences between (and among) the SEE and the CEE countries, as measured by statistics. They include the late start of economic growth mainly driven by domestic demand, low level of exports and foreign direct investments, dangerous levels of trade and current account deficits, wide-range poverty, mass migration due to economic and security reasons, high share of illegal activities, and many other elements. Evidently, the wars in the WB have exacerbated these trends. However, it would be a mistake to think that the differences are overwhelmingly due to this factor, since the outbreak of violent conflicts has had its historical roots deep in the mentality of societies. In addition, some countries of the region were saved from wars, yet they too were unable to follow the CEE transformation pattern from the beginning of the 1990s.

Transformation indices regularly prepared by international organizations point to a clear evidence of the delayed adjustment by emphasizing non-economic factors as some of the key explanatory elements of the well-known development. In early 2005, the Freedom House created a ranking based on selected political, legal and institutional criteria that are critical to sustainable and high growth rates. They included election procedures, the development of civil society, independence of the media, efficiency of governance, constitution, legal and judiciary framework and corruption. On a scale of 1 to 7, where 1 is the "perfect" situation, Slovenia, Poland, Estonia and Hungary are best placed, with marks below 2. In turn, SEE countries' performance ranges between Bulgaria (3.25) and Kosovo (5.50), with Romania (3.58), Croatia, Serbia and Montenegro (each of 3.83), Macedonia (4.00), Albania (4.13) and Bosnia (4.29) in between.[5]

II.2.2. Without an awareness of the legacy of history, the behaviour, objectives and policy choices can be hard to understand. The differences between them and the CEE countries did not start in 1990, but go back to several centuries of historical developments. This "discovery" became manifest at the moment of the dissolution of former Yugoslavia, a country that both in political and economic terms used to be considered a success story, at least in the societies of the CEE countries living under Soviet domination for decades.

The (European) peripheral position of SEE differs in several aspects from the semi-peripheral situation of the CEE.

First: it is true that the two regions of Europe had been living for centuries under foreign occupation, but there was a basic difference between German-Austrian and Turkish values.

Second: although none of the CEE or SEE countries was able to start a genuine and sustainable development based on their own efforts, the external factors of development produced different results. Certainly, the external modernization impact experienced by the CEE was larger and more lasting. At the same time, the absorption capacity of the CEE societies was higher as well. In other words, there was a way to (partial) economic modernization from the semi-peripheral pattern of CEE development that could create a special interface between different socio-economic and political models. This interface was much less evident in the case of SEE, so this peripheral model seemed largely unable to be adjusted to the mainstream European models. Obviously, several decades of economic orthodoxy and separation from the world market have further "consolidated" this pattern. It is interesting, however, that the more open Yugoslav model was unable to overcome historically fixed "systemic" rigidities as well.

5 Quoted by Calic (2005), with reference to www.freedomhouse.org.

Third: both CEE and SEE were constantly at the mercy of the Great Powers, but their interests differed over centuries, also due to the geographic differences between CEE and SEE. They considered the CEE region as their genuine backyard of expanding market outlets and, partially, of production possibilities. Therefore, there was a fundamental interest in incorporating these countries into the genuine reproduction system of the developed "core". In turn, the Great Powers' basic interest in SEE remained motivated mainly by political and security considerations, and was not economy-driven. In case of regional insecurities, efforts focused on (re)creating apparent stability without fostering the potentially lasting economic pillars of sustainable security and peace. One has to add that the potential for conflict in the SEE region was always generated by a lack of ties to Europe's mainstream development and could also be attributed to rivalry among leading European powers.

Fourth: modern nation-state development was more delayed in SEE than in CEE. In fact, this process was interrupted several times either by domestic or external developments and could not be completed until now. As a result, weak, and, in some cases, failed states emerged with serious questions of viability in the future. It may not be an exaggeration that at least part of the SEE "has to be catapulted into the 21st century after having remained predominantly in an everlasting 19th century". (Mintchev, 2001)

Fifth: for historical reasons, SEE remained much more heterogeneous in ethnic, religious, mental and behavioural terms than CEE (which did not contain ethnically homogeneous societies either). This gave sufficient fuel to different conflicts and violent actions, including wars, ethnic cleansing and 19th century nationalism, as well as the emergence of authoritarian regimes with little sense of democracy and "globally open(ed) mentality".

Sixth, and finally: external powers with high capacity to intervene in emergency situations did not understand that long-term stabilization of the SEE, particularly the WB cannot be successful by using the same instruments that may have generated positive results in other parts of the world, including the CEE countries. The most frequent and mistaken assumption used to be that economic development in itself could provide meaningful contribution to political stabilization and the long-term solution to open conflicts.

II.2.3. Of course, similar to CEE, SEE cannot be considered a homogeneous region either. Both historical developments and previously indicated macroeconomic performances have varied substantially. Consequently, based on different criteria, such as the level of economic development, the capacity of the national public administration to tackle priority issues, ethnic composition, etc., different subgroups can be created. The EU's strategy, considering the region, primarily the WB as a "package", has created such groupings (two accession countries, one country in the process of accession negotiations, others in different stages of institutionalized relations with Brussels). Such differences were certainly widened by the WB war that led to substantial disintegration and to completely new political and geographic realities in the region.[6] New political (state) borders were drawn, new countries emerged as successor states of the former Yugoslav Federation, "traditional" production and trade relations were abolished and fundamentally reorganized in part. No less importantly, the ethnic (and demographic) composition of the population of several countries has changed dramatically, both as a result of wars and also as a consequence of migration and immigration, as well as highly different birth rates in different parts of the SEE region.

Only if these factors are always kept in mind in a basically economy-focused analysis, and if the interdisciplinary approach is followed consistently can one expect to provide a realistic analysis with viable policy recommendations.

II.3. Barriers to Sustainable Development

After reviewing the main characteristics of the starting situation in the SEE economies and their similarities with or differences to the transforming CEE countries, some of the basic barriers to sustainable development have to be pointed out. We do not intend to draw a comprehensive picture but will concentrate on two issues. First: what are the barriers to generating or maintaining a viable path to macroeconomic development. Second, which are the basic factors that may hinder successful adjustment to EU patterns, a precondition for future integration. In most cases, the two areas overlap. Of course, a number of additional barriers will have to be discussed. Some of them will be addressed in the next chapter that analyzes selected, high-priority sectors and socio-economic activities in the context of sustainable development. Another part seems to be characteristic of just one or a few countries and has been highlighted in the attached country studies.

II.3.1. One set of barriers is related to the slow progress in the transformation process. Of course, different SEE countries have reached different stages in transformation. Thus, the quality of reform needs and the reform-targeted areas may substantially differ. While in the WB, in many areas we can still speak of a lack of reforms or a very early period of effective transformation, the EU accession countries of 2007, Bulgaria

6 The "velvet" break-up of Czechoslovakia cannot be compared to the developments in the WB, either in its antecedents, or concerning its consequences. This is another important difference between SEE and CEE.

and Romania face different challenges in the transformation. In a critical analysis prepared two years after the "democratic" political change in Serbia, the Free Market Center in Belgrade stated that not so much concrete steps toward reform as even "the commitment to reforms is missing".[7] Similarly critical are the findings of the *Croatian country study*.[8] Although Croatia started negotiations with the EU, its reform readiness and its level of economic transformation were far behind those of the CEE countries at the moment they initiated official talks with Brussels.

The challenges for Bulgaria and Romania are different, since, after years of delay and hesitation, they do not stem from the lack of reforms but partly from the growing pressure in areas yet to be reformed (pension system, healthcare, education, regional development, etc.), partly from the unavoidable negative consequences of the reform process. In the forefront of the barriers one can identify specific structural problems, such as the inadequate or insufficient response of the private sector to already implemented reforms, the insufficient depth of the financial markets, the lower quality of public administration, and similar issues.

One of the real "crossroads" of transformation is the attitude of a given country towards privatization in general, and the chosen pattern of privatization in particular. In this respect, the CEE countries opted for different ways in the first half of the 1990s as well. However, after a period of mistakes or ambiguous successes (with serious backlashes even in case of apparently positive results), all of them, except Slovenia, became committed to market-conform privatization accompanied by a massive inflow of foreign capital. Also the so-called "strategic" sectors were opened up to privatization. Looking at the SEE countries, Bulgaria consistently opted for market-conform privatization following fundamental reforms and macroeconomic stabilization in mid-1997. Similarly, Romania has substantially liberalized its privatization practice in the last few years, even if some bottlenecks remain, mainly in the banking sector. In turn, the privatization process proved much more uneven in the WB. Old oligarchic or monopolized structures have been preserved, even though, on paper, privatization has taken place. The main objective of privatization was not to achieve higher economic efficiency and domestic and international competitiveness, *i.e.*, improving the conditions of resource allocation, but to redistribute economic assets in order to maintain old structures and networks.[9] Put in a historical context, it is clear

---

7 See Hernádi, *Serbia-Montenegro country study*, 2006, p. 7. *Free Market Center: Two Years of Reform in Serbia: A Wasted Opportunity*, Belgrade, 2002.

8 *Preparation for and Accession Process to the European Union of Croatia* (Lakatos, *Croatia country study*, p. 41.)

9 In Gligorov's (2005) appropriate terminology, how to create "non-standard corporate structures", p. 17.

that, among other factors, old-fashioned nationalism and the delayed building of the nation-state may have played an important role in shaping privatization, particularly in Serbia-Montenegro and Croatia.

This privatization pattern has substantially impaired the rapid bottom-up development of new small- and medium-sized firms, key pillars of sustainable growth, particularly in case of lacking transnational companies involved into the domestic manufacturing and service industries. Certainly, other factors, such as the bureaucratic measures and the splitting-up of Yugoslavia as a larger "domestic" market have also had a negative effect on the SMEs. For instance, already in the early 1990s, thousands of small firms were established in Serbia-Montenegro. However, as a result of the fragmentation of the Federation, half the registered firms have gone out of business. In addition, for many years, until most recently, it was much more difficult to set up a new company and by far not just because of the smaller market.

Although inefficient, uncertain, unreliable and unpredictable legislation is a major barrier to sustainable development for all actors on the market, it hits, evidently, SMEs much more than other players (*e.g.* the absence of a reliable cadastre and land registration, high collateral requirements when the legality of the collateral is questioned, etc.).

II.3.2. Barriers to sustainable development do not arise from the inevitable negative processes accompanying fundamental transformation. To a different degree in each country, previous patterns of development and deeply rooted historical heritage affect both the policy mix and the expected outcome. This legacy is all the more "burdensome" if apparent and perceived "success stories" are linked to its implementation. In this context, the special character of the so-called "Yugoslav model" is a unique burden to fundamental economic and social transformation of the WB countries in general, but of Serbia-Montenegro and Croatia, in particular. In fact, the Yugoslav model tried to create a "third way" between central planning and the market economy in the 1970s and 1980s. Although its results were not outstanding (Yugoslavia did not increase its competitiveness either on the global or the European scale), it served as an interesting attempt in a politically, ideologically and economically divided Europe. One could argue that the Yugoslav Federation, and even its successor states (could have) started the new era in Europe and the transformation period with a clear advantage in comparison to all other CEE countries. However, the legacy became a real brake, "first-comer's advantages" rapidly turned out to be obvious disadvantages, and not as a result of the Balkan wars. Slovenia, widely considered as the most successful new EU member country, still suffers from this legacy.[10]

This negative heritage can be identified at least in three fields. First, employee-managed firms are very reluctant, or openly opposed, to be privatized (not least by foreign owners). Therefore, the preferred way of privatization became the joint venture, with obvious drawbacks for sustainable development, company growth, market orientation, technological renewal or new labour market policies. Second, high and increasingly uncompetitive wages remained, since wages used to be resistant to downward movement in all European countries. It has clearly hampered structural changes in different economic activities and blocked the overdue transformation of the labour market. Third, the mental barrier is particularly hard to be overcome. Namely, it is very difficult to mentally adjust from the former "pioneering" position to "lagging behind" and then quickly back to the "pioneering" status within half a generation. It has to be emphasized that war alone cannot be blamed for this dramatic change in the ranking of the transforming countries. As in several cases in European history, wars could have been used to overcome negative or outdated heritages earlier. Just the opposite happened in the WB. The consequences of wars did not accelerate the process of modernization, opening up, liberalization and widespread international cooperation. On the contrary, they had strengthened old attitudes that, seen from today, have already become substantial barriers to sustainable development under the conditions of global competition and an expanding European Union.

II.3.3. The structure of central budgets represents another barrier to lasting development. The centralization degree of the budgets (share of the budget in GDP) varies from country to country, the lowest being in Albania and Macedonia (around 30% of GDP). The key problem is, however, not just the size of the budget, although the low level of tax revenues (mainly due to tax evasion and a lack of tax collection mechanisms) reduces the funds available for financing public utilities and an efficient administration. No less important is the structure of the budget, since it remained mainly redistributive instead of allocating part of the available resources to future-oriented activities (education, better environment for innovative and entrepreneurial activities, etc.). Moreover, the consequences of the wars (most of them fought in order to protect "national interests" or to reach "national independence") have resulted in a sizeable budgetary burden, since war veterans and "national heroes" had to be compensated adequately. Entrepreneurship is, however, not only

10 This is clearly seen in the declining relative competitiveness of Slovenia as compared to other CEE countries in the key Western European markets.

impaired by the well-known crowding-out impact of the centralizing and redistributional budget, but also due to high interest rates that punish the people who would like to start a private venture.

II.3.4. A barrier that, unfortunately, got little attention in the past years, is the emergence of additional regional disparities. SEE, similar to CEE, although on a lower income level, was characterized by substantial regional disparities, both in terms of GDP *per capita* figures and the structure of main economic activities. These differences began to widen once the economic transformation started and resulted not only in huge income (and ownership) disparities[11] but also in the emergence of visible poverty. The dissolution of Yugoslavia added another feature to this picture. Namely, the financial support provided through the central budget by more prosperous members of the Federation to less developed members (mainly by Slovenia and Croatia to Kosovo, Macedonia and Bosnia) stopped at the moment the Federation was dissolved.

Catching up to the EU and, even more, EU membership may aggravate this problem, at least initially. It is a general experience that available resources are better used in a more developed economic and administrative environment than in less developed regions. Thus, the "efficiency gap" may be widening in the next few years, provided EU resources will be used efficiently and not become a support to bottomless undertakings in underdeveloped sectors and geographic areas. Due to the modest amount of financial resources provided by the EU to the WB countries, this problem does not seem an imminent issue. However, both Bulgaria and Romania, facing the challenge of spending much higher amounts of EU resources as of 2007, have to be prepared for this potential barrier to sustainable development.[12]

II.3.5. Finally, another neglected factor of sustainability has to be mentioned. In the last decade, human capital has become the key "production factor" and the main element of competitiveness all over the globe. Sustainable development in the SEE countries desperately requires the critical mass of human resources for successful socio-economic modernization. There are two dangers, both of them acute in most countries. On the one hand, the provision of public money available for educa-

---

[11] Still, the difference is not higher than in several old EU member countries, particularly if one takes into account not only current incomes but also the value of individual property, a much more "diverging" factor than registered income differences.

[12] This statement may seem paradoxical and contradictory, since development economics generally considers the availability of financial resources as one of the key elements of accelerated and sustainable development. The problem is not with the amount of money, not even with its efficient allocation but with the temporary gap between booming regions (developed "islands") and the lack of the required absorption capacity in underdeveloped areas of the same country.

tion, training, retraining and research and development is insufficient in most cases. Also, due to budgetary constraints, other priorities and structural rigidities, it is not clear where additional resources can be found to finance education. On the other hand, the impact of large-scale emigration of young, flexible and, to a large extent, skilled people from practically all SEE countries in the last ten to fifteen years, may have already created a lasting barrier to sustainability.

II.4. The Main Actors of Modernization and Sustainability

Sustainability does not only depend on viable economic and social policies but also on the commitment of different players to successful modernization. In this section, a short overview of the crucial real and potential players in the region will be offered in order to identify the driving forces behind development and the right mixture of the key players ("modernization alliance") that is likely to emerge in the next few years.

II.4.1. More than the CEE countries, SEE is heavily influenced by international actors. They include at least four different groups and also approaches to create the conditions for sustainable development. First, international financial institutions have been playing a key role in ensuring stable macroeconomic framework in all countries. IMF programs have been accepted everywhere, although their validity and strength differs from country to country. However, in the least developed SEE countries the IMF still plays a decisive role in determining the basic macroeconomic conditions for development. Second, mainly in those countries where the influence of the IMF is stronger, the activity of the international donor community is stronger as well. Most likely, Bosnia and Kosovo, but also Macedonia and Serbia-Montenegro could not have survived the wars without international financial and technical support. Third, the role of international businesses linked to the inflow of foreign direct investment has to be pointed out. This sector had played a crucial role in the successful modernization and EU accession of most CEE economies. Therefore, the same positive impact can rightly be expected in the SEE region as well. However, at the moment, FDI does not represent a strong policy-shaping lobby except in Bulgaria and Romania. The reasons for its limited influence can be found in their modest share in the total production, investment, employment or exports of the target country, due both to serious barriers to economic transformation and to substantial restrictions to market entry and the normal functioning of the economy. Nevertheless, there is a widespread view that the role of FDI will be growing in the coming years all over the SEE region. Finally, the EU as the main external actor has to be mentioned. Prospective EU membership is a major hope and the key catalytic agent for policy-makers and societies.

Regarding the future of economic and social development, the role of the individual external actors shows important differences despite the fact that everybody underlines and, most probably, is deeply convinced of, its personal fundamental and positive impact on creating the framework for sustainable development. International financial institutions used to stress their contribution to financial stability. Correctly, their patterns imposed on (accepted by) the target countries of SEE have largely supported macroeconomic and mostly financial stability, a precondition for accelerated growth. However, by shaping framework conditions, they were not able to generate the basic components of sustainable growth. As international experience proves, sometimes just the opposite happened, and the apparent stabilization collapsed and had to be followed by another (more or less fragile) financial and economic "consolidation". Moreover, it has to be added that imposed and quick (forceful) macroeconomic consolidation may strangulate some potential factors of sustainable growth and produce a wide gap between monetary stability and real economic progress (convergence). If this gap, or in a more positive formulation, the monetary framework cannot be filled by "contents", *i.e.* real and competitive economic players, activities and products within a certain time, stabilization may prove unsustainable and the imposed system may collapse with serious economic, political and social consequences.

The international donor community's outstanding role in supporting the survival of selected SEE countries cannot be denied. One of the basic dilemmas of future development is, however, to what extent and in what timeframe can this kind of financial contribution be replaced by other factors, including, first of all, by the genuine revival of the domestic economy. Short-term and badly needed help may also bring about negative consequences. On the one hand, in some cases, foreign assistance is unable to convert failed states into viable states. On the other hand, lasting financial support tends to generate a subsidy mentality instead of mobilizing domestic resources and strengthening the entrepreneurial, risk-taking, responsible attitude of the society. Part of other transfers, essentially private remittances from citizens working in the EU and in overseas countries may produce the same, ambiguous impact (helping to survive or even live on a decent level, but, and at the same time, freezing new economic endeavours).

Foreign direct investments, as well as export revenues of companies and growing revenues from tourism and other services are at the heart of economic development, since they are produced by actors of the real sector and flow back to the economy. Despite some negative and mostly temporary phenomena, such as dismissing some employees in the first phase of restructuring following privatization, previously flourishing local producers and suppliers dropping behind, or its contribution to (temporarily) growing regional disparities, FDI has been playing a crucial role in the rapid modernization and economic catching up of less developed countries with structural deficiencies. However, its efficiency indicated a high level of dependence on a number of framework conditions, such as, among others, the quality of the host country's legal and institutional system, the availability of human resources, the state of physical infrastructure, the development level of the business culture, including potential domestic partners (and competitors). Moreover, its interests sometimes conflicted with the consequences of macroeconomic stabilization. However, their international network, both concerning potential suppliers and necessary financing could generally overcome rigidities and shortcomings of the host economy.

Finally, beyond undeniable political and psychological effects, the EU's main role lies in creating a functioning public administration, the rule of law, a transparent regulatory framework and in contributing to higher levels of business confidence. Brussels' financial support is an additional, although modest contribution to the SEE countries. The gradual implementation of the *acquis communautaire* in the SEE region can be considered a benign external pressure as compared to the rather "drastic" requirements and conditionalities involved in IMF stabilization packages. Still, some conflicts may emerge between the institutional-legal approach of the EU and the obvious interests of the business sector, both domestic and foreign. Specific rules related to environmental standards, consumer protection, competition policy, etc., may be felt too restrictive by different actors of the business community, at a lower level of overall economic development.

II.4.2. The impact of domestic players used to be more limited, at least in the first stage of transformation. Many of the traditionally influential lobbies became the losers of transformation, while new actors did not know a lot about the characteristics of the "real" market economy. In addition, rapid and, according to some experts, overhasty liberalization and opening up deprived potential new domestic actors of the possibility of "growing up" and become competitive after a certain time of "artificial" protection.[13] As of today, it is premature to try to identify those domestic economic groups that could become the drivers of long-term economic growth in SEE. Most probably, the sector will consist of some

[13] Unlike fellow Western European SMEs, mushrooming SMEs in CEE, and even more in SEE, had to face intensive international competition from the very beginning of their existence. They did not have a "grace period" to become stronger in technical, financial or managerial terms. Neither could they enjoy the state-level protection of the domestic market, due to the rapid implementation of the free trade agreements with the EU. In turn, the companies that survived seem to be highly competitive both on the domestic and on the international markets.

large restructured and privatized domestic firms, competitive SMEs, domestic suppliers of transnational companies and selected firms with regional influence (the so-called regional transnational companies). This trend is already apparent in CEE countries and there are signs that, with some delay, selected SEE economies will also follow this path. However, something important has to be noted here: whatever the reasons may be, the longer a SEE country wants to keep its "strategic" enterprises alive and block the way to market-conform privatization or forbid the sale of companies to foreign owners, the less probable is the emergence and consolidation of the described pattern of development. This point has to be stressed particularly when looking at the half-hearted privatization in some ex-Yugoslav countries, let alone the general attitude – from hesitation and reluctance to open opposition or even hostility towards potential foreign buyers.

The relative influence of the individual groups depends on their position in the production, reallocation and distribution of value added. Sectors with high value-added contribution may become important market players. They include selected manufacturing companies (mainly with international market orientation), competitive SMEs, specialized service providers and, in several countries of the region, the rapidly developing tourism industry. In addition, the main beneficiaries of EU funds have to be taken into account, provided they will make efficient use of the available resources.[14]

II.4.3. Developmental economics ascribes great importance to the role of the State in the catching-up process. Unfortunately, one of the main victims of the transformation was the public administration. In order to enhance the modernizing role of the State, at least three requirements have to be fulfilled. First, the quality of public administration has to be substantially improved, not only at the central, but also the regional and local levels. Among others, this task is closely linked to the efficient utilization of EU resources, since a large part of them will directly reach regional and local actors (communities). Second, public administration has to become free from any kind of (party-)political influence. Excepting the minister and the political state secretary, all public administrators should be protected by law against party-political and coalition-driven considerations. Third, the traditional role of the State as the collector and redistributor of a (generally large) part of GDP, has to be reconsidered. Without giving up a certain level of protection, particularly to the needed people, the State has to become increasingly a generator and not only a

[14] In contrast, agriculture, once the provider of domestic financial resources in the early stages of (mis)industrialization, at least in the medium term can be considered the net recipient of resources in the framework of the inevitable revival, restructuring and modernization of this important sector all over the SEE region.

(re)distributor of values and welfare. At present, very few European countries meet these conditions. Certainly, SEE countries are still far away from these standards. But some of them, to some extent as a result of the learning process from negotiations with the EU and adjusting to EU requirements, are expected to become stronger players of the economic development in their respective countries. In turn, some others will keep on struggling with the predominantly failed character of (mis)created and "artificial" States. In the latter case, no meaningful role will be played by representatives of the State and by the public administration at large.

Regions and rapidly developing sub-regions or municipalities may become other interesting "public" actors. Strengthened in the struggle for power, competence and economic resources with state organizations and backed by EU contacts and money, some of them may acquire larger influence. The pattern of their "networks" including EU institutions, domestic governmental organs but also foreign (and domestic) investors can offer a challenging topic for further socio-economic analysis in the coming years. Particular attention should be paid to regional actors in the two acceding countries of SEE.

II.4.4. Development scenarios for SEE in general, and for WB in particular, do not rule out the possibility of the emergence of ethnicity-based players. Ethnic roots of building State, economy and society are rather strong in several countries of the region. Such a development could, however, be extremely dangerous both for the sustainability of domestic development and for regional security and stability. Unfortunately, but understandably in the given historical context, the most committed groups can be identified in the least developed countries or in failed (or not-yet "full-fledged") nation-states.

II.4.5. No less dangerous is the scenario that includes actors of illegal production and services, as well as criminals in the "mixture" of driving forces behind development. Criminality is already widespread in all SEE countries and could easily become an organizing element of everyday life and economic activities, with emerging special structures and interest networks. If these activities cannot be curbed and their representatives cannot be excluded from the "special mixture of driving lobbies" responsible for the sustainability of favourable and EU-conform development and policies, major setbacks in SEE may result with a high degree of probability. This could certainly be seen as a big obstacle on the way to upgrading institutionalized relations with the EU, including full-fledged membership as the ultimate goal.

II.5. Main Uncertainties and Dilemmas Accompanying the Macroeconomic Development

EU efforts aim to maintain and further strengthen the already attained level of stability in SEE. Several policy instruments by Brussels have been developed in order to serve this basic objective. An analysis of their efficiency will follow in Chapter V. Here, attention will be directed at those uncertainties and dilemmas that are part of the transformation and EU-related adjustment and, even contrary to current EU policies, may raise serious questions of sustainability and further progress.

II.5.1. The first dilemma emerges between apparent stabilization and the availability of the critical mass of resources (human, financial, institutional, political-social alike) and their own initiatives required for a genuine and lasting development process. Return to the past system is unlikely everywhere, but progress is by far not clear and uniform. In addition, recurring, albeit geographically limited, return to ethnic hostilities and violence cannot be excluded at all. None of the current structures can be considered as fully consolidated, particularly if the relevant political and social impact of urgent or indispensable reforms is anticipated (mainly the consequences of fiscal and budgetary restructuring). Still, Bulgaria, Romania and Croatia can manage these tasks and challenges. Much less predictable is the pattern of development in Serbia (particularly with respect to the ongoing negotiations about Kosovo and the aftermath of Montenegro's referendum in favour of independence), as well as in Albania and Macedonia. Bosnia and, independently of its future status, Kosovo are far from a situation that could be described as "self-stabilization". Their stability depends crucially on further and sizeable external resources without anything like the start of genuine economic development in sight.

II.5.2. Economic recovery reflected in higher growth rates and sustainable growth process for a few years can prove fragile already in the next period if the key driving forces of growth will not change. Currently, favourable growth is fundamentally nourished by domestic demand involving both domestic commodities and services (housing) and imported goods. However, this situation is unsustainable for a longer period.[15] In fact, domestic markets are very small, solvent domestic demand

---

15 In this context, both Bosnia-Herzegovina and Kosovo are in a special situation, since a large part of domestic consumption is generated by foreign troops, experts and members of the international community. In addition, citizens employed by international organizations contribute to higher consumption. Moreover, the largest part of private transfers is spent on consumer goods and basic services as well. Disregarding the two extreme cases, the risky Albanian situation can be mentioned. Here, high private transfers have been accompanied by a 70% expansion of credit activities of banks in the last

cannot be increased meaningfully (even if part of it is generated by remittances that finance private construction but also everyday life) and a large part of the aging population has a rather small, if any, share in aggregate purchasing power. Also, tight fiscal policies and external constraints (high trade and current account deficits) put evident limits to the longer-term continuation of such policies. As in some CEE economies, investment- and export-led development could become the key driving force. However, both require not only a much stronger cooperation with FDI but also a different structure for foreign investments. With the partial exception of Romania, FDI in the manufacturing is relatively underrepresented, and if available, it mainly produces for the domestic market (or low-skilled labour-intensive textile and clothing industry for external markets). In countries with stricter regulation, such as Croatia, for example, FDI is definitely domestic-market oriented. One of the biggest question marks is to what extent international capital will consider SEE as an important location for export-oriented activities and as a potential partner in the global (and European) production and service network of leading transnational companies. Until recently, foreign business focused on privatization deals on the one hand, and on the acquisition of public utilities and banking, on the other. Large-scale green-field investments with predominantly export-oriented production, a major engine of sustainable growth in CEE countries, are (still) rare, or, in the WB countries, practically non-existent.[16]

II.5.3. Sustainability may be questioned or threatened by voluminous trade and current account deficits in all countries. Without finding new and sustainable revenue sources, either by markedly strengthening the export potential or by developing parts of the service sector (tourism, where available), or, no less importantly, by attracting more foreign capital investment in value-added activities, in the short or medium term external financial constraints may become a major barrier to development. This challenge particularly hits countries with great reliance on external financing by the international donor community, including Bosnia, Albania, Kosovo, Macedonia and Serbia. In addition, the current level of private remittances, a highly sensitive and volatile element of financial sustainability for most countries (but mainly in Albania and Macedonia) cannot be taken for granted, either. Thus, also in this context, the reconsideration of FDI-related policies is extremely timely in several SEE countries.

---

year alone. Needless to say, the rapidly increasing money supply has overwhelmingly financed the booming but artificial and unsustainable demand for consumer goods.

16 It is noteworthy that a recent World Bank study sees the main factors of sustainable development in Albania in such areas as tourism, agrobusiness, light manufacturing and transit trade. See: Mladenova, *Albania country study*, 2005, p. 9.

II.5.4. Tight monetary policies in general, and fixed exchange rates in particular, have already resulted in another dilemma. For domestic inflation rates are regularly higher than the average inflation in the Eurozone, appreciation of fixed currencies cannot be avoided. Certainly, there has been a substantial "appreciation reserve" in all countries of the region, either by pegging the national currency to the DM and the Euro at an undervalued rate, and/or by mobilizing large productivity reserves. However, this process does not last forever, and further appreciation resulting in overvalued exchange rates[17] may impair not only the competitiveness of already existing production but, and no less importantly, hinder the inflow of foreign capital for production (and not exchange rate-related speculative) purposes. Romania and Serbia have been able to avoid this trap until now, with varying impact on competitiveness. Serbian export has remained at a very low level and favourable exchange rates have been unable to compensate for basic obstacles to and uncertainties in the legislation and market entry conditions for potential foreign investors. In turn, Romania could considerably benefit from its exchange rate policy by attracting wage-sensitive foreign investors. However, on the negative side, it has to be added that foreign-owned production became concentrated in low value-added, low-technology segments of the production chain, in the best case a factor of sustainability of economic development based on sensitive sectors and weak structures.

II.5.5. With the exception of Croatia, all countries are facing growing pressure for wage increases, partly over the growth rate of labour productivity. In fact, wages (and even more, pensions) in all countries are desperately low, even in comparison with the CEE countries. The double negative impact on price-based competitiveness, resulting from appreciating exchange rates and growing wages, challenges economic policy makers and raises some key issues of further restructuring as well as open dialogue and new agreements (consensus) between the government, the business sector and the employees.

II.5.6. Beyond the generally well-known economic dilemmas listed in the above paragraphs, a mainly political consideration has to be mentioned. This can be described as the dilemma of imported stability against generating domestic instability. The issue is closely linked to preparation for EU accession and the mandatory implementation of a large number of EU rules and regulations before membership. If a country is not prepared

---

[17] Real exchange rate distortions towards overvalued exchange rates can be found in several SEE countries, as in Croatia (with an overvaluation of 16%), Serbia (9%) or Albania (8%). In turn, all CEE countries still have an undervalued exchange rate (with a margin between 6% for Slovenia and 33% for Slovakia). Among the SEE countries, and despite an eight-year history of currency board, Bulgaria's exchange rate indicates the highest degree of undervaluation (22%). For details see: Holzner (2005).

to face the consequences of quick and massive introduction of EU rules but still insists on rapid accession, it may find itself in a very dangerous situation. On the one hand, membership in the EU can certainly be interpreted as additional stability, a guarantee of security. However, the consequences that the economy and the society of the new member country are not prepared for may create serious domestic problems leading to substantial internal instability (*e.g.* high levels of unemployment, closing of factories, massive bankruptcy of uncompetitive SMEs, etc.). All factors taken into consideration, the (immediate) balance of membership may easily turn to the negative.

II.5.7. Finally, a similarly neglected social dilemma has to be addressed. Sustainable development requires active, flexible societies. There is a potential danger that societies largely dependant on external resources and not on personally produced revenues/incomes will be less able to change their behaviour. Dependence not only on international donors but, even more, on relatives living abroad and sending back sufficient money to live on without any personal effort or work, can create a dangerous and highly passive attitude. This kind of "self-marginalization", obviously on a higher level of living standard than that of many other citizens, but decoupled from the real economic processes of the country can question the sustainability of the system in several ways. Evidently, there are justified questions concerning the economic sustainability of high-dependency patterns. Moreover, in the longer term, the social and political sustainability of the given system may be at stake, since deep cleavages may be produced within the texture of the given society. Economic and social tensions between active workers and rent-seekers are likely to increase, as the conflict potential between poor people with long years of employment and wealthy citizens without any meaningful personal efforts.

II.6. Domestic Tasks of Sustainable Economic Development

This section aims to provide some general recommendations in the light of three basic sets of requirements: the domestic agenda of further transformation, adjustment to the EU conditions and consideration of the key Lisbon goals (in their renewed form as of 2005). Depending on the level of economic development, progress made in the process of transformation and the quality of institutional relations with the EU, individual SEE countries have partly similar, partly different priorities to be addressed. In addition, not only the priorities but also the timing and sequencing of major policy reforms and measures may vary. It is not the aim of this study to offer country-specific proposals in this section. Special features will be addressed in more detail in other parts of the survey. Here, emphasis is laid on summing up the most important domestic tasks to be performed in order to ensure sustainability (even if, in several cases and to different degrees, sustainability includes an external factor and responsible attitude of out-of-the-region actors as well).

II.6.1. Economic policy has to remain credible both to domestic and international players. Since SEE countries cannot be put into a homogeneous package, some country-specific priorities will be mentioned here.

In Bosnia-Herzegovina, a better business environment requires more permeable boundaries between the entities of the country. Also, the large role of the public sector has to be reduced and public utilities have to be reformed and restructured. Labour market flexibility, a common problem of several countries, has to be enhanced and at least part of the labour force working in the informal sector should be reintegrated into the primary labour market. Policies have to put special emphasis on creating new jobs.

Bulgaria faces partly different challenges. In that country, beyond successful membership in the EU, the government's goals include an active participation in the Lisbon programme. On the one hand, priority is given to poverty reduction and higher wages. On the other, and simultaneously, knowledge-based sectors of the economy have to be supported, with special attention on reforming the education system.[18]

Despite low inflation and the apparent macroeconomic stabilization, Macedonia is facing serious challenges deriving from the still high level of political risk threatening long-term business opportunities. In addition, the business environment is poor, the banking system is largely incompetent and foreign direct investment is low. The key task involves developing a more favourable business climate and the substantial reduction of political and administrative risks.

Romania's economic assessment has been improving in the last years. The better climate is indicated both by the larger inflow of foreign capital and the more favourable rating of the country in different international surveys.[19]

Serbia's economic policy makers have to get prepared for a period of lower levels of official international support and turn to other external sources of financing, including bringing back Serbian savings held in

18 Interestingly, Bulgaria has developed a detailed plan of adjustment to the Lisbon goals. For more detail see: Petkova, *Bulgaria country study*, 2006, pp. 9-10.

19 A recent evaluation of the World Bank states that in some key areas, such as sustainable private sector growth, infrastructure, agriculture, poverty reduction, the Romanian situation has improved and reached a level qualified as "satisfactory". The only area in which notable improvement could not be registered was institutional reforms. In detail see: Novák, *Romania country study*, 2006, p. 14.

foreign banks[20] as well as encouraging FDI inflows. This, however, requires a substantial restructuring of the economy, legislation, but also a change in the public's mentality. In addition, the privatization process has to be speeded up and the banking sector has to be made more transparent.

II.6.2. Although with different priorities concerning individual sectors, and partly with different policy instruments, structural reforms are in the forefront of domestic tasks everywhere in the region. Particularly in the WB countries, they have to address both product, labour and financial markets. Perhaps the biggest difference or delay as compared to the CEE countries can be detected in these same areas. This set of objectives includes several special policy areas.

First, liberalization has to be extended to current account and capital movements. At the same time, trade liberalization has to be widened not only in WB countries far away from EU membership but also in Croatia. Analyzing details of the commodity market's liberalization in Bulgaria and Romania on the one hand, and in Croatia, on the other, it is clear that there are still large differences indicating Croatia's long way to achieving this goal.

Second, privatization needs further impetus. SEE countries stand at different levels of privatization, with Bulgaria well advanced and WB countries much less open to domestic or foreign investors. Despite some delays and non-transparency in several privatization deals, Romania now seems to enter a new stage in which energy utilities will be offered for sale. Also, the creation of a new state authority for privatization (AVAS) is expected to streamline the process of privatization.[21] In contrast, privatization remains a difficult policy task in Croatia, for ambitious privatization plans to sell minority stakes in the Privatization Fund by the end of 2004, and all companies with majority ownership by mid-2005, have not been implemented. Not only institutional and legal problems but an inherited mentality of protecting "national champions" (*e.g.* loss-making shipyards) and the erroneous and narrow-minded attitude to save jobs instead of implementing badly needed restructuring and getting ready for international competition have blocked the process.[22] Even more contra-

---

[20] "Remonetization", *i.e.* the return of foreign exchange assets from foreign banks has been calculated by the World Bank in the magnitude of 10% of GDP. At the same time, international donor support reached 5%, and privatization revenues from foreign and domestic buyers totalled another 4% of GDP in 2003. For more detail see: Hernádi, *Serbia-Montenegro country study*, 2006, pp. 9-10.

[21] In 2004, the new agency privatized 62 large and medium-sized companies, based on transparent and competitive tendering procedures, in the amount of Euro 170 mn. Still, there remained on the list about 1,500 firms to be privatized. See: Novák, *Romania country study*, 2006, p. 18.

[22] For a detailed analysis see: Lakatos, *Croatia country study*, 2005, pp. 10 and 20.

dictory is the privatization process in Serbia, where less than 50% of the GDP is produced by the private sector.[23] Missing property rights protection and the lack of an effective bankruptcy mechanism, the continuous insistence on selling minority shares, the overdue task of consolidating the banking system and legal uncertainties concerning the purchase of state-owned infrastructure companies are among the most important barriers to speeding up privatization. In addition, the ambitious effort to restructure about 60 large, insolvent state-owned companies before selling them may turn out to be a big mistake, since restructuring generally costs a lot of taxpayers' money without eliminating the networks of vested interests. Further uncertainties are caused by the loss of time, since domestic and potential foreign markets are rapidly changing and the technological upgrading holds additional risk factors in a world of unprecedented modernization. As a consequence, substantial financial, technical and human resource inputs may end up in a worse situation than if the loss-making company had been either closed or sold several years ago. Finally, the outdated but deeply rooted "economic nationalism" can be mentioned as a major obstacle. Similar experience has been reported from Montenegro.[24] In addition, privatization may become hostage to political deals. A large-scale privatization in Serbia (the petrochemical plant in Nis) fell, at least temporarily, victim to a government crisis. Namely, the government would have needed the partial support of the opposition to sell the plant to one of the well-known foreign bidders (Shell, BP, Lukoil, MOL, among others). However, support was made dependent on the government's willingness to stop legal procedures against the son of Milosevic.[25] This case is not only proof of direct interdependence between politics and economics in most countries of the region but also the lasting influence of former politicians (sitting in The Hague) on domestic (economic) developments. This is certainly not the form of "positive sustainability" this study has repeatedly addressed.

Third, the banking system needs basic reforms in several countries. While Bulgaria has privatized more than 80% of its banks, and the positive impact is already felt, the situation is less encouraging in other SEE countries. Certainly, Croatia and Romania have made sensible progress recently, but some deals are still pending and the motives of expected decisions not quite transparent. Again, Serbia shows substantial delays,

---

23 In contrast to the EBRD estimate, other calculations point out that, based on the capital value of the companies, just about 5% has been privatized, while 95% remains in state ownership. In total, about 900 companies should be privatized and another 2000 should be closed. As compared to the initial pace, the speed of privatization has substantially slowed down in the last two years (Reuter, 2005b).

24 Hernádi, *Serbia-Monenegro country study*, 2006, pp. 10-11.

25 Reuter (2005b), p. 386.

with less than 40% of private ownership in the banking system in mid-2005. In addition, the Serbian government has forbidden green-field foreign investments in the banking sector, in order to provide "better opportunities" for the (partial) sale and survival of existing Serbian banks.

Fourth, the traditional role of the State has to be redefined. It is interesting that fundamental changes in the assessment of the role of the State, both at the political and social level were more rapid in ex-Soviet-dominated countries than in the successor states of Yugoslavia that disposed of an extensively publicized "mixed system". Certainly, the Balkan wars have reinforced the role of the State, both as a result of building new nation-states and as a necessary factor of preserving or fighting for "national independence". Even more, the natural reaction of "failed states" has been, apparently, a general effort to create more, not less, "State". The lack of a new approach is apparent everywhere in the WB countries, but, due to the long way to EU membership, it does not seem to be too urgent. In turn, the problem may become acute very soon in negotiations between Croatia and Brussels. Accommodation to the *acquis communautaire* requires radical steps in removing administrative and judicial obstacles to the business community in general, and a dramatic change in national rules of competition policy, in particular. In this context, large-scale state aid programs have to be cancelled.[26]

II.6.3. Institution-building is another basic task of sustainable development. Even more, it is an outstanding target of accommodation to the EU requirements, since, from the beginning, and due to its basic structure and priorities Brussels has been devoting more attention to institution building in conformity with EU rules than to taking into account and supporting "real" economic convergence.

A comparative study on the "institutional quality" of selected SEE (and Black Sea) countries reveals substantial deficiencies and cross-country differences (Hammermann-Schweickert, 2005). The survey based on the structure and performance of legislative, administrative and judicative institutions comes to several relevant conclusions. First, to no one's surprise, it states that SEE countries lag behind CEE countries in all institutional aspects, while the latter joined the EU at a lower level of institutional maturity than Mediterranean countries.[27] Second, progress made in creating efficient legislative institutions is considered greater than in judicial and administrative fields. Third, in terms of the speed in

[26] In the last few years, while taking essential political steps to prepare for accession to the EU, Croatia has increased the amount of direct state aid from 2.8 to 3.4% of GDP (Lakatos, *Croatia country study*, 2005, p. 20).

[27] Probably this was the only area, however crucial for the successful adjustment to EU structures, where (most of) CEE was less prepared for membership than Spain and Portugal in the first half of the 1980s, a few years before their accession.

preparation, Croatia and Bulgaria have registered the greatest progress in recent years, with Romania lagging behind but still better placed than any other WB country. The lowest grades were given to Macedonia, Bosnia and Albania with respect to legislative institutions, to Bosnia and Serbia concerning administrative institutions and to Albania, Bosnia and Serbia in the area of judicial institutions. The overall picture shows a relatively positive development in Croatia and Bulgaria and worst performance in Bosnia, Serbia and Albania.[28] For more details see Appendix Tables II.6.3/1-5.

II.6.4. Finally, reforms with a long-term impact have to be mentioned. Although their implementation did not form part of the first stage of transformation and macroeconomic stabilization, in the longer run the sustainability of already achieved results may substantially depend on additional and long-range reforms, as it is clearly indicated by the experience of several CEE countries (partly reinforced by EU membership and adjustment to EMU conditions). Although these issues covering the radical restructuring of the central budget can be identified everywhere in the region, in some countries, for different reasons, they do not form part of the current priorities. However, Bulgaria, Romania and Croatia have to make serious efforts in order to reform their pension system, the health care system and the tax regime. In the latter case, some steps have already been taken[29] (see Romania's 16% tax rate), but individual measures can hardly offer a viable solution to the general restructuring of the budget (both on the revenue and the expenditure side). Apparently, these reforms do not form an organic part of EU adjustment, since most of these fields have remained under national competence in the EU. Thus, despite the progress made in creating the internal market, substantial cross-country differences can still be identified within the current EU. Nevertheless, as the experience of the CEE countries shows, fundamental reforms have a number of integration-related implications, not least in relation to the successful preparation for introducing the Euro as the official currency in the new member states. Examining the sustainability criteria from this angle, it has to be stressed that three major "playing fields" have to be taken into account. First, looking at the growing financial pressure, the economic and socio-political conditions of the fundamental reforms have to be clarified. Second, most long-range budgetary reforms require a high

---

[28] All indicators are based on Kaufmann-Kraay-Mastruzzi (2005), *Governance Indicators for 1996-2004*. The World Bank, as quoted by Hammermann-Schweickert (2005).

[29] In 2005, corporate profit tax rates fluctuated in the SEE countries between 10 and 30%, a bit lower than in CEE countries. Interestingly, seven SEE countries had nine different tax rates. Not only Serbia and Montenegro have autonomous tax regimes, but also the Republika Srpska differs from the tax system of the Federation of Bosnia-Herzegovina (ICEG EC Corvinus, 2005b, p. 3).

level of consensus between government and opposition (most of the draft laws need a two-third majority of support in the national parliaments). Third, and no less importantly, the acceptance, if not the open support, of the measures by the majority of the society is needed. Thus, sustainability is an interplay of technical, economic, political and socio-psychological factors. It is an unprecedented challenge to keep stability and, thus, sustainable framework conditions, in transforming economies at a relatively low initial level of economic development and with a pressing desire for rapid improvement in living standards. Most probably, and foremost in SEE countries, longer-term macroeconomic stability is more dependent on social tolerance and political agreement than on the implementation of adequate economic policies. To put it more precisely: the latter is a precondition for any kind of sustainability, but, most probably, not a sufficient instrument that could in itself guarantee the achievement of predetermined objectives.

CHAPTER III

Selected Special Issues Influencing Relations between the EU and SEE

The analysis of the macroeconomic development of the SEE in Chapter II, covering both progress made and tasks and challenges ahead, highlighted on the margin a number of special subjects that are supposed to essentially influence the future of relations. They will undergo a deeper and more detailed survey in this chapter, with special reference to the capacity of selected areas to contribute not only to sustainable growth but also to the upgrading, *i.e.* higher quality relations between the EU and the SEE region.

Due to the basic character of the study, topics of predominantly economic nature have been selected. However, the complex situation, particularly in the WB, made it imperative to include some areas with relevant political and social implications as well. Of course, none of the issues to be addressed in the following can be considered as "purely" economic, social or political. There is a network of interdependences that cannot be ignored when dealing with the respective topics. Just to mention a few: trade prospects cannot be decoupled from the legacy of the Balkan wars; visa policies substantially affect regional business opportunities; agriculture has a lot to do with social degradation and poverty. Moreover, migration has a number of political, social and economic motives and consequences. Beyond some macroeconomic consequences, private financial transfers (remittances) have manifold implications on income levels, consumption patterns, investment priorities, social behaviour and future developments.

Despite a high level of interdependence, Chapter III is divided into two basic parts. In the first section, in nine subchapters, key economic and social factors characterizing the SEE countries will be dealt with. In turn, the second section containing three additional subchapters addresses mainly political, institutional and social questions related to the consequences of the dissolution of the Yugoslav Federation and of the Western Balkan wars.

The SEE-related issues include trade with the EU; intraregional trade among the SEE countries, in general, and among the WB countries, in particular; foreign direct investments, unemployment, physical infrastructure, agriculture, human resources including migration, private financial transfers and poverty. All of them have a fundamental impact both on the future of regional stability and cooperation, and the quality of relations with the EU in the framework of the overall prospects for an enlarging Union.

The second section dedicated to special problems of the Western Balkans opens with an analysis of the consequences of territorial disintegration as well as wars and hostilities. The following subchapters deal with distorted institutions, widespread criminality and ethnic issues.

III.A. SEE-related Issues

III.1. Trade Relations with the EU

III.1.1. From the very beginning of the EU's establishment, European integration considered trade policy as the most important instrument both for its own, internal development and for influencing other actors. The impact of this key instrument of policy implementation can be particularly felt in shaping political and economic relations with countries (or groups of countries) at a lower level of economic development and that represent low economic bargaining power. No doubt, the SEE countries belong to this category. They are policy-takers while Brussels is the unquestionable policy-maker.

This imbalance is aggravated by the fact that small countries are generally more dependent on external economic relations, including foreign trade, than large economic units with an important domestic (internal) market. This statement applies to all small and open economies, irrespective of their development level. Thus, it is not a special feature of SEE. However, the degree of economic leverage may be influenced by the relative economic power of the policy-taker country (*e.g.* the manoeuvering room of Switzerland is different from that of Slovakia or Albania). In this respect, SEE is at the bottom of the EU's pyramid of policy-taker relations. This pyramid can be constructed in two different ways. One pattern is based on the lack or availability of trade preferences and, also, on different levels of preferences. In this comparison, SEE countries fare better than many other countries in the world (excluding member states). Second, based on economic bargaining power, SEE seems to be in a worse position than most other countries not only at the same or similar level of trade preferences but also without preferences (East Asian emerging economies). In fact, they can be placed in this pyramid of bargaining power immediately above the ACP (African, Caribbean and Pacific) countries that include ex-colonies of developed EU member countries, but below all other groups with which Brussels has preferential trade contacts.

III.1.2. In the next paragraphs, in a three-level structure, a detailed analysis of trade relations of the SEE will be provided. First, overall features of SEE trade development will be addressed. Next, trade relations with the EU will be discussed with select comparative figures of Central European new members. Finally, status and trends in intraregional trade will be highlighted. The basic statistics used in all surveys have been provided by different publications of the United Nations and the relevant foreign trade-related Eurostat documents. In addition, the database of the Vienna Institute for Comparative Economic Studies (WIIW) was used, particularly with respect to intra-regional trade flows. Despite the application of different statistical sources, figures are generally comparable and wide discrepancies that would question the relevance of the survey could be avoided.

III.1.3. Both the economic literature and practical experience have repeatedly demonstrated the positive correlation between economic growth and openness to international flow of commodities, services and capital. Moreover, export-oriented development in small and open economies has always been underlined, since exports used to be one of the key engines of rapid growth and, in successful cases, also the main engine behind structural change and enhanced global and regional competitiveness. Looking at the dimensions of the national markets of SEE countries, all of them need large, stable and expanding external markets for sustainable development. Still, there is a large difference in the degree of openness of the CEE and SEE economies, as measured by the share of trade in GDP.

The most important indicator shown in the table below is the substantial difference exports are playing in the generation of GDP in individual countries. The lower level of openness, *i.e.*, the lower level of competitiveness, is particularly manifest in the difference between the SEE countries, on the one hand, and the comparable figures for the Czech Republic and Hungary. As a result, there is still large potential in increasing both the volume and the share of exports. Moreover, different export/GDP ratios characterize the comparison of individual SEE countries. While Bulgaria's export amounts to 40% of GDP, and, based on its share in GDP, is nearest to the two Central European countries, other countries show a much lower degree of "openness". A second group is formed by Romania and Macedonia, with about one-third of export/GDP ratio (but, as we will see, with very different geographic orientation, with Romanian export mainly going to extra-regional markets, and Macedonian exports remaining within the SEE region). A third group is represented by Bosnia-Herzegovina and Croatia, with exports accounting for about one-quarter of the GDP. Finally, Serbia-Montenegro and Albania can be considered as "closed" countries, with a marginal role of exports in the production of GDP. Taking into account that all SEE countries are economies with small domestic markets, the low level of export indicates a mainly inward-looking economic structure with an unsatisfactory level of competitiveness.

Table III.1
Theoretical trade openness of CEE and SEE countries (merchandise exports to GDP in PPP in USD)

Country	Actual 1995	Openness 2003	2003 realization ratios (a)
Albania	10.5	15.8	0.53
Bosnia-Herzegovina	14.6	20.6	0.56
Bulgaria	21.8	29.6	0.94
Croatia	39.6	40.5	0.98
Macedonia	27.7	23.9	0.61
Romania	14.5	25.9	1.02
Serbia-Montenegro	.	.	.
Czech Republic	33.2	62.3	1.41
Estonia	45.0	75.4	1.63
Hungary	30.2	61.0	1.78
Latvia	24.2	35.1	1.04
Lithuania	28.8	43.7	1.09
Poland	19.3	27.4	0.92
Slovakia	39.2	60.5	1.40
Slovenia	74.2	70.1	1.33
SEE-7	21.5	26.0	0.77
CEE-8	36.8	54.4	1.33

(a) figures above 1 indicate high level of openness, while figures below 1 suggest unused reserves of further opening up.

Source: computations based on UN COMTRADE statistics.

A comparison of country figures between 1995 and 2004 shows the main trend in gradual opening up to foreign markets. There has been a dramatic development both in Hungary (where the export share of the GDP almost doubled) and in the Czech Republic. In turn, SEE countries provide rather contradictory figures, with Romania being the only country with a gradual and substantial opening up (with export accounting for 22 and 32% of GDP, respectively). Bulgaria's previously high share of export/GDP remained on the same level (in 1995, this country was still "more open" than either Hungary or the Czech Republic), while Croatia's figureindicates a slight decline. The same trend can be observed in Albnia, from a very low initial level. Figures for Macedonia and Serbia-Montenegro, although at a quite different level of export shares, are volatile.

Table III.2
Share of exports in GDP (at official exchange rate, in %)

Country	1990	1995	2000	2004
Albania	10.1	8.1	7.1	7.5
Bosnia-Herzegovina		1.2*	24.0	24.1
Bulgaria	23.3	40.9	38.2	40.6
Croatia		24.6	24.1	23.4
Macedonia		26.9	36.9	31.6
Romania	15.1	22.3	28.0	32.1
Serbia-Montenegro		10.3	15.5	12.2
Memorandum items:				
Czech Republic		39.2	52.3	62.5
Hungary	26.6	28.7	60.4	54.7

* prior to 1998, data refer to the Federation of Bosnia-Herzegovina only.

Source: UN. Statistical Division. National Accounts, http://unstats.un.org/unsd/snaama/selectionbasicFast.asp, and UNCTAD Handbook of Statistics, 2005.

The main conclusion to be drawn is that, except Romania, exports could not be converted into an important engine of economic growth. Growth of the domestic economies, if any, was fuelled by other factors, mainly by domestic consumption. The fundamentals of export-oriented growth have not been created which, as mentioned in the previous chapter, results in serious doubts about the sustainability of the current pattern of growth in the region.

III.1.4. The basic pillar of the EU's trade policy towards SEE consists of autonomous trade measures (ATMs) that came into force in 2000 as part of the SAP. These measures were granted for a period of five years and were prolonged for a second five-year period in 2005. The measures implied the right to export to the EU without customs duties and quantitative restrictions, except certain categories for textile and food products. Wine, fisheries products and sugar enjoy preferential tariff quotas, while tender beef benefits from reduced custom duties. Quotas on the import of textiles continue to apply to Montenegro and Kosovo.[1] Free trade agreements, already in place with Croatia and Macedonia (although not yet fully implemented, due to a transition period covering several years) represent a higher level of trade liberalization for two reasons. First, they are less exposed to "conditionality" considerations and time constraints (5 years and waiting for prolongation), in case a SEE country fails to fulfil commitments made to the EU in the framework in which ATMs were

1 Following the enlargement of the EU in May 2004, the measures were extended to the ten new member countries as well.

introduced. Second, at the end of the day, they will create a free-trade zone without any restrictions and partial exemptions, which are part of the ATMs, since the latter do not (automatically)include some sensitive industrial products and all agricultural commodities.

Despite dramatic trade liberalization on the EU side, there have remained some commodities that face market access barriers. Most of them are of minor importance as compared to the total volume of production or export of a given country. However, some may have a negative effect on overall growth and export performance. It has to be noted that select protectionist measures have been applied by Brussels even to acceding countries.[2] Finally, they had to be lifted completely at the moment of accession. (However, some safeguard measures have remained in place, mainly in agricultural trade.)

Another set of EU-imposed barriers includes the application of restrictive rules of origin. According to this regulation, products exported by the Western Balkan countries but containing non-EU-originated imported inputs are not covered by the ATM regime.[3] The fact that the WB is not part of the "European cumulation" area creates five different bilateral trade regimes, one for each of the WB countries. The applied rules of origin may largely impede trade among the WB countries. This contradicts the objective of the EU aimed at enhancing regional trade, since it disrupts even that part of trade and cooperation contacts among ex-Yugoslav republics that could (have) survive(d) the negative developments of the last decade (see more in Chapter III.2). According to specific trade-related studies, more than 50% of Croatia's exports to the EU do not enjoy tariff-free market access (Calic, 2005, p. 23).[4] In this context, the multilateralization of bilateral free trade agreements as of 2007 may have a positive impact, since it would abolish the rules of origin-related restrictions.

However, the potential benefits offered by the preferential market access largely depend on the economic realities of the (would-be) exporting country. The EU has a decade-long negative experience with ACP countries that have been unable to make use of the generous benefits offered, due to domestic economic problems (both in quantitative, qualitative and structural terms). They could have exported practically all kinds of finished manufactured products to the EU markets, but very few new commodities appeared. In turn, East Asian countries, without practically any trade preferences, could gain substantial market shares in the EU. Some-

2 For instance, Brussels imposed anti-dumping restrictions on urea imported from Bulgaria. In April 2004, the EU adopted definitive safeguard measures on import of preserved citrus fruits from Bulgaria.

3 Bulgarian and Romanian exports have the same treatment as those of the new member countries before accession, as stipulated in the bilateral Association Agreements.

4 With reference to a World Bank study prepared by Kaminski and de la Rocha (2003).

thing similar has been happening when we compare the CEE and the SEE export performance on EU markets. In fact, there is little difference concerning market access conditions. However, there is a large performance gap reflected in the sluggish export by SEE (and particularly by WB) countries. The basic causes include still restrictive trade policies both concerning import and export. For several reasons, SEE countries are reluctant to open their markets to foreign competition. First, they fear that domestic companies enjoying high protection of the domestic market will be crowded out. Since export-orientation remained limited, these firms do not possess additional external (export) opportunities to compensate for the partial and potential loss of the domestic market and to switch to a new growth path based on exports. Second, the artificially high share of agriculture and the large number of small-scale agricultural producers, partly a forced answer to cope with the negative impact of transformation and the consequences of regional wars, could not successfully face import competition on the domestic food and agricultural markets. The social and domestic political implications are considered by many politicians to be disastrous. Third, tariff revenues form a relevant part of the government's total budgetary revenues that could not be replaced by other income sources in an economy of low level of development and a high level of tax evasion.[5] On the export side, and mainly as a result of the "war economy", domestic self-sufficiency plays a role, particularly as far as agricultural goods are concerned.

In addition, non-trade related factors have to be considered as well. Here, special attention has to be paid to the level of cooperation with international capital. The low level of FDI in the SEE (except in Bulgaria and Romania) is a major barrier to qualifying SEE economies to make better use of open EU markets. Moreover, inefficient customs administration in the WB countries may be a factor of hindering higher export volumes.

Only some of the SEE countries are members of the WTO (Albania, Bulgaria, Croatia and Romania). Kosovo and Bosnia-Herzegovina are regulated by international administration, while Macedonia and Serbia are not members of the WTO. This may not be a fundamental handicap in making better use of EU trade preferences. However, it is much more telling that, for instance, Serbia officially does not support the country's membership in the WTO because if would imply further and extensive liberalization of foreign trade with increasing international competition on the domestic market. The supporters of an autocratic trade policy, backed by economic lobbies with vested interest in the (very limited)

---

5 Tariff revenues are very important for Kosovo and Montenegro. Also, in Bosnia-Herzegovina, they account for a third of the entities' budget (Michalopoulos, 2001).

domestic market and, not least, by nationalists and "patriots" in the political field, represent a clear majority against the interests of exporters who are not or only poorly organized.[6]

Fundamentally, the low level of export response in most WB countries has domestic economic (and political) reasons. The region has not only considerably been falling behind the rapid export response of the CEE since the early 1990s, but also as compared to its own trade history. Export of goods and services accounted for less than one-fourth of GDP in Serbia in 2004, far from the 42% in 1989. The negative development is even more striking if we consider that in 2004 the ex-Yugoslav domestic trade became foreign trade and is part of the one-fourth performance of trade and services in GDP.[7]

III.1.5. The EU is the most important trading partner in the region. Its share in the total export of SEE amounts to more than 60% and has shown a growing trend in the last decade. The new member countries of the EU indicate a somewhat higher share of the EU in their total export, but the trend is similar both in the SEE and in the new member states. The worldwide and regional geographic composition of total export has been summarized in Table III.3.

---

6 In fact, Serbia applied for WTO membership in 2001, but after a long process fraught with political and technical difficulties, it had to apply again in 2005. The country might become a member in 2008. See Begovic and Mijatovic (2005), as quoted in Hernádi, *Serbia-Montenegro country study*, 2006, pp. 25-26.

7 For more details, see an enlightening study prepared by the World Bank on Serbia (2004) and quoted in Hernádi, *Serbia-Montenegro country study*, 2006, pp. 29-30. Please note that the much lower share given in Table III.1 does not contain trade in services.

Table III.3
Global geographic distribution of the merchandise export of SEE (in % of total export)

Country group	Year	Region (a)	CIS	SEE	EU-8 (b)	EU-15	NAFTA	Asia	Rest of the world
SEE	1993	30.9	13.6	5.2	9.8	53.9	4.1	5.2	5.9
	1996	27.7	8.3	5.9	10.2	59.3	2.6	4.5	5.9
	2000	28.4	8.0	6.0	11.6	61.2	2.1	3.4	4.9
	2003	27.9	6.2	5.1	12.8	62.2	1.7	3.8	4.4
Memorandum item									
EU-8 (b)	1993	27.5	12.4	1.9	11.4	61.7	3.4	4.5	2.9
	1996	25.1	11.5	1.3	11.9	65.1	2.2	4.8	2.8
	2000	25.0	13.0	1.0	10.6	65.3	2.1	5.2	2.4
	2003	23.7	10.0	1.1	12.0	65.4	1.6	6.7	2.6

(a) Central and Eastern Europe, including ex-Soviet republics, SEE and new member countries.

(b) Central and Eastern European countries that joined the EU in 2004.

Source: computations based on UN COMTRADE statistics.

As for the value of trade between the EU and SEE, two different statistical sources have been used. One is based on United Nations documents and gives figures in USD, while the other is the Eurostat, with figures calculated in Euro.

Table III.4
Development of exports by SEE countries to the EU (USD mn)

Country	1990	1995	2000	2004	Country share SEE7 = 100	
					2000	2004
Albania	140	165	244	501	1.6	1.5
Bosnia-Herzegovina(x)		17	814	1,361	5.2	4.2
Bulgaria	2,488	2,219	2,352	5,653	15.0	17.5
Croatia		3,516	3,058	5,150	19.5	15.9
Macedonia		514	619	741	4.0	2.3
Romania	2,356	4,635	7,247	16,674	46.3	51.5
Serbia-Montenegro		893	1,331	2,299	8.5	7.1
Memorandum items:						
Czech Republic		17,219	24,827	55,684		
Hungary	4,923	9,128	22,955	43,584		
Slovenia		6,021	6,259	10,276		
Yugoslavia	8,341					

Note and source: see Table III.2.

Total exports of SEE to the EU reached USD 32.4 bn in 2004, or just 58% of the Czech or 74% of the respective Hungarian figures. A decade earlier, total exports of USD 12 bn were still higher than Hungarian exports to the EU. Particularly ex-Yugoslav exports declined (except Slovenia), since they amounted to less than USD 5 bn, as compared with USD 8.3 bn, in the last year before the dissolution of the federation.

From a very low level, partly due to wars and delayed starting (or not-yet-starting) of economic transformation, exports to the EU started to gain dynamism after 2000. Between 2000 and 2004, exports by the two accession countries, Bulgaria and Romania more than doubled. In turn, export dynamism of the Western Balkan countries, including Croatia, remained less impressive but positive, especially as compared to the period between 1995 and 2000. Most probably, better access to EU markets, as provided by Brussels' trade policy instruments, has been playing a relevant role in increasing exports (with the least impressive growth in Macedonia).

Table III.5
Development of imports by SEE countries from the EU (USD mn)

Country	1990	1995	2000	2004	Country share SEE7 = 100	
					2000	2004
Albania	239	576	853	1,644	3.6	2.8
Bosnia-Herzegovina (x)		379	2,201	3,959	9.3	6.7
Bulgaria	2,901	2,372	3,187	8,568	13.4	14.6
Croatia		5,910	5,466	11,442	23.0	19.5
Macedonia		861	1,018	1,592	4.3	2.7
Romania	3,091	5,787	8,499	23,518	35.8	40.1
Serbia-Montenegro		2,000	2,494	7,995	10.5	13.6
Memorandum items:						
Czech Republic		19,472	24,073	53,394		
Hungary	4,856	10,533	20,855	42,640		
Slovenia		7,214	7,718	13,695		
Yugoslavia	11,671					

Note and source: see Table III.2.

As a result, relative shares in total SEE exports to the EU have been changing in the last years. Romania is the dominant player with more than half of total exports by SEE to the EU, followed by Bulgaria and Croatia. Other WB countries have marginal shares. Another important feature is that within the total exports by SEE to the EU, only the two candidate countries could increase their relative participation ratio, while that of all WB countries has shown a declining trend. Moreover, between

2000 and 2004, Bulgaria became the second largest exporter, overtaking Croatia. This development can only partially be ascribed to Bulgaria's better position in the EU trade policy framework. To a large extent, a more open economic policy, including large-scale privatization and better investment climate as compared to the Croatian situation, have contributed to the above change.

In contrast to the export figures, in 2004 total imports of SEE from the EU amounted to USD 58.7 bn, or 10% more than imports by the Czech Republic and 38% more than by Hungary. This indicates the high import needs of the region, but without a similar impact on exports. In the Central European countries, imports and exports developed simultaneously, or with a rather short time gap between higher imports and their impact on export generation. The underlying reason was the strong correlation between imported inputs and rapidly growing export-oriented and competitive production, facilitated both by appropriate economic policies and by the massive involvement of foreign capital that helped link imports and exports within a very short time. In turn, this correlation does not exist in the case of the SEE countries in general, and in the Western Balkan countries, in particular. Exports and imports became decoupled to a large extent. Imports mainly serve domestic consumption and not production. Moreover, the relatively low activity of foreign direct investments does not enable most countries to change the structure of imports and establish direct links between imports and exports.

Romania is the largest importer, with 40% of total SEE imports from the EU, followed by Croatia, Bulgaria and Serbia-Montenegro. In 2004, Croatia's imports alone reached as much as the total imports of ex-Yugoslavia in 1990. In the period between 2000 and 2004, Serbian imports increased more than three-fold, Romanian imports grew by 177%, while the respective figure for Bulgaria was 169%. Croatian imports doubled as well.

Regarding the participation of the individual countries in total SEE imports from the EU, Romania, Bulgaria and Serbia-Montenegro increased their share, the other countries register a relative decline. The aggregate share of Albania, Bosnia-Herzegovina and Macedonia accounts for 12% of the total imports only.

Similar trends can be identified in Eurostat data as well. Table III.6 summarizes changes in export and import between 2001 and 2005, by each of the SEE countries.

Table III.6
EU trade with SEE countries (Euro mn)

Country	EU Exports		Export Growth 2001-2005 (%)	EU Imports		Import Growth 2001-2005 (%)
	2001	2005		2001	2005	
Albania	1,114	1,320	18	336	459	37
Bosnia-Herzegovina	2,047	2,703	32	696	1,324	90
Bulgaria	4,436	7,133	61	3,741	5,282	41
Croatia	7,042	10,371	47	3,128	3,968	27
Macedonia	1,409	1,340	-5	693	954	38
Romania	12,103	21,789	80	10,135	15,278	51
Serbia-Montenegro	3,179	4,945(a)	56	1,266	1,744(a)	38
Western Balkans	14,791	20,679	40	6,119	8,449	38
SEE total	31,330	49,601	58	19,995	29,009	45

(a) figures for 2004.
Source: Eurostat. Comext.

In the first half of the decade, trade between the EU and SEE grew substantially. However, EU exports, from a higher starting level, increased more rapidly than imports. This is particularly true for trade relations with Bulgaria and Romania, both having had free trade agreements with Brussels well before membership. Also, these countries represent by far the largest share of the EU's trade with the region. Romania alone is a more important market for EU products than the total of the Western Balkans. Even more importantly, Romanian exports to the EU almost twice as much as the five Western Balkan countries combined. Finally, the heavy imbalance in trade has to be mentioned, which reflects two facts at the same time. On the one hand, the substantial import demand of the war-ridden and belatedly restructuring Western Balkans can be noted. On the other hand, the modest export potential of all ex-Yugoslav countries (including that of Croatia) has to be underlined.

III.1.6. In the first decade of transformation, CEE countries carried out an unprecedented geographic reorientation of their foreign trade from collapsing "Eastern" markets towards the EU. Many international experts doubted in the early 1990s that such a change could be possible, particularly within a short time.[8] Several factors played an important role in the successful geographic reorientation, such as the opening up of the EU market (although with more transitional restrictions than in the case of Western Balkan exports), early and courageous reform steps in several CEE countries and large-scale cooperation with international direct

[8] For an analysis of changes in geographic and structural patterns, see Inotai (2001).

capital and rapidly growing FDI. In the case of the SEE-7, this process is illustrated in Tables III.7 and III.8.

Table III.7
Share of the EU in total exports of the SEE countries
(% of total exports)*

Country	2000	2004	2005
Albania	93.4	84.5	84.1
Bosnia-Herzegovina	47.6	60.0	58.0
Bulgaria	51.2	57.0	55.3
Croatia	50.5	62.8	62.0
Macedonia	46.1	44.6	52.7
Romania	60.6	71.0	68.4
Serbia-Montenegro	37.7	51.6	50.1
Memorandum items:			
Czech Republic	68.6	83.3	84.4
Hungary	70.0	78.6	76.8
Slovenia	63.9	66.0	67.0

* United Nations figures are not comparable with EU statistics. Therefore, in this and the next table, figures taken from the wiiw database have been used.

Source: WIIW, http://www.wiiw.ac.at/balkan/files/data/export_dot, various years and Eurostat.

Table III.8
Share of the EU in total imports by SEE countries
(% in total imports)

Country	2000	2004	2005
Albania	75.6	72.5	70.4
Bosnia-Herzegovina	33.2	59.7	58.2
Bulgaria	44.0	59.4	56.8
Croatia	54.3	69.6	65.2
Macedonia	49.4	59.5	57.9
Romania	63.0	72.0	68.4
Serbia-Montenegro	40.9	56.3	51.2
Memorandum items:			
Czech Republic	61.9	77.5	70.9
Hungary	66.4	71.4	67.8
Slovenia	67.4	80.5	79.5

Note and source: see Table III.7.

The export orientation to the EU as the major market of all SEE countries is evident, since in 2005 all countries sold more than half of their total exports in the EU. Particularly high EU concentration can be seen in Albanian exports that are as heavily concentrated on the EU as those of the Czech Republic. Romania's EU-directed export orientation is at the same level as that of Slovenia. Other SEE countries sell 50 to 60% of their total exports in the EU.

Between 2000 and 2005, all SEE countries, except Albania with an unprecedented high level of EU share in total exports already in 2000, have increased their EU orientation in a meaningful way. Moreover, Bosnia-Herzegovina, Croatia and Serbia-Montenegro indicate a more than 10 percentage point increase of exports to the EU. From a higher starting level and less dramatically, but also the comparable Central European countries registered increasing EU orientation.

In imports, "dependence" on EU deliveries is even more pronounced than in the geographic orientation of exports by SEE countries. The EU's share is clearly above 50% in all cases, with similarly high figures for Albania, Croatia and Romania as well as Hungary and the Czech Republic (but still lower than Slovenia). It has to be added that longer term developments are better demonstrated by 2004 figures, due to the distorting impact of high oil prices in 2005 that has necessarily increased the share of suppliers outside the EU, since most energy imports originate in third countries.

Between 2000 and 2004, reliance on EU imports has fundamentally increased in all SEE countries (except Albania with the highest EU share anyhow), and introduced a new quality of trade relations, for in several cases imports from the EU surpassed in this period the 50% mark with the exception of Albania. The speed and size of reorientation is indicated by a 10 to 15 percentage point higher EU share in total imports within four years, and an even more dramatic reorientation in the case of Bosnia-Herzegovina (26.5 percentage points).

In comparing export and import shares of the EU in total trade of the individual countries, some interesting differences will become manifest. Both the Czech Republic and Hungary show higher EU orientation in exports than in imports. This is partly due to the fact that they cover most of their energy needs from Russia, *i.e.* from an extra-EU source. Partly, both countries have been incorporated into an international production network based on competitive imports from non-EU (mainly Asian) sources and on competitive exports to the EU. This pattern cannot be observed in the case of the SEE. The phenomenon that imports from the EU have a higher share in total imports than exports to the EU in total exports is not surprising since the less developed Balkan countries are far away from EU accession.[9] However, it raises some additional issues

[9] Interestingly, in this case, Slovenia also seems to follow the Western Balkan more than the CEE pattern. Slovenia has a lower level of "EU dependency" in its exports than in its imports. This discrepancy can be partly explained by the different geographic direc-

concerning the two acceding countries as well as Croatia, since they also have a higher EU share in imports than in exports, despite the fact that they are heavily (or partly) dependant on energy imports from Russia. The answer lies in the low degree of incorporation into the global network of transnational companies, and it is also a result of the domestic consumption-driven growth in the last period.

In summary, approaching the trade issue from SEE countries' perspective, most figures show an increasing role of EU-related trade, with the EU-15/25 being already the predominant trading partner of all SEE countries. On the contrary, the share of these countries' trade is of marginal importance in total EU trade flows. Some figures have been collected in Table III.9.

Table III.9
Share of the SEE countries in total EU exports and imports (in % of total EU trade, including intra-EU trade)

Country	EU Exports			EU Imports		
	1995	2000	2004	1995	2000	2004
Albania	0.026	0.035	0.045	0.008	0.010	0.015
Bosnia-Herzegovina(x)	0.017	0.090	0.109	0.001	0.035	0.041
Bulgaria	0.109	0.131	0.236	0.111	0.101	0.172
Croatia	0.272	0.224	0.316	0.176	0.131	0.157
Macedonia	0.040	0.042	0.044	0.026	0.027	0.023
Romania	0.266	0.349	0.649	0.232	0.311	0.507
Serbia-Montenegro	0.092	0.102	0.221	0.045	0.057	0.070
SEE-7 total	0.822	0.973	1.621	0.599	0.672	0.985
Memorandum items:						
Czech Republic	0.895	0.988	1.474	0.862	1.064	1.693
Hungary	0.484	0.856	1.177	0.457	0.984	1.325
CEE-5	2.948	3.907	5.376	2.856	3.864	5.802

Note and source: see Table III.2 and own calculations.

The five Central European EU members represent 5.8% of total EU imports (including intra-EU imports as well) and offer market for 5.4% of total EU exports (including intra-EU exports as well). The seven SEE

tion of energy imports. However, contacts with ex-Yugoslav republics is also manifest in its export orientation. The latter can be assessed as a clever trade strategy in order to make use of the traditional advantages in regional trade. However, it can also be interpreted as a sign of declining competitiveness leading to trade diversion from more to less demanding markets.

countries have a less than 1% share in total EU imports and a 1.6 share in total EU exports. Thus, the differences are manifold.

First, in 2004, CEE-5 exported six times more to the EU than SEE-7, while the difference in EU exports to the two groups amounted to less than four to one. As a result, the export-oriented development of the CEE-5 is clearly in contrast with the import-driven trade relations of the SEE-7 with the EU.

Second, the export share of CEE-5 in total EU imports is higher than the import share in total EU exports. Just the opposite development can be observed in the SEE-7 figures. Third, the share of both regions were gradually increasing in total EU trade figures. However, the export share of CEE-5 in total EU imports more than doubled between 1995 and 2004, while, it only grew by two-thirds in the SEE-7, starting from a very low level. On the contrary, the share of imports by SEE-7 doubled in this decade, while that of the CEE-5 grew by about 80% "only". Fourth, at the level of individual countries, Croatia and Macedonia lost relative market shares in total EU imports pointing, particularly in the first case, to declining competitiveness in the key developed market of the country. In turn, Romania could double its share in EU imports between 1995 and 2004. On the import side, each SEE country increased its share in EU total exports, led by a rather dynamic growth in Romania, but also in Bulgaria and in Serbia-Montenegro.

III.1.7. Another manifest difference to the CEE countries can be identified in the commodity structure of exports. CEE countries, although at a different degree and in diverging structures, have become important suppliers to the EU market of increasingly higher value-added and higher-technology goods. The original specialization pattern towards EU markets over decades of the socialist system was based on the predominance of agricultural goods and sensitive semi-finished goods and light industry consumer products (iron and steel, petrochemicals, textile and clothing, some other low-skilled commodities). This pattern, however, could be rapidly overcome first by Hungary, then by the Czech Republic and Slovakia. (Slovenia's export pattern differed from that of the other CEE countries, while Polish structural change remained a bit ambiguous, due to reluctant opening to foreign capital and to the "fallacious" attraction of the larger domestic market.)

This structural upgrading in the exports of the SEE countries to the EU ahs not taken place. The dominant export articles are still agricultural goods, minerals, raw materials, semi-finished industrial products and light industry commodities. The share of machinery and higher-demand consumer goods is very low. Similarly, high-tech and higher value-added products are lacking in most countries' commodity composition of exports. In sum, instead of reorientation towards intra-industry production and trade pattern, the dominant part of trade relations remains characterized by inter-industry division of labour (see Tables III.10. and III.11).

Although in different degrees, all CEE and SEE countries export mainly manufacturing goods to the EU. The share of these products (SITC 5, 7 and 6+8) fluctuates around 80% in most SEE countries, with a downward movement in Serbia-Montenegro (71%) and a substantial upward trend in Romania (90%). The same figures amount to 90% and more for the selected CEE countries. However, the fundamental difference lies not here but in the share of machinery in total exports as compared to other manufactured products (including labour intensive light industry goods such as textile and clothing, shoes and leather products and material-intensive commodities such as steel, metal products, rubber, paper etc.). Commodities belonging to the main group of SITC 7 used to represent higher technology and are based on higher skill-intensive work and, as a rule, they incorporate higher added value. Generally, the share of machinery exports is considered to be an important feature of technological development and competitiveness of a national economy. From this perspective, there is a substantial difference between CEE and SEE countries, but also among countries within both groups. Almost two-thirds of Hungary's exports to the EU consists of machinery products, while half of the Czech and 44% of the Slovene exports are in this category. In turn, the highest share of machinery among the SEE countries represented by Romania is still below 30% (and Croatia with just 30% in 2004 but a downturn in 2005 probably indicating high level of structural vulnerability).

In all CEE countries examined in the comparison, machinery exports are (substantially) higher than exports of other manufactured goods (6+8), while the latter dominate exports of the SEE countries, with 60 to 77% of total exports in many cases. Any substantial upgrading in the SEE economies would require a radical change in export structure in favour of higher technology content and higher value added machinery products. Some countries have started to reveal the first stage of this development trend, with a rapidly growing share of machinery in total exports (Croatia, Romania and, to a lesser extent, Bulgaria). Other SEE countries indicate a very low share of machinery exports, without apparent signs of structural catching up.

The real difference between CEE and SEE countries can not only be identified in different commodity structures but also in the value of exports. Total machinery exports of the SEE-7 group to the EU amounted to about Euro 5.5 bn in 2004, slightly more than one-quarter of Hungary's machinery exports to the EU.

Agricultural exports play a minor role, except by Macedonia, Bulgaria and Serbia-Montenegro (and Croatia in 2005), as expressed in % of total exports to the EU. Although on a higher level of agricultural exports, similar trends can be observed in the Czech Republic and Hungary as well.

Table III.10
Commodity pattern of SEE exports to the EU (in Euro mn)

Country	Year	0-9	0+1	2+4	3	5	7	6+8
Albania	1995	151	11	24	1	2	5	107
	2000	279	12	27	3	1	12	222
	2004	397	19	38	12	1	21	300
Bosnia-Herzegovina	1995	23	1	3	0	0	3	16
	2000	610	15	124	3	9	38	418
	2004	1,001	22	160	6	10	160	617
Bulgaria	1995	1,836	184	159	20	238	142	1,074
	2000	3,281	217	186	105	227	333	2,176
	2004	4,636	376	259	142	206	623	2,999
	2005	5,289	436	304	246	224	759	3,268
Croatia	1995	1,893	70	161	113	304	174	1,044
	2000	2,860	120	291	260	381	425	1,336
	2004	3,942	181	364	147	353	1,207	1,585
	2005	3,973	321	373	204	351	980	1,565
Macedonia	1995	664	132	34	0	5	140	349
	2000	813	67	31	0	6	112	596
	2004	778	83	42	14	6	34	597
	2005	946	116	52	3	7	35	730
Romania	1995	3,390	106	77	59	190	322	2,598
	2000	8,281	202	449	67	304	1,611	5,603
	2004	14,149	305	500	393	385	3,516	8,956
	2005	15,303	351	408	620	425	4,317	9,032
Serbia-Montenegro	1995							
	2000							
	2004	1,744	323	135	10	146	150	941
Memorandum items:								
Czech Republic	1995	8,997	258	717	353	667	2,544	4,299
	2000	26,549	789	1,119	724	1,679	12,095	9,786
	2004	39,236	1,319	1,271	1,054	2,288	19,505	13,131
Hungary	1995	7,610	794	422	202	590	2,743	2,754
	2000	24,181	1,357	589	446	1,539	146,412	5,444
	2004	32,198	1,773	792	583	1,762	0790	6,118
Slovenia	1995	4,245	59	125	3	184	1,470	2,378
	2000	7,072	71	169	10	540	2,764	3,360
	2004	8,747	112	217	146	698	3,866	3,592

Note: 0-9 total exports; 0+1 food, beverages and tobacco; 2+4 raw materials; 3 energy; 5 chemical products; 7 machinery and transport equipment; 6+8 miscellaneous manufactured goods.
Source: Eurostat, Easy Xtnet, Online Database, http://epp.eurostat.cec.eu.int.

Table III.11
Commodity pattern of SEE exports to the EU
(% of individual commodity groups in total exports)

Country	Year	0-9	0+1	2+4	3	5	7	6+8
Albania	1995	100	7.1	15.9	0.8	1.1	3.5	70.7
	2000	100	4.1	9.7	0.9	0.4	4.4	79.4
	2004	100	4.7	9.5	3.0	0.3	5.3	75.6
Bosnia-Herzegovina	1995	100	3.9	12.7	0.3	0.3	11.7	70.1
	2000	100	2.4	20.2	0.5	1.5	6.2	68.5
	2004	100	2.2	18.0	0.6	1.0	16.0	61.6
Bulgaria	1995	100	10.0	8.7	1.1	13.0	7.7	58.5
	2000	100	6.6	5.7	3.2	6.9	10.2	66.3
	2004	100	8.1	5.6	3.1	4.5	13.4	64.7
	2005	100	8.2	5.7	4.7	4.2	14-4	61.8
Croatia	1995	100	3.7	8.5	6.0	16.1	9.2	55.1
	2000	100	4.2	10.2	9.1	13.3	14.9	46.7
	2004	100	4.6	9.2	3.7	9.0	30.6	40.2
	2005	100	8.1	9.4	5.1	8.8	24.7	39.4
Macedonia	1995	100	19.8	5.2	0.0	0.8	21.1	52.6
	2000	100	8.2	3.8	0.0	0.7	13.7	73.3
	2004	100	10.6	5.4	1.8	0.7	4.4	76.7
	2005	100	12.3	5.5	0.3	0.7	3.7	77.2
Romania	1995	100	3.1	2.3	1.7	5.6	9.5	76.6
	2000	100	2.4	5.4	0.8	3.7	19.5	67.7
	2004	100	2.2	3.5	2.8	2.7	24.8	63.3
	2005	100	2.3	2.7	4.1	2.8	28.2	59.0
Serbia-Montenegro	1995	100						
	2000	100						
	2004	100	18.5	7.8	0.6	8.4	8.6	54.0
Memorandum items:								
Czech Republic	1995	100	2.9	8.0	3.9	7.4	28.3	47.8
	2000	100	3.0	4.2	2.7	6.3	45.6	36.9
	2004	100	3.4	3.2	2.7	5.8	49.7	33.5
Hungary	1995	100	10.4	5.5	2.7	7.8	36.0	36.2
	2000	100	5.6	2.4	1.8	6.4	60.5	22.5
	2004	100	5.5	2.5	1.8	5.5	64.6	19.0
Slovenia	1995	100	1.4	2.9	0.1	4.3	34.6	56.0
	2000	100	1.0	2.4	0.1	7.6	39.1	47.5
	2004	100	1.3	2.5	1.7	8.0	44.2	41.1

For notes and source see: Table III.10 and own calculations.

Background country studies contain more details about the export pattern of the individual SEE economies. Only some issues will be discussed in this section.

Albania's EU-oriented export industries include textiles, clothing, footwear and leather products, mainly based on subcontracting agreements with Italian companies and a modest FDI inflow primarily from Italy and Greece to the Albanian economy. No other industry has progressed significantly and, consequently, failed to become part of the more sophisticated supply chains of European companies. The furniture industry is expected to make substantial progress in exports to EU markets in the near future.

In Bosnia-Herzegovina's exports, natural resource-based products (iron, steel, wood, non-ferrous metals) account for almost half of exports to the EU. Goods requiring intensive unskilled labour (clothing footwear, furniture, hides, textiles) have almost the same importance. These two groups represent nearly 90% of total exports.

Also, the *Romanian country study* comes to the conclusion that, in spite of the very rapid growth of exports, the commodity pattern did not change significantly. The key components of the export development are still the labour-intensive industries (textiles, clothing and footwear representing about 30% of total exports). In addition, energy and semi-finished goods kept their importance in exports (petroleum products with 13, chemicals and metallurgical products with 8% each). However, most recently, and connected to accelerated privatization, machinery and electric industry products have gained in importance and now represent about 17% of total exports.

No such encouraging developments can be seen in the exports of Serbia-Montenegro. On the contrary, today, the commodity pattern of exports is "less developed" than it used to be two decades ago. Unskilled labour-intensive and natural resource-intensive products represent 75% of exports, despite high labour costs in regional comparison. The labour-intensive character of EU-related exports can be further strengthened by a recent agreement (April 2005) that grants free access to the EU market for Serbian textile and clothing articles. The importance of the agreement is not only attached to the high share of such companies in Serbia and their role in employment creation, but should be considered also in the light of the WTO liberalization of global textile trade as of the beginning of 2005 (Serbia is not a member of the WTO).[10]

III.1.8. Finally, the trade balance between the EU and the SEE has to be addressed. Free trade between countries on different levels of eco-

[10] It has to be noted that Serbian textile and clothing exports to the EU reached USD 1 bn two decades ago, while, in 2004, they only amounted to USD 156 mn. In addition, the EU rules do not apply to Montenegro (the agreement was signed with Serbia only), and do not offer free market access to those products that are not manufactured in Serbia (*i.e.* to potential re-exports from other SEE countries).

nomic development generally results in (substantial) trade surplus for the more developed countries. Therefore, the high trade deficit of the SEE countries is not surprising. However, here again we can find a marked difference in some CEE countries that, in the last few years, could achieve a surplus in trade with the EU (mainly due to their high level of incorporation in the international subsidiary networks of multinational companies). Of particular interest is the balance of agricultural trade. On the one hand, the SEE countries may have comparative advantages in this sector. Even more, these apparent advantages could be mobilized first and simplest in order to start an export-oriented growth. On the other hand, the EU's agricultural protectionism is well-known. It is instructive to look at agricultural trade figures more in detail in order to assess the real impact of ATMs on trade liberalization in agricultural products (Tables III.12. and III.13).

Table III.12
Development of the trade balance between the EU and the SEE countries (Euro mn and coverage ratios)

Country	1996-2000	2001-2005	Coverage ratios (export/import)	
			1996-2000	2001-2005
Albania	-2,312	-3,973	32.6	32.4
Bosnia-Herzegovina	-4,040	-6,243	27.2	41.9
Bulgaria	-784	-5,837	93.8	78.5
Croatia	-13,386	-26,027	44.4	39.2
Macedonia	-2,577	-2,560	53.6	58.7
Romania	-5,150	-15,901	84.3	79.7
Serbia-Montenegro		-12,199		42.9
SEE average	-28,249	-72,740	66.4	62.2
Memorandum items:				
Czech Republic (a)	-13,397	+11,202	86.2	106.5
Hungary (a)	-7,027	+18,679	91.8	113.8
Poland (a)		-28,711		87.1
Slovakia (a)		-2,059		103.0
Slovenia (a)	-7,926	-9,661	77.4	79.9
CEE-5 (a)	-82,405	-6,432	79.0	99.0

(a) for 2004 and 2005 EU-25 figures.

Source: see Table III.10 and own calculations.

Trade relations of the SEE countries with the EU are characterized by huge and persistent deficits. Moreover, the cumulated deficits were rapidly growing between the second half of the 1990s and the first half of this decade. While the aggregate deficit (without Serbia-Montenegro) reached Euro 28.2 bn between 1996 and 2000, the figure increased to more than Euro 46 bn between 2001 and 2004, just covering a four-year period. CEE-5 also registers deficit in trade with the EU (mainly due to Poland and to Slovenia), but its deficit was halved between 1996-2000 and 2001-2004, as a result of successful export-oriented development and growing competitiveness. More importantly, CEE-5 deficit in the first four years of this decade was already smaller than that of the SEE-7 (between 1996 and 2000, the former was still three times higher than that of the SEE-7). The Czech Republic could substantially cut its previous deficit, while Hungary's trade with the EU started to show slight surplus between 2001 and 2004. In turn, the aggregate deficit of all SEE countries kept growing (with the exception of Macedonia).

The figures reveal an important source of surplus in the global trade relations of the EU. In fact, in the period between 2001 and 2005 the EU exported to the SEE region commodities worth almost Euro 200 bn (Euro 192.4 bn exactly), while cumulative imports remained below Euro 120 bn (Euro 119.7 bn). As a result, the share of imports covered by exports (X/M coverage ratio) shows a two-third coverage on average in the SEE-7 (without Serbia-Montenegro) between 1996 and 2000. This indicator has declined in the last five years, partly due to the inclusion of Serbia Montenegro data. Interestingly, the figures are more favourable for the two acceding countries, with about 80% in each case. In turn, imports were three times higher than exports between 2001 and 2005 in Albania. Also, Bosnia-Herzegovina and Croatia have shown dramatic trade deficit with the EU. As a result of rapid export growth, the comparable CEE figures increased from less than 80% of coverage in the second half of the 1990s to almost 100% in the last five years. In addition, Hungary, the Czech Republic and Slovakia registered a trade surplus with the EU. In turn, Slovenia and Poland remained more similar to the Bulgarian and Romanian performance. The figure indicating the share of imports covered by exports improved between 1996-2000 and 2001-2005 for Bosnia-Herzegovina and Macedonia alone (and, evidently, for all CEE countries as well). In contrast, deteriorating data can be registered for each of the three more developed countries of the SEE region. The underlying reasons are structural change and preparation for EU membership in case of Bulgaria and Romania, and structural rigidities (temporarily compensated for by tourism and other transfers) in case of Croatia.

Table III.13
Agricultural trade between the EU and the SEE countries (Euro mn) (a)

Country		1996-2000 cumulative	2001-2005 cumulative	Coverage ratios (export/import)	
				1996-2000	2001-2005
Albania (b)	Exports	62	77	7.6	10.6
	Imports	812	727		
	Balance	-750	-650		
Bosnia-Herzegovina (b)	Exports	31	75	2.9	4.4
	Imports	1,064	1,696		
	Balance	-1,033	-1,620		
Bulgaria	Exports	1,050	1,743	113.9	116.8
	Imports	921	1,492		
	Balance	+128	+251		
Croatia	Exports	430	1,142	21.4	32.2
	Imports	2,008	3,550		
	Balance	-1578	-2,408		
Macedonia	Exports	287	423	44.2	49.4
	Imports	648	857		
	Balance	-361	-434		
Romania	Exports	747	1,465	44.8	39.4
	Imports	1,668	3,722		
	Balance	-921	-2,257		
Serbia-Montenegro	Exports				
	Imports				
	Balance				
SEE-7(b) (c)	Exports	2,606	4,925	36.6	41.0
	Imports	7,121	12,044		
	Balance	-4,514	-7,119		
Memorandum items:					
Hungary	Exports	5,269	8,729	246.8	156.2
	Imports	2,135	5,587		
	Balance	3,135	3,142		
Poland	Exports	5,943	14,451	81.7	124.5
	Imports	7,277	11,605		
	Balance	-1,334	2,846		
Slovenia	Exports	341	602	16.6	21.6
	Imports	2,058	2,782		
	Balance	-1,717	-2,180		
CEE-5	Exports	14,419	32,741	79.9	96.7
	Imports	18,040	33,864		
	Balance	-3,621	-1,123		

(a) SITC 0+1 (food, beverages and tobacco); (b) cumulative figures covering the period between 2001 and 2004; (c) except Serbia-Montenegro.

Source: see Table III.10 and own calculations.

Despite the fact that trade theory would assume high(er) export potential of less developed countries, SEE's agricultural trade with the EU shows a dramatic deficit. The deficit reached Euro 4.5 bn between 1996 and 2000, and increased to more than Euro 7 bn between 2001 and 2004-2005. With the exception of Bulgaria, all countries registered a deficit in agricultural trade with the EU, and all of them, except Albania, showed a growing deficit between the two periods (despite the fact that the cumulative figures cover only four years as compared to the same data covering a five-year period). Country specific coverage ratios fluctuated between 4(!)% for Bosnia-Herzegovina and 49% for Macedonia (except the higher than 100% ratio for Bulgaria). In order words, agricultural trade with an average coverage ratio of 41% behaved substantially worse than total trade, with a coverage ratio of 65%. Compared with the CEE countries, Poland's agricultural exports to the EU were almost three times higher than the cumulated agricultural exports of the SEE-7 group, while the total exports of the CEE-5 were 6.5 times higher than those of the SEE-7. In addition, the previous deficit in agricultural trade with the EU was substantially reduced due to the traditional surplus generated by Hungary and the reversal of trade deficit to trade surplus by Poland.

As a result, at least until now, agricultural exports could not become a major source of foreign currency in order to co-finance "modernization imports" by SEE countries from the EU. The problems can be identified both in the fragmented and disintegrated agricultural production of the individual countries, as well as in the prevailing agricultural protectionism of the EU, irrespective of the better market access opportunities offered in the framework of the ATMs after 2000.

III.2. Regional Trade: Inception, Results and Barriers

III.2.1. The idea to create an institutionalized framework for regional trade flows has many authors. First it emerged after the Dayton agreement with the objective that recreating former and establishing new trade links among the war-ridden countries could have a double positive impact. On the one hand, it could help overcome problems and bridge deep gaps generated by regional wars and violence. On the other hand, improved trade relations were expected to contribute not only to the partial restoration of the previously strong economic cooperation between now independent ex-Yugoslav countries but also to act as a new engine of growth and a medium-term instrument to overcome economic and social underdevelopment.

A few years later, the idea of fostering regional trade became part of the EU's strategy towards the Western Balkans. Trade liberalization, and later, possible EU membership was closely linked to the signing and enforcement of bilateral free trade agreements among the SEE and particularly among the WB countries. In fact, the conditionality of regional free trade appeared in a much more pronounced form than in the "classic" Association Agreements concluded with the CEE countries, a decade ago.[11] Moreover, they were considered as a prelude to EU membership by several years and without any clear accession date.

Finally, the Stability Pact identified the signing of bilateral free trade agreements as one of its main objectives. As a first step, Memoranda of Understanding (MoU) on future trade liberalization were prepared not only with the five WB countries, but also with Bulgaria and Romania, the two countries that did not have a chance to join the first wave of "Eastern" enlargement of the EU in 2004.[12]

The MoU was considered an important step to improve political and economic relations among the countries of the Balkans. First, it was supposed that this instrument could revive broken economic (and trade) relations between some of the previous members of the Yugoslav Federation (mainly between Croatia and Serbia-Montenegro). Second, and concerning the economic impact, MoU laid down standards for product coverage for free trade agreements among the participating countries. Within a gradual process of six years, it intended to include at least 90% of all products traded or to be traded, both based on the value of trade and the number of tariff measures, under the umbrella of free trade.

III.2.2. The above described approach is not at all new. The same recommendations were given by international organizations and influential experts to CEE countries at the beginning of the 1990s. Reorganization of lost regional trade relations was considered by these experts more important than a rapid opening up to the world in terms of both trade and capital flows. Probably, this position was essentially based on the facts and experience of decades-long poorly structured economies and the well-known difficulties of overcoming structural bottlenecks and deeply rooted and distorted trade structures rapidly. This approach became "suspicious" the moment when major trading partners on a much higher level of economic development and without the burning problems of systemic transformation signed up for this idea. Immediately, justified or not, all CEE countries became aware of another reality. Namely, that the support to more regional cooperation may be a useful instrument to divert

---

11 In fact, all "Europe Agreements" mentioned the desire to establish free trade conditions among the associated countries, simultaneously with the signing and implementation of the free trade agenda with the EU. However, it was never considered a mandatory conditionality criteria of membership. Moreover, the Copenhagen criteria did not contain this element as a necessary precondition of accession.

12 Since another country, Moldova belonged to the SP. However, due to the very modest trade it has with other SP countries (except the future EU member, Romania), respective trade data will not be included into this survey.

competitive economic actors from Western European to regional markets. In turn, from the very beginning of the transformation, it was absolutely clear for all CEE countries that the success of their socio-economic modernization and catching-up in living standards and technological development crucially depend on considering the developed countries' markets as the key target of export-oriented growth. A logical link was created between global competitiveness and regional cooperation, based on widespread international experience.[13]

Experience with regional integration based on, and expected to be driven by, more extensive trade relations has clearly shown that, for many reasons, no direct road leading from national import-substitution through regional free trade still based on (regional) import-substitution to global competitiveness. CEE countries under Soviet domination and many Latin American regional integration attempts prove the failure of this approach. In turn, there is a way to enhanced regional cooperation, but as a result of sustainable global competitiveness. This path was followed by the successful East Asian economies that consolidated their competitiveness in the most open, largest and most competitive domestic market: that of the USA. In a second step, particularly in the last years, they have been aggressively pushing ahead with regional cooperation in order to further improve their global (and, of course, also regional) market positions.

The only regional integration that could escape this trade policy trap was the EU. First, it is an integration of highly developed countries, with a substantial competitive edge (despite declining competitiveness in some areas). Second, the EU is the largest trading bloc in the world that cannot be ignored by any other country or group of countries. Third, despite the emerging deficiencies in global competition and an increasing propensity for protectionism, the EU is correctly considered by all CEE and SEE countries as the basic modernization anchor of the less developed part of Europe. Therefore, unrestricted trade relations (mainly market access) are one of the key elements of sustainable growth in the European "periphery".

It is evident that regional trade can rightly be evaluated as an important source of growth, particularly for SMEs "growing out" of the domestic market. It is an additional factor of attracting FDI by offering a larger regional market, both for exports and imports Moreover, regional trade may strengthen large national companies in their orientation towards additional business possibilities in the region (the so-called regional

---

13 These lessons were not only known but even first formulated by those experts who, this time, tried to press the CEE countries to reconsider the sequencing of steps in how to become competitive on the international markets. This cynical behaviour will hardly be forgotten by those who happened to be direct participants in these policy discussions.

multinational companies). However, from a macroeconomic point of view, it ranks second to the main development anchor. Any approach that would like to change this linkage is expected to find widespread suspicion and mistrust in the countries that feel they should follow external, imposed patterns. In addition, the wrong sequencing can derail the otherwise promising way of export-based growth.

Resistance does not come from political or psychological considerations (feelings) only, but is also based on hard economic facts. Regional trade liberalization dictated (or, in milder terms, conditioned) from outside, at least in the first and decisive period of the transformation process, cannot generate a genuine bottom-up development of the respective economies. On the contrary, sustainable growth has to be based on an approach that is anchored to the most important external markets that are definitely outside the Central, Eastern and Southeastern European region.[14] This reality is clearly reflected in the trade orientation of all CEE and SEE countries. Larger shares of regional markets in exports are generally a sign of lacking or lower levels of external competitiveness and, consequently, not a success story, as supporters of the idea of more regional trade would like to qualify it.

In fact, the approach to, and EU conditionality of, regional free trade did not generate much enthusiasm among the respective countries, even if there were arguments in favour of more cooperation, at least on paper and for those who have never become really familiar with the basic factors of successful development, in general, and the specific features of the Balkan countries' history and reality, in particular.

It was widely believed that more regional cooperation can dismantle existing trade barriers and reduce the risk of violent conflicts as well. However, arguments were not limited to the negative aspects, that is, on what should be overcome, but also a number of positive points were made. They included common geography and neighbourhood, the common experience under Communism (however different in Yugoslavia, Bulgaria and Romania, let alone Albania), the solution of urgent regional problems related to environmental protection and the development of physical infrastructure. Also, joint actions were expected to enhance the attractiveness of the Balkan region towards foreign capital and create, on a regional basis, competitive conditions for large-scale activities of

[14] Several centuries of Central and Eastern European economic history prove that, for different reasons, this part of Europe has not been able to start a genuine, region-based modernization process. Modernization impact always came from outside the region, either in the form of favourable business cycles affecting foreign trade, or by imposed "modernization patterns" with very different consequences. Enforcement of the *acquis communautaire* and membership in the EU can be considered as a benign (and hopefully successful) form of "imposed and imported patterns".

multinational companies. Moreover, the EU considered regional cooperation as a precondition for future EU membership. Therefore, each country tried to cope with these requirement as all of them considered membership their first priority (or among the top priorities) in their future development agenda.

Nevertheless, the basic objectives the SEE countries wanted to achieve by meeting these EU criteria varied. For Albania, political motives were clearly paramount. It was expected that a favourable settlement of the "Albanian question" both in Kosovo and in Macedonia may depend on emphasizing the country's commitment to regional cooperation. In Croatia, where fears about the impact of regional cooperation prevailed, positive elements of an "imposed cooperation" were found by emphasizing the chance of regaining lost regional markets and in highlighting Croatia's political, social and economic achievements and selling them, as a benchmark pattern, to other countries of the WB. In turn, from the very beginning Romania viewed regional cooperation within the context of international politics. First, it considered itself within the regional cooperation scheme as a NATO country capable of contributing to (and, maybe, even invited to serve as) regional stabilization in the process of expanding NATO to WB countries as well. Second, already in full negotiations on accession with Brussels, but in a handicapped position compared to CEE countries, Bucharest expected additional support from Brussels in order to finalize negotiations and approach full membership as soon as possible.

Despite this "package" of positive arguments, some of them real, some of them artificially created in order to let institutionalized regional cooperation palatable to domestic opponents with relevant influence on politics and public opinion, concerns were voiced in all these countries openly.

The most widespread concern was the possibility that more regional cooperation would be considered as a substitute for EU membership. The Amato-report rightly stresses that if the SEE countries "suspect that regional integration is really a substitute for EU membership, it will be a non-starter" (Amato, 2005, p. 178). Still, before coming to such a conclusion, it states that "before the opening of accession negotiations free trade in the region, leading to a customs union with the EU, should be complete… The common economic space should compensate for the costs related to the emergence of new, small and economically unviable states in the region" (Amato, 2005, p. 178). It is not difficult to discover the basic contradiction between the two statements separated by a few lines from each other in the referred document. Regional free trade, even if fully implemented, would never be able to compensate for the costs of expensive and partly uncertain and even dangerous nation-building (based on 19th century ethnic criteria). In the 21st century, even strong states with a strong national bourgeoisie and efficient public administration would face serious global challenges if they wanted to implement such policies. The WB countries definitely do not belong to such a category of states.

Less developed member countries in the regional free trade zone feared that their tiny domestic markets may become "colonized" by more developed countries of the region.[15] This fear was apparently felt by Croatia, an economically more developed and politically more stable country, with a competent public administration, at least in regional comparison.

In turn, particularly more developed Croatia expressed fundamental uneasiness about more intensive regional cooperation, because it wanted to avoid any move or sign that would indicate a potential return to the previous Yugoslav federation, first in the economic area, but later, also in the form of a political "union". Therefore, according to several Croatian documents and statements, all instruments have to be used for avoiding the return of "Serbian dominance" and for blocking any form of institutionalized cooperation on the regional level. First of all, Croatia's historical (geographic and political) ties to Central Europe, and not to the Balkans, have been emphasized in all forums. On the way to EU accession, Croatia's main supporters and "benchmark countries" were not those in the WB, but those in Central Europe, such as Austria, Hungary, the Czech Republic, Slovakia, and, to a lesser extent, Poland.[16]

The fear of getting trapped in the framework of regional SEE cooperation instead of joining the EU remained moderate to non-existent in Bulgaria and Romania, particularly after having signed the Accession Treaties and waiting for (almost) immediate accession. Similarly, and at the other end of the scale, bilateral free trade agreements with SEE countries did not represent a big barrier in those countries that, at the moment, are far away from EU membership. The subject was more controversial and problematic for in-between countries like Croatia and Macedonia.

III.2.3. Starting in 2001, the SP countries (SEE-7 and Moldova) have signed bilateral free trade agreements with the aim of concluding all 28 bilateral treaties by the end of 2005. In fact, by mid 2005 all but one bilateral agreements were signed and implemented. The only exception

[15] "Neo-colonization" through the EU would still be accepted in exchange of EU membership. But regional "colonization" was definitely opposed by all countries.

[16] According to the Croatian elite, the EU notion of the Western Balkans is not based on objective criteria but rather on Brussels' own internal considerations and the negative legacy of the Tudjman era, when the country was isolated from the "West" (see: Lakatos, *Croatia country study*, 2005, p. 37).

was the treaty between Serbia-Montenegro and Macedonia initialized in May 2005. The legal background of most treaties is based on WTO principles, with two exceptions. One is represented by the bilateral documents implemented by CEFTA countries (Bulgaria, Croatia and Romania). The other special case is represented by agreements between Serbia-Montenegro and Croatia and Serbia-Montenegro and Bosnia-Herzegovina, respectively, which lack a reference to WTO principles. In the meantime, bilateral trade agreements with Kosovo under UN administration have become part of the agenda. However, this goal had not to be reached by the original deadline of end of 2005. In fact, trade negotiations only started between Kosovo and Bosnia-Herzegovina as well as Macedonia, while, for several years, the issue was "under review" in Bulgaria and "under preliminary analysis" in Romania, notably the two EU accession countries.

The timing of signing bilateral trade agreements perfectly illustrates the special relations and interests of the participating countries. Although most such documents were prepared and approved by the national parliaments between 2003 and 2005, some agreements date back to previous times. For instance, a free trade treaty between Romania and Moldova was signed in 1994, the first version of the document between Croatia and Macedonia in 1997, and between Bulgaria and Macedonia in 2000, that is, before the SP process actually started. Furthermore, Serbia-Montenegro concluded such an agreement with Bosnia-Herzegovina, and Albania and Bosnia-Herzegovina with Macedonia in 2002. Evidently, CEFTA-based agreements were signed at the very moment of membership of the given country in this regional cooperation scheme (1997 for Bulgaria and Romania and 2003 for Croatia). Until now, only one bilateral treaty had to be revised and re-implemented in its modified form (between Croatia and Macedonia in 2002).

A summary of valid bilateral treaties, including those in the pipeline (with Kosovo) is provided in Table III.14.

Table III.14
Free trade agreements between SEE countries

	Albania	Bosnia-Herzegovina	Bulgaria	Croatia	Macedonia	Moldova*	Romania	Serbia & Montenegro**	UNMIK/ Kosovo***
Albania		Applied 01/12/04 WTO ****	Applied 01/09/03 WTO	Applied 01/06/03 WTO	Applied 15/07/02 WTO	Applied 01/11/04 WTO	Applied 01/01/04 WTO	Applied 01/08/04 WTO	Applied 01/10/03 WTO
Bosnia-Herzegovina	Applied 01/12/04 WTO		Applied 01/12/04 WTO	Applied 01/01/05 WTO	Applied 01/07/02 WTO	Applied 01/05/04 WTO	Applied 01/12/04 WTO	Applied 01/06/02	II round FTA negotiations Q2/05
Bulgaria	Applied 01/09/03 WTO	Applied 01/12/04 WTO		CEFTA 01/03/03 WTO	Applied 01/01/00 WTO	Applied 01/11/04 WTO	CEFTA 01/07/97 WTO	Applied 1/06/2004 WTO	Under examination
Croatia	Applied 01/06/03 WTO	Applied 01/01/05 WTO	CEFTA 1/03/2003 WTO		Applied 11/06/97 Revised 11/06/02 Applied 11/07/02 WTO	Applied 01/10/04 WTO	CEFTA 01/03/03 WTO	Applied 01/07/04	
Macedonia	Applied 15/07/02 WTO	Applied 01/07/02 WTO	Applied 01/01/00 WTO	Applied 11/06/97 Revised 11/06/02 Applied 11/07/02 WTO		Applied 01/01/05 WTO	Applied 01/01/04 WTO	Initialised 31/05/05	IV round FTA negotiations 08/06/05
Moldova*	Applied 01/11/04 WTO	Applied 01/05/04 WTO	Applied 01/11/04 WTO	Applied 01/10/04 WTO	Applied 01/01/05 WTO		Applied 17/11/94 WTO	Applied 01/09/04 WTO	
Romania	Applied 01/01/04 WTO	Applied 01/12/04 WTO	CEFTA 01/07/97 WTO	CEFTA 01/03/2003 WTO	Applied 01/01/04 WTO	Applied 17/11/1994 WTO		Applied 01/07/04 WTO	Under preliminary analysis
Serbia & Montenegro**	Applied 01/08/04 WTO	Applied 01/06/02	Applied 01/06/2004 WTO	Applied 01/07/04	Initialised 31/05/05	Applied 01/09/04 WTO	Applied 01/07/04 WTO		
UNMIK/ Kosovo***	Applied 01/10/03 WTO	II round FTA negotiations UNMIK/Kosovo Q2/05	Under examination		IV round FTA negotiations 08/06/05		Under preliminary analysis		

* Moldova is associated to the process with an extended timeline.
** Serbia & Montenegro started negotiation process when it was known as FR Yugoslavia; therefore, both names may appear on the agreements.
*** All agreements in line with UNSCR 1244
**** FTA notified to WTO

Source: http://www.stabilitypact.org/trade/FTA%20Matrix%20_9%20June%202005.xls.

III.2.4. Both in international and in CEE comparison, regional trade in SEE is characterized by modest turnover. The reasons range from low export potential over sluggish liberalization and opening of the economy to clear orientation to non-regional, mainly EU markets. Still, the importance of regional trade should not be underestimated, particularly in case of some countries that have some of their most important partners within this region. Basic trade data are highly contradictory for several Western

Balkan countries, particularly for Serbia-Montenegro. In order to illustrate the differences, figures provided by two different sources will be shown in Tables III.15 and III.16 (one in Euro, one in USD terms).

Table III.15
Regional trade among SEE countries (a) (in Euro mn)

Country	Exports to SEE Region			Exports to the World		
	2002	2004	Growth %	2002	2004	Growth %
Albania	13	15	15	348	426	22
Bosnia-Herzegovina	164	267	63	874	1,174	34
Bulgaria	570	727	28	5,942	7,204	21
Croatia	839	1,066	27	5,111	6,215	22
Macedonia	421	512	22	1,101	1,196	9
Romania	519	763	47	14,634	17,560	20
Serbia-Montenegro	60	70	17	1,519	1,673	10
Total SEE	2,586	3,420	32	29,529	35,448	20

(a) Excluding mostly insignificant trade with Moldova (except Romania).
Source: European Commission calculations based on IMF (DOT) data.

According to Table III.15, exports to the region, based on volume data, can be grouped into several categories. Croatia accounts for the largest exports, followed by the two accession countries, Romania and Bulgaria. Starting from the modest performance of the economies of Bosnia-Herzegovina and Macedonia, SEE-oriented exports may be meaningful. In turn, Albania and Serbia-Montenegro show very low export figures. In another comparison, regional exports show a more positive picture. As compared to global exports, the dynamics of regional exports exceeded the growth of global exports by 60% (32 and 20% growth rate between 2002 and 2004, respectively). In fact, all SEE countries, except Albania, registered higher growth rates in their SEE-related exports than in their global trade. As a result, intra-SEE exports increased from 8.8% to 9.7% of the total exports of the region. In contrast, Table III.16 differs from the previous table by registering much higher regional trade figures for Serbia-Montenegro and also higher figures for Bosnia-Herzegovina (and partly Macedonia). At the same time, Romanian figures are lower, due to the exclusion of trade with Moldova (a Stability Pact country).

Still, in terms of intensity and real importance of regional trade, the share of SEE in the total exports and imports of the individual countries is more telling than figures expressed in Euro. Table III.17 provides these data.

Table III.16
Regional trade among SEE countries (in USD mn)

Country		2001	2004
	exports	8	19
Albania	imports	72	140
	balance	-64	-121
	exports	338	617
Bosnia-Herzegovina	imports	902	1,928
	balance	-564	-1,311
	exports	497	920
Bulgaria	imports	215	448
	balance	+282	+472
	exports	777	1,625
Croatia	imports	260	856
	balance	+517	+769
	exports	485	664
Macedonia	imports	414	617
	balance	+71	+47
	exports	369	809
Romania	imports	233	408
	balance	+136	+401
	exports	547	1,074
Serbia-Montenegro	imports	1,054	1,520
	balance	-507	-446
	exports	3,021	5,728
SEE total	imports	3,149	5,917
	balance		

Source: as for Table III.7.

The figures allow us to draw some basic conclusions. First, regional trade, as expressed in total trade, is highly important for Bosnia-Herzegovina, Macedonia and Serbia-Montenegro, with 32 to 39% of total exports staying in the region. The next group is formed by Croatia with more than 20% of total exports directed to SEE countries. Another category is represented by Bulgaria, with about 10% of total exports going to SEE. In turn, Albania and Romania do not consider the SEE market an important recipient of their exports.

Second, between 2000 and 2005 the share of regional trade was on the increase for Bosnia-Herzegovina and Macedonia, both on the export and the import side. Although on a lower level, similar tendency could be observed in Croatian trade development (and in Romania, but with a marginal share of SEE trade). Serbia-Montenegro increased the share of SEE in exports, but turned more to non-SEE markets with respect to its imports.

Higher intra-SEE trade shares indicate regional trade creation. In a positive interpretation, this trend can be attributed to the trade policy measures aimed at establishing a free trade zone in the Balkans. Also, following years of destruction and slow recovery, the revival of traditional trade contacts between the independent republics of the ex-Yugoslav federation may have played a role in enhanced regional trade. However, statistical figures contained in Table III.17 can also be interpreted in a less positive way. Regional trade creation can express the inability of SEE countries to remain or to become competitive in more demanding markets in general, and in the EU, in particular. Most probably, as CEFTA experience has clearly demonstrated, the technical conditions of market access were not worse in case of the EU than in case of the SEE market. If, under such conditions, a trade diversion towards the regional market can still be registered, it points to the lower level of competitiveness of the economies of the region. This hypothesis seems to be supported by the fact that the share of intra-regional exports is regularly higher or much higher than the share of intra-regional imports (except the marginal figures of Albania). In other words, everybody tries to sell its products in less demanding regional markets, while everybody seeks to import commodities from more developed third countries, either because they cannot be acquired regionally or because they are – rightly or wrongly – perceived to be of better quality. Whether, in the second stage, exports to the region will result in higher export competitiveness to third countries, mainly to the EU, remains to be seen.

In fact, CEE countries also increased their regional trade in 2004, as a result of EU accession. This, however, was due to the adoption of the EU's common trade policy as of May 1st, 2004, the date of their accession. According to the new trade regime, no restriction can be applied to the exports of any member country. Thus, previous trade barriers among CEFTA countries that became EU members had to be dismantled immediately. To a large extent, this impact is reflected in growing intra-regional trade figures. In addition, intra-regional exports reveal higher shares in total exports than intra-regional imports in total imports. This, however, can hardly be attributed to lower levels of competitiveness, but is the result of a longer-term regional market strategy of key transnational companies (and also of some domestic "regional multinational firms") implementing regional production, service and distribution networks.[17]

[17] It has to be noted that high intra-regional exports of the Czech Republic still reflect special relations with Slovakia dating back to the period of federation. In turn, Slovenian orientation to the SEE regional market may include both the revival of traditional contacts and the growing problems with competitiveness in developed market economies.

Moreover, the "gap" between intra-regional export and import shares is lower than in most SEE countries.

Table III.17
Share of regional trade in total trade of the SEE countries (exports and imports in % of total trade)

Country	2000	2003	2004	2005	EU 2005	CEE-5(a) 2005
Albania						
Exports	2.1	3.9	3.6	3.6	84.1	0.7
Imports	6.1	6.7	6.1	6.1	70.4	3.8
Bosnia-Herzegovina						
Exports	30.5	32.1	35.2	32.4	58.0	19.2
Imports	21.4	32.4	34.9	35.4	58.2	22.2
Bulgaria						
Exports	12.6	9.5	10.1	11.2	55.3	3.6
Imports	4.4	3.0	3.2	4.3	56.8	7.4
Croatia						
Exports	12.0	19.5	20.1	21.8	62.0	11.7
Imports	2.0	3.8	5.2	6.5	65.2	14.8
Macedonia						
Exports	30.9	32.6	43.6	38.6	52.7	2.7
Imports	19.8	20.8	24.2	26.8	57.9	13.3
Romania						
Exports	2.3	3.2	3.6	4.9	68.4	8.2
Imports	0.7	0.9	1.2	1.4	68.4	11.9
Serbia-Montenegro						
Exports	28.2	30.7	31.7	34.6	50.1	6.1
Imports	20.9	13.6	15.4	18.8	51.2	9.4
Memorandum items:						
Czech Republic (a)						
Exports		17.4	20.3		84.4	17.4
Imports		12.5	13.1		70.9	13.1
Hungary (a)						
Exports		10.7	13.1		76.8	10.1
Imports		8.2	10.7		67.8	9.4
Slovakia (a)						
Exports		26.0	25.2		84.8	27.8
Imports		25.5	29.4		79.8	33.0
Slovenia (a)						
Exports		16.6	18.4		67.0	8.2
Imports		12.5	12.8		79.5	9.0

(a) trade with CEFTA countries in total trade.

Source: WIIW, http://www.wiiw.ac.at/balkan/files/data/export(or imports)_dot_see_200. and IMF Direction of Trade Statistics.

Evidently, regional trade is not evenly spread across member countries. There are some bilateral "density links" that are responsible for the bulk of regional trade turnover. The bilateral trade flows are illustrated in Tables III.18 and III.19.

Table III.18
Bilateral trade flows among SEE countries: exports (country shares of total exports in %)

To \ From	Year	ALB	BiH	BUL	CRO	MAC	ROM	SM
Albania	2000		0.0	0.5	-	1.3	0.1	0.0
	2004		0.1	0.4	0.3	1.2	0.1	0.4
Bosnia-Herzegovina	2000	-		0.2	10.6	1.7	0.1	14.7
	2004	0.1		0.1	14.1	1.9	0.1	17.7
Bulgaria	2000	0.0	0.0		0.1	1.8	1.8	1.2
	2004	0.0	0.1		0.3	1.8	1.7	1.2
Croatia	2000	0.1	7.2	0.1		3.7	0.2	-
	2004	0.1	18.5	0.5		6.8	0.8	4.2
Macedonia	2000	1.9	1.0	2.3	1.3		0.1	12.2
	2004	0.8	0.4	2.2	0.9		0.1	7.2
Romania	2000	0.0	0.7	1.8	0.1	0.2		-
	2004	0.0	0.0	3.3	0.7	0.2		1.0
Serbia-Montenegro	2000	-	21.6	7.8	-	22.2	-	
	2004	2.6	16.2	3.6	3.6	31.6	0.9	
SEE – 7	2000	2.1	30.5	12.6	12.0	30.9	2.3	28.2
	2004	3.6	35.2	10.1	20.1	43.6	3.6	31.7

Source: see Table III.17.

Both export and import tables indicate that the importance of intraregional SEE trade mainly consists of a few bilateral trade flows. According to 2004 figures, Bosnia-Herzegovina and Macedonia direct a substantial part of their exports to Serbia-Montenegro, while for Croatia and Serbia-Montenegro it is the Bosnian market that represents a meaningful share. In addition, Bosnian exports to Croatia have to be mentioned. In imports, Bosnia-Herzegovina is an equally important market for Croatian and Serbian products and Macedonia for Serbian goods.[18]

[18] Unfortunately, key data on the commodity pattern of intra-regional exports and imports was not available. However, based on regional and international experience and findings of the background country studies, the trade structure is most probably dominated by food items, semi-manufactured industrial goods and selected consumer products.

Table III.19
Bilateral trade flows among SEE countries: imports
(country share of total imports in %)

From \ To	Year	ALB	BiH	BUL	CRO	MAC	ROM	SM
Albania	2000		-	0.0	-	0.2	-	0.1
	2004		0.0	0.0	0.0	0.2	0.0	0.2
Bosnia-Herzegovina	2000	0.0		0.0	1.0	0.5	0.1	4.7
	2004	0.1		0.0	2.1	0.3	0.0	2.9
Bulgaria	2000	2.5	0.3		0.1	5.7	0.6	8.7
	2004	2.3	0.3		0.3	8.7	0.9	3.6
Croatia	2000	1.0	14.4	0.1		3.0	0.0	-
	2004	1.3	22.7	0.2		3.2	0.2	3.0
Macedonia	2000	1.9	0.7	0.4	0.7		0.0	3.5
	2004	0.9	0.6	0.2	0.7		0.0	3.5
Romania	2000	0.7	0.4	3.5	0.2	0.5		3.9
	2004	0.9	0.5	2.4	1.2	0.7		2.2
Serbia-Montenegro	2000	-	5.7	0.4	-	10.0	-	
	2004	0.6	10.9	0.3	0.8	11.2	0.1	
SEE – 7	2000	6.1	21.4	4.4	2.0	19.8	0.7	20.9
	2004	6.1	34.9	3.2	5.2	24.2	1.2	15.4

Source: see Table III.17.

Turning to some important statements included in the country studies, Albanian politicians stress the limits to regional trade among less-developed countries. In turn, Macedonia considers SEE free trade as a useful instrument not imposed by foreign powers. However, Macedonian experts see that the enforcement of bilateral agreements has not changed either the volume or the structure of trade substantially. In addition, most of them are burdened with legal details, additional regulations and unnecessary administration. Furthermore, it is surprising how little trade has been going on between the two largest economies of the WB, namely Croatia and Serbia-Montenegro. The drive to recapture lost regional (mainly ex-Yugoslav) markets is already present, but still in its initial stage. The exceptional case of Bosnia-Herzegovina and Macedonia can be explained to some extent by the inflow of international and private transfers that happened to create additional domestic demand. Especially the international administration in Bosnia-Herzegovina can be considered as a consumer of regional goods. Therefore, part of the SEE trade is fuelled by transitional (and artificial) import demand more than the real needs of genuine economic development. Thus, there is a real danger that the current level of intraregional trade may markedly decline once international forces leave some areas (mainly Bosnia). In turn, such demand may continue or even grow in Kosovo, also depending on its future status.

III.2.5. A realistic picture of SEE trade opportunities has to take into account a number of constraints, some of it will stem from the low level of economic development and the limited purchasing power of the society (despite remittances and international aid). Another part is linked to the real needs of a modernizing economy that cannot be met by regional imports since this kind of input is largely unavailable in any of the SEE countries. However, more and more countries and companies are becoming aware of their limited competitiveness in non-SEE markets, they will make efforts to gain additional outlets for their products at least in the region. As a result, export and import trends and priorities have already started to vary. Looking at further liberalization of the overall trade relations of the WB countries, such export gains may quickly prove illusory and short-lived. Stronger pillars of sustainable regional trade would require rapid modernization and adjustment to competitive pressures at least on the European markets.

Moreover, barriers are not only attributed to deficiencies at the macroeconomic and corporate level. Regional trade is hampered by a number of non-tariff barriers and administrative burdens. It is well known that CEFTA has never become a real free trade area. Certainly, most tariff barriers have been abolished or significantly lowered, but non-tariff barriers have stayed in place and have been widely used by all member countries. The same is happening in SEE trade, mainly with respect to sensitive products such as agricultural commodities, semi-manufactured or consumer goods that are believed to generate imported competition for countries with little industrial base, a weak private sector, high level of unemployment and a limited domestic market. In such situations, the "natural" response is trade protectionism.

Albania announced in the spring of 2006 that it would like to "review, re-evaluate and revise" its bilateral free trade agreements with SEE countries. The government argues that the conditions that prevailed a few years ago when such agreements were prepared and signed have fundamentally changed. The rapid development of the domestic construction material industry is mentioned as an example. Years ago, such production did not exist in that country. Therefore, it was easy to offer to the partner countries of the region tariff- and quota-free access to the Albanian market. Today, however, the emerging national manufacturing sector requires more protection. Thus, emphasis should be on "fair trade" instead of "free trade".[19]

---

19 Gibson-Shaw (2006).

Bosnia-Herzegovina applies long transitional periods of varying duration for each country. In addition, liberalization of agricultural trade is very limited with Albania, Bulgaria and Romania, but, in contrast, is practically 100% with Croatia, Macedonia and Serbia-Montenegro. However, the latter practice of liberalization had to be temporarily suspended because of difficulties in the agri-food sector. Missing or improper regulation of property rights, land registration, intellectual property questions, entry and exit laws, bankruptcy procedures, competition regulations, treatment of foreign investors are common barriers in most countries of the region. In fact, they are easier to be accepted, absorbed or compensated for by large and financially strong companies than by small and medium-sized firms of neighbouring countries in the SEE trade framework. Serbia-Montenegro reports a liberalization rate of 80 to 99% with all SEE countries, except with Albania where the share of liberalized trade remains below 40%.[20] The political obstacle based on the fear of getting decoupled from mainstream European developments, *i.e.* EU accession, should not be ignored either, particularly in the case of Croatia.

III.2.6. Looking at the modest impact of regional free trade on growth and economic modernization, let alone on improving competitiveness, as well as taking note of the emerging difficulties, it is more than striking that some influential EU politicians still insist that regional trade integration of SEE (and mainly of the Western Balkans) is "the key to the region's economic revival". In addition, a customs union, similar to that established with Turkey, is suggested between Brussels and the Western Balkan countries.[21] In fact, all countries of the region are expected to have free trade with the EU and the SEE group. However, there are powerful economic arguments why different national tariffs *vis-à-vis* third countries should not be abolished immediately (or in the near future). Fiscal considerations are just one reason, since customs duties form an important part of government revenues. Also the (temporary) role of customs in the protection of emerging national businesses has to be mentioned. Last but not least, each country may consider its customs policy as an important instrument to attract foreign investors. The customs-union approach would be another conditionality on the path of the Western Balkan countries towards EU membership. It has to be stressed that the new member countries had to adopt the EU's common external tariff at the moment of accession. Until then, they could keep their national tariff policies towards third countries. In addition, the very development of European integration shows that the common external tariff has been at the end of a long process of trade liberalization.

---

[20] See: Hernádi, *Serbia-Montenegro country study*, 2006, p. 29.

[21] Bildt (2006), p. 6.

III.2.7. It is much more realistic to start with more modest projects that promise success in the shorter term and may have a palpable positive impact on trade, growth and regional cooperation. One indirect but gradually more important source of regional trade can be the utilization of special EU funds earmarked to regional (cross-border) development. First, the creation of "Euroregions" between and among neighbouring countries can have a positive impact. As an example, the tri-lateral cooperation around Lake Prespa among Albania, Macedonia and Greece can be mentioned. Similar initiatives can be seen among Serbia, Bulgaria and Macedonia (Nis-Sofia-Skopje), Serbia-Croatia-Bosnia-Herzegovina (Novi Sad-Osijek-Tuzla) or Croatia-Montenegro-Bosnia-Herzegovina (Dubrovnik-Herceg Novi-Trebinje).[22] Second, positive experience with selected PHARE-financed programmes can be underlined. The financial memorandum signed in 2005 between Bulgaria and the European Commission under the Phare Cross-Border Programme supports several bilateral projects between Bulgaria and Greece, Romania, Macedonia and Serbia-Montenegro, respectively, in the total amount of Euro 33 mn.[23]

III.2.8. Besides current developments future conditions will also be shaping the environment and everyday practice of regional free trade. As of January 2007, Bulgaria and Romania have left the SEE framework. Consequently, the free trade area, recently renamed to Central European Free Trade Area (CEFTA) has not only been "deprived" of two of its largest markets, but the remaining countries may face additional trade barriers that could even threaten their already established market positions and force them to redraw individual investment and trade policies. Croatia's accession, with the implications of free trade with the EU can be another, although provisional but not negligible, risk factor in regional trade.

If, namely, the timetable (roadmap) for the implementation of bilateral free trade agreements varies from country to country, and, especially, between the individual SEE country and the EU, additional trade barriers could arise both in the form of higher tariffs and several non-tariff barriers. Therefore, it is imperative that the EU support free trade among SEE countries by offering all of them equal conditions on the EU market. Another important but regional measure can be the conversion of 28 bilateral free trade agreements into one multilateral free trade scheme. In this context, two urgent steps have yet to be taken. One is the ratification and implementation of those bilateral treaties that still lack this procedure

22 Lopandic (2002), pp. 7-8.

23 Priority areas include improvement of transport infrastructure, environmental protection, tourism, human resource development, small-scale projects, technical assistance. For more detail, see: Petkova, *Bulgaria country study*, 2006, p. 26.

but should be in place as soon as possible. The other is the ratification of all trade-related documents by the European Parliament that require such a legal step as a result of Bulgaria's and Romania's joining the EU. In order to avoid temporary disruptions of free trade (as stipulated by CEFTA and SEE agreements), this action has to be taken immediately upon accession and not be delayed for several months, as it, unfortunately (and inadvertently), happened following the first phase of "Eastern" enlargement in 2004.[24]

III.3. Development, Features and Perspectives of Foreign Direct Investments (FDI) in SEE Countries

III.3.1. The growing role of FDI in global development in general, and in the transformation and modernization process of CEE in particular, is well-known. As a major player of economic development in the early 21st century, FDI not only contributes to growth, investment, export, technology transfer and the transmission of modern management methods, but it increasingly influences labour markets, both in terms of dismissal and hiring of employees, both directly and indirectly, through the process of delocalization or outsourcing. Most importantly, however, FDI integrates national economies or selected actors of national economies into the global network of production and services.

Since the systemic transformation in CEE and SEE has been simultaneous with dramatic changes in the world economy and the process of European integration, success or failure of the transformation cannot be separated from the pattern and volume of cooperation with FDI. Some CEE countries, mainly Hungary, and a bit later the Czech Republic, Slovakia and the Baltics considered the inflow of foreign capital not only as a necessary transfer of financial and other resources but also as a pillar of competitiveness-related structural changes, sustainable high growth and successful catching-up to the performance level of more developed EU countries. Unfortunately, SEE countries, similar to most other key areas of transformation, were lagging behind and started to cooperate with foreign capital only in the last few years at rather different degrees and with reluctance or even open opposition.

This chapter surveys basic figures and trends of FDI in the SEE region by looking not only at the stock or yearly inflow of foreign capital but also at the structure, motivation, geographic origin and regional concentration. Moreover, it addresses FDI-related policies of individual countries by pointing out real or potential advantages as well as suspected

[24] The ratification by the European Parliament took place early 2005, after more than eight months of membership and following the emerging difficulties of trade relations between the new member countries and the not-yet EU-member CEFTA countries.

disadvantages and other concerns. Finally, special attention will be paid to the ongoing outsourcing process, of which several SEE countries expect more (and upgraded) FDI, not least from the more developed CEE region. It has to be noted that, as part of a larger study focusing on the future of relations between the EU and the SEE, only some key developments are highlighted in this section. More detailed analyses have been prepared in recent years that serve as basic reference for the next paragraphs (see: Hunya (2004), Inotai (2005a), Inotai (2005b), Inotai (2005c), OECD (2006), UNCTAD (2005), Vienna Institute for International Economic Studies (2005)).

III.3.2. As Table III.3.20 shows, SEE countries have been relying on FDI rather differently.

The difference between the SEE and the CEE region is striking, since the latter received four times more FDI than the SEE countries by the end of 2004, with a population of 65 mn as compared to 55 mn. Consequently, *per capita* FDI stock in the CEE countries was, on the average, more than three times higher than the SEE average.[25]

Behind average figures in the region, however, substantial differences can be identified. Romania represents 36% of total FDI stock in SEE, followed by Croatia (26%) and Bulgaria (16%). Other WB countries had not attracted larger amounts of FDI until most recently. FDI stock in Hungary or in the Czech Republic alone was higher than the combined stock in the SEE region. However, it is interesting to note that the only ex-Yugoslav country that already became member of the EU has not performed well, since it only attracted FDI in the amount of Euro 5.5 bn, or less than Bulgaria and less than 60% of FDI stock reported by Croatia. Here, once again, the legacy of the Yugoslav system and the comfortable level of development in the first decade of the transformation process have to be taken into account.

[25] Based on 2004 figures, *per capita* inward FDI stock reached Euro 2,310 on average in CEE-5, as compared to Euro 715 in the SEE-7 average. Disaggregated country dates indicate that Hungary registered Euro 4,381 *per capita*, while the Czech Republic reported Euro 4,052, or twice as high as the outstanding figure of Croatia in SEE comparison (Euro 2,150). Despite dynamic development in the last years in select countries, respective figures for all other SEE countries remained below Euro 1,000 (wiiw, 2005).

Table III.20
Stock of FDI in SEE countries (2004)

Country	In Euro mn (a)	In USD mn (b)
Albania	1,339	1,514
Bosnia-Herzegovina	1,537	1,660
Bulgaria	6,000	7,569
Croatia	9,544(c)	12,989
Macedonia	1,179	1,175
Romania	13,193	18,009
Serbia-Montenegro	3,763(d)	3,947
SEE-7 total	36,550	46,863
Memorandum items:		
Czech Republic	41,415	56,415
Hungary	44,226	60,328
Slovenia	5,500	4,962
CEE-5	152,141	197,633

(a) WIIW database on FDI 2005.

(b) UNCTAD (2005).

(c) according to official Croatian figures, the stock figure at the end of 2005 reached Euro 11.3 bn.

(d) of which Serbia Euro 3,574 mn and Montenegro Euro 189 mn.

The 2004 stock figures result from rather different annual inflows of FDI in the last years. An overview is provided by the next table.

On average, a clear upward trend can be seen in the figures, for annual FDI inflows were increasing in the reviewed period between 1998 to 2004. This process is particularly apparent after 2002. However, the trend is not without contradictions, since some countries had registered peak years of FDI inflow previously, followed by a more or less sharp decline in FDI in the following year(s). The volatility of FDI inflows can be explained by two basic factors. First, the uneven process of privatization sometimes results in large inflows as a consequence of selling state-owned companies, mainly in the telecommunication and banking sectors. Since, however, privatization cannot be repeated, and green-field investments are still rare, the level of FDI inflow cannot be sustained. As a result, and in contrast to most CEE countries, economic policy making and strategic planning cannot yet be based on a genuine and permanent cooperation with FDI. Second, fluctuations in inflow of fresh FDI in the CEE countries could be largely compensated for by the rapidly increasing reinvestment of profits which, for many companies, made the import of fresh money superfluous, for further development could be financed from profits earned in the host country. Such an "outlet" or counterbalancing factor did not exist in the SEE countries in the last few years, since later and slower inflow of FDI has not produced large-scale profits to be reinvested.[26] Therefore, higher annual inflows were followed by much lower FDI activity in the following period (see Croatian and Serbian figures).

Table III.21
FDI inflow into the SEE countries between 1998 and 2004 (annual figures in Euro mn)

Country	1998	1999	2000	2001	2002	2003	2004
Albania (a)	40	39	155	232	151	158	278
(b)	45	51	143	204	135	178	343
Bosnia- Herzegovina (a)	60	166	159	133	282	338	400
(b)	67	177	150	130	266	382	490
Bulgaria (a)	605	866	1,103	903	980	1,851	2,278
(b)	537	802	998	803	876	2,070	1,232
Croatia (a)	843	1,369	1,142	1,503	1,195	1,788	980
(b)	835	1,420	1,085	1,407	591	2,025	899
Macedonia (a)	114	31	189	493	83	85	127
(b)	128	32	175	441	78	96	156
Romania (a)	1,763	964	1,147	1,294	1,212	1,946	5,183
(b)	2,079	1,025	1,051	1,154	1,080	2,156	5,020
Serbia-Montenegro	101	105	55	197	593	1,243	829
(a)	113	112	25	165	562	1,405	1,031
(b)							
SEE-7 total (a)	3,526	3,539	3,950	4,754	4,496	7,480	10,075
(b)	3,804	3,619	3,627	4,304	3,588	8,313	9,172
Memorandum items:							
Czech Republic	3,317	5,933	5,404	6,296	9,012	1,863	3,596
Hungary	2,988	3,106	2,998	4,391	3,185	1,909	3,365
Slovenia	194	99	149	412	1,750	299	422
CEE-5 total	12,805	16,364	20,974	19,240	22,716	8,366	13,178

Sources: (a) wiiw (2005); (b) EBRD (2006a).

Nevertheless, there are some encouraging signs as well. First, annual FDI inflow figures show that the region in general, and some countries in particular (mainly Romania and Bulgaria, and, with reservations, Croatia) are converting themselves into more important host countries of FDI.

[26] In turn, profit repatriation, due to uncertain political and economic climate, changing policy instruments and a lack of further expansion in the limited domestic markets, could be observed in several cases.

According to 2004 flow figures, Romania accounted for more than 50% of total FDI into the SEE, and Bulgaria ranked second with almost 23%. Second, mainly as a result of transparent economic policies and the introduction of new incentives to attract FDI, the annual upward trend of inflows is evident in Romania and Bulgaria, and, on a lower scale, in Bosnia-Herzegovina as well. Third, in 2003 and 2004 Romania could attract more capital than the leading FDI importers of Central Europe, namely the Czech Republic and Hungary. Furthermore, figures for Bulgaria and partly Croatia are comparable with those of the Czech Republic and Hungary.

The macroeconomic importance of FDI can be measured in different comparisons (its contribution to growth, job creation, investments, exports and imports, current account position, etc.). Two widely used indicators have been gathered in Table III.22, namely the role of inflow of FDI in gross fixed capital formation (practically in total domestic investment), and the share of FDI stock as expressed in percentage of GDP.

Table III.22
Macroeconomic importance of FDI in SEE countries

Country	FDI inflow in % of gross fixed capital as a % of GDP (annual averages)			FDI stock in % of GDP		
	1998-1999	2000-2002	2003-2004	1998	2001	2004
Albania				13.3	15.8	20.4
Bosnia-Herzegovina				1.6	9.2	23.2
Bulgaria	44.0	38.8	52.9	12.0	20.6	30.9
Croatia	25.1	25.5	18.8	8.6	21.7	34.5
Macedonia	13.0	43.0	14.6	5.5	23.2	27.3
Romania	21.1	13.6	24.3	10.2	19.3	22.4
Serbia (a)				.	9.2	20.0
SEE	26.0	23.3	31.2	10.5	18.1	25.6
Memorandum items						
Czech Republic	30.7	36.4	12.1	22.6	45.2	48.0
Hungary	29.5	25.5	15.2	42.4	53.7	55.1
Poland	17.2	16.9	12.3	12.8	22.5	25.7
Slovakia	8.0	41.6	9.9	12.5	27.1	33.2
Slovenia	3.2	14.2	5.9	12.7	13.5	21.2
CEE-5	20.0	24.4	12.1	19.0	31.1	36.2

Source: wiiw (2005).

Several interesting conclusions can be drawn from the above figures. First, despite the much lower amount of FDI inflows into SEE countries, its role in total investments is generally higher than in the CEE countries. In other words, less developed SEE countries require FDI in order to finance investments more than CEE countries that seem to dispose of domestic savings and other resources as well. Second, after years of large inflows of FDI as part of the fixed capital formation, the importance of foreign resources in the CEE region has started to decline in recent years, partly as a result of efficient investments and successful structural changes brought about by the crucial role of FDI in previous years. Also, the near completion of privatization and saturating markets with well-established networks of production and service activities have contributed to declining shares. In contrast, SEE is still in the process of structural change and, in most cases, in the early stages of privatization. Therefore, the relative role of FDI as measured in total investments is high and rising. In this context, the different trends reflected in the growing share of FDI in gross fixed investments in SEE countries and the declining in the CEE countries, represented by figures for 2003-2004, is quite clear. Third, FDI stock as a share of GDP has been growing everywhere. There is, however, still a substantial difference between the figures released by Hungary and the Czech Republic, and other countries. However, it has to be added that, in this comparison, SEE countries reveal similar patterns as less FDI-intensive CEE economies, such as Poland and particularly Slovenia.

III.3.3. One basic difference between SEE and CEE countries lies in the main forms of FDI going to transforming countries. In principle, FDI can be involved in privatization deals (including mergers and acquisitions), brown-field investments (investing in already existing ventures), green-field activities (completely new production or service lines), reinvestment of profits and, finally, loans from the international or domestic financial market to finance the implementation of business objectives. In the early stage of liberalization and opening up, privatization and smaller-scale brown-field ventures (often in the form of minority or majority-owned joint companies) used to be the prevailing forms of investments. Depending, however, on the degree and speed of opening, the available market's size and the host country's cost advantages in international comparison, large-scale green-field investments should follow. Finally, an ever larger share of new investments may be financed by the reinvestment of profits earned both by privatized and green-field firms. This "upgrading" has been successfully carried out in some CEE countries, first in Hungary, later in the Czech Republic and Slovakia. The process is still going strong in Poland and hasn't yet followed the above described pattern in Slovenia.

For several reasons, SEE countries are still at the beginning of this "journey". First, privatization started later, although Bulgaria and also Romania have achieved meaningful results in recent years. In turn, privatization remains a half-hearted objective in the WB countries, due to fears of even higher levels of unemployment, growing external influence and social opposition to foreign capital and ownership. Second, again with the exception of both EU accession countries, the opening up of weak and small national economies was carried out reluctantly, with many market access barriers. Under such conditions, and with the incorporation of selected CEE countries into the global and regional production network of transnational companies by developing large and competitive export-oriented structures, there is little room for export-oriented green-field investments in the SEE countries. (Delocalization and outsourcing are certainly a prospective but by far not an unlimited possibility, as it will be discussed later in this chapter.) Finally, reinvestment of profits can only be considered seriously if investments in general, and production in privatized companies in particular start to generate not just nominal but real profits.[27]

Unfortunately, cross-country comparisons are only partly possible, for national statistics do not provide in-depth surveys. Thus, investments generated by privatization, expansion or green-field activities are not separated (all figure under the heading of "equity capital"). Moreover, most countries do not report reinvested earnings, either because the amount is negligible, or because of missing statistical registration. Nevertheless, even a partial comparison may be interesting.

In the early phase of FDI, equity capital plays the most important role (sometimes accompanied by loans). Later, however, as foreign ventures start generating profits, the financing of new investments includes increasing shares of reinvested profits. This was the case in Hungary in the second half of the 1990s, and it has become a common feature in both Hungary and the Czech Republic in the last few years. In contrast to financing about 70% of FDI inflows by reinvested earnings in these two countries, FDI inflow to SEE still is dominated by fresh money, either in the form of equity capital or of loans.[28] In other words, the profit generating capacity of the SEE economies is still relatively low, or worse: earned

---

27 The benchmark is generally the break-even point of a business. Profits, even if earned in the first years of activities, need to cover the original investment costs. They remain "nominal" unless this level is reached. Only after this stage can we speak of "real" profits, either for repatriation or for reinvestment, depending both on the overall or regional corporate strategy and on the investment climate in the host country.

28 Data on other SEE countries are not available. However, they would most probably confirm our findings and would indicate low levels of profit reinvestments (at much lower levels of annual FDI inflows).

profits are repatriated. Most probably more time is necessary for "maturing" investments. Moreover, a more appropriate investment policy is required as well in order to convince foreign companies to increase their reinvestment activities. Finally, the lacking or underdeveloped state of green-field investments (mainly in the manufacturing sector) can be an explanation for the modest contribution of reinvested earnings to total FDI inflow volumes.

III.3.4. Sustainable economic growth requires not only constant and high level inflow of FDI but also a healthy structure of FDI-related economic activities. In most SEE countries, the lion's share of FDI stock can be found in selected areas of the service sector, with special regard to banking, telecommunication and selected utilities (energy, water, housing). Relatively less attention was paid to different manufacturing sectors, except the privatization of some large-scale state-owned companies with decisive domestic market shares and meeting growing domestic consumption demands. Contrary to the Czech Republic, Hungary and Slovakia, export-oriented FDI in manufacturing remained rather modest but with substantial potential to be exploited in the coming years.

Sectoral statistics of FDI, even if available, are difficult to compare. In addition, they are based on different national sources with substantial differences in the total volume of FDI stock as compared to international and comparable statistics.[29]

Table III.23 shows the different sectoral activities of FDI among selected SEE countries and, no less importantly, between SEE and selected CEE countries. The most important difference is represented by the share of manufacturing in total FDI stock. It amounts to almost half of total investments in the Czech Republic and Hungary, while comparable figures fluctuate between one-fourth and one-third of total stock in selected SEE countries. Romania makes an interesting exception, partly due to the larger domestic market that is supposed to have been a major factor in attracting investment as compared to other SEE markets. To some extent, export-oriented manufacturing can also be observed, supported by increasing export figures (see the previous subchapter). One additional remark, however, has to be made. The statistically registered share of manufacturing is significantly influenced by the volume of FDI active in other economic sectors. In this context the liberalization and opening of basic non-manufacturing sectors, such as telecommunications, public utilities and banking and insurance, have to be considered. For, if these sectors are not yet fully open and privatization is still in progress the

---

[29] For instance, wiiw data, based on our own estimates, report about Euro 6 bn FDI stock in Bulgaria, while Bulgarian National Bank figures, contained in the key material for elaborating sectoral statistics, register almost Euro 8 bn by the end of 2004.

share of manufacturing may be temporarily higher than its "normal" share would be in total FDI stock. In turn, advanced or almost full privatization of non-manufacturing sectors may produce the opposite result by indicating a lower than "normal" share of foreign investments in manufacturing businesses. Nevertheless, the basic difference between the SEE and the Czech Republic or Hungary lies in the predominantly domestic market- vs. export-orientation of FDI in manufacturing in general, and in technology- and in labour-intensive vs. skill-intensive industrial sectors in particular. This structural difference is demonstrated in Table III.24.

Table III.23
FDI inflow by form (Euro mn)

Country		Amount (a)			Share in % of total		
		1998-1999	2000-2003	2003-2004	1998-1999	2000-2002	2003-2004
Bulgaria	total	1,471	2,986	3,965	100.0	100.0	100.0
	(b)	1,097	2,098	2,646	74.6	70.3	66.7
	(c)	353	731	967	24.0	24.5	24.4
	(d)	21	158	352	1.4	5.3	8.9
Croatia	total	2,212	3,840	2,709	100.0	100.0	100.0
	(b)	1,783	2,359	1,027	80.6	61.4	37.9
	(c)	109	437	865	4.9	11.4	31.9
	(d)	319	1,042	818	14.4	27.1	30.2
Romania	total	2,727	3,653	1,946(e)	100.0	100.0	100.0
	(b)	2,636	3,162	691(e)	96.7	86.6	35.5(e)
	(c)	.	.	572 (e)	.	.	29.4(e)
	(d)	91	491	683 (e)	3.3	13.4	35.1(e)
Memorandum items							
Czech Republic	total	9,250	20,712	5,459	100.0	100.0	100.0
	(b)	6,861	14,226	1,296	74.2	68.7	23.7
	(c)	808	4,818	3,841	8.7	23.3	70.4
	(d)	1,601	1,667	321	17.3	8.0	5.9
Hungary	total	6,094	10,574	5,274	100.0	100.0	100.0
	(b)	2,807	3,763	444	46.1	35.6	8.4
	(c)	2,063	4,525	3,637	33.9	42.8	69.0
	(d)	1,224	2,287	1,192	20.1	21.6	22.6
Slovenia	total	293	2,311	721	100.0	100.0	100.0
	(b)	228	2,002	196	77.8	86.6	27.2
	(c)	65	122	262	22.2	5.3	36.3
	(d)	.	188	261	.	8.1	36.2

(a) cumulative two- and three-year figures; (b) equity capital; (c) reinvested earnings; (d) other capital (loan); (e) 2003 only.

Source: wiiw (2005) and own calculations.

In all SEE countries, except Romania, manufacturing is not only much less represented in total foreign investments, but there are substantial differences in the pattern of manufacturing investments alike. While such activities are concentrated in the Czech Republic and Hungary requiring higher skilled labour and technology-intensive activities, mainly represented by the manufacture of electrical and optical devices as well as transport equipment, these sectors have practically remained outside the sectoral orientation of FDI in SEE (with Romania being a partial exception). With generally modest amounts of FDI, labour- and material-intensive sectors represent the highest shares in overall FDI in manufacturing (textiles, chemicals, refined petroleum products, basic metals). Another common characteristic is the relatively high share of FDI in the food-beverages-tobacco sector, with principal orientation towards the respective domestic markets.

Table III.24
FDI stock by economic activities (as of end-2004, in % of total)

Sectors	Bulgaria	Croatia	Maced.	Romania(a)	Czech Rep.(b)	Hungary(a)
Agriculture, fishing	0.2	0.5	0.8	.	0.7	0.6
Mining	0.8	3.5	1.6	.	1.2	0.3
Manufacturing	27.5	34.7	24.3	51.6	42.5	45.8
Electricity, gas, water	11.2	1.0	0.2	.	7.1	4.1
Construction	2.0	0.8	3.4	2.0	2.3	0.9
Trade, repair	18.5	8.3	3.0	11.4	12.7	9.8
Transport, storage, communication	13.2	14.7	43.7	16.2	5.4	8.5
Financial intermediation	14.7	27.2	18.0	9.2	16.3	10.1
Real estate, renting	6.5	3.9	2.1	6.6	9.3	17.0
Hotels, restaurants	1.3	4.9	1.3	1.1	0.7	0.8
Other activities	4.0	0.6	1.5	1.9	1.8	2.2

(a) 2003.

(b) figures calculated by the author on the basis of 2003 stock and 2004 flow data.

Source: wiiw database.

Table III.25
FDI stock in the manufacturing industry (a)

Sectors	Croatia	Macedonia	Romania(b)	Czech R.(c)	Hungary(b)
Food, beverage, tobacco	14.5 (5.0)	28.6 (6.9)	18.8 (9.7)	10.2 (4.3)	13.0 (6.0)
Textiles, clothing	1.6 (0.6)	3.9 (0.9)	8.4(f) (4.3) (f)	2.1 (0.9)	1.8 (0.8)
Leather, shoes	0.6 (0.2)	.	(f) (f)	0.1 (0.0)	0.4 (0.2)
Wood products	0.6 (0.2)	2.6(d) (0.6) (d)	5.0 (2.6)	1.9 (0.8)	1.0 (0.5)
Pulp, paper, printing	3.7 (1.3)	(d) (d)	.	5.9(b) (2.5)	3.5 (1.6)
Chemicals	35.9 (12.5)	5.6 (1.4)	16.6 (8.6)	6.4 (2.7)	16.6 (7.6)
Rubber, plastics	1.2 (0.4)	0.8 (0.2)	.	6.6 (2.8)	3.4 (1.6)
Other non-metallic mineral products	18.3 (6.4)	.	.	11.5 (4.9)	3.9 (1.8)
Basic metals	1.0 (0.3)	18.7 (4.5)	23.0 (11.9)	12.2 (5.2)	6.0 (2.7)
Machinery and equipment	1.3 (0.5)	0.1 (0.0)	8.9 (4.6)	5.6 (2.4)	5.7 (2.6)
Electrical and optical equipment	8.6 (3.0)	0.1 (0.0)	4.3 (2.2)	13.9 (5.9)	19.8 (9.1)
Transport equipment	0.5 (0.2)	0.2 (0.0)	10.4 (5.4)	21.9 (9.3)	24.7 (11.3)
Other manufactured products	12.3(e) (4.3)	39.3(e) (9.5)	4.7 (2.4)	0.9 (0.4)	0.5 (0.2)

(a) share of the given sector in total FDI stock in parentheses.

(b) 2003.

(c) Our own calculations based on 2003 stock and 2004 flow data.

(d) wood, pulp, paper, printing combined.

(e) of which 11.4 (4.0)% due to coke and refined petroleum products for Croatia and 17.8 (4.3)% for Macedonia.

(f) textiles, clothing, leather and shoes together.

Source: wiiw database and our own calculations.

III.3.5. Similarities and differences characterize the geographic origin of FDI in SEE, as compared to CEE, as well. Obviously, EU member countries take the largest share of FDI in all cases. However, there are some special features, both in the ranking of the individual EU countries, and the relative importance of non-EU sources of capital.

Table III.26
Geographic origin of FDI (based on 2004 stock data, country shares in total FDI registered in the respective host country)

Country of FDI origin	ALB	BiH	BUL	CRO	MAC	ROM (a)	CZR (b)	HUN (a)
Austria		13.3	17.5	27.0	2.5	6.2	11.7	11.2
Belgium-Luxembourg			4.7	6.1		2.5	5.3	6.4
Denmark			0.8	0.6			0.7	0.5
France			1.9	1.6	0.3	10.4	7.6	4.3
Germany		7.5	8.7	16.2	3.4	7.2	20.5	29.2
Greece	48.0		9.6		24.1	11.4		
Ireland			0.3	0.2	0.5		0.3	
Italy	43.0		5.4	9.1	1.5	7.8	1.2	1.8
Netherlands			10.9	7.7	7.4	18.6	30.3	19.5
Sweden			0.8	1.1	0.1	2.0	1.4	1.5
United Kingdom			4.9	2.6	3.6	2.0	4.1	0.9
EU-15	More than 90	More than 30	65.8	72.4	43.5	69.3	70.6	79.4
Czech R.			4.9	0.1				
Cyprus			5.4		5.9	4.2	0.9	0.8
Hungary			4.9	4.3	31.6	1.4	0.3	
Slovenia		9.1	0.4	5.0	2.7			
Switzerland			3.6	1.8	4.0	3.2	2.8	1.2
Turkey	2.2 (c)		1.2		1.5			0.2
Russia			0.8	0.1	0.4	1.8		0.2
USA			6.8	9.8	2.5	3.4	5.3	5.2
Japan			0.4				2.2	1.7
Tax paradises (d)			2.4	3.4	1.7	9.3	0.7	0.3
Others		About 60	3.7	3.3	6.0	8.8	5.0	15.4

(a) 2003.

(b) own calculations based on 2003 stock and 2004 inflow figures.

(c) Turkey and Macedonia together.

(d) includes Isle of Man, Virgin Islands (British), Liechtenstein, Cayman Islands, Netherlands Antilles.

Note: Luxembourg is included in the figures of Belgium-Luxembourg, and Cyprus appears separately.

Source: wiiw database, country studies and our own calculations.

The above figures show that, in most cases, the European Union countries are the key investors in the SEE and the selected CEE countries alike. The EU's share in the total stock of FDI accounts for 65 to 80% (or even more than 90% in Albania). In this context, there is no big difference between SEE and CEE countries. Of course, one has to be aware of two basic differences. First, the total volume of FDI in the Czech Republic and Hungary is several times higher than in the SEE countries. Second, due to the lower, and in some cases, a very low level of FDI, a few big investments in the SEE countries can substantially alter the figures indicating the geographic origin of foreign capital. Therefore, country-related shares have to be considered and evaluated accordingly.

Among the leading EU investor countries, Austria, Germany, Italy and the Netherlands have top positions almost everywhere. The difference between SEE and CEE lies in the relatively low but still most relevant share of Austria (a leading role in some SEE countries and among the important investors in CEE), and, in turn, in the leading role of Germany (and the Netherlands) in the CEE as compared to their relatively low but important share in the SEE. Moreover, Italian investments are more oriented towards the SEE countries than to the CEE region.[30] French investments are not particularly large, but they are important in some sectors both in SEE and CEE countries.

The basic difference between FDI investments in SEE and in CEE is the relevant activities of Greek capital in SEE, while it is practically non-existent in CEE. To a much smaller extent, Turkish interests are also concentrated in selected SEE countries. While Greek investments have targeted large-scale privatization deals (banking and telecommunications), Turkish investors have cast their glance at smaller ventures, mainly in manufacturing, retail trade and agriculture.

Other developed countries have shown modest interest in the SEE countries. Measured in the share of total foreign investments, US and Swiss companies are represented both in SEE and CEE countries, with similar shares but, obviously, with highly different volumes of invested capital. Japan (and some other Asian countries) started to invest in CEE but are still reluctant to enter new ventures in SEE (except emerging Chinese investments in Romania). In addition, and despite some overly publicized information in mass media, Russian capital remained at a very modest level, with low representation in all countries.

An interesting difference between SEE and CEE countries can be seen in the higher share of tax paradises in investment activities in SEE coun-

[30] The picture was different in the first years of transformation, when substantial Italian investments came to Hungary. Most of them have already been closed or moved towards lower wage countries, such as Romania, Bulgaria, Albania or Ukraine.

tries than in CEE countries. Investments originating in Luxembourg and Cyprus included (with different and sometimes unclear national origins), foreign capital from these countries has a much more important role in the total investments in SEE than in the Czech Republic or Hungary.

Finally, the fact that net capital flowing into emerging and transforming economies became partly important sources of FDI in almost all SEE countries has to be mentioned. In turn, CEE countries register investments coming almost exclusively from more developed countries. To be sure, the origin of FDI does not in itself imply any prejudice concerning the structure, motives and efficiency of the imported capital in SEE countries. However, international business used to make a difference between a Western European bank, insurance company or telecommunications firm and, for instance, a Greek or Turkish venture in the same sector. The lower level of economic development in the SEE region, along with historical, ethnic, psychological and geographic factors, and the initially lower business interest shown by Western Europe and other OECD countries are reflected in the differences of the geographic origin of imported capital. There is no evidence at the moment to assess and compare the efficiency of foreign capital stemming from different geographic regions or to draw conclusions concerning its contribution to sustainable growth and structural modernization in individual SEE economies. Such evaluations would always remain subject to certain prejudices, even if more than a few individual cases seemed to support the view that the basic motives, management methods, technological standards, attitudes towards local employees and long-term strategic considerations show similarities at the country- and development level.

The higher share of regional (or non-traditional) capital of FDI imports by SEE countries is not only a new phenomenon in the pattern of FDI flows in the last 15 years in Europe, but it may become an interesting new factor in the unfolding regional cooperation beyond free trade agreements. First, it could become an important element of supporting regional trade flows. Second, it can pave the way for sustainable regional cooperation in selected production and service areas. Third, it represents a genuine bottom-up business approach to economic development, in contrast to free trade agreements concluded by states of the region and to be implemented in the framework of a top-down process. Finally, regional (cross-country) investments are expected to overcome political, social and psychological obstacles and prejudices caused both by hostilities in recent years and stemming from deeply-rooted historical developments. Therefore, despite the generally small volumes of such cross-country investments, a statistical overview seems to be overdue.

The most important regional investor is Greece with more than Euro 2 bn stock in the countries listed in the table (figures on Albania and

Serbia-Montenegro were not available). Turkey is also present in several countries of SEE, but the reported amount of Turkish investments lags behind the Greek figure with about Euro 300 mn.

With regard to the new EU member countries, three of them have shown substantial interest in SEE economies, partly by participating in the privatization process, but also by establishing joint or new ventures. The longer term economic interests of Hungary are clearly manifested by more than Euro 1.3 bn registered stock in various countries (and other ventures in the not-listed SEE countries, as well as much higher volume of investment in Romania than reported in official Romanian statistics). Also the Czech Republic started to turn more attention to SEE not only due to its traditionally strong trade relations but also by investment in privatization deals of public utilities.[31] Slovenia, as a previous member of the Yugoslav Federation, was able to preserve part of its business relationships. This is reflected in an FDI stock of Euro 700 mn, as shown in Table III.27. In addition, Slovenian firms are working hard on renewing previous economic ties by new investments in several WB countries. At the same time, other new member countries, such as Poland and Slovakia, has not considered investments in SEE as a lucrative business. The reasons may be found in the lack of traditional economic relations, different geographic orientation (Polish capital going rather to Russia and the Ukraine), as well as in the relatively earlier stage of economic development, where capital imports, but not yet capital exports, play an important role in the overall economic strategy. As a surprising exception, the strong presence of Lithuanian capital in Bosnia-Herzegovina has to be mentioned, due to the privatization of one large Bosnian aluminous earth producing factory – this is the biggest single foreign investment in that country for the time being.

Currently, the accession countries (Bulgaria and Romania) have weak direct investment positions in SEE. Most probably their economic development has not reached the level where capital imports, a key issue to successful catching up, is accompanied by increasing capital exports. The first signs of modest efforts can be seen in Bulgarian investments in Macedonia and in Romanian investments in Croatia.

31 The largest Czech investment in the region was the purchase of a Bulgarian energy company in 2004. Czech public utility companies pay special attention to the ongoing privatization in SEE.

Table III.27
Regional FDI flows into SEE countries (2004 stock, in Euro mn, share in total FDI imports in %, in parentheses)

From \ FDI exports to	Bosnia-Herzegovina	Bulgaria	Croatia	Macedonia	Romania
Greece		759.5 (9.6)		275.4 (24.1)	1,159.1 (11.4)
Czech Republic		391.3 (4.9)	10.8 (0.1)		
Hungary		385.2 (4.9)	410.2 (4.3)	360.5 (31.6)	144.7 (1.4) (a)
Turkey		93.2 (1.2)		16.8 (1.5)	179.3 (1.8)
Russia		62.8 (0.8)	14.0 (0.1) (b)	4.7 (0.4)	
Slovenia	185.7 (9.1)	29.1 (0.4)	476.0 (5.0)	30.4 (2.7)	
Bosnia-Herzegovina			88.1 (0.9)	1.0 (0.1)	
Romania			8.1 (0.1)		
Bulgaria				18.3 (1.6)	
Serbia-Montenegro	95.9 (5.1)			10.3 (0.9)	
Croatia	275.5 (15.9)			4.2 (0.4)	
Slovakia			11.4 (0.1) (b)	3.6 (0.3)	
Albania				3.3 (0.3)	
Poland				1.3 (0.1)	
Lithuania	252.4 (15.2)				

(a) according to other figures, Hungarian investments in Romania are several times higher.
(b) 2003 and in USD mn.
Source: wiiw database, national statistics and our own calculations.

As the main objective of this study, special attention is being paid to the unfolding network of regional capital, an important element of long term regional stability and economic cooperation. In this context, Slovenia is way ahead of other WB countries. However, capital flows between Croatia and Bosnia-Herzegovina, as well as between Serbia-Montenegro and Bosnia-Herzegovina can also be termed as significant. Almost all such capital flows, however, remain strictly within the ethnic boundaries of the entity. In other words, Serbian capital is financing projects in the Republika Srpska, while Croatian capital flows to the ethnic Croat areas of Bosnia-Herzegovina. It is quite clear that ethnicity-based capital flows do not follow global trends and, in addition, can become instruments of further separating ethnic groups instead of contributing to the creation of a sustainable multiethnic state. In turn, in official statistical data they appear as an element of fostering regional cooperation and providing more fuel to regional trade flows. An important conclusion to be drawn from this is that, similarly to fundamental trade orientation towards external (mainly EU) markets, regional capital will not be able to replace global capital inflow, both from the enlarging EU and from non-European sources.

III.3.6. The regional concentration of FDI is extremely high in all these countries. This development pattern was not unfamiliar to CEE countries in the first decade of cooperation with FDI. It is evident that profit-oriented foreign (and domestic) ventures prefer central regions with an adequate supply of (skilled) labour, a well-developed physical infrastructure, proximity to public administration, service and banking sectors and political decision makers, as well as higher than average living conditions. However, as the development process becomes sustainable, investment activities broaden and adequate labour will be in short supply, FDI starts to move to less developed regions of the given country as well. The resulting longer-term government-level regional policies, improving the quality of public (local) administration, the emergence of competitive small- and medium-sized businesses as potential partners for large foreign corporations, investments in physical and human infrastructure and, not to be forgotten, tax incentives contribute to creating the necessary and favourable conditions for the geographic expansion of foreign businesses in the host country. This has clearly been the case in both the Czech Republic and Hungary, even if the key business activities remain based in the capital cities and metropolitan areas.

In some SEE countries, mainly in Bulgaria and Romania, a similar process is expected to start soon. Privatization of companies outside the capital areas and the selling of regional public utilities (energy, water, heating, etc.), as well as improving physical infrastructure and a growing need for skilled labour are among the driving forces. In turn, WB countries, with low levels of FDI and without attractive offers to foreign capital, face a dramatic concentration of foreign capital to the key region of the country, either because of a lack of such companies or due to still prevailing restrictive privatization policies. As a consequence, the positive impact of FDI is difficult to spread over other regions and, no less importantly, differences in income and living standards keep growing between the central and the peripheral regions. (The growing lure of the capital and increasing poverty in the regions further fuel labour flows from the peripheral to the central regions and, thus, further strengthen and deepen the development gaps within the given domestic economy.)

In Albania, more than two-thirds of FDI-related activities are concentrated in Tirana and Durres (the biggest port of the country). In Bosnia-Herzegovina, regional income differences are exacerbated by the ethnic origin of "foreign" capital, since the Croatian dominated parts of the country report a relatively high FDI inflow from Croatia, while the less developed Republika Srpska does not get substantial investments from Serbia, and does not consider FDI as an important element of economic development. As a result, original (and inherited) differences are expected to grow in the future, due to the above mentioned factors, among others. In Romania, more than half of the foreign equity investments can be found in Bucharest, while the least developed Eastern regions fell practically outside the interest of foreign business.

III.3.7. Following the general and, as far as possible, comparative surveys, some important findings of the country studies have to be summed up.

In Albania, two countries, Greece and Italy dominate the FDI landscape. Investments from both countries are concentrated in neighbouring geographic regions (south-southwest and Adriatic seashore, respectively) and mainly consist of small- and medium-sized enterprises. Italian-owned firms are involved in construction (35%), textile and footwear manufacturing (21%), trade and services (16%) and agri-food industry (8%). In turn, Greek companies are almost absent in manufacturing, but overwhelmingly present in trade.

In contrast to other countries, the majority of the small amount of FDI in Bosnia-Herzegovina targeted the manufacturing sector linked to production related to the post-war reconstruction needs (steel and cement). At the same time, no FDI flowed into higher value-added, technology-intensive or export-oriented ventures. As another difference with Croatia, Bulgaria and partly also Romania, the banking sector could only draw smaller investments from a wider range of countries.

Bulgaria is one of the few countries that reported green-field investments in the amount of about Euro 1 bn in 2004.[32] As a result of rational economic policy and a focus on comparative advantages, the country became an interesting destination for worldwide offshore activities (13th place among 60 potential offshore locations in 2004). With the opening up of the energy and other public utility sectors to FDI, Bulgaria may be able to continue to attract larger amounts of foreign capital in the coming years. Moreover, FDI may reach various regions of the country and, as a consequence, reduce the current concentration of FDI in and around Sofia and create new regional engines of sustainable economic growth.

Croatia is one of the leading host countries of FDI in SEE. However, most of the foreign capital was absorbed by non-manufacturing activities, such as telecommunications and banking. The relatively low share of FDI

---

[32] Green-field investments between 2003 and 2005 include Turkish (SISECAM, USD 220 mn), US-American (C3i, Tumbleweed), Austrian (Palfinger, USD 31 mn), Dutch (Royal Frans Maas, Euro 15 mn) and Swedish (Consilium, Euro 5 mn) ventures.

in manufacturing (about 37% of total investments) is in itself problematic for future and sustainable development. However, more critical is the fact that investment in manufacturing is largely constrained (sometimes ambiguous and restricted) to privatization, minority-owned foreign shares, and domestic-market-orientation. Large-scale export-oriented activities are missing, nor has there been a spillover effect of FDI so far.

In Macedonia, the only large investment occurred in the telecommunication sector. Investments in manufacturing, a potential source of job creation and export growth in a country plagued by extremely high unemployment are rare.

Romania is not only by far the largest host country of FDI in SEE, but a pioneer in working not only with foreign investors coming from different countries but with the EBRD, as a major investor and temporary owner of Romanian assets. Commitments of the EBRD amount to Euro 2.5 bn, with participation in more than 100 projects.[33] On the other hand, most FDI is still interested in low wage costs instead of becoming an efficiency and strategic asset-seeking partner, a key factor of structural modernization and enhanced competitiveness.

Serbia-Montenegro has been lagging behind in attracting FDI in recent years. Moreover, FDI has almost completely avoided Montenegro, while Serbia has been able to get some investments in the framework of a sluggish, stop-and-go privatization process subject to direct or indirect political influence. In turn, green-field investments and cross-border acquisitions represented an almost negligible share of the total inflow of FDI.

III.3.8. Comparing national economic strategies of the SEE countries, FDI is given a high priority in creating the preconditions for sustainable growth. As a consequence, most countries have developed and partly implemented special plans to attract foreign investors. As a first step, obvious obstacles to FDI have been eliminated and investment-related international agreements signed (avoiding double taxation, guaranteeing the protection of foreign assets, ensuring the free repatriation of earned profits, etc.). Also, the general business climate has shown signs of improvement. As a result, in the last couple of years, several SEE countries have been able to secure their relative position in the World Bank's Doing Business list. Nevertheless, with the exception of Bulgaria overtaking Slovenia, all SEE countries substantially lag behind the CEE countries' performance. In another comparison based on the Growth and Competitiveness Index (GCI) produced by the World Economic Forum,

33 Romanian statistics on the geographic origin of FDI report EBRD figures separately. It is the EBRD's strategy to offer its share for selling to other investors, both domestic and international ones, after the projects enter an advanced stage.

all SEE got lower grades than CEE countries. Within the SEE group, Bulgaria has the best position in both comparisons. In general, the GCI shows a better situation than the Doing Business index, possibly suggesting a difference between better overall macroeconomic conditions and the everyday experience of market players (except for Bosnia-Herzegovina and Macedonia). The most shocking difference can be seen in the case of Croatia that ranks second behind Bulgaria in general competitiveness while it has the worst business climate (even worse than that of Albania). Recent experience of potential and already active foreign investors can only support the extremely poor grade given to Croatia. Details can be found in Table III.28.

Table III.28
Rankings of the SEE and CEE countries based on selected composite indices

Country	Doing Business (World Bank index)	Growth Competitiveness Index (World Economic Forum)
Bulgaria	62	58
Romania	78	67
Macedonia	81	85
Bosnia-Herzegovina	87	95
Serbia-Montenegro	92	80
Albania	117	100
Croatia	118	62
Memorandum items:		
Lithuania	15	43
Estonia	16	20
Latvia	26	44
Slovakia	37	41
Czech Republic	41	38
Hungary	52	39
Poland	54	51
Slovenia	63	32

Source: World Bank Doing Business, WEF Competitiveness Index, as quoted by ICEG (2005) monitoring, No. 19.

Albania bases its FDI strategy on low production costs due to low labour costs. Foreign investors enjoy government-level, preferential treatment. In addition, restrictions in so-called sensitive sectors (transport, banking, etc.) have been lifted. Membership in the WTO and preferential trade privileges granted by the EU are also part of the "attractivity basket". Further improvement of the legal and institutional framework, upgrading human capital, better physical infrastructure and the removal of administrative barriers figure among the short- and medium-term objectives to make the country more attractive to investments in general, and FDI in particular.

Bulgaria's FDI strategy is based on the requirement of sustainable high annual inflows of FDI even after almost finishing the privatization process. Labour-intensive foreign operations requiring low skilled workers are expected to become gradually replaced by higher-skilled ventures. More investment in education, the rapid development of the physical infrastructure and more efficient public administration are among the key objectives of the next period.

Macedonia has already implemented 27 bilateral Investment Protection Agreements with a large number of non-OECD countries included. Government-level treatment to foreign investors has been granted already in 1999. Most sectors are open to FDI, including banking, insurance, and public utilities. More importantly, from the beginning of 2005, a one-stop registration procedure has been in place for new companies. As a result, the time required to start up a new company can be reduced from several weeks (48 days on average in previous years) to five days.

Among the Romanian arguments the relatively large domestic market is considered a convincing factor of attracting foreign investors. Other factors include a stable political environment, new opportunities in the still open privatization process, NATO membership and EU accession, the geographic location of the country, strong cooperation with international institutions (including their participation in investment projects as a confidence-building instrument), proximity to energy suppliers, as well as the low cost of skilled labour.

III.3.9. Despite undeniable progress made in most countries, FDI still faces a number of barriers in several SEE economies. Some of the obstacles are not associated with bureaucratic inefficiency or inadequate legal and institutional frameworks. They include the small size of the national, and also the regional market (even if free trade agreements are fully implemented), the low purchasing power of the population, an underdeveloped business environment, as well as the lack of promising business opportunities, including the small number of interesting ventures offered for sale in the privatization process.

In several WB countries, the legacy of ex-Yugoslavia, *i.e.*, the survival of self-management companies is a big obstacle both to privatization and cooperation with FDI. Also, murky property and real estate rules reduce the attractivity of several countries as future host countries for foreign investments.

In Albania, the tax burden is high in SEE-CEE comparison, and the behaviour of the tax authorities is unpredictable. Registration for small business is particularly complex (therefore, maybe unwillingly, illegal activities are indirectly encouraged).

One of Croatia's handicaps is the relatively high wage level that does not attract FDI based on wage differences, at least not in the labour-intensive sectors. Starting from the current wage level, Croatia could qualify as the only SEE country for efficiency-seeking foreign investments (instead of wage-cost-based considerations). However, a number of preconditions are unfavourable, such as the distorted economic structure caused by the high level of state intervention, complicated market entry and exit procedures,[34] unclear rules of privatization, protection of several market segments in favour of (inefficient) domestic producers, etc.

In Macedonia, some "strategic" sectors are not allowed to be fully owned by foreign companies. Foreign insurance companies may have a maximum share of 65% (with special permission this can go up to 80%). The absence of reliable property registration records and the lack of certainty about property rights have already discouraged several companies from investing in the country. In order to start operating a business, a potential investor needs to go through 13 procedures that take 7 weeks and are accompanied by high costs to be paid in cash. According to business representatives, corruption of the public sector and the unreliability of regulations belong to the most important barriers.

Similar obstacles are reported from Serbia-Montenegro, but probably with even more restrictions, both on the level of macroeconomic regulation (*e.g.* the partial liberalization of short-term capital movements) and in the business sector (where the legacy of the Yugoslav economic system is even stronger felt than in other ex-Yugoslav republics).

Two additional and overall concerns have to be added to the country-specific barriers. They do not affect Bulgaria and Romania, but are widespread in the WB. First, due to the very high level of unemployment, policy makers are concerned with the negative impact of privatization, since, at least in the first stage, it would generate not more but less jobs, and, consequently, even higher levels of unemployment (see in detail, Inotai, 2005a). Therefore, governments want to include employment clauses in several privatization deals, which dooms the deal to failure, or creates a venture with initial disadvantages in domestic and international competition. Second, several societies manifest mixed or sometimes

[34] By the end of 2004, a total of 12 administrative procedures and 49 days were needed to start normal business operation. However, average registration time was expected to cut to 16 days in 2005, while the number of procedures has already been reduced to five.

unfriendly, even hostile feelings and attitudes towards foreigners in general, and foreign investors in particular. It is generally felt that foreign ownership may reduce national sovereignty and lead to unilateral and crucial "dependence" on transnational companies. Moreover, the potential disappearance of "well-known" (but certainly uncompetitive) domestic companies causes concerns. In addition, it is feared that national economic-policy making may become fundamentally influenced by "foreign interests". Such perception is rather strong in Serbia-Montenegro, Croatia and Macedonia. Interestingly, and probably partly for similar reasons, this feeling is present in Slovenia as well.

III.3.10. In the last few years, FDI to some SEE countries seems to have reached a new stage. Still, at present, it is more represented by rapidly increasing investment volumes than by much needed new investments. Annual inflows to Romania and Bulgaria have been steadily increasing, while Croatia, although with substantial annual ups and downs, could also attract meaningful capital investments. The situation is much less promising in other WB countries, despite the improving political situation and the apparent macro-economic stability. Yet, the big challenge is still ahead, and it consists of several components. First, all SEE (as also CEE) countries have to keep relying on massive capital inflows in the coming decade. As, however, income from privatization is expected to decline, as large-scale privatization enters its last stage, new sources have to be tapped. Evidently, Croatia, Serbia and Romania still have major "privatization reserves", and the level of capital inflow mainly depends on the respective national economic (and political) decisions. Bulgaria may privatize most large assets by 2007. In turn, smaller WB countries can hardly find state-owned companies that foreigners would be ready to buy, or at least not at the desired selling price. Second, and not only for finding new sources of FDI but also in order to ensure sustainable development in small national economies, export-oriented, predominantly green-field investments can be considered as the key international contribution to successful modernization. Since in the last decade such investments went to selected CEE countries (mainly Hungary, the Czech Republic and Slovakia), it is not self-evident that such a process will be reproduced in the SEE countries, even if they try to offer similar conditions. Large-scale export-oriented ventures usually cover the whole regional, sometimes even the European market or an important section of the global market. New capacities are not always needed, and (hopefully increasing) SEE market demand can easily be met by subsidiaries of transnational companies operating in CEE countries. Third, and again interrelated with the previous points, the reinvestment of profits has to be taken into account. There seems to be a sectoral difference with regard to the reinvestment propensity of foreign capital. Given a favourable environment, manufacturing and some service companies (*e.g.* retail chains) tend to reinvest profits easier than banking or public utilities. The reason is quite understandable, for market sizes are different. The saturation of the national market establishes clear limits to further investments (at least in the same sector) for banking, insurance or energy, while manufacturing and many service activities may not feel constrained by the small size of the national market, since, provided they have comparative advantages, their products can be sold in third countries as well (usually within the global intra-firm distribution network of the same foreign company).

In sum: favourable political and economic environment of the potential host country is an indispensable but, most probably, not sufficient argument for attracting fresh international capital. In this context, global and regional market developments and strategic investment plans of transnational companies are supposed to play a crucial role in the next period.

III.3.11. Although to a different degree, all SEE countries reckon with the possibility of attracting foreign capital currently located in CEE countries. They expect that SEE economies will become part of the global and particularly of the intra-European outsourcing process, including the "delocalization" of production and service facilities. Similar to the CEE countries a few years ago, SEE can now enter the same path of FDI-driven development, hopefully with the same and generally positive results. The EU enlargement to the eastern and southeastern borders of Europe may have created major cost, transportation and logistical advantages to SEE countries. According to UNCTAD, this "new frontier" could potentially become a magnet for efficiency-seeking investment. (UNCTAD 2005)

However, it seems more realistic that production relocation from CEE to SEE countries will not happen on a massive scale. Of course, part of the previous production activities in CEE countries have already moved to other locations, well before, and practically independently from, EU accession (most labour-intensive sectors were relocated from Hungary and the Czech Republic to SEE and the Ukraine, or, not infrequently, to China). Obviously, other sectors, or some segments of other sectors may follow. Still, the size of outsourcing has its clear limits on both sides.

Membership in the EU is hoped to stimulate investments, since producers can rely on a large internal market. However, this market has already been there for several years, as free trade preceded membership. Most forward-looking companies have taken the necessary strategic decisions and carried out investments several years before membership materialized or is expected to materialize in the case of Bulgaria and Romania. SEE regional free trade is an additional element, but neither the size of the market nor the evident barriers to implement free trade agreements seem to convince transnational companies to set up a new venture or relocate production capacities from other countries if the new demand can easily be covered by production in already established subsidiaries. There are few reasons to create parallel capacities, with the possible exception of definitely domestic-market oriented production (construction materials, food, local services).

Also, the assumption that rapidly growing production costs in the CEE countries would force transnational companies to move to lower cost production sites seems to be exaggerated. Of course, such a scenario cannot be fully ruled out. Nevertheless, several restricting factors have to be considered (for a detailed analysis see Inotai, 2005b). First, total production costs do not depend only on labour costs but on a number of other cost factors as well (the state of the physical infrastructure, price of basic utilities, value-added production of the labour force, productivity, tax regimes, etc.).[35] Second, legal, political and institutional conditions, and increasingly, the socio-cultural environment have become important factors influencing investment decisions. Third, geographic proximity to major markets matters a great deal. In this sense, regrettably, SEE countries have a comparative disadvantage, at least with regard to the EU market. Fourth, transnational companies that have outgrown their early development stage characterized by "footloose" production (*i.e.* when most production inputs were imported), have started to develop a domestic network of suppliers (both of national and foreign ownership). The stronger this production and service network is, the more such companies are likely to remain bound to the current production location, even if direct cost advantages could be expected in another location. In other words, it is extremely costly and time-consuming (and carrying business risks) to build up a new network in another country. Companies well embedded into a given environment are less keen to move to other countries. Of course, some activities can be relocated as part of the company's overall upgrading strategy. But massive shifts cannot be anticipated. As a partial exception, new companies not yet present in CEE may start their regional ventures in SEE countries (some US, Canadian or even Asian firms may appear here as pioneers). Finally, host country FDI-related policies and general economic strategies influence the decision-making process of foreign companies. Failed or misguided economic policies resulting in major macroeconomic crises in selected CEE countries may give priority to moving out over the positive impact produced by reasonable FDI-attracting policies of SEE countries (particularly if FDI-related policies of the competitors, in this case those of the CEE countries are also reasonable).

---

[35] A table containing selected cost factors influencing investment decisions can be found in the Appendix (Appendix Table III.3.11./1).

III.3.12. Maintaining the net capital importing position over a longer period seems to be a must to all CEE and SEE countries, even if budgetary resources from the EU are expected to grow dramatically in the next years. However, as the example of several CEE countries shows, at a given level of development capital flows cease to be a one-way street. The export of capital will emerge and, thus, the net capital balance, so vital for the external financial situation of all SEE countries, may become the result of inflow and outflow of capital.[36] At the moment, none of the SEE countries, except Croatia, is threatened by such a development. However, one has to take into account that globalization has widened the horizon of capital owners all over the world. In addition, a large number of new investment opportunities have opened up and many new countries, still being massive capital importers, have entered the "club" of capital exporters recently. Moreover, all countries may have some larger (even partly or fully state-owned) companies that feel the narrow limits of the national market. Thus, they perceive the potential benefits of expanding mainly to neighbouring markets. In other cases, they are aware of the fact that becoming more and more international is the key instrument to remaining competitive. In recent years, Hungary became a sizeable capital exporter, basically within the CEE and SEE region. The Czech Republic and Poland are following suit, while Slovenian business always considered the new countries of SEE as its "natural zone" for investment activities. However, capital exports can not only be generated by positive factors (growing competitiveness, larger markets, cost advantages, etc.) but also by negative, so-called push-effects. This may happen if a given SEE country cannot offer a favourable business environment or, even more, hostility against capital in general, or against a given company in particular becomes manifest. In such a case, the reaction of capital is not the well-known and traditional "capital flight"[37] but a kind of "protest investment" outside the national boundaries. In the case of Croatia, part of the capital export certainly falls into this category, and is largely supported by the Croatian community living in selected European countries. A comparison with some CEE figures is provided in Table III.29.

36 Capital exports in the form of repatriating profits are not considered here.

37 Generally, capital flight has not produced direct investments (excepting housing in some cases) but remained within the framework of "financial transactions".

Table III.29
Capital exports of selected SEE and CEE countries (end-2004 stock data in Euro mn) (a)

To \ Capital exporter	Czech Republic	Hungary (b)	Poland (b)	Slovakia	Slovenia (b)	Croatia
Total	2,248(c)	2,566	1,495	507	1,849	1,783(d)
Slovakia	619	558			15	3
EU-15	526	618	691	141	365	119
Slovenia	62	18				351
Poland	57	59		22	98	161
Switzerland	37	3	88	6	17	477
Russia	29	12	22	12	63	5
Hungary	10		2	29	9	18
Romania	7	166	15	0	29	2
Bulgaria	298	136	2	0	20	1
Serbia-Montenegro	2	5			102	111
Croatia	2	352		2	610	
Czech R.		81	40	235	19	14
Ukraine		20	91	32	17	
Macedonia		266			79	9
Turkey		12	80			
Lithuania			23	1		
Belarus			6			
Latvia			1			
Bosnia-Herzegovina				10	207	201

Note: End-of-2004 figures in the World Investment Report (UNCTAD, 2005) are substantially higher (*e.g.* USD 4,472 mn for Hungary, USD 3,061 for the Czech Republic, USD 2,661 for Poland, USD 2,450 mn for Slovenia, USD 618 mn for Slovakia and USD 2,426 mn for Croatia. Unfortunately, no comparable geographic breakdown of the summary figures is available. Therefore, as a "second-best" solution, wiiw figures have been used.

(a) Data are not available for Bulgaria and Romania. As compared to their economic size and capital imports, figures for the Baltic countries report relatively significant capital export flows, with Euro 1,024 mn for Estonia, Euro 166 mn for Latvia and Euro 310 mn for Lithuania (all stock data for 2004); (b) Figures for 2003; (c) Based on stock data for 2003 and inflow data for 2004; (d) Euro 1,651 mn only, according to Croatian national statistics at the end of 2005.

Source: wiiw database (2005) and own calculations.

Due to rapidly increasing capital exports in the last couple of years, several figures listed in the table may be outdated,[38] however, both the

[38] According to year-end 2005 estimates, the stock of Hungarian capital abroad may have reached Euro 6 bn (Inotai, 2005b). Hungarian investments in Croatia alone surpassed Euro 900 mn, while the stock of capital in Bulgaria was nearing the level of Euro 500 mn. Also, being the largest investor in Montenegro, Hungarian statistics register a capital stock of more than Euro 150 mn. For more details see Appendix Table IV.3.4.

volume and geographic distribution of capital exports allow us to draw some interesting conclusions. First, all CEE countries started exporting capital after the first decade of transformation. The relatively most "advanced" stage (in terms of capital exports *per capita*) has been reached by Slovenia, followed, surprisingly, by Croatia, and then by Hungary. Second, most of the exported capital was directed to neighbouring countries. The EU-15's share was rather low, between 20 and 25% in most cases, except the less than 10% share of Croatia at one and, and almost half of foreign investments by Poland, at the other end of the scale. While the EU is the key investor in the CEE and most of the SEE region, the two-way flow of capital remains largely unbalanced with strong EU dominance, both in terms of share and, even more, in terms of volumes expressed in Euro. Third, the main target of capital exports were neighbouring countries. This trend is particularly strong in the WB countries that took almost half of total FDI by Slovenia, almost 40% of Croatia and one-fourth of total Hungarian capital exports. In turn, Poland and Slovakia has not shown interest in this region. With the exception of a massive Czech privatization deal in Bulgaria, a similar pattern emerges if Bulgaria and Romania were included in the table. However, in this case Hungary is catching up to Croatia, with almost 40% of total FDI stock in the SEE-7 countries. The regional concentration of capital exports can be also seen in cross-country capital flows among the CEE-5 countries. They absorb 56% of the total Slovak, 33% of the total Czech and 26% of the total Hungarian capital exports. Again, Poland is the exception without meaningful capital export activities in this region (3% of the total), while Croatia, a non-EU country located 31% of its capital exports in the CEE-5 (not only in Slovenia, but also large amounts in Poland). Slovenia's SEE orientation is underlined by the fact that only 8% of its capital exports was directed to other CEE countries.

In the future, SEE and CEE capital is expected to turn increasing attention both to the Western Balkan and the two new EU member countries of SEE. In the first case, attractive privatization offers will play the key role, while Bulgaria and Romania, as new EU members may offer interesting investment possibilities both for expansion of already established capacities and for green-field investments. In several cases, such capital exports may be the result of the southeastern expansion of transnational companies already located in CEE countries, and financed by profits earned at CEE production sites.[39]

---

[39] Usually, such exports are registered by National Bank statistics as capital exports from the respective CEE country, even if capital exports were not carried out by a "domestic capital-owned" firm. For instance, the largest foreign investment in Macedonia is r the privatization of the local telephone company by the Hungarian telecom company MATÁV. However, MATÁV is owned by Deutsche Telecom. Nevertheless, the trans-

III.4. Labour Market, Unemployment

For several reasons, unemployment is one of the most critical issues of sustainable development and stability in SEE in general, and in the WB countries in particular. First, in most countries its level, measured as a percentage of the total active population, is extremely high. Second, there is no viable strategy available, primarily in the WB countries, which would reduce unemployment significantly in the foreseeable future. Third, it can become (and, in fact, has already become) a hotbed of corruption, illegal activities, tax evasion, all of them risk factors for the normal and predictable functioning of a democracy. Fourth, particularly youth and long-term unemployment are likely to create a general attitude that deprives large segments of the society of a "normal working culture", and strengthens "subsidy mentality".

The section is organized as follows. First, general information will be provided on the employment and unemployment situation in the SEE countries. Second, some of the key factors of high unemployment will be identified. In the next part, the structure of unemployment will be analyzed. Finally, government and business policies directed at the reduction of unemployment will be outlined.

III.4.1. It has to be stressed that official unemployment rates may vary widely, not only due to the varying conditions of the individual national economies and labour market policies, but also because of the different statistical methods used to measure unemployment. Moreover, as it is well known from the experience of the CEE countries, official unemployment figures at a given moment do not tell a lot about the general situation of the labour market. High level unemployment may be the reflection of a deep structural reform already started but not yet completed, while, in turn, lower levels of unemployment may illustrate a pre-reform situation, with artificially maintained outdated production and labour market structures. In the latter case, much higher unemployment figures can be expected in the coming years. Evidently, high unemployment rates are not only the consequence of deep structural reforms in the first stage of transformation. As the situation in some WB countries indicates, it can appear without such structural reform as well.

Despite the methodological difficulties in comparing national unemployment rates, SEE countries can be divided into three main categories. Bosnia-Herzegovina and Macedonia struggle with extremely high unemployment, between 35 and 42% of the labour force. The second group includes Albania, Bulgaria (until 2004), Croatia and Serbia, with two-

---

action was carried out from Hungary by the Hungarian subsidiary of Deutsche Telecom. Thus, it is considered (and officially registered) as a Hungarian investment in Macedonia.

digit unemployment rates, but in the lower spectrum of 11 to 15%. Romania (and, as of 2005, Bulgaria) seem to belong to the third group, being the only SEE countries with a one-digit unemployment rate, similar to the EU-25 average, and not higher than in several large EU member countries (Germany or France, for instance).

Still, a lot of caution is needed in evaluating making up the above categories. On the one hand, as already mentioned, similar unemployment rates may be the result of both already implemented reforms and no-reform policies. Second, and clarifying the former statement, the direction of the unemployment trend has to be carefully analyzed. Stagnating or growing unemployment can be interpreted as a sign of no-reform or the start of the reform process, while declining unemployment figures (certainly from a high initial level) can be assessed as an important indication of improving labour market conditions following the implementation of basic structural reforms in the domestic economy. Again, three groups can be distinguished. In the first group that includes Bosnia-Herzegovina, Serbia and Macedonia the annual unemployment figures have dramatically increased from an already high or very high starting level. Albania, Croatia, and particularly Bulgaria, in the second group shows declining unemployment rates that, mainly in the case of Bulgaria, are linked to higher growth rates, new job opportunities in a restructured or restructuring economy. Finally, Romania represents the third group with a slowly declining unemployment rate (still in the one-digit range), most probably as the result of accelerated privatization and delayed restructuring of the economy. Some basic figures are contained in Table III.30.

Labour market statistics are, however misleading in two opposite directions. On the one hand, many experts argue that real unemployment is lower, since many people find some employment in the grey economy, while, officially, they remain registered as unemployed. In turn, the real number of unemployed can be higher than that of those registered. Unregistered unemployment is an essential factor of the labour market situation in the SEE countries. Once these people try to return to the official labour market and are registered, unemployment figures would be higher than the official statistical data.[40]

---

40 For instance, as a result of new regulation to receive unemployment benefits in Hungary, people have to register at a labour office as unemployed, *i.e.* looking for a job. Consequently, the official unemployment rate increased in the last year not as a result of a higher level of unemployment (or net job loss in the economy) but as a consequence of higher unemployment registration.

Table III.30
Official unemployment figures in the SEE countries (based on labour force statistics) (a)

Country	Unemployment figures '000 persons				Unemployment rates share in total labour force		
	2000	2002	2004	2005	2002	2004	2005
Albania	215	172	157	155	15.8	14.4	14.0
Bosnia-Herzegovina	421	442	491	523	40.9	43.9	46.9
Bulgaria	567	592	400	330	17.8	12.0	10.0
Croatia	298	266	250	236	14.8	13.8	13.1
Macedonia	262	284	309	330	31.9	37.2	37.5
Romania	821	845	800	695	8.4	8.0	7.0
Serbia	426	460	665	.	13.3	18.5	20.0

(a) Economic Commission for Europe (2005b) contains different figures, based on using different statistics. Generally, its unemployment figures are higher than those indicated in this table.

Source: wiiw database and national statistics.

In all countries, transformation was accompanied by a dramatic decline of official employment. In the CEE countries (excluding Hungary) employment levels declined by 15 to 20% in one decade. In turn, SEE countries suffered an even more dramatic decline in employment, fluctuating between 50% in Macedonia and 21% in Serbia-Montenegro, a country that is still facing major restructuring. Between 1989 and 2004, total employment declined by 39% in Bosnia-Herzegovina, 35% in Albania, and between 26 and 28% in Bulgaria, Croatia and Romania, respectively. In the manufacturing industry, the main target of transformation and labour market changes, job loss amounted to more than 50% (which means that one out of every two jobs were eliminated) in Bosnia-Herzegovina, Macedonia but also in Bulgaria (Economic Commission for Europe, 2005a).

Table III.31
Employment rates between 1996 and 2003 in selected SEE countries (based on labour force statistics, % of employed people in total active population)

Country	1996	2000	2003
Albania total	60.3	55.1	51.1
male	72.6	66.0	62.6
female	47.9	44.1	39.1
Bulgaria total	54.0	49.9	52.5
male	57.7	53.6	56.0
female	50.4	46.3	49.0
Croatia total	61.6	53.2	54.7(a)
Macedonia total	41.7	40.8	38.5
male	52.7	50.4	45.6
female	30.7	31.3	31.3
Romania total	65.5	63.3	57.6(b)
male	72.6	69.1	63.6
female	58.4	57.5	51.8
Serbia-Montenegro total	51.3	50.0	47.4
Memorandum:			
EU-15 total	60.3	63.4	64.4
male	70.4	72.8	72.6
female	50.2	54.1	56.0

(a) 2004.

(b) 2002.

Source: Eurostat. Employment in Europe 2000, national labour force statistics, wiiw database.

It is well known that one of the key challenges for the European Union in catching up with the Untied States in the coming years is higher employment levels. According to the Lisbon Agenda, employment rates should reach 70% by 2010, and, within it, female employment is to reach 60%. Although the EU has made some progress in the last few years, the figures are far from the objectives defined in the document. With respect to the SEE countries, the situation is disappointing for two reasons. First, employment rates are much lower than in the EU-15 (and also in comparison with the CEE countries). Second, and probably more important, employment rates were falling in the period under discussion in each country. There is no sign at the moment of how this trend could be reversed in the short term.

Some country-specific remarks taken from the country studies have been summarized below.

In Albania, the most backward and autocratic country in Europe, political and economic transformation produced massive shifts in the labour market. Most state-owned industries were closed, and public administration was scaled down as a result of budgetary constraints. Albania is the SEE country with the lowest level of GDP centralization (lower than 30%). Since, from the beginning, agriculture was the leading economic sector with a 50% share in total employment, and, in addition, agricultural cooperatives were abolished and land was returned to individual farmers, workers dismissed from jobs in industry and public administration could not be temporarily absorbed by villages. Just the opposite happened. Most people believed to have better employment chances in urban areas. As a result, and contrary to developments in Bulgaria or Romania in the 1990s, and also due to rural poverty, a massive flow of labour began from rural to urban regions. However, the inadequate (unskilled) supply of, and low demand for, labour immediately generated a high level of structural, thus lasting, unemployment. According to recent figures, less than half the population over 15 years of age is employed, and only 14% of the unemployed are actively seeking jobs. 38% are inactive. No less important, even among those registered as employed persons, more than half of them are in fact underemployed. The situation is further aggravated by the rapid increase of the Albanian population. Probably the only country in Europe with a rapidly growing native population, more than 50% are younger than 30 years. In terms of future developments, special attention has to be paid to the fact that a quarter of Albanians belong to the age group of 0 to 14 years. In statistical terms, in the next 5 to 18 years they will enter the labour market without any real perspective of solid job opportunities.

The unprecedentedly high unemployment rates in Bosnia-Herzegovina are rooted in several factors. The almost total paralysis of economic activities during the war was not followed by a boom period of reconstruction and restructuring. Domestic and foreign capital did not consider the new state as a safe terrain for longer-term investments. Refugee flows (both inflows and outflows) have aggravated the contradictions between supply and demand on the labour market. In addition, state companies were artificially maintained, and restructuring (privatization, selling) of public utilities did not really start at all. The presence of international organizations has created an artificial demand for some jobs, but with a longer-term negative impact on the structure of the domestic labour market.

After heavy economic and social losses in the 1990s, Bulgarian unemployment rates started to decrease in recent years. The labour market is still in a difficult position, albeit slowly leaving the double digit unemployment rate. Nevertheless, the much higher youth unemployment and regional problems remain a fundamental challenge. According to national statistics, up to one-third of the registered unemployed are younger than 30 years. Similar to most other countries, rural unemployment (13.6%) is much higher than urban unemployment (8.8%), which generates a permanent flow of mostly younger people towards major economic centres, particularly to Sofia.[41] A further problem is caused by the contradiction between the still relatively high level of public education and the imminent need of adequate labour by different businesses. The structural gap is not only contributing to higher unemployment but is a powerful incentive for migration and results (at least temporarily) in a loss of investments in human capital financed by taxpayers' money in a country with rather limited internal development resources.

At first glance, the Croatian labour market has started to improve a bit in the last couple of years. Although the official unemployment rate remained double-digit, it showed some decline, accompanied by a slight reduction of long-term structural unemployment (to about half of the total of registered unemployed people). The basic problems continue, as expressed in the very low participation rate (only 42% of the population over 15 years are employed), high youth unemployment (over 40% of the respective age group), and the high share of inactive people over 50 who are still within the working age group (due, at least partly, to the consequences of war and the ample benefits received by "veterans"). A further and increasingly important barrier aggravates the difficult labour situation. Namely, under the conditions described above, the labour market is extremely inflexible. On the one hand, labour market rules are characterized by very high hiring and dismissal (entry and exit) costs. On the other hand, high wages (accompanied by lower level of productivity, *i.e.*, high unit labour costs) prevent both domestic and foreign companies from starting new investments with considerable positive impact on job creation. In addition, the rigid and costly laws represent a big barrier to new entrants into the labour market who, despite being well educated, cannot be employed for it is very difficult to dismiss less skilled and less committed employees. Similarly, inflexible structures make it very difficult to re-enter the labour market once somebody becomes unemployed. Thus, in Croatia a special social strata called "discouraged workers" has emerged, with repeated and failed attempts to find a new job. Finally, the unfavourable business climate characterized by slow and ambiguous privatization, half-hearted restructuring and an uncooperative attitude toward potential foreign capital (and owners) play a relevant role in supporting or fostering labour market rigidities.

---

41 At the same time, it is surprising that booming construction in Sofia and in preferred holiday and recreation areas cannot or is not ready to absorb part of this labour supply and has been contracting more and more foreign, mainly Ukrainian guest workers.

Macedonia has the relatively highest level of registered unemployment among the SEE countries. In fact, the country incurred part of its unemployment as a member of the Yugoslav Federation. National independence started with 150,000 unemployed and with an equal number of over-employed persons having worked in different (mainly unproductive) administrative positions in the former Yugoslavia. As the only country in the SEE region, the number of the unemployed exceeds that of the employed in Macedonia. This is the combined outcome of low labour force participation, disproportionately high rates of long-term unemployment (particularly among women and young people), low levels of education and professional training, ethnic minorities and socially disadvantaged people. The regional disparities in unemployment and job opportunities are very large. In addition, and as a "logical" consequence of the situation, the share of the grey economy is dominant in several regions.

Official statistics of the Romanian unemployment seem more favourable. This SEE country has the lowest level of registered unemployment, similar to some CEE countries and much lower than figures reported by Poland or Slovakia. Several factors can explain this. First, the fundamental restructuring of the economy started only in the last few years, with some selected areas without serious structural change until today. Second, Romania was able to attract significant foreign capital in some areas of manufacturing that require low level skills but offer many job opportunities (including textile and clothing, leather and shoes manufacturing and other labour-intensive industries). Third, a massive migration to Western Europe and overseas countries has certainly alleviated labour market pressures. Fourth, although the unemployment rate is lower than elsewhere in the region, according to experts, real unemployment is substantially higher than the level reported in official statistics. As for the future, there are at least two factors that may raise unemployment (much) higher in the coming years. On the one hand, accession to the EU requires the termination of many state subsidies that have sustained large unproductive manufacturing companies. Most of these factories have to be closed with a substantial negative impact on employment in general, and generating very high levels of regional unemployment in particular.[42] On the other hand, higher wages resulting both from further restructuring and EU membership can easily make investments in low-skilled (or unskilled)

---

[42] There are dozens of towns and larger villages with one factory that used to be the only significant employer in the given settlement. By closing this employment source, whole towns and villages are likely to remain without an alternative job opportunity. Rapid restructuring generated by new investments is unlikely, and even if it happened, there would be a large gap between the structure of demand and supply of labour. In consequence, both unemployment and migration from depressed regions to apparently more attractive areas will experience an increasing trend.

activities less profitable. As a result, part of the capital invested in labour-intensive industries may leave the country, with serious impact on the general labour market (and to less developed regions where, again, these investments proved to be the major source of keeping or even creating jobs).

According to official statistics, both labour participation and employment rates in general remained relatively higher in Serbia than in most other SEE countries. However, the process of restructuring of state-owned enterprises on the one hand, and the gradual shrinking of the informal economy, on the other, will contribute to hidden unemployment turning into official, documented joblessness lowering both rates. The unusually high youth unemployment rate (2.5 to 3 times higher than the EU average) poses a special problem. A special feature of the Serbian labour market is the similar level of official unemployment in urban and rural areas, mainly as a result of large state-owned entities in the whole country. However, there is another explanation, and not very promising for the future of the country, namely the very low share of self-employed people in total non-agricultural employment. This figure, an important indicator of the business climate, entrepreneurial spirit and future-oriented mentality, hardly reaches 5% or half of the average figure in CEE and other SEE economies. This is particularly surprising since in the early 1990s thousands of small firms were established. However, most probably, these firms were hardest hit by the dissolution of the Yugoslav Federation and by the subsequent wars, because they have been not only running short of capital but, most importantly, lost the market they initially targeted. About half of these firms went bankrupt and may have become discouraged to relaunch their previous activities, especially in a market with a much smaller purchasing power. Moreover, for many years, practically until most recently, and contrary to accepted economic rationale, the administrative and financial costs to set up a new company have become much higher. Additional pressure on the labour market is exerted by the massive inflow of refugees (estimated at 300,000) and internally displaced people (around 250,000). Beyond its obvious, direct negative impact on the labour market by raising unemployment, this factor also has a long-term, indirect effect on the uprooted ("entwurzelt") people's social status and further solidifies the interrelation between unemployment and poverty, as well as unemployment and growing illegal activities (in detail see Calic, 2005).

III.4.2. Beyond the well-known factors of declining employment, experienced also in the CEE countries in the last fifteen years, SEE countries face some specific problems which have to be noted briefly.

a The recession stemming from the transformation to market economy was more serious and lasted longer, and restructuring was much slower (if any) than in CEE countries, leading not only to high levels of unemployment but also to widespread, long-term unemployment.

b Both due to the delayed and half-hearted privatization and the reluctant opening to foreign capital, the double positive impact of FDI could not be felt until most recently. On the one hand, job creation, both direct and indirect, did not start in the second stage of privatisation linked to efficient restructuring. On the other hand, green-field investments remained scarce, thus its job creating impact was, in most cases, minimal (if any).

c Traditionally, some WB countries used to have some unemployment well before the transformation, due to structural problems (*e.g.* the high share of agriculture in the GDP, the low level of manufacturing, fragmented services, etc.). In order to mitigate the negative effects of structural unemployment, many ex-Yugoslav citizens looked for jobs in Western Europe in the 1960s and 1970s.

d The Western Balkan war had a very negative impact on employment as well. Many jobs, mainly in industry, were destroyed, and massive forced migration and refugee flows added to tensions in the labour market. The necessity of rebuilding the national economies as well as the establishment of new institutions as a result of the disintegration of the Yugoslav Federation were not sufficient to create more jobs, partly due to the lack of physical capital (reconstruction) and/or to the obvious structural (skill) difference between supply and demand in the labour market.

e Inflexible labour markets inherited from ex-Yugoslavia, accompanied by high labour costs (not necessarily of wages!), *i.e.* lower levels of productivity, can be identified as other serious obstacles to increasing employment levels. Although all SEE countries, except for Croatia, have much lower minimum wages than the CEE countries, they have not been able to generate large FDI flows that created jobs.[43] Minimum monthly wages fluctuate between Euro 73 in Serbia and Euro 91 in Romania, as compared to more than Euro 230 in the Czech Republic and Hungary. The only conspicuous SEE exception is Croatia where minimum wage reaches Euro 285, an obvious obstacle to higher level of employment (and of investments as well) (ICEG-Corvinus, 2005).

f Labour markets have been influenced by different forms and directions of migration as well. Intra-regional migration, mainly as a re-

[43] In fact, international experience shows that the largest part of job creation cannot be expected from FDI but is the result of increasing business activity of small- and medium-sized enterprises, both domestic and foreign-owned.

sult of the Western Balkan wars, has contributed to higher unemployment and aggravated the problems of structural unemployment. This phenomenon can be observed not only in areas with large-scale immigration (refugee inflows) but also in the economic development of those regions and new states that badly need skilled and experienced workers who were forced to leave their former domicile in the last decade. Another disputed impact of migration has been the massive outflow of young and flexible labour from all SEE countries to Western Europe and overseas. It is extremely difficult to generate sustainable development without the critical minimum of well-trained human resources. In this context, the difference between most CEE countries (Poland being a partial exception) and the SEE countries is remarkable, or, perhaps more precisely, shocking.

g High and persistent unemployment is also generated by high birth rates in the Albanian community that makes its impact on the longer-term development of the labour market not only in Albania but also in Kosovo and Macedonia.

h Finally, the possibilities of survival outside the official labour market were to some extent different. Certainly, CEE countries have also "lost" a substantial part of their previously registered labour force by withdrawing from the official labour market. However, the main survival strategies could be identified, including returning to the household (to subsistence level agriculture, for example), utilizing early retirement schemes, and starting new businesses outside the "legal" economy (based on large-scale tax evasion in the form of the so-called "forced entrepreneurship"). In SEE, these opportunities were only partially available. In fact, a return to agriculture could be observed simultaneously with the increasing migration of the rural population to towns, offering the only (slight) opportunity to get a legal or illegal job. Also, due to the larger share of agriculture in GDP and employment, as well as its low level of productivity (in some countries as a result of returning land to the "original" owners) the substituting role of subsistence agriculture remained more limited than in selected CEE countries. In addition, early retirement schemes were not widely applied, partly due to labour market inflexibilities (old workers were not allowed to be dismissed), partly stemming from the limited burden-taking capacity of central budgets. Finally, forced entrepreneurship is not only linked to some kind of personal business affinity but also to a certain level of starting capital (either in cash or in kind), the general level of social welfare network, and, no less importantly, to the overall economic environment, including growth, investment, the size and structure of demand, etc. In the last case, the overwhelming answer in SEE was emigration instead of "forced entrepreneurship" at home.

III.4.3. A deeper assessment of unemployment and the medium-term outlook of the labour market (a key element in the successful adjustment to EU requirements and the start of sustainable growth with social tensions under control) require the analysis of some specific features. They include the sectoral characteristics of the labour market, youth unemployment, long-term unemployment trends, regional imbalances and the role of the "shadow" economy.

The sectoral survey shows that manufacturing was the real victim of the transformation. Manufacturing employment both in total employment and as compared to previous levels declined dramatically. Inflexible labour markets, delayed privatization, reluctant liberalization could, in fact, produce a slower speed of decline. However, this attitude did not prevent job losses and only postponed the time of dramatic changes, while delaying the start of restructuring and industrial revival, probably connected with new (net) job creation. Unofficial employment in agriculture increased as a temporary survival shelter (from the beginning it was extremely high in Albania, namely 50%) against high unemployment. Expectations that the rapid development of the service sector would be able to absorb most of the unemployed coming from the manufacturing industry proved largely unrealistic, since job creation in the service sector remained limited and the structure of labour demand did not correspond to the labour supply that was available. The economic recovery in Bulgaria and Romania in the last few years may recreate some of the lost industrial jobs but certainly at a much lower level than the pre-transformation period.

Youth employment is a very serious problem in all countries, but particularly in those with very high general unemployment rates and a relatively high share of younger population. In addition, inflexible labour market rules generally discriminate against young job seekers, for elder people cannot be dismissed, and new job opportunities are scarce. In Bosnia-Herzegovina, 56% of the population aged 18 years, and 44% of the age group between 19 and 24 years are reported unemployed. At the same time, about 20% of the working population is younger than 24 years. Sociological surveys point out that extremely high level of youth unemployment can also be explained by the special attitude of these people, since they prefer to wait for a job opportunity abroad than to look for job at home.[44] In Bulgaria, youth unemployment (the share of unem-

44 In fact, 62% of young Bosnian people want to work abroad (see: Bassa, *Bosnia-Herzegovina country study*, 2005, p. 10).

ployed people younger than 30 years of age) has reached one-third of total unemployment at times, affecting 40% of people with secondary education and 6% of young people with a high-school degree. The situation is even worse in Albania where one-third of the young people with higher education are reported unemployed (or do not participate in the official labour market).[45] Unemployment among young skilled workers is a serious problem for two reasons. First, it means that, either as a result of a misguided education system or the low demand for new labour by business in general, taxpayers' money is invested in activities that do not generate additional value. Second, such investments encourage migration, even seeking jobs that do not require the education and training these young people have received.

Long-term unemployment (*i.e.*, unemployment lasting longer than 12 months[46]) is another common feature of the SEE countries. Combating long-term unemployment successfully is a long process. In Croatia, this figure stood at 53% of total unemployed persons a few years ago and could be reduced slightly to the 50% mark most recently. In Macedonia, more than one-fourth of the unemployed people have been looking for a job for more than eight years and another almost 40% for a period between 3 and 8 years. The share of unemployed people finding a job within one year is as low as 6%. Similarly, almost three-fourth of the unemployed in Serbia have been looking for a job for more than one year.

Similar to the differences in growth rates, the speed and depth of structural change, FDI orientation (if any) and new investments, most SEE countries show large regional differences in employment as well. In general, unemployment is higher in rural areas and structurally depressed regions struggle with the legacy of large-scale but inefficient industrialization, and lack new job opportunities locally. The only difference seems to be Serbia, where urban and rural unemployment rates are similar (11.4 and 10.7%, respectively). Surprisingly, the highest official unemployment rate is registered in the most developed part of the country (Vojvodina), which is due to the highly distorting impact of Serbian refugees from other, (much) less developed parts of ex-Yugoslavia.

A common feature in all SEE countries is the extensive presence of the shadow economy. According to reliable estimates, it accounts for

45 One-fifth of the Albanian population, mainly young people have left the country after 1990.

46 Long-term unemployment figures are not always reliable, since in some countries unemployment benefits are paid for less than 12 months. Also, ILO-standardized labour force statistics are based on active job-seeking, and once job search is abandoned after 12 months, no further registration as "long-term unemployed" is available. As a consequence, many unemployed people are not included in the long-term unemployment statistics.

about one-third of the GDP and employs 23 to 30% of the total labour force (it is 37% in Bosnia-Herzegovina), as compared to 20-25% in selected CEE countries (Novák, 2005). In fact, the personal experience of people living in the SEE region seems to indicate that the real size of the shadow economy is larger than what the official figures indicate.

III.4.4. Until now, most SEE countries have failed to develop credible and long-term employment and labour market policies. On the one hand, this is surprising, since unemployment is one or just the most important economic problem policy-makers are facing. On the other hand, it has to be noted that, under current conditions, it is very difficult to design a policy that would promise a radical decline of the high level of unemployment. Thus, most governments try to stem further job losses. However, as already pointed out, restricted restructuring, mainly to be carried out in the framework of a large-scale privatization process that includes enhanced participation of foreign capital as well, has been given priority. The underlying hope is that, as a consequence, unemployment will not worsen, and, at some point, economic growth will generate more jobs, while most of the jobs in uncompetitive companies can be preserved. This hypothesis, however, hardly works in reality. As widespread experience shows, restructuring managed by the State does not lead to international competitiveness, even if the required financial resources are available (which, generally, is not the case) and the process could be carried out in a relatively short time. Therefore, delaying restructuring and privatization with the aim of keeping jobs usually turns out to be a short-sighted and failed approach. At the end of the day, restructuring proves to be unavoidable or the entire company is threatened with bankruptcy and elimination. Most state-owned or half-heartedly "privatized" companies in the ex-Yugoslav countries are facing this destiny. According to estimates, privatization of the large Serbian public utility companies (electricity, oil refinery, telecommunications, airport, forestry, railways) that at present employ 135,000 people will result in dismissing about 45,000 employees in total (in contrast to the official version of "only" 18,000) (Reuter, 2005b). A similar situation can be seen in Croatia where state-owned companies prevail. Their deficiencies were not remedied by the rationalization of the labour force but by growing indebtedness.[47] Neither did this solution facilitate mass privatization. Instead, it created a structure with a

[47] According to the so-called Markovic law, still in force, the mass conversion of state-owned enterprises into joint-stock companies was allowed. Its main characteristics were the following: (a) only natural persons and pension funds were eligible to receive the shares issued on preferred terms by a converted enterprise, (b) the conversion was only optional for each socially-owned enterprise, and the decision was to be made by the workers. Should they opt for conversion, they (and retired employees) would be entitled to up to 60% of the equity in the new company.

high number of insider workers equipped with a lot of safeguard measures.

Another expectation is linked to resumed and sustainable high growth. In fact, all countries have returned to a relatively high growth period but, except Bulgaria and Croatia, without significant or any positive impact on the labour market. The positive correlation between growth and job creation surely exists, but in countries with a low level of productivity and, consequently, large productivity reserves, growth can be generated in the long term primarily or exclusively by a continuously high growth of productivity.[48]

Further hope is associated with the badly needed inflow of foreign capital. However, most countries have not yet created the necessary political and legal stability that could attract sizeable amounts of foreign investments. In addition, large-scale investments are more productive and less labour-intensive, so that their impact on the labour market, although not negligible, remains modest. (This impact has been analyzed in detail by Inotai, 2005a.) Moreover, foreign capital, after the initial stage, starts to become a job creator and a job destructor simultaneously, as structural change progresses, wages increase and the international environment for investments changes.

Finally, although nobody has stated it openly, many politicians expect the problem of unemployment to be alleviated by mass migration, with a highly questionable impact on sustainable development and successful catching up in the respective countries (see in more detail in III.7).

In most SEE countries, labour market policies, if available, are partial, fragmented and rudimentary. There have been some initiatives in Croatia to make the labour market more flexible (without much result), and, at the same time, facilitate the establishment of new ventures. However, these steps remained very timid, as shown by the slow pace of setting up new ventures, as compared to the CEE countries. Despite the very cautious privatization that prevented companies from dismissing some of the labour force, newly established private companies were not able to absorb even the small number of people who lost their previous job. Figures show that until 2002, employment in state-owned companies decreased by 12%, while private firms could increase their employment capacity by 11% only. Macedonia is trying to increase job opportunities by providing small- and medium-sized firms with tax privileges. Serbia's labour market policy, aimed at bringing people back from the informal to the legal

48 In developed economies, in the last two decades a 3% annual growth has been able to create new jobs. In less developed countries,, particularly in the first stage of transformation, substantially higher growth rates are needed to produce increasing employment.

labour market, improving the quality of jobs and facilitating the reallocation of labour to more efficient sectors is in contradiction with another instrument described in the same document, namely, that the existing overall level of employment and participation have to be sustained.

Experience in CEE countries fighting unemployment with different degrees of success (and failure) provides several lessons to be considered in the process of shaping labour market strategies in SEE countries as well.

First, the overall level of unemployment can only be reduced if passive and active labour market policies are combined, with policy emphasis on the latter.

Second, active labour market policies do not suffice, since they address the supply side of the market only. One may train an adequate labour force, but without a simultaneous and positive response on the demand side represented by the business community, the expected favourable impact cannot be achieved. Therefore, active labour market policies have to go hand-in-hand with the establishment of a favourable investment climate for existing and potential entrepreneurs.

Third, the creation of an adequate supply of the labour force requires a fundamental change in the education policies of the individual countries. The different structures of supply and demand on the labour market can create a large number of "mis-educated" young people. The negative impact may not only be manifested in the mis-allocation of scarce resources but also in the development of growing social discontent of educated people.

Finally, there is widespread agreement on the basic role of small- and medium-sized companies in the job creation process. However, in this context, CEE (and SEE) countries face some specific problems that were not experienced by their Western European counterparts in the critical stages of their development process. On the one hand, small- and medium-sized firms started to develop after the transformation has begun. Until now, they have not had sufficient time to go through the different stages of company development (single-proprietor enterprises, small family businesses, genuine small companies, medium-sized firms, etc.). On the other hand, their development process was not accompanied by temporary or lasting protection by their respective national governments. Company building and large-scale trade and capital liberalization represented simultaneous processes. Thus, the new companies had to face international competition from the very beginning of their existence, and could not rely on strong governmental support. In fact, most of the potential (and protective) instruments were forbidden due to the competition rules of the *acquis communautaire* or were given up as a result of reciprocal trade liberalization and of creating a larger free trade area. Evidently, there was no other viable alternative for them, since those countries that did not (quickly) follow this way are struggling with much higher unemployment today than those that joined this approach, certainly not without a painful (but in many cases rather successful) adjustment. In sum, the job creation capacity of small- and medium-sized companies (both domestic and foreign-owned) has not been lost, but it is more modest than in Western Europe. However, the process takes time. In turn, large transnational companies located in different CEE and SEE countries can generate an important positive, although indirect, impact on the labour market by creating a dynamic sector of small and medium-sized firms that are a part of their expanding local production and service-based network.

III.5. Physical Infrastructure

Physical infrastructure can rightly be considered the blood system of the economy (as human capital-based infrastructure could be called the nerve system of the economy). Besides the traditional areas of transportation, such as motorways, railways, rivers, ports and airports, it includes several other fields, mostly linked to other economic activities as well. So, water economy has strong links to environment and health safety. Energy, one of the key engines of economic growth, is also closely linked to the level of welfare of the population, competitiveness of the economy and environment. Moreover, it raises a lot of policy issues well beyond the national economies competence (volume, price and geographic origin of imports, ways of delivering different energy sources). Most recently, as a result of spectacular growth, the expansion and rapidly increasing influence of the e-economy on overall economic activities have to be reckoned with as well. Each aspect could be analyzed in detailed comparative studies related to the SEE region. However, our objective is much more limited. As part of their legacy, current developments and prospects of the SEE countries, with special regard to their closeness to and accession to the European Union, this chapter offers an overview of the state of physical infrastructure and major plans for its further development. Thus, the chapter is divided into three parts. First, short remarks will be made on the interdependence between sustainable economic growth and the development and performance levels of the physical infrastructure. Second, the current situation will be described, both as a result of previous development (and destruction) and in the context of comparable statistics. In the third part, different development approaches at the national, regional and EU-level will be examined.

III.5.1. There is widespread theoretical and practical evidence for the strong interrelationship between economic development and the performance of physical infrastructure, both in quantitative and qualitative terms. Historical experience shows three different patterns of development of the physical infrastructure. In the first case, it follows the general economic growth, mainly generated by manufacturing activities, and used to be subject to a continuous catching-up pressure. In consequence, the poor condition of the infrastructure can become a brake on faster economic growth and enhanced competitiveness. In the second and more fortunate case, overall economic development and progress made in the development of physical infrastructure are well balanced and mutually harmonized. In many cases, however, and this is the third pattern, the quantitative and qualitative development of the physical infrastructure is considered a precondition for sustainable growth and improving welfare. This is largely characteristic of all SEE (and most CEE) countries. In other words, investments into the infrastructure should, to some extent, precede overall economic growth. Consequently, only the "normal" pattern described as the second case, can be lastingly established.

International experience in general, and specific lessons provided by the transformation process in CEE in particular, have highlighted close interdependence between overall growth and the state of physical infrastructure and ongoing investment plans in this field. The most obvious correlation can be seen between the infrastructural environment and the propensity of capital, both domestic and foreign, to make new investments. Since foreign direct investments has become a major factor in sustainable economic growth in selected CEE countries, experience with its geographic location is particularly instructive. The Hungarian, Czech and Slovak developments underline the close relationship between the geographic expansion of FDI and the availability of modern physical infrastructure. The latter plays a crucial role in upgrading potential locations for foreign (and also domestic) investments.[49] According to general experience, FDI does not wait for large infrastructural investments to be completed. On the contrary, once investments in infrastructure are decided with a clear and reliable timetable for integrating them into the national (and international) network, decisions on new investments follow right away. Namely, FDI (but also domestic investors) want to take full advantage of the new opportunities (be it market opening or cost reduction) offered by an improved infrastructure, from the very beginning of its operation. Needless to say, high-quality infrastructure affects the company's economic performance, profit outlooks and competitiveness favourably in several ways. First, it reduces production costs by saving on transportation expenses. Second, it increases the predictability and reli-

---

49 For instance, two maps of Hungary, one indicating the current (and planned) state of physical infrastructure, mainly that of the highway system and the other representing the geographic location of FDI have a close to 90% overlap.

ability of production (from different types of manufacturing to the service sector). As a result, it becomes a key factor in the decision-making process of domestic and international investors looking for appropriate geographic location for their future ventures. Third, it reduces the security risks stemming from the geographic distance both in terms of the supply of material ensuring smooth production in a given enterprise and the delivery of manufactured goods and services to selected markets.

Another positive impact of well-performing physical infrastructure can be identified in the development of the labour market. One of the key instruments to combat high level unemployment in selected regions is the development of physical infrastructure. Consequently, the physical mobility and the chance for potential employees to join the primary labour market can be substantially enhanced. Therefore, the development of physical infrastructure has a doubly positive impact. It not only enhances the mobility of labour but, by attracting new investments to a given region, it also increases the number of jobs for people living within the "magnet area" of the improved infrastructural network.[50]

With regard to SEE, development of the physical infrastructure cannot be separated from the future of regional trade. Bi- and multilateral trade agreements can be helpful for sure, however, the legal framework is only as good as the extent of the production and transport capacities. In many cases, one of the most serious barriers to substantially higher regional trade can be found in the poor state of physical infrastructure. Furthermore, the availability of physical infrastructure not only provides a good environment for the regional flow of commodities and services produced at the current level of productive capacities, but it generates further demand as well. Therefore, the supply-side approach of infrastructural development has to be emphasized as a major priority in future investment plans.[51]

III.5.2. Physical infrastructure inherited from the past was, with the partial exception of the Yugoslav Federation, underdeveloped and characterized by a one-sided external orientation. Bulgaria and Romania mainly used their Black Sea ports to carry out the lion's share of their foreign trade with the ex-Soviet Union. Regional railway and highway links were not only underdeveloped but in most cases inefficient as well. Oil and gas

---

[50] We are fully aware of the fact that labour mobility is influenced by several other factors as well. However, the availability of a good physical infrastructure is a basic (although in many cases not sufficient) precondition of higher mobility.

[51] Unfortunately, many feasibility studies to asses the potential traffic on a planned highway draw conclusions on the basis of the current traffic (and may, therefore, reject the investment plans for lacking profitability). Instead, they should, from the very beginning, take into account the additional impact of such investments on increasing and re-orienting traffic.

pipelines connecting the ex-Soviet Union and the Central and Eastern European countries (to a large extent as transit countries towards Austria, Germany and Italy) were missing in SEE, with serious impact on using cheap and clean energy for energy production, industry and communal heating. Conditions for domestic transportation were somewhat better but without practically any highway built in the pre-transformation period.

The situation was markedly worse in Albania, a country that declared self-sufficiency and "independence" from the outside world as a basic pillar of its development policy. Until 1991, private vehicles were banned and buses and trucks travelled only limited routes with the aim to shift most of the traffic to railways. Rural communities were not connected to the main road (and railway) network. Also, the capacity of the major Adriatic port in Durres was not used adequately at all.

The clear exception was Yugoslavia that started to modernize its physical infrastructure already in the late 1960s with loans partly provided by the European Investment Bank.[52] Similar to the developments designed and carried out a century ago in the Austro-Hungarian monarchy, the basic approach was to look at the added regional value that an all-Yugoslav construction of the infrastructure could offer. Necessarily, it focused on the advantages of a federal Yugoslavia and did not give priority to local or subregional needs. After the break-up of the federation, the otherwise logical network of physical infrastructure could not fit into the new geography of the Western Balkans.

Another important difference in the development of physical infrastructure of the CEE countries was the main geographic orientation of the "arteries". In CEE the dominant direction was West-East, both to directly connect the neighbouring countries to the ex-Soviet markets and, at varying degrees from country to country, to the Western European railway and highway networks. Hungary and partly Slovenia were (and still are) the only new EU member countries that have been fully linked to the European highway network.[53] In ex-Yugoslavia, an important corridor linking Western Europe with Greece (the only EU member country still without common continental EU border), Turkey and the Middle East had been partially constructed (the section covering Zagreb-Beograd via Skopje and Nis). However, highway development has never got the

[52] Yugoslavia, as the only CEE country at that time, signed a trade agreement with Brussels and established diplomatic relations with the European integration. As a result, access to loans of the EIB became available. For all other CEE countries, EIB credits were denied until the end of the 1980s.

[53] Prague will soon be connected to the German highway system, but Warsaw is far away from being part of the European highway network. Also, little work has remained for Bratislava, less than 60 km from Vienna, to finally become a part of the highway system.

priority of linking a Balkan country to Western (and Central) Europe. If such constructions were implemented, they mainly served domestic purposes (Bucuresti-Ploesti, from Sofia to the northeast) and only in a few cases were they considered as part of a trans-European corridor with highly uncertain deadlines for their completion both at home and in the neighbouring countries (Sofia-Plovdiv, Beograd-Nis).

While the accelerated development of the West-East corridor became an imperative in the new EU member countries, and substantial work has been done in the last few years both in Hungary (to the East and the South), in Slovakia and in Slovenia, the lack of West-East connection is increasingly felt as a disadvantage in the SEE countries. In fact, the new corridor linking the Adriatic Sea with the Black Sea could offer an important instrument for sustainable development. However, its construction is not even on the drawing table as of now. It seems more probable that the Balkan countries will be linked to the EU through a combination of East-West and South-North axis, in which Hungary and Slovenia (plus Croatia) may become the key transit countries. The missing genuine North-South infrastructure will remain a major bottleneck for most CEE and SEE countries alike (the corridor from Helsinki/ Tallinn crossing the other Baltic countries, Poland, Slovakia, Hungary and going to the south-eastern part of Europe).

The poor initial conditions were further worsened in the last fifteen years by several developments. First, the wars in the Western Balkan countries destroyed part of the previously existing physical infrastructure (highways, railway links, bridges and energy systems as well). In addition, the bombarding of Serbia by NATO has cut off Balkan countries, mainly Bulgaria but partly also Romania, from the Western markets, due to damage in the physical infrastructure. In addition, a lot of time was lost during the period of Western embargo against Milosevic's Yugoslavia, when the borders were practically closed. Second, the dissolution of Yugoslavia created a situation with a highly fragmented infrastructure. Within the new state borders, the previously built network often proved illogical or poorly designed, at least in not covering the imminent and basic needs of restarting sustainable growth in the newly created states.[54] Third, more than 5,000 km of a new border line was "created" with

[54] For example, Bosnia-Herzegovina needs a road network linked to the Zagreb-Beograd highway as well as to the ports of the Adriatic sea. The railway system has to be linked to the European network. The Sava river that is suitable for shipping cannot be used because of a lack of agreement with neighbouring countries. Reliable supply of electricity, a major precondition for foreign and domestic investments, could not yet be reestablished. Moreover, many municipalities are unable to provide 24-hour drinking water (what's more, many users are not able or ready to pay for such services) (In detail see Bassa, *Bosnia-Herzegovina country study*, 2005, p. 20).

substantial impact on previous transport flows (European Commission, 2003). Fourth, a large number of new border crossings had to be established among the new states. Financial and technical costs, huge delays in transportation, people crossing the borders with new identity cards, unpredictable customs procedures, inadequate road and railway connections within the former Yugoslav Federation, particularly among its less developed territories (Bosnia-Herzegovina, Kosovo, Montenegro, Macedonia), became the inevitable consequences of the new reality in the Western Balkans. Finally, all countries of the region facing the above challenges in physical infrastructure are not only historically poor but became even poorer either in the first (and mostly prolonged) stage of transformation or as a result of years-long wars.

Looking at the current situation of the physical infrastructure in the Western Balkan, the following main features can be identified.

Table III.32
Number and type of border crossings in the SEE region

State border	Length in km	Number of		Total number of crossings	Number of		Total number of crossings per 100 km
		railway crossings	road crossings		railway crossings per 100 km	road crossings per 100 km	
Slovenia-Austria	330	3	18	21	0.91	5.45	6.36
Slovenia-Italy	232	3	10	13	1.29	4.31	5.60
Slovenia-Hungary	102	1	7	8	0.98	6.86	7.84
Slovenia-Croatia	501	7	24	31	1.40	4.79	6.19
Croatia-Bosnia	932	5	25	30	0.54	2.68	3.22
Croatia-Hungary	329	3	7	10	0.91	2.13	3.04
Croatia-Serbia	241	3(a)	6	9	1.24	2.49	3.73
Serbia-Hungary	164	2	5	7	1.22	3.05	4.27
Serbia-Romania	546	2	7	9	0.37	1.28	1.65
Serbia-Bulgaria	506	1	5	6	0.20	0.99	1.19
Serbia-Macedonia	232	2	3	5	0.86	1.29	2.15
Serbia-Albania	220	1	3	4	0.45	1.36	1.81
Serbia-Bosnia	380	2	12	14	0.53	3.94	4.47
Romania-Moldova	681	2	5	7	0.29	0.73	1.02
Romania-Bulgaria	609	3(b)	7(c)	10	0.49	1.15	1.64
Romania-Ukraine	549	4	5	9	0.73	0.91	1.64
Romania-Hungary	448	5	14	19	1.12	3.13	4.25
Bulgaria-Macedonia	165	-	3	3	-	1.82	1.82

Bulgaria-Greece	493	2	2	4	0.41	0.41	0.82
Bulgaria-Turkey	259	1	1	2	0.39	0.39	0.78
Macedonia-Albania	191	-	2	2	-	1.04	1.04
Macedonia-Greece	262	2(d)	3	5	0.76	1.15	1.91
Albania-Greece	294	-	2	2	-	0.68	0.68

(a) out of the three railway crossings, at present, one is out of operation;

(b) out of the four railway crossings one is a ferry that, at present, does not function;

(c) out of the seven road crossings four are ferry services across the Danube;

(d) out of the two railway crossings, one is transporting goods only.

Source: Erdősi (2005), pp. 44-45.

Deficient physical infrastructure is a major obstacle to improved regional cooperation. Despite the newly created state borders between ex-Yugoslav republics that multiplied the number of international border crossing points, the difference in the coverage of physical infrastructure between the SEE region and selected CEE countries is striking. The best and internationally comparable indicator is the number of continental (road and railway) border crossings in a 100 km section of border lines. All international border lines of Slovenia (with Austria, Croatia, Hungary and Italy) stand out with high border crossing figures (between 7.84 and 5.33 crossing points per 100 km of borderline). The number of border crossing points among the previous ex-Yugoslav republics can mostly be considered average, between 3 to 4 crossing points for 100 km of borderline. In contrast, all other international border sections, except the border between Hungary and Romania, indicate a substantially lower level of "infrastructure intensity". Often, border sections well above 100 km long lack any border crossing points. This points to the autocratic economic development and infrastructure planning of each SEE country, including Greece, a member of the EU.

Beyond the low density of the physical infrastructure network in the SEE region, the dramatic change in the relative importance of the main transportation modalities in the last decade has to be underlined. Similar to the developments in CEE in both passenger and commercial transportation, highway transportation has gained in importance. Its share in total passenger transportation is above 80% (except in Romania), and, in little more than a decade, its position increased by 10 to 20 percentage points (excluding Greece and Slovenia, where road transportation was the overwhelming way of physical movement already in 1990). In commercial transportation, highway usage is less important than in passenger transportation. Nevertheless, its share increased substantially in many countries of the region and became the leading form of transportation. The only exception is Bulgaria where, along with Romania, transportation of goods by railway still plays a more important role than road transportation. (For statistical figures see Appendix Table III.5.2/1.)

Road networks, although relatively extensive, are far from the quality required not only by the EU but also by the safety of local traffic. In the SEE countries, primary and secondary roads have a total length of over 200,000 km. However, only about 1,300 km can be qualified as highways (excepting the most recent highway construction in Croatia).[55] This road network has to serve a rapidly increasing number of passenger cars mainly imported from Western Europe, despite all kinds of economic problems.[56] (Most of these cars belong to the category of "over-used" vehicles.) In contrast to the rapidly increasing number of cars, the quality of the roads has been gradually deteriorating, due to a serious lack of regular maintenance. In Serbia-Montenegro, it is estimated that only 30% of the roads are in good condition and the lack of maintenance can be observed even in parts of the highway system (*e.g.* between Beograd and Nis). In addition, most roads do not comply with requirements for European trucks (axle loads up to 11.5 tons), while practically all traffic going to Turkey and the Near East uses these roads contributing to further deterioration. Another problem is that most roads are too narrow and need a widening of up to 7 m. Major roads generally lead to larger towns and cities and create huge traffic jams. By-passes should be constructed immediately.[57]

The railway network consists of about 25,000 km of lines, 3,500 km of which have double tracks and the share of electric lines varies between 76% in Bosnia-Herzegovina and 66% in Bulgaria on the one hand, and about one-third for all other countries. Network density is quite different in each country. Romania (4.8 km per 100 km²), Croatia (4.8) and partly Bulgaria (3.9) and Serbia-Montenegro (3.8) have relatively high density (Slovenia has a density of 6 km per 100 km²), while Albania, Bosnia-Herzegovina and Macedonia have a much less developed railway system (less than 3 km per 100 km²). In addition, the break-up of Yugoslavia

55 For more detailed information see Appendix Table III.5.2./2.

56 Between 1990 and 2003, the total number of passenger cars more than doubled in Romania, while it increased by 89% in Bulgaria, 84% in Croatia, and by 65% in Macedonia. In contrast, the growth remained modest in war-ridden Bosnia-Herzegovina (28%) and, even more so in Serbia (11%). In 2003, the number of passenger cars per 1,000 persons reached 331 in Croatia, 292 in Bulgaria, while it only amounted to 37 in Albania (where, before 1990, private ownership of passenger cars was forbidden) and to 72 in Bosnia-Herzegovina. The comparable Slovenian figure was 468 (Erdősi, 2005).

57 The Core Regional Network of the Western Balkan includes about 6,000 km of roads, with 58 border crossing points as well as major Adriatic ports and airports in several ex-Yugoslav cities. According to a study by the European Commission, 70% are in need of renovation (European Commission, 2003).

resulted in the creation of new "national" (meaning state-owned) railway companies and, evidently, further barriers to smooth traffic. Reform, in accordance with EU directive 91/440, to separate the network infrastructure from operational activities is far from completed (sometimes not even started). Investments and maintenance have been seriously neglected which led to the disruption of the smooth functioning of some major "corridors". As a consequence of war damage, unpredictable travel time and a dramatic fall in trade (that used to be domestic trade before the split of the Federation), current operation accounts for 10% of the pre-1990 levels in Bosnia-Herzegovina and to 30% in Serbia (Stability Pact, 2003). At the current level of demand, it is impossible to carry out profitable activities in the railway sector.

Before 1990, all Balkan countries had direct access to sea (Adriatic and Black Sea). As a result of the dissolution of Yugoslavia, four landlocked countries were created: Macedonia, Kosovo, as well as Bosnia-Herzegovina (with a tiny and artificial access to the Adriatic Sea, without major commercial importance), and Serbia, following the independence of Montenegro. It's beyond doubt that Croatia has turned out to be the big "winner" of this "geographic game", however, its main ports can hardly work efficiently without a "hinterland" that, based on its growth and living standard, generates sufficient demand for services in Croatian ports. In turn, the importance of the port of Thessaloniki may have grown for Macedonia. The three SEE countries with long coasts, Bulgaria, Croatia and Romania have important commercial fleets, consisting of 243 (Croatia), 240 (Romania) and 172 (Bulgaria) ships (as compared to 1,529 ships in Greek ownership). In turn, the volume of transported goods declined in the past decade.[58]

All SEE countries, except Albania, have more than one airport.[59] Several of them serve not only domestic but also international traffic. However substantial upgrading, including a lot of safety-related modernization, is needed for most of them. In addition, all new countries created their own national airlines (some of them more than one), with few flights, high operating costs and probably huge losses. The embargo against Serbia led to the cancellation of most direct flights from Western Europe to Beograd and certainly added to the negative balance.

The electric power network also suffers from the consequences of the break-up and the succeeding wars. Before 1990, the whole of SEE was

58 In 2001, the total transportation performance reached 25 mn tons for Romania, 16 mn tons for Bulgaria and less than 13 mn tons for Croatia (as against 60 mn tons for Greece) (Erdősi, 2005).

59 Romania has 17 airports, while Croatia has 13 airports with paved taxiways, followed by Serbia-Montenegro (8), Bulgaria (5) and Bosnia-Herzegovina (4).

adequately interconnected, electric power from exports and imports within the region and coming from outside suppliers. In the last decade, however, traditional networks have been disrupted, mainly in the WB. Bosnia-Herzegovina is hit hardest, but the main connection between Croatia and Serbia was cut as well. Furthermore, Albania badly needs a better and more reliable electric power supply system. The establishment of a regional energy market is more than imperative (see later in this chapter).

Finally, oil and gas pipeline networks need integration. Traditionally, two different supply sources have determined the geographic orientation of the pipeline network. Bulgaria and Romania (and partly Serbia) relied on Soviet/Russian sources, while Croatia and Slovenia on imported oil from other sources and shipped into the Adriatic ports. Albania only had a modest domestic pipeline system, while Bosnia-Herzegovina and Macedonia became heavily dependant on external and one-sided dependence.[60]

III.5.3. The few facts mentioned in the previous chapter make it clear that the overall modernization of the physical infrastructure is a fundamental precondition for the sustainable growth, competitiveness, attraction of large amounts of foreign capital and sizeable increase of regional and EU-oriented trade. National and regional initiatives have been launched in this area.

On the national level, Croatian efforts to implement an ambitious highway-construction plan have to be pointed out. In recent years and mainly financed by credit from the World Bank, Croatia launched a spectacular program that dramatically increased the extent of highway system from 36 km in 1995 to almost 850 km in 2005). This policy was generated largely by the U-shape geography of the country, the needs of the growing tourist industry and the upgrading of services offered by ports to the mainland and to neighbouring countries.

Total public expenditure on the transport sector accounts for about 6% of the GDP (out of which half is directly pegged to highway construction), a very high figure in international comparison.[61]

Highway construction in other SEE countries is much less ambitious. Although several countries of the region are "hosting" important sections of various European "corridors", developments are far from convincing. Just the opposite, some previously built corridor sections reveal serious problems due to the years-long lack of maintenance (mainly in Serbia). In

60 Corresponding maps have been included in Appendix III.5.2/3 and III.5.2/4 (maps).

61 By 2013, the total length of the highways shall reach 1,365 km, which would imply a highway density of 24 km/1,000 km². The comparable figure for the EU-15 was 16 km/1,000 km² in 1999. For more details, see: Lakatos, *Croatia country study*, 2005, p. 28.

Romania, highway construction is considered an important element of growth and competitiveness, but construction work had to be cancelled due to legal, financial and other problems. Furthermore, the itinerary of East-West highways became a subject of political debate, since the Hungarian-populated Transylvania would like to see this highway cross the region, while the Bucharest government designed another route (south of the Carpathians, and probably at much lower construction costs). Another bottleneck is represented by the poor connection between Romania and Bulgaria, sharing a 400 km section of the Danube river, with only one bridge. Although the need for one or more bridges has repeatedly appeared among the topics discussing priorities in the last twenty years, no real progress has been made. A disagreement between the two countries concerning the location of the bridge has so far proven to be an insurmountable obstacle.[62]

Evidently, one of the most important barriers to infrastructural development is the lack of financial resources. However, some additional problems mainly due to the national economic and social environment should not be forgotten either. In the successor states of ex-Yugoslavia, new national authorities were established to manage the daily operation of public utilities. Most of them remained in state ownership and accumulated heavy losses from the very beginning. Therefore, the only way to attract fresh capital both to repay debts and inject money into modernization seems to be the privatization of these companies. However, at least four important barriers have to be taken into account in this context. First, there is a low level of interest by potential foreign investors in buying bankrupt, run-down companies and meet the double objectives of repaying debts and investing in modernization. The way out of this blind alley could be the streamlining of the companies and the cancellation of their debt to the major domestic banks. This, however, would strictly contradict the current legal rules in most Western Balkan countries where employment in state-owned companies in general, and in public utility firms in particular, is highly protected and any major dismissals are practically impossible. Second, privatization by a foreign owner faces a number of legal obstacles or can only be carried out under conditions that make the business highly risky, unprofitable and therefore undesirable for potential investors (minority ownership or majority ownership with strong restrictions, preserving the jobs, etc.). Third, most privatization efforts run against a social and psychological environment that is either reluctant or openly hostile to foreign ownership, particularly in so-called "strategic sectors" of the national economy (no doubt, energy and water

62 Now, the bridge will be built between Vidin (Bulgaria) and Calafat (Romania), with a total amount of Euro 266 mn, including EU support of Euro 70 mn. It is expected to be completed by 2008.

supply, the railway, highway systems, ports belong to this category). These sentiments are particularly strong in Serbia, but the Croatian society is not exempt from this attitude, either. Fourth, there is widespread concern that any kind of privatization would result not only in growing unemployment but in price increases, and many domestic consumers with low income levels would not be able to pay their utility bills.[63]

Comprehensive national infrastructural strategies are difficult to be identified in the region, at least those that are based on solid financial foundations. Bulgaria and Romania make a certain exception not only due to their development reached in recent years but also because they have not suffered war damages and, no less importantly, NATO membership forces them to give priority to some infrastructural investments that are considered to be vital for NATO.[64]

It is striking that almost no document deals with the rapidly growing importance of the internet-infrastructure. All SEE countries lag seriously behind in this field. According to the E-Readiness Ranking prepared by the Economist Intelligence Unit, in 2004 Bulgaria occupied the 42nd position and Romania the position No. 50, while Estonia is No. 26, the Czech Republic No. 27, Hungary No. 30 and Slovenia No. 31 and Turkey No. 45. Western Balkan countries were not ranked at all.

Looking at the very high costs of infrastructural developments and the clear interdependence among the SEE countries based on sharing common continental borders, it is not surprising that key attention has been devoted to the international players. In this context, the European Union plays a pivotal role not only as a provider of financial assistance to acceding (after 2007 member) countries but also to candidates and would-be candidates. Also, big hopes are nourished for the implementation of ambitious plans for the trans-European corridors and the ongoing activities in the framework of the Stability Pact that was considered from the very beginning regional infrastructure planning and implementation as its main contribution to peace, stability and sustainable growth in SEE.

The EU has identified ten pan-European corridors, several of which cross the SEE region. Table III.30 summarizes their main itineraries.

---

63 Even at present, a large part of the population does not pay for electric power, water or heating. According to estimates, the share of non-payers is the highest in Albania, followed by Bosnia-Herzegovina, Macedonia and Serbia. It has to be added that more and more people, particularly those with long-term unemployment and practically without any chance to find a job, try to avoid payment in Bulgaria and Romania as well.

64 For example, among the key investment projects underway in Bulgaria several have direct or indirect importance for NATO (reconstruction and extension of the Sofia airport, a new Danube bridge, new break water and bulk cargo at the port of Bourgas, winter camp for Danube river ships in Rousse).

According to the table, all SEE countries are involved in the regional development of physical infrastructure. Taking into account all main and branch routes to be developed, Bulgaria is involved in six projects, while Romania, Croatia[65] and Serbia each participate in four projects. Moreover, the modernization and extension of the rail and road network is vital for Albania and Macedonia, even if these countries host two projects respectively. The connection of the Adriatic with the Black Sea, the key "horizontal" axis in the Balkans, is a major precondition for sustainable growth and economic attraction. Compared to other SEE countries, Bosnia-Herzegovina seems to be less integrated into the trans-European projects.

Table III.33
Overview over the trans-European corridors crossing SEE

Number and itinerary of the corridor	Mode of transportation	Length (in km)
Corridor IV (a) Branch: Arad-Bucuresti-Constanta Branch: Arad-Sofija-Istanbul Branch: Sofija-Thessaloniki	Rail Road	4,340 3,640
Corridor V (b) Branch: Rijeka-Zagreb-Budapest Branch: Ploce-Sarajevo-Budapest	Rail Road	3,270 2,850
Corridor VII Danube	River	2,415
Corridor VIII Durres-Tirana-Skopje-Sofija-Varna/Bourgas	Rail Road	1,270 960
Corridor IX (c) Chisinau-Bucuresti-Alexandroupolis	Rail Road	6,500 5,820
Corridor X (d) Ljubljana-Zagreb-Beograd-Nis-Skopje-Veles-Thessaloniki Branch: Budapest-Novi Sad – Beograd Branch: Nis-Sofija Branch: Veles-Florina	Rail Road	2,528 2,300

(a) starts in Dresden, via Prague, Bratislava/Vienna, Budapest, Arad, with branches from Arad.
(b) from Venice, through Trieste/Koper, Ljubljana, Budapest to Lvov, with branches from Rijeka and Ploce.
(c) starts in Helsinki through St. Petersburg, Kiev and reaching Chisinau.
(d) starts in Salzburg to Ljubljana.
Source: European Commission (2002).

65 Part of the ambitious highway construction in Croatia remains outside the trans-European network (*e.g.* the highway between Zagreb and Split). Moreover, the economic benefits expected of such projects have not been evaluated using internationally recognized investment appraisal techniques.

One should not forget that trans-European corridors have been under planning for 30 years, with rather modest results. While there has been a high-level political support, the economic feasibility of several projects remains questionable. Thus, until now, it has been impossible to raise the necessary funds that could finance such large-scale and multi-annual project. Most recently, the EU had to cancel several infrastructural projects as well. In addition, money available in the EU financial framework (as part of the structural and cohesion funds) has been distributed among member countries. As a result, very little money has remained to finance cross-border infrastructural development, a major precondition for sustainable growth in SEE.

In this context, the efforts made by the Stability Pact in the last few years deserve special attention. Started in 2001 and based on a strategy paper prepared by the European Commission (European Commission, 2001) in June 2004, the Stability Pact countries could sign a Memorandum of Understanding on the Development of a South East Europe Core Regional Transport Network. It designated Belgrade as the headquarters of the REBIS (Regional Balkans Infrastructure Study) Secretariat. The document includes 4,300 km of railways, 6,000 km of roads, major ports and airports, as well as the inland waterways of the rivers Danube and Sava. The main tasks of the Stability Pact-launched initiative covers the following:

(a) strengthen the regional approach in the development of physical infrastructure,

(b) raise money from national and international sources,

(c) develop and update the database on regional infrastructure projects twice a year,

(d) address environmental issues of physical infrastructure development, with special regard to cross-country waterways (European Commission/World Bank, 2005).

Table III.34
Regional infrastructure projects by countries involved

Country	Number of projects	Costs (Euro mn)	Country share in %
Albania	9	506	9.7
Bosnia-Herzegovina	5	532	10.3
Bulgaria	6	782	15.1
Croatia	4	403	7.8
Macedonia	4	132	2.5
Romania	7	914	17.6
Serbia-Montenegro	8	933	18.0
Kosovo	1	1	0.0
Moldova	2	31	0.6
Turkey	2	738	14.2
Region	6	219	4.2
Total	54	5,191	100.0

Source: http://www.seerecon.org/infrastructure/projects/summary/country-euro.cfm.

As of mid-2005, the current database includes 54 projects with a total cost of Euro 5.19 bn, out of which more than Euro 3 bn is linked to rail and road, Euro 1.7 bn for energy, Euro 322m for water and environment and Euro 140m for cross-border trade facilitation (European Commission/World Bank, 2005). The participation of the individual countries is shown in Table III.34.

Not all of the projects registered by the Stability Pact are part of the trans-European corridors. However, more than half of the projects initiated and about 40% of the total costs are related to these corridors.

According to a study financed by the European Commission, Euro 4 bn would be needed to upgrade the existing road network to a level compatible with the planned traffic by 2015. Moreover, as much as Euro 12 bn has been estimated for the upgrade of the railway network. Substantial investments would be required to develop the Danube into a major West-East corridor in Europe (not only in the SEE countries but, for instance, in Hungary and Slovakia as well). In GDP terms, priority investments into the physical infrastructure would amount to 1% for Albania and Croatia, but they would reach 2.5 to 3% of the GDP in the case of Bosnia-Herzegovina, Macedonia and Serbia (Stability Pact, 2003). For comparison, the Transport Infrastructure Needs Assessment (TINA) package determined 1.5% of GDP as the maximum amount of investment in the regional road and railway infrastructure. In reality, much less has been spent until now (European Commission, 2003).

Table III.35
SEE infrastructure projects by trans-European corridors (excluding Romania and Bulgaria, in Euro mn)

Corridor	Ongoing Projects		Completed Projects		Total	
	Number	Cost	Number	Cost	Number	Cost
IV	1	15	0	0	1	15
V	5	554	2	118	7	672
VII	0	0	1	26	1	26
VIII	5	163	0	0	5	163
X	4	638	1	11	5	649
Air	2	126	1	55	3	181
Unspecified	4	139	5	213	9	352
Total	21	1,635	10	423	31	2,058

Source: European Commission/World Bank (2005).

A realistic estimate was prepared by the European Commission covering the period between 2004 and 2009. It took into account the potential costs of committed, ongoing and new projects by countries of the Western Balkans. It concluded that about Euro 3.8 bn would be needed in this period which, assuming a relatively high growth rate of the countries of the region, would require between 0.5 and 1.4% of the annual GDP in individual countries. Anticipating sustained growth, these investments will likely to come from domestic sources.

Table III.36
Investment costs and GDP development

Year	Estimated GDP 2003	Total GDP 2004-2009	Assumed real growth 2004-2009	Estimated investment costs 2004-2009	Investment /GDP 2004-2009
Unit	Euro bn	Euro bn (a)	Real growth (%)	Euro mn (a)	In % of GDP
Albania	5.5	40.9	45%	555	1.4%
Bosnia-Herzegovina	6.1	49.2	28%	531	1.1%
Croatia	25.3	206.4	27%	981	0.5%
Kosovo (b)	1.7	14.7	33%	105	0.7%
Macedonia	3.8	39.3	26%	482	1.2%
Serbia-Montenegro	12.3	108.1	32%	1,165	1.1%

(a) at 2003 prices.

(b) based on IMF estimates.

Source: European Commission (2003). The forecast is based on World Bank GDP figures for 2001. An annual growth between 3.7 and 6.5% has been projected for the individual countries. (For additional figures see Appendix Tables III.5.3/5 and III.5.3/6.)

At the same time, we have to be aware of the fact that a number of infrastructure projects have already been financed or are in the process of financing from international sources. As of June 2003, the World Bank, the European Investment Bank, the European Commission, the European Bank for Reconstruction and Development were participating in a large number of projects in all Western Balkan countries. (For a detailed list see Appendix Table III.5.3/7.)

Beyond the development of the physical infrastructure dominated by road and railway projects, the Integration of the SEE countries to the all-European structures showed significant progress in two important areas, namely the interconnection of the national energy systems and participation in the common European space.

The Treaty establishing the Energy Community in SEE (Treaty, 2005) includes all Stability Pact countries, irrespective of their current institutional status with the EU. This document was signed on October 2005. Its main objectives are:

- creating a stable regulatory and market framework,
- ensuring access to stable and continuous energy supplies,
- taking on the *acquis communautaire* related to energy, environment and competition,
- enhancing the security of supply with regard to the connections to Caspian, North African and Middle East reserves,
- developing Network Energy market competition on a broader geographic scale and exploit economies of scale,
- improving the environmental situation.

According to the Treaty, customs duties and quantitative restrictions on the import and export of Network Energy shall be prohibited. Mutual assistance in case of disruption of energy supply is foreseen. The institutional framework consists of the Ministerial Council, the permanent high-level group, the regulatory board and the Secretariat to be established in Vienna. The budget of the Energy Community will be covered overwhelmingly by the European Community (94.9%), while the total contribution of the SEE member countries accounts for 5.1% of the total sum (out of which Romania contributes 2.2 and Bulgaria 1%, and all WB countries combined 1.9%).

This Treaty is the first one that incorporates the whole SEE region into an important area of the *acquis communautaire*. As a result, all participating countries become members of the EU energy *acquis*, well before full-fledged membership. Most probably, the Energy Community will support a more balanced energy supply, particularly in those countries that still struggle with everyday supply problems (Albania and Bosnia-Herzegovina, and especially Kosovo). Moreover, it is expected to streamline investment projects, since calculations will be increasingly made on the basis of the common energy market and not with regard to small, disrupted (and several times also distorted) domestic market requirements. Thus, until 2015, investments in the magnitude of about Euro 25 bn can be attracted to the energy sector of the SEE countries by enabling them to reach the technical and quality levels of the EU within one decade. No less important is the strategic geographic situation of SEE between the (current) EU and the potential long-term suppliers of Europe located in the Caspian Sea region, as well as in several Middle Eastern countries. This connection is considered crucial both for the long-term security of supply and the more balanced geographic distribution of the key energy import sources for the European economy. The large-scale geographic approach has been underlined in the Treaty by including into the operation of the network energy markets all five EU members located in the direct geographic neighbourhood of the SEE region (Austria, Greece, Hungary, Italy and Slovenia).

Although the Treaty does not mention it, we have to stress that this document provides excellent opportunities to large Western European energy companies to enter the energy markets of SEE, either by direct sales (or purchases) or, and most likely, by buying large parts of the national energy producing companies. In this context, some years ago, Bulgaria already started a liberal privatization policy and could sell some of the major energy companies to various new owners (including US and Czech companies). The privatization process seems to be much more difficult and slow-going in most Western Balkan countries. Therefore, one of the hardest tests of the effective implementation of the Treaty establishing the Energy Community may be the opening up of some national energy markets as required by this document.

Most recently, during the Austrian Presidency of the EU, the agreement on creating the common European space was signed in June 2006. The agreement includes the EU member countries, eight SEE countries (including Kosovo), as well as Iceland and Norway. According to the document, the common European space will be established by 2010, based on unified safety regulations and common competition and consumer safety rules. By extending the *acquis communautaire* to 35 European countries, a common market of more than 500 million citizens will be created. At the same time, uniform technical and safety standards could guarantee the better utilization of the European space and avoid temporary congestions, as well as reduce safety risks. Moreover, the agreement offers better framework conditions for the rapidly increasing tourism industry in the Balkans and could lead to the more efficient use of several airports in the region. Last but not least, the common European space is likely to encourage international capital to consider further large-scale investments in the SEE countries.

III.6. Agriculture

Several factors prompt us to briefly cover some specific agricultural issues in the SEE countries. Three issues will be discussed. The first section provides arguments why the current and future state of the agriculture are a key element in the sustainable stability and development in the SEE countries. The second section illustrates the macroeconomic importance of the sector, while the third section analyzes agriculture-related policies, with special regard to the main tasks before or at the threshold of EU membership.

III.6.1. First, during the most difficult years of transformation in general, and of the Western Balkan wars in particular, agriculture showed a highly ambiguous picture. On the one hand, it was seriously damaged. On the other hand, it served as the last resort for survival. Despite its "last resort" function, it has to be stressed that, most probably, the economic and social costs of transformation were (among) the highest in the agricultural sector, with the most serious disintegration and degradation of production as compared to the pre-transformation period.

Second, and simultaneously, the heavily affected state of the sector offered survival opportunities for many losers of the transformation process in the form of subsistence agriculture. Hundreds of thousands of unemployed people with family roots in the rural areas of the respective countries could at least provisionally return to their villages. Most of them belong to the first- or second-generation industrial workers, without specialized skills but nevertheless employed in different stages of industrialization during the Communist era. Legal unemployment would have been much higher without the protective role of agriculture.

Third, in almost all SEE countries agriculture is considered to have comparative advantages due to fertile soil, long sunny periods, low land and labour costs and, ultimately, and the much lower level of chemical contamination than in the large-scale (industrialized and heavily subsidized) Western European agricultural production systems. Looking at the main pillars of sustainable economic growth, agriculture is expected to become a highly competitive sector in several SEE countries. Except for the tourism industry in some countries, there are few other sectors of the national economy that could provide such a lasting and important boost to growth, higher living standards and external equilibrium as agriculture can. Its role is particularly important in reducing the substantial trade deficit that, in some cases, has been approaching levels that may threaten the sustainability of the socio-economic development.

Fourth, overall modernization of the agriculture is imperative in the context of EU accession. To be sure, membership in the EU in general, and in the Common Agricultural Policy (CAP) in particular, is likely to offer some advantages to new members (direct payment to farmers, export subsidies, unlimited access to the EU market). In turn, all countries have to face fierce competition from old and new member countries, as well as from third countries with which the EU has free or preferential trade agreements that include selected agricultural products as well. Moreover, Western European farmers enjoy a much higher financial support and used to be much stronger both in financial, technical and marketing terms. Since agriculture, as describe above, is one of the fundamental pillars of long term and sustainable development, it has to be able to withstand the competitive pressure from the EU countries after or even before accession. At present, as pointed out in chapter III.1, the region's trade in agricultural commodities with the EU demonstrates a substantial deficit. This situation can only be remedied if meaningful modernization of the sector takes place in the coming years, hopefully before membership in the EU. (This path is not open to Bulgaria and Romania any longer, thus their agricultural modernization has to be implemented within the enlarged EU – with all the positive and negative effects that may accompany the process.)

Finally, it has to be remembered that rural development in general, and agriculture in particular, contribute to social peace in countries with large ethnic minorities and characterized by deep poverty in rural areas.[66] The situation has become much more complex as a consequence of ethnic cleansing and the expulsion or flight of the traditional population. The new refugee map of former Yugoslavia has had a lasting impact with yet unknown longer-term consequences on the future of the rural population and of those engaged in agricultural activities.

III.6.2. Macroeconomic figures demonstrate the importance of agriculture in terms of output, employment and foreign trade. Unfortunately, some indicators found in internationally comparable statistics differ substantially from national figures. Moreover, there is a wide gap between official figures and estimates, since part of the agricultural production remains within the framework of the subsistence economy and does not enter the market (and, consequently, statistical registration). Even

---

66 For instance, in Bosnia-Herzegovina, rural areas are dominated by Serb farmers who suffered already in the Yugoslav Federation from the large-scale and over-ambitious industrialization that led to increasing gaps between urban and rural areas and to the (relative) underdevelopment of the latter ones. See: Bassa, *Bosnia-Herzegovina country study*, 2005, p. 10.

wider is the gap between the number of registered agricultural employees and the number of people effectively involved in some kind of agricultural activities (be it on the subsistence level).

Despite the sometimes contradictory and confusing figures, some general remarks can be made. First, the significance of agriculture in GDP production is rather high and, except for Croatia, it reaches two-digit levels. The shares are two to four times higher (disregarding Albania) than the share of agriculture in the new member countries (except in Poland and Lithuania), and even higher than in the EU-15. The figures partly reflect the relative importance of agriculture in SEE, both due to favourable climatic and topographic conditions in some countries, and the lower level of economic development. However, the figures cannot be separated from the dramatic decline of non-agricultural activities, which, statistically, has increased the weight of agriculture in the gross national output.

Table III.37
Macroeconomic importance of agriculture in the SEE countries

Country	Share of agri-culture in GDP in %	Cumulative growth of agricultural output between 1999 and 2003 (1998 = 100)	Employment in agriculture (in % of total employment)	Agricultural	
				exports (% in total exports) (a)	imports (% in total imports (a)
Albania (b)	33	112.7	More than 50		
Bosnia-Herzegovina	11	83.2	.		
Bulgaria	10 11.4 (b)	96.2	25.1	8.8	4.8
Croatia	6.9 8.2 (b)	82.4	7.1 16.0 (b)	13.7	7.8
Macedonia	9.9 18.0 (b)	93.5	4.2 15.0 (b)	16.7	12.9
Romania	11.7	112.8	36.2	2.4	6.6
Serbia-Montenegro	19.9 14.4 (b)	110.8 (c) 108.6 (d)	4.5	20.3	9.0

(a) SITC 0+1 commodity groups; (b) Taken from national statistics; (c) Serbia only; (d) Montenegro only, average of 2000-2003, base year 1999.

Source: WIIW Database and national statistics.

Second, output growth in recent years has shown a varied picture. In some countries such as Albania, Romania and Serbia-Montenegro, agricultural production increased by 10 to 13% in a five year period. In other countries, however, the 1999 level could not be reached (in Bosnia-

Herzegovina, Bulgaria, Croatia, Macedonia). However, all comparisons have to be considered with utmost care. Some countries that could increase agricultural output started from a disappointingly low level in 1999 (*e.g.* Serbia). Others have shown very sharp annual fluctuations in both categories (higher or lower output than in 1999). Both Bulgaria and Romania belong to this group. The main conclusion is that the figures reflect the unsatisfactory (in some cases dramatic) situation of agriculture. Even if domestic supply could be covered to great extent by domestic production, the registered growth can hardly serve as a basis for sustainable competitiveness of the sector and, no less importantly, as a basic pillar of export-oriented growth and a contribution to the reduction of the trade deficits in the coming years.

Third, the role of agriculture in employment is crucial. However, the figures in this area are widely diverging, and in some cases they are impossible to interprete. According to general international experience, productivity in agriculture is lower than the national average, therefore, the share of this sector in total output (GDP) should be lower than its share in employment.[67] This correlation is more than clear in Albania, Bulgaria, Romania and, with some limitations, Croatia. However, it is hard to believe that 15 (or 20)% of the GDP in Serbia is produced by 4.5% of the population. Similarly, Bosnia-Herzegovina's agricultural output accounting for 11% of GDP is unlikely to be generated by 4% of the labour force employed. Also, agriculture in Macedonia appears to be more productive than other sectors of the economy. If we consider that both in Bosnia-Herzegovina and Macedonia, agricultural output in 2003 lagged behind 1999 levels by 17 and 6.5%, respectively, the picture conveyed by statistical figures becomes even less credible.

Fourth, agricultural exports play an important role in total exports of all countries, except in Romania. The share of agricultural commodities in total exports is higher than that of imports (again, with the exception of Romania). At first glance, it might lead to the conclusion that the SEE countries have a surplus in agricultural trade. However, looking at the huge overall imbalance between exports and imports (the coverage ratio is below 50% in many cases), this conclusion should be regarded as wrong. With the exception of Bulgaria, all SEE countries have – partly substantial – deficits in their agricultural trade (as well). Therefore, at least at present, agriculture could not convert itself into an engine of export-oriented growth.

67 In socialist Yugoslavia, productivity per active farmer did not reach the 1939 level until 1963. By the end of the 1970s, agricultural productivity reached about 10% of the British and 16% of the French figure, and was at about the same level as that of Pakistan.

Further information on the individual countries sheds more light on the condition and outlook of agriculture.

Albania was one of the few countries that has attained a relatively steady growth of agricultural production. This is to a large extent due to the abolition of a fully collectivized system after 1990, which was characterized by an extremely low output and inefficient distribution. All collective farms were dismantled and about 98% of the land was distributed to small farmers. A majority of the farms is cultivated by families just for their own consumption. Market access is further hampered by the poor physical infrastructure and processing capacity. Even if production on scattered farmlands remains highly inefficient in European comparison and large portions of agricultural land are abandoned and uncultivated, there is some progress compared to the extremely low starting levels.

Bosnia-Herzegovina, where half a century ago three-quarters of the population depended on subsistence agriculture, is not an ideal land for agricultural activities, since only 14% of the country's territory can be cultivated. As a result of war damages, agricultural output fell by about 40% by the end of the 1990s, partly due to land mines that are still to be found on a significant part of arable land. Production incentives were further reduced by the high level of imports, not least for the consumption of the large number of international staff stationed in the country.

By the end of the 1990s in Bulgaria, about 75% of the agricultural land had been restored to its previous owners or their heirs. This "transformation policy" resulted, as in all other countries of the region, in fragmented ownership structures with low efficiency levels and, in many cases, the lack of cultivation. According to the 2003 census, the total number of farms amounted to more than 684,000, out of which physical persons were in the possession of 677,000 farms. They utilized 30% of the total arable land, with 1.3 hectares per farm on average. In contrast, the remaining 7,110 owners (legal entities) cultivated 70% of the land, including 2,000 cooperatives. The average farm size reached 285 and 586 hectares, respectively.

Croatia reports 450,000 agricultural farms in a country of 4.4 million inhabitants. Total farmland area accounts for 3.14 million hectares, but only one-third of this land is used effectively. Within this framework, 55% of the arable land is utilized. The size of the average family farm is 2.4 hectares, which, excluding some very special products, is absolutely inappropriate for competitive production.

In the last few years, and despite increasing output, the share of the Serbian agriculture in GDP production went down substantially (from 23 to 15%, according to national statistics). However, this trend reflected three distortions. First, that of nominal adjustments due to energy and service prices; second, poor harvests; and third, no similar changes have taken place in the structure of employment.

III.6.3. Although to a different degree, but the agriculture of all SEE countries face several challenges, regardless of their performance in recent years. They can be classified in four groups.

First: the consequences of agricultural "reforms" (in many cases simply the breakup of the previous production system) have to be managed. These can be best identified in the current ownership structure and the sometimes complete lack of land registration, or the missing legal basis of new ownership. In Albania, around 30 laws and regulations have been passed in order to create a comprehensive legal and regulatory framework for land administration. Also, an Immovable Property Registration System (IPRS) for real property titling and registration was established. Moreover, a comprehensive, donor-supported program to provide first-time registration to new land owners was introduced. In Bulgaria, a state-owned institution (National Land Company) is in charge of maintaining a transparent market mechanism, competitive land prices and to create consolidated areas in order to overcome (further) land fragmentation.[68] Macedonia also faces the challenge of land fragmentation, since 75% of the agricultural land (1.3 mn hectares) is in the hand of small farmers. The favourable climate and soil conditions can be adequately utilized only if production efficiency increases. In this respect, land concentration or at least more cooperation among individual farmers is a precondition. In Romania, privatization led to the creation of a rather fragmented land market, too. In the first wave (1991), a large number of former owners got their land back, up to 10 hectares per family. This way, 9.34 mn hectares of arable land was turned into 3.9 mn small private farms. In the second wave of privatization, former owners of up to 50 hectares per family were entitled to get land back. Since the sale of agricultural land has been forbidden for several years, the newly created fragmented structure started to get consolidated. As a result, private ownership amounts to more than 97% of agricultural land. Small farmers dispose of two-thirds of Romania's arable land, with a very low level of productivity and limited market access.[69]

Second: all countries suffered serious market losses both in the domestic and the international context. The rapid shrinking of the domestic

68 After 2002, the arable land market already has revealed signs of stabilization with annual transactions amounting to 35,000 cases and with stabilized and increasing agricultural land prices (around Euro 730 per hectare). For details, see: Petkova, *Bulgaria country study*, 2006, p. 20.

69 At the same time, land owned by agricultural companies that could not be privatized until now, are managed by the Agency of the State Domain and are waiting to be leased.

market, as a result of declining living standards and the growing importance of subsistence activities, was accompanied by the appearance of foreign agricultural commodities. They entered the market either as a result of rapid (and sometimes overhasty) trade liberalization or were highly subsidized by EU sources. Also, foreign companies (both in the food industry and in retail trade) have increased the pressure of imported goods on the shrinking domestic markets. At the same time, the most important external markets have been largely lost (*e.g.* the ex-Soviet Union for Bulgarian agriculture). As a special development, the ex-Yugoslav republics have largely lost their traditional domestic market as a consequence of the break-up of the Federation. This has hit Macedonia especially hard since it was a major exporter of agricultural goods to other Yugoslav republics. Of course, loss of the market was only one side of the coin. The dissolution of previous forms of production and the break-up of well-organized vertical links from different stages of agricultural production up to the marketing of commodities can also be blamed.

Third: in the first decade of the transformation practically no attention was paid to agriculture. It was widely admitted that all countries were facing more important issues (especially the war-ridden WB countries), and agriculture was considered a hidden, built-in stabilizer in terms of physical survival and labour market tensions. Similarly, international assistance has largely ignored agriculture. Looking at different EU documents, it is striking how little space has been devoted to agriculture in the reform proposals. Except for some general recommendations as institutional and legal changes, no concrete proposals have been developed for agriculture and the food industry, and even less financial resources have been made available for this purpose.

Fourth: the most important challenges that may influence the medium-term development pattern of the SEE countries originate in the labour market. Agriculture has been playing an ambiguous role in this context. On the one hand, in situations of highest emergency (war, transformation crisis), it provided additional and temporary protection to a large number of refugees or unemployed people. On the other, however, it cannot guarantee long-term employment and acceptable living standards. Just the opposite, even some of those who used to work in agriculture may be threatened to lose their current occupation in the future. As soon as the limited survival and protective capacities of agriculture become manifest (and they already have in recent years), people have started to migrate back to towns and cities looking for jobs. This is a particularly hot issue in countries where historically the rural population used to represent a higher share than in many more developed parts of Europe. Since new job opportunities are unlikely to be created at such a speed, urban unemployment may be rising as official unemployment figures do, since part of hidden unemployment (covered by subsistence agriculture) will become evident.

There is large-scale migration from rural to urban areas in Albania, due to the very high number of people who used to work traditionally in agriculture. In Bosnia-Herzegovina (partly due to the shortage of agricultural land) the rural-urban ratio of the population changed in a few years from 60 to 40 to its opposite, namely to 40% rural and 60% urban population. One feature of the Bulgarian population is that some rural areas that used to be home for 43% of the total population show critical signs of depopulation. Moreover, the rural population is aging, especially those people who work in agriculture. Only 5% of land owners are younger than 35 years, while 66% are above 55 years. Under the current conditions, the capacity of agriculture to keep young people employed is very modest.[70] As stated in the background country study, "jobs in the agrarian sector are not considered a success but a temporary occupation for times when there are no other jobs".[71] 36% of Croatia's population lives in rural areas that, in the current economic system and agricultural conditions, are hardly in a position to offer normal and sustainable living conditions in the long term. Romania, with one of the highest population employed in agriculture, requires fundamental reforms, since neither the actual nor the more competitive future agriculture will be able to support so many active workers. In addition, the age structure of the farmers is rather unfavourable, and, similar to Bulgaria, it is difficult to convince young people to commit themselves to agricultural activities as their main occupation. In recent years, Serbia-Montenegro has seen a modest return of young people who started to produce organic food to rural areas.[72] However, such an activity is linked to high risks in an environment in which financial support is unpredictable, the domestic market is very limited (already due to the low purchasing power of the population) and vertical links (to reliable traders) are not protected from sudden disruptions.

It is not surprising that most countries have started to devote more attention to agriculture in the last few years, even if major results are not to be expected soon Almost all countries have discovered some of their comparative advantages, and that to utilize them they need substantial legal and economic changes, a good education and, last but not least, meaningful financial resources. In addition, most of the modernization

---

70 In 2002, 11.2% of village dwellers sought employment in small towns and more and more seek to findwork in or around Sofia or the major construction sites at the Black Sea coast.

71 See: Petkova, *Bulgaria country study*, 2006, p. 22.

72 The massive migration from rural to urban areas took place already in the 1970s, when many villages, mainly in East and South Serbia became either completely abandoned or inhabited by old people.

plans have to take into account not only the obvious positive outcome but also the negative side-effects that have to be managed in order to avoid potential backlashes (mainly concerning employment policies and rural development). In the light of agricultural reforms, SEE countries can be classified in two groups based on their road to EU membership. The WB countries do not have to build a lot of EU requirements into their agricultural strategy, while Bulgaria and Romania have already considered the impact of membership on their agricultural sector.

Albania has a strong growth potential due to its geographic location, low wages, fertile soils and favourable climate. Also, the rural population seems to be rather adaptive and fast learning, as indicated by the mushrooming of greenhouses built in recent years.[73] Furthermore, many Albanians used to work in developed European countries in the agricultural sector. Some of them may return and use their acquired know-how in the Albanian agriculture. Better physical infrastructure, as well as open markets in the EU and in the SEE region could further encourage enhanced agricultural activities. Bosnia-Herzegovina has already specified some agricultural sectors that should get additional attention and may become internationally competitive, not least as a result of the more dynamic inflow of foreign capital in selected food processing branches.[74] Croatia wants to focus on high-yield cultivation and pays special attention to the livestock sector. Large investments are planned for the storage and distribution of basic agricultural products. The profitability is expected to increase as a result of new regulations that differentiate between agricultural support for commercial farms and non-commercial units. Moreover, a successful agricultural policy requires the consolidation of the fragmented agricultural land and politically sensitive decisions on the future ownership of (still) state-owned agricultural land. In Croatian, an equally sensitive issue is what role foreign investors will be allowed to play in the agri-food industry. Also, it has to be noted that, as a candidate country, Croatia has started to set up the payment agency in order to channel SAPARD money to its agriculture. Taking into account that the country is already entitled to pre-accession funds (including SAPARD resources), progress has been rather modest until most recently. Delays, however, can jeopardize the availability of such resources just in the crucial years of transformation and adjustment to EU rules. Serbia-Montenegro concentrates on creating an efficient framework for agricultural activities, such as better transport infrastructure, the establishment of vertical cooperation

---

73 It is not known how such establishments face electricity shortages regularly (let alone whether or not they are paying for electricity).

74 Fruits, vegetables, juices, jams, tobacco, cattle breeding, fish farming, wine, spring water and organic food, as well as timber are on the list (Bassa, *Bosnia-Herzegovina country study*, 2005, p. 14).

between producers and traders, sustainable rural development and environmental protection and the setting up of more efficient institutions. In the international arena, Serbia-Montenegro is preparing to face the opportunities and challenges of the country's expected WTO membership.

A few years ago, Bulgaria and Romania started to meet the requirements of EU membership. Agriculture became part of the preparation, especially since it started to benefit from EU financial resources in the framework of the SAPARD project embedded into the EU's current seven-year budget covering the period between 2000 and 2006.

Bulgaria has gradually liberalized its agricultural market and met its WTO commitments (already in accordance with EU rules, *e.g.* the introduction of export subsidies for selected food products). Bulgarian wines became a success story in several EU and overseas markets, not least as a consequence of a wine fund created by the intra-professional organization of wine producers. EU-conform quality control was introduced at all milk collection points and in all milk processing plants. Moreover, Bulgaria was one of the first pre-accession countries that had established and was authorized as a national SAPARD payment agency.[75] One of the most urgent tasks is the completion of the Agricultural Land Information System (ALIS) by clearing all data necessary for the agricultural parcels identification system and the equipment of the system with remote sensing services: a precondition to getting access to direct payments to Bulgarian farmers immediately following membership.

Romania's most interesting initiative, in cooperation with Brussels, may be the implementation of an early retirement scheme for farmers. According to this document, farmers over 55 years of age will have to stop commercial farming activities and cede the land to younger farmers. 27% of the rural population hopes that, as a result of this measure, supported in the framework of the Common Agricultural Policy, their chances to carry out profitable farm activities will increase. Concerning EU-conform legislation, Romania lags behind Bulgaria, as indicated by the large number of transitional measures discussed in the agricultural chapter.[76] Nevertheless, taking into account the large rural population, direct payments may have a qualitatively higher (and, in the short term,

[75] The utilization of SAPARD (and national co-financing) resources can be considered effective. There is a constant need to recruite new labour and continuously train former staff (by the end of 2006 about 450 new staff is needed). SAPARD supported several programs in Bulgaria, including the development of a concept for rural development, semi-subsistence farming, and specific measures concerning the setting up of producer groups and technical assistance.

[76] For instance, the modernization of meat and milk processing units or an eight-year transition obtained for the reclamation of 30,000 hectares of land on which forbidden hybrids were grown.

definitely positive) impact on Romanian farmers than the generally favourable effect in other new member countries (except in Poland where these payments have turned around the fundamentally hostile attitude of farmers towards the EU and created large support for the Union in this very social strata).

In sum: from large-scale free trade agreements to membership, the EU can certainly help the agricultural sector in the SEE countries. However, the deeply rooted structural problems, including scattered ownership, low productivity levels, inefficient marketing methods, the politically sensitive problems of employment, poverty and rural (under)development, will need long-term policies and genuine national strategies. European integration cannot and will not solve these problems. On the contrary, in case of deficient preparation current problems and tensions may be aggravated further. Since agriculture is much more than just one economic sector and has wide-ranging political and social implications (similar to the situation in some old EU member countries), adequate EU policies have to be developed to support the gradual and sustainable transformation of agriculture in the SEE countries before and after accession alike.

III.7. Migration: Facts, Potential Consequences and Policy Requirements

III.7.1. Historically, Southeastern Europe has been a region with intensive migrations of two basic patterns. First, emigration from this area to other, more developed parts of the world started in the 19th century, parallel to the overall European trend in search for better life overseas. Second, intra-regional migration were recurrent as a result of local wars, invasions and liberations, and, more importantly, as a consequence of two world wars. All these events have certainly shaped the ethnic composition, neighbourhood policies, human resource potential and availability of the individual countries. This study, however, does not cover past periods, instead it focuses on recent developments.

In the last 40 years, the migration record of the region can be divided into two basic periods. The first one started in the 1960s and lasted until the start of systemic transformation. It was characterized by the intensive outflow of manpower from ex-Yugoslavia to Western Europe in general, and to Germany in particular, especially as construction labour ("guest workers"). In turn, the other countries of the region, namely Albania, Bulgaria and Romania were under communist rule, without any individual visits (let alone for work purposes) to market-economy countries of Europe. Yugoslavia's openness provided several advantages for the Yugoslav economy and society for two decades. First, the flow of workers to Western Europe substantially eased the problem of unemployment.[77] Second, workers' remittances played a significant role in hard currency revenues and thus contributed to the viability of the current account for many years. Third, after several years of working abroad, many Yugoslav citizens returned to their native country with the purpose of starting small (private) ventures (in fields where this was allowed), using financial means, professional knowledge and personal experience acquired in foreign countries. Fourth, a strong network could develop among guest workers and family members and friends who remained in ex-Yugoslavia. This generated a strong two-way flow of workers and network members and created adequate conditions for additional guest workers and family members to migrate to Western Europe. And finally, for decades, the migration-driven interaction established a cultural link between Yugoslavia and Western Europe, an obvious advantage over all other Central and Eastern European countries.[78]

This situation changed dramatically after 1989/1990. The second migration period of the last 15 years is rooted in three basic factors. First, ex-Yugoslavia ceased to be the only (and preferred) country sending people abroad. Albania, Bulgaria and Romania started to see huge outflows of citizens, as the borders were opened, visa requirements were (partly) lifted, and the serious economic problems of transformation became part of everyday life. Second, the main pattern of migration changed as well. Except for some specific forms of intergovernmental agreements on employment (which was the basic framework of employing Yugoslav guest workers), (e)migration took spontaneous and unregulated forms, in most cases without any previous commitment to job opportunities. In addition, the number of migrants substantially increased due to social and human reasons. Some of the migrants were not looking for (better-paid) job opportunities, they only seemed to be interested in better social benefits. Others, mostly coming from ex-Yugoslav republics, were forced to leave their country as a consequence of wars, ethnic cleansing and the loss of their property. Others, mainly young people, seized the opportunity to study abroad. Third, migration could be increasingly observed not only on the international level but also within the region, between ex-Yugoslav republics, again as a result of wars and ethnic atrocities.

---

77 In contrast to all other socialist countries, Yugoslavia never imposed the obligation of full employment on the economy. Registered unemployment, even if very low compared to current figures, was always acknowledged.

78 Certainly, the relatively free travel of Hungarian and partly Polish citizens to Western Europe in the 1970s and 1980s differed very much from the strict and prohibitive rules applied elsewhere in the region. However, this "freedom", both in its form and consequences, generated a lower quality of cultural and business interaction than in the case of the ex-Yugoslav society.

III.7.2. According to estimates reported in a recent study prepared by the United Nations, worldwide about 191 mn people have left their native country in search of a better life in another country. This accounts for about 3% of the world population, and a very low figure compared to the much more intensive global flows of other production factors, such as capital, commodities and services. Official estimates on worldwide migration between 2000 and 2005 do not indicate specific data for Southeastern Europe. If we take Southeastern European emigration as part of the Eastern European figure, the average annual net emigration amounts to just 105,000 people, which is very much below the real figures (considering that Eastern Europe also reveals net emigration data).[79]

Based on national estimates made in the countries of the region, in the last 15 years, gross emigration from Southeastern Europe outside the region (not counting intra-ex-Yugoslav migration) may have reached the level of 4 mn people, or more than 7% of the total population. (Net figures do not vary much, since few people returned to their native country in this period, and immigration from third countries remained low.) Since almost all of them belong to the working-age group, the share of emigrants in the total active population may be double this figure. (Moreover, in some specific sectors, as well as many young people, skilled labour or university students, the share is substantially higher.)

In the 1990s, in two different waves, about 14% of the Albanian population, or about 450,000 people emigrated. The first wave started in 1990 with 4,000 emigrants who "occupied" Western embassies and continued with the massive illegal border crossing to Greece and Italy. While the first wave was largely motivated by political considerations, the second one that started in 1997 was generated by predominantly economic motives and increasingly by family ties between first-wave and second-wave migrants.[80] At present, at least about 35% of the Albanian labour force works abroad (of which, based on official figures, 600,000 does so in Italy and 200,000 in Greece).

According to international estimates, Bosnia-Herzegovina's population shrank by almost one million, with heavy fluctuations during and after the war. At least 300,000 Bosnians are now living in countries outside ex-Yugoslavia.[81]

---

79 United Nations (2006).

80 Albanian Institute for International Studies (2005), pp. 18-19.

81 During the war, about half of the original population became displaced. Many of them left for neighbouring "ethnic" countries (Croatia and Serbia), or returned later to the same ethnic-dominated areas of Bosnia-Herzegovina. *The Economist*, November 26, 2005, p. 36.

Official Bulgarian figures indicate that about 200,000 people left the country between 1992 and 2001. Nevertheless, real figures are several times higher, reaching 600,000 to 700,000 (including the emigration of Turks and Muslims in the early years of transformation), many of them working abroad illegally. Preferred foreign locations are the United States, Australia, as well as Southern Europe (Italy and Spain).

The number of Croatian migrants is estimated at about 400,000, including those who left the country well before the 1990s. The country's main domestic political and socio-economic problem is not outward migration but the outflow and inflow of huge numbers of displaced people due to the Balkan wars.

Romanian statistics suggest that about 2 to 2.5 million Romanian citizens are working abroad (but only 10% has a labour contract). Most of them live in Italy, Spain and France.

The Serbian and Montenegrin community abroad counts numbers 4 mn people, out of which 30% live in overseas countries and in Western Europe, respectively, while almost 1.6 mn are hosted in the neighbouring (mainly new) countries, such as Bosnia(n Serb Republic), Croatia, Macedonia. Figures on migration outside Southeastern Europe after 1990 are not available. Certainly, a large part of the community left the country still in the era of the Yugoslav Federation (and did not want to return after the 1990s).

Unfortunately, the current figures cannot be considered reliable. Certainly, one driving force behind migration, namely open hostilities and wars, has been, for the time being, eliminated. However, other motives remain strong or became even stronger in the last few years. Economic considerations rank first, but not only concerning higher wages but also better prospects for future jobs, more efficient and rewarding utilization of professional knowledge, higher social standards. In addition, two factors have to be mentioned. One is linked to the persistently high level of unemployment in most countries (particularly in the Western Balkans) and the rigid employment structures that force mainly young people to look for survival abroad. The other is the still the palpable political uncertainty (sometimes latent hostility) related to the incomplete institutional structure of the region (the independence of Montenegro, the future of Kosovo, unstable governments and failed states in the territory of ex-Yugoslavia).

It is quite telling that, according to a survey in 2002, 20% of high-skilled young people in Serbia have decided to emigrate, while another 54% said they favoured emigration (Reljic, 2003, p. 35). According to a Bulgarian study, about 1 million of working age citizens (out of a total of

5 mn) are willing to look for a job abroad.[82] Finally, in Albania, more than half of the young population would prefer to live outside the country (Albanian Institute for International Studies, 2005, p. 18).

III.7.3. Concerning political stability and sustained economic development, several aspects of regional or internal migration have to be taken into account as well. In this context, by far the most far-reaching impact stemmed from the consequences of the Western Balkan wars. Bosnia-Herzegovina, Croatia and Serbia were particularly hard hit by the internal and regional displacement of huge numbers of people. According to the United Nations High Commission of Refugees, in 2005 almost 20 mn people worldwide were in a critical situation, out of which about half were registered as refugees and another 28% as internally displaced persons. In a geographic breakdown, 23% (or about 4.5 mn) lived in Europe,[83] to a large extent coming from or located in the Western Balkan countries.

There is no question that multi-ethnic Bosnia-Herzegovina suffered most. Out of a total population of 4.4 mn, about half had been displaced by the war, and, out of them, about 1.2 mn went abroad (mainly to Croatia and Serbia, following their ethnic roots). The UN Refugee Agency estimates that about 1 mn have returned home, but half of them can be classified as "minority returns", meaning that they did not come back to their original homeland but to the respective national minority (either the Croat- or the Serb-dominated part of the country). Many others just returned to take possession of what, in a fortunate case, might have remained from their personal belongings after the war, or to sell their property before moving on. Croatia has struggled with about half a million displaced persons, both in Croatia and in neighbouring Bosnia-Herzegovina. Most Croats have in the meantime returned, as about 150,000 ethnic Croats fleeing from Bosnia have received Croatian citizenship. The return of the Serbian population originally living in Croat territory proceeds much slower, due to persistent ethnic hostilities on the local level, but also because their original home had been destroyed during or after the war. Finally, according to international estimates, Serbia-Montenegro registered 277,000 refugees and 248,000 internally displaced persons.[84] Regrettably, this story is far from finished. Montenegro's independence is unlikely to generate massive and direct outward migratory flows. In turn, inward migration can be intensified in special sectors, as for instance, the return of Montenegrin university students

---

82 See: Petkova, *Bulgaria country study*, 2006, p. 29.

83 UN sees the neglect of 25m internally displaced as a global failure. *The Financial Times*, April 20, 2006 and www.unhcr.org.

84 *The Financial Times*, April 20, 2006.

from Serbia, not without negative consequences. However, the most important impact on the Western Balkan migration can be expected from the future status of Kosovo, which can create new regional tensions and a new wave of migration (or massive flight) from Kosovo to Serbia.

The overriding political (and human) relevance of the issue of internally or regionally displaced persons hides two additional elements of domestic (or regional) migration. Both of them may be gaining in importance in the next period and could affect the sustainability of political and economic stability.

One is the already mentioned migration between urban and rural areas. Transformation produced a two-way migration, due to fundamental economic reasons. On the one hand, the massive bankruptcies of state-owned industrial companies and high urban unemployment drove many people, albeit temporarily, back to rural areas and to agriculture promising physical survival (in Serbia, but also partly in Romania). On the other hand, the miserable situation in the agriculture in some countries, aggravated by bad or almost nonexistent physical infrastructure forced younger people in particular from villages to larger towns or the capital city. This trend is most manifest in Albania.

The second form can be called "irregular transit migration", including human trafficking. The Balkan region is the source, transit road as well as destination of criminal enterprises. Such cross-border (regional) "migrations" can be found in each country. However, the majority of such activities have been observed between Albania and the Albanian-populated neighbouring regions in Kosovo and Macedonia (Grecic, 2004). (For more details, see the forthcoming sub-chapter III.9.)

III.7.4. A vast literature is available on the diverse impact of migration both on the host and the originating countries (regions). This section only deals with some selected effects on the originating country. Even here, a limitation has to be made, since one of the major (and, according to common wisdom, generally positive) effects, namely financial transfers (remittances) will be elaborated on in the next sub-chapter. Our attention is focused on those consequences that are likely to have a negative influence on long-term and sustainable economic growth in the Southeastern European countries.

Although most studies highlight brain drain as the most important negative development, this section starts with the demographic changes. In all Southeastern European countries, except in Albania, the population started to shrink in the last decade. This process was worsened by migration. Individual countries lost 8 to 15% of their population.[85] The figures are, however, higher if the active population or, more importantly, young and skilled labourers are taken into account.

Moreover, migration does not only accelerate the process of shrinking and aging population, but it restructures regional population balances as well. Already today, in the Western Balkans the Albanian population is the second largest only preceded by the Serbs but ahead of the Croatians. Medium-term forecasts envisage the Albanian population as the largest one in the Western Balkans, with unpredictable consequences for the stability and modernization of the whole region, and most probably, for the future of Europe as a whole, as well. Another negative demographic impact is that, in most countries, it is young men who emigrate, at least in the first wave of migration, while elderly people and women are left behind. Within half a generation (10 to 15 years) it could create huge imbalances not only between working and elderly people but also in the sexual composition of the society of the originating countries.

As for the issue of brain drain, let us mention just a few examples. Between 1996 and 1998, Bosnia-Herzegovina lost 42,000 highly skilled persons, three-quarters of them under the age of 40. According to the UNDP Human Development Report, at least 92,000 young people left the country between 1996 and early 2001 and ten thousands were waiting for emigration visas.[86] Despite serious barriers to emigrate, due to, among others, strict visa policies imposed by EU (but also overseas) countries, the outflow of skilled and young people could not be stanched. More and more people consider the real possibility of leaving the country and the region. A special and ambiguous form of brain drain is longer-term tertiary education abroad. Certainly, it may generate substantial added value if young graduates return to their home country after finishing their university studies. However, most of them remain in the country they studied in or find another opportunity to prolong their student period. In this context, Albania is no exception. Based on Albanian sources, every year about 3,000 Albanians, or 30% of the total number of university students at home, enrol in Western higher education institutions. In recent years, about 12,000 Albanian students were studying at Italian universities alone (Albanian Institute for International Studies, 2005, p. 23).

Brain drain, while building up human resource potential on the individual level, may deprive the originating country of the most important factor of sustainable growth and socio-economic modernization. In many

---

[85] The situation is even more serious in Moldova, a Stability Pact country but not part of Southeastern Europe. Here, about 600,000 persons left the country to work abroad, mainly in Western Europe and, to a large extent, illegally.

[86] Bassa, *Bosnia-Herzegovina country study*, 2005, p. 20.

cases, it is accompanied by "intangible" investments in human resources, if young and skilled people educated in their native country and with the support of tax-payers' money (budgetary expenditures generated by the production of national income) leave for jobs in other countries.[87] This is a particularly dangerous development in the era of globalization, when the overwhelming majority of wealth-creation is attributed to the human factor. Moreover, countries lacking the minimum of critical mass of human resources will unlikely to be able to catch up and generate a sustainable path of development. Although not yet recognized at the highest political level, several (Western) Balkan countries may already facing this unique challenge. However, negative influences do not end here. A labour market with poorly skilled supply cannot create and sustain an efficient public administration, one of the preconditions of modernization and successful (or any kind of) EU integration. Instead, it produces weak structures with low-quality performance (including low level professional skills, lack or insufficient knowledge of foreign languages, etc.). In addition, "underdeveloped" human resources in the respective countries have a negative impact on the development of social attitudes and mentality, with the real danger of returning to the past, with all of its vicious cycles (including 19th-century nationalism, ethnic priorities, etc.), instead of making use of new opportunities and facing future challenges. Ultimately, the lack of adequate domestic (national) human resource potentials may result in weak governments, public institutions and states. As a consequence, the country will not be able to resist the pressure of foreign political actors or reject certain recommendations and conditions to be imposed by international financial institutions. Interestingly, this fear has been figured most prominently in Serbian studies (Begovic and Mijatovic, 2005).[88]

III.7.5. Recently, the fundamental medium- and long-term negative impact of the current massive brain drain has been recognized by most countries of Southeastern Europe. As a result, different approaches have been conceived to reduce the volume and intensity of this process, and, as far as possible, reverse it in the medium-term. Also, plans have been prepared to get the best of the brain drain by converting it into "brain gain". At the same time, all studies dealing with Southeastern Europe in general, and with the Western Balkans in particular, have to reckon with the fact that they have to struggle with migration on two fronts at the same time. One of them is represented by the "brain gain" efforts. The

87 Investments in soccer players have been recognized in monetary terms, once they are sold and bought. For several reasons, such a practice could not be developed in the market of high-quality human labour.

88 As quoted in Hernádi, *Serbia and Montenegro country study*, 2006, p. 22.

other, no less important for short-term stability, is the facilitation of the return of refugees.

Brain gain-related action programs have identified two basic goals: bring talented people back to the home country or develop channels through which home country business, public administration and academic life get access to the knowledge, financial resources and networks of fellow citizens living abroad.

Due to the unprecedented level of emigration of skilled people and the large gap between the relatively small minority of skilled and the large majority of unskilled people that make up the society, it is no surprise that Albania has put together the most comprehensive and ambitious plan. It consists of three major efforts: (a) promote the return of Albanian citizens educated abroad, (b) bring together the community of Albanians that have returned to Albania, and (c) provide logistical and advisory support to foreign educated Albanians if and when they try to reintegrate into the Albanian society. The concrete proposals were based on an opinion poll that resulted in partly unexpected findings. It turned out that most respondents listed "inappropriate work ethic" as the primary reason against returning, while low living standards (including low wages) and the difficulty to find adequate employment ranked lower. Therefore, the following measures were put forward by the Albanian Institute for International Studies:

- improving the quality of higher education in Albania by creating new, business-related faculties and, at the same time, ending the process of further "liberalization" of founding new and undemanding universities that only create a "massive lumpen-intelligentsia", a "ticking social time bomb", since such an education generates a large gap between personal expectations and the real need of the society,
- breaking up the inflexible and hierarchy-based, gerontocratic system of higher education,
- implementing a civil service reform that could qualitatively upgrade public human resource management and end the supervisors' right to choose candidates at their discretion (source of nepotism),
- mandating employees educated abroad to return to their workplace upon completion of their studies abroad,
- decreasing the high level of "politicization" in the civil service, a major disadvantage for foreign-educated Albanians that otherwise would like to return,
- drawing up a clear strategy to deal with the informal economy,

- and reversing the long-term decline of research and development funding (Albanian Institute for International Studies, 2005, pp. 8. and 13-15).

It is obvious that the implementation of the above aims needs different time horizons. In an optimal case, some of them can reap some benefits in a relatively short time, while others, such as the elimination of the informal economy or the higher quality of tertiary education require more time. Moreover, social and professional resistance to the plans has to be taken into account, particularly in status-quo-oriented public administration and hierarchically organized universities.

Bosnia-Herzegovina has formulated much less ambitious plans. One of them was launched in cooperation with the Austrian Federal Ministry for Foreign Affairs and the Austrian Committee on World University Service. In this structure, Bosnian academics living abroad have been invited to return to local universities for temporary lecturing. Another indirect way of bringing young Bosnian citizens back is through the international organizations working in the country, basically as employees of foreign institutions. Obviously, this system has the handicap of skilled Bosnians leaving the country once international organizations end or suspend their local activities.

Bulgarian initiatives started in the late 1990s, when, on the occasion of Bulgarian Easter, the President of the Republic invited successful young Bulgarians to come together during that holiday. This and other steps resulted in the positive development, many young Bulgarians returned to participate in the 2001 parliamentary elections and several of them accepted high-level government jobs (some of them even became ministers in the new government). The return to Bulgaria by others led through foreign companies setting up businesses in the country. However, a long-term strategy of converting brain drain, at least partially, into brain gain is still absent.

Similarly, there is no Romanian initiative either. The basic reason may be that about 90% of immigrants are engaged in different undocumented activities. As long as there is no clear and detailed picture on the immigrants' activities, it is difficult to draw up a strategy to try to bring them back to the home country.

Based on a different and historically longer pattern of migration, Serbia has developed a special approach. It consists of two options. One is driven by the return of expatriates to the country of origin (return option), while the other tries to mobilize expatriates in order to contribute to the economic development of the country, since it is obvious that they would not like to return and settle down in Serbia (diaspora option). For ex-Yugoslav (and not least Serbian) citizens started to migrate way before the 1990s, and there are about 2.4 mn Serbian (and Montenegrin) citizens living in developed countries (and Latin America). It is understandable that heavy emphasis has been laid on the diaspora approach. In this context, so-called diaspora networks have been created. However, substantive results are conditioned on the fundamental improvement of the domestic political and economic situation.

A special way of replenishing manpower may lie in "importing" people from other countries. Since all Southeastern European countries struggle with high or very high levels of unemployment, the structure of importing labour would substantially differ from the Western European pattern, in which many low-skilled or unskilled workplaces have to be filled by immigrants (not least from Southeastern Europe and by skilled workers without any use of their skill in the new but better paid job). Therefore, policies to import labour have to be based on acquiring highly-skilled labour. This, however, is not always easy because the potential source countries may also need this labour or the target groups may already have followed the same route as their colleagues in Southeastern Europe and have emigrated to Western Europe and overseas countries (young engineers, computer technicians, doctors, nurses, academics, etc.). Nevertheless, in principle, there are two different approaches that could be implemented. One is based on "ethnicity" (and partly geographical neighbourhood), while the other can be called the "global" approach. Until now, the first one has been launched by some countries. However, it cannot be considered as part of a genuine strategy of brain drain. More realistically, it can be put in the context of national visa policies. Hundreds of thousands of Moldavians have applied for Romanian citizenship as that country was preparing to join the EU in 2007. Similarly, application for Bulgarian citizenship by tens of thousands of Macedonians has been reported. Of course, these applicants do not represent a closed group of people that would like to emigrate to Romania or Bulgaria. More likely, they would like to open up a channel to move further away, mainly to Western Europe by having national (Romanian and Bulgarian) documents. It is even less probable, that this group consists of high-quality people, since most of those may already have found a way to more lucrative Western European and overseas jobs. Despite all these limitations, some observations could be made on how national visa policies could be put in the service of genuine brain gain objectives.[89]

[89] Hungary has widespread experience in this field, since many Hungarians from Romania, Slovakia and Serbia have been employed in Hungary in the last decade. Romanian citizens are mainly employed in agriculture, construction (many of them without valid working contracts) but also in medical services. Most Slovaks work in Hungarian or Hungary-based multinational firms with legal contracts. The Serbian diaspora (both Hungarians from the Voivodina and Serbs) is composed of refugees but also of tal-

It is interesting that, until now, no Southeastern (or Central) European country has dealt seriously with the possibility of "global" brain gain. Evidently, the massive inflow of foreign direct capital to some Central European countries has been accompanied by substantial brain gain in the field of management and marketing knowledge and services. Also, new technologies have been adopted. But a clear vision of replacing high-skilled people who emigrated by bringing similarly high-skilled and motivated young people and businessmen from rapidly developing countries, such as India, China, Brazil, Russia or the Ukraine, has not yet been developed. The identification of the reasons may lead too far and is certainly not the objective of this study. However, it has to be underlined that this "global" approach is open to Southeastern European countries as well, and could become part of the "migration policy mix" in the future.

Until recently, and understandably, immigration policies in the Western Balkan countries were clearly dominated by the return of refugees. Many of them returned to Croatia and Serbia, as well as to the respective ethnic communities of Croats and Serbs in Bosnia-Herzegovina. As a result, the ethnic lines that were mixed (diluted) in ex-Yugoslavia, became more evident and fixed, not only between Croatia and Serbia, but also in Bosnia-Herzegovina as well. Many of those who used to live in ethnically mixed communities have been more than reluctant to return to their home where they would have belonged to the ethnic minority (either Croatian or Serbian).

Most affected Bosnia-Herzegovina formulated an Action Plan in 1999 (supported by the EU) that consisted of tools such as the creation of housing for refugees, establishing a safe (social) environment, strengthening social services, etc. However, several problems have prevailed. First, many refugees cannot return to their original home because their property (house, apartment) fell victim to war and previous ethnic atrocities. Second, memories of the war and ethnic cleansing are still very vivid and prevent people from accepting and trusting the new situation. Third, economic decline resulted in the lack of employment opportunities. This particularly affects young people who prefer to stay in larger towns and are not ready to return to their previous home in villages and rural areas. Fourth, the struggle for jobs has already created a cleavage not only

---

ented and well-established business people. One has to take into account that brain gain for a country generally means brain drain from another country. If such a flow takes place between two neighbouring countries, short-term gains for the host country can result in long-term losses for the entire region, as the lagging behind of the country deprived of the critical mass of human resources could represent a source of social, economic and political instability. In addition, special considerations of keeping the ethnic balance in the originating country may play a role in shaping migration policies by potential host countries.

between ethnic groups by favouring the employment of citizens belonging to the "state-creating nation" (be it Croatia or Serbia), but also within the same ethnic group, between firmly rooted citizens and returning refugees. According to several plans, the latter should have been given special support in order to get reintegrated – but, as many feel, not at the expense of other Croats or Serbs who are also looking for jobs. Since high-level unemployment can hardly be reduced substantially in the next few years, these problems will remain in the limelight or may even become aggravated. A reverse, but not less problematic development could be seen in recent years in Kosovo, where Serbs have been continuously dismissed from public utilities, previously employing both Kosovar Albanians and Serbs.[90]

In sum, migration abroad or within the region or the country, is fraught with a large number of problems and conflict potential. Moreover, ex-territorial immigration raises serious doubts about the human resource potential of several Southeastern European countries that would be definitely required both for starting a sustainable socio-economic development and for creating the necessary preconditions for future successful accession to the EU. However, in a short-term approach, it has to be acknowledged that migration has had a stabilizing impact as well. By generating financial resources abroad and transferring part of them back to the home country it could mitigate social and economic problems and poverty, and contribute to the survival of large social groups. Nevertheless, its long-term impact is by far not unanimously positive, since it generates economic and social distortions and may lead to firmly-rooted rent-seeking activities. The next chapter is dedicated to the financial implications of migration, with its potential or real, short- and long-term economic, political and social consequences.

III.8. Financial Transfers

III.8.1. In principle, financial transfers from one country to another, and more importantly, from more to less developed countries, can be considered an important element of growth, employment creation and additional investments. In contrast to this comprehensive macroeconomic approach, most beneficiary countries concentrate on the impact of financial transfers in the context of financial stability and increasing private income. An important role is attached to transfers in keeping the balance-of-payments in stable or sustainable conditions and increase the amount of available cash for a large part of the domestic population.

90 Originally, the staff of the electricity company was 50-50 between Serbs and Kosovar Albanians. Today, the proportion has been shifted to 90 to 10 in favour of Kosovar Albanians, and certainly not because of professional considerations.

As a methodological remark, it has to be pointed out that financial transfers, under the heading of "current transfers" in national bank statistics, include several other transfers as well, such as grants, gifts, inheritance, prizes won from lotteries abroad, pensions, current taxes, social security contributions of persons (including foreign ones) living in the given country, and by far not only remittances from citizens working abroad. In addition, and this is an important issue for the region, this heading contains EU pre-accession and other aid transfers as well.[91] Even personal remittances can be classified into three different types, such as workers' remittances, compensation received by employees temporarily living abroad and migrants' transfers arising from the change of residence from one country to another.[92] (Remittances by native citizens living and working outside SEE belong to the two former categories.)

The macroeconomic importance of remittances from citizens working abroad can be measured in different ways. First, the total amount of the transfer is an important indicator. Second, it can be compared to the size of the GDP, with total exports, its contribution to cover the deficit or generate or increase the surplus of the current account. Concerning the sustainability of economic growth, a comparison between yearly private transfers and the annual inflow of FDI can also be considered as an interesting indicator.

According to the latest study published by the United Nations,[93] worldwide money transfers may have reached more than USD 300 bn, as against USD 31 bn in 1990. World Bank calculations for 2005 amount to USD 173 bn, as the total amount of transfers by migrants to their native countries and citizens. However, a large part of the transfers is not channelled through banks but from person to person. Thus, in reality, the total transfer may amount to USD 250 bn. In addition, not only migrants from less developed countries remit part of their income, but also citizens of developed countries. Everything taken together, the World Bank arrives at an estimate of USD 300 bn. The country-related statistics contain just the officially documented remittances plus a part of the estimates. According to these figures, two important comparisons can be made. One is based on the total volume of transfers, while the other measures remit-

---

91 Other components of transfers, including EU support, official bilateral and multilateral aid, etc. will not be dealt with in this chapter. Most of these elements, some of them vitally important in the different stages of political stabilization and economic reconstruction for the Western Balkan countries, have been included in other parts of the present study.

92 While the first two categories appear on the current account, the third (and smaller one) is included in the capital account. For details see EBRD (2006a), p. 3.

93 United Nations. *International Migration and Development*. New York, May 2006, and Rössler (2006).

tances in % of the GDP of the respective country. Needless to say, two rather different rankings result.

Concerning the total volume of transfers, India and China top the list, both with incoming transfers of more than USD 21 bn each in 2004. Among the leading 20 countries one Southeastern European country only, namely Serbia-Montenegro can be found, with USD 4.1 bn (between Morocco and Pakistan, on place 11). However, based on the share of transfers in GDP, three of the Southeastern European countries plus Moldova can be identified in the list of the "leading" 20 countries. Moldova ranks just second, with 27% of GDP transferred from abroad, while Bosnia-Herzegovina is in 5th place with 22.5. Serbia-Montenegro occupies place No. 8 with 17.2%, while Albania is 17th in this ranking with 11.7% of GDP.[94] (For an international ranking see Appendix Table III.8.1/1) Thus, it can be seen that the macroeconomic relevance of remittances from abroad ranges from important to vital to several Southeastern European countries even in global comparison. In turn, CEE countries and, until most recently, Bulgaria and Romania reported a contribution by remittances to the GDP in a magnitude of less than 2%.

Beyond the relative importance of remittances, its dramatic increase in the last few years has to be pointed out. According to EBRD figures (EBRD, 2006a, pp. 3-4) between 2001 and 2004 total inflows to SEE countries grew by 84%, while the region's GDP only grew by 74% (in USD). In other words, high domestic growth (from a very low initial level) was accompanied by an even higher increase of remittances.[95]

III.8.2. Turning to the individual countries of Southeastern Europe, national statistics referred to in the individual country studies, show other important characteristics.[96]

In Albania, the volume of remittances has been growing more rapidly than other foreign exchange earnings. In 2005, they represented 14% of the GDP, 70% of exports and covered just one-third of imports. Also, this

---

94 EBRD (2006a) contains slightly different figures without changing either the ranking of the countries or the macroeconomic weight of remittances.

95 The EBRD concludes that remittances to SEE do not behave in a counter-cyclical way, since they used to increase in periods of economic hardship (EBRD, 2006a, p. 4). However, it is obvious that all Western Balkan countries face serious economic problems despite relatively high growth rates. In addition, a country-by-country survey would prove that remittances increased substantially over average to Bosnia-Herzegovina and Serbia, two countries in the most critical economic situation. Finally, the initial and rapidly growing trend of remittances to Bulgaria and Romania has to be taken into account, too.

96 A table containing partial comparative figures based on IMF statistics is in the Appendix, Table III.8.2./1.

financial transfer has been clearly higher than the respective inflow of FDI.[97]

The picture is similar in Bosnia-Herzegovina, where in 2003 private remittances accounted for 16.9% of the GDP, 67% of exports and covered 30% of the trade deficit. Moreover, they were more than three times higher than the inflow of FDI and more than double the amount of foreign aid. In *per capita* terms, Bosnia-Herzegovina received the highest private transfers in the Southeastern European region (about USD 285 per person). The above data may be underestimated, since it does not contain the informal (or direct, non-banking) ways of bringing money into the country.

Bulgaria started to register substantial amounts of private remittances just in the last ten years. Due to their rapid rise, however, they currently represent almost 3% of the GDP and about 85% of total current transfers, while pre-accession money from the EU only amounts to 11%. For many years, private transfers developed in line with FDI (excluding the last three years, when FDI entered a new and upgraded stage).

Similar contribution to the GDP could be observed in Croatia as well, where private remittances look back to a much longer history.

Although in ex-Yugoslavia, Macedonian citizens were also allowed to accept jobs abroad, the share of private transfers saw a spectacular increase in terms of GDP only in the 1990s, when the economic situation of broad social strata worsened substantially. The increase of private transfers in GDP from less than 2% in 1993 to 12.3% in 2000, and to 13.8% in 2004, was largely due to transfers by Macedonian citizens who had been living abroad for a longer period, and only a small part can be explained by remittances by new migrants. (Behind the growing proportion a rapidly growing volume of transfers can be detected as well, since transfer payments were less than USD 60 mn in 1993 and more than USD 720 mn in 2004.)

Similarly, Serbia-Montenegro also had a decade-long experience with private transfers from guest workers. However, these sums were much lower than those registered during the war and in the post-war period, including at present. After 2000, remittances represented 10 to 12% of the GDP annually and equalled a growing share of exports of goods and services (from 35 to 60%). Thus, the balance on current transfers could usually cover more than half of the trade deficit. Interestingly, Serbia-Montenegro belongs to those countries that do not only show an increasing inflow but also an outflow of private transfers. To be sure, the difference between inflows and outflows kept increasing. While inflows grew

---

97 According to Fullani, Governor of the Bank of Albania (2006).

from USD 670 mn in 1999 to more than USD 3.5 bn in 2004, in the same period outflows increased from USD 280 mn to USD 620 mn. Most probably, a large portion of the outflows was directed to Serbian citizens living in other parts of ex-Yugoslavia, mainly in Bosnia-Herzegovina, Croatia or Macedonia.

The following table summarizes some major interrelations between the trade balance, the balance of services and the balance of transfers.

Table III.38
Components of the current account in % of GDP

	Balance of goods		Balance of services		Balance of transfers	
	2002	2004	2002	2004	2002	2004
Albania	-23.9	-19.6	-0.1	-0.6	12.9	13.6
Bosnia-Herzegovina	-59.2	-554	3.3	4.5	24.6	22.2
Bulgaria	-10.2	-14.0	2.9	3.7	3.4	4.6
Croatia	-24.6	-24.3	13.6	17.7	4.8	4.3
Macedonia	-21.3	-20.9	-0.6	-0.8	13.2	14.7
Romania	- 5.7	-9.0	0.0	-0.4	3.3	4.2
Serbia	-24.7	-31.7	1.9	1.8	10.0	15.3
Montenegro	-32.7	-28.1	7.6	9.1	6.7	2.9

Source: wiiw database as quoted in Gligorov (2005), p. 3.

Balance of transfer figures point to quite different positions of the individual Southeastern European countries. In terms of GDP, they are very significant in Bosnia-Herzegovina, Serbia, Macedonia and Albania (in this order). At the same time, they only play a minor role in the three largest economies of the region, namely Bulgaria, Croatia and Romania. However, in terms of the absolute volume of transfers, it has to be taken into account that these are the economies with the largest GDP, therefore smaller shares may hide large amounts of transfers. In addition, the relatively low share in these countries can partly be explained by the late start of migration (Bulgaria and Romania) and the higher *per capita* GDP in Croatia that made substantial transfers less vital than for other Western Balkan countries.

Another interesting characteristic is that the share of transfers in GDP has not changed substantially in most countries. It points to the relative stability of transfers. The only remarkable exception was Serbia, with a large increase, due to the growing deprivation of citizens in that country. The gradually increasing figures for Bulgaria and Romania seem to confirm that the rapidly growing number of new migrants started to raise transfer payments in recent years.

The third conclusion can be drawn when transfer shares in GDP are compared with the share of the trade deficit in GDP. Between 2002 and 2004, trade deficit was growing as a share of GDP in both accession countries (Bulgaria and Romania), as well as in Serbia and remained steady at a high level in Croatia. As a consequence, non-trade income plays a vital role in having more or less sustainable current account balances everywhere. Remittances to Albania covered more than 160% of the trade deficit, while they remained slightly above 100% in Bosnia-Herzegovina and slightly below this level in Serbia-Montenegro (EBRD, 2006a, pp. 4-5). In other SEE countries, the role of remittances in covering the trade deficit was much smaller (below 20%). This is partly due to the smaller gap between exports and imports and partly to the availability of other revenues (*e.g.*, Croatia could cover 91% of its trade deficit by revenues from tourism).

Graph III.39
Ratio of remittances to export revenue in selected transition countries, 2004

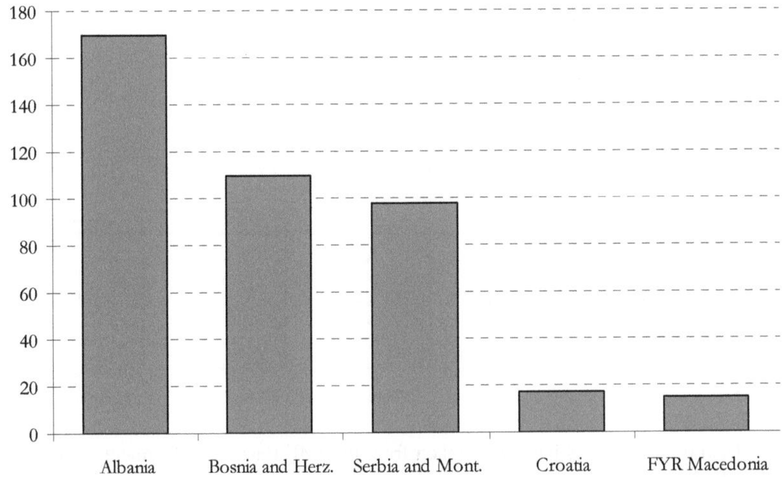

Note: Data on remittances have been taken from the IMF Balance of Payments Yearbook, unless otherwise stated.

Source: EBRD and IMF Balance of Payments Yearbook (2005).

Another interesting comparison can be made between the volume of remittances as compared to revenues from exports and the inflow of FDI, respectively. Concerning the relationship between remittances and exports, the WB countries can be divided into three categories. In Albania, officially registered remittances are substantially higher than export revenues. In Bosnia-Herzegovina and Serbia-Montenegro remittances and exports are more or less on the same level. In turn, in Croatia and Macedonia export revenues prove to be much more important than the volume of annual remittances (*Graph III.39*).

The relative role of remittances is much more important if these sums are compared to FDI figures. Moreover, remittances proved to be more stable than FDI flows (that were mainly linked to larger or smaller privatization deals). According to the EBRD (2006a, p. 4) survey, remittances exceeded net FDI in 2004 by three to five times in Albania, Bosnia-Herzegovina and Serbia-Montenegro. In addition, they were almost 50% higher than the registered FDI inflow in Macedonia and Croatia, respectively (see *Graph III.40*).

Graph III.40
Ratio of remittances to net FDI in selected transition countries, 2004

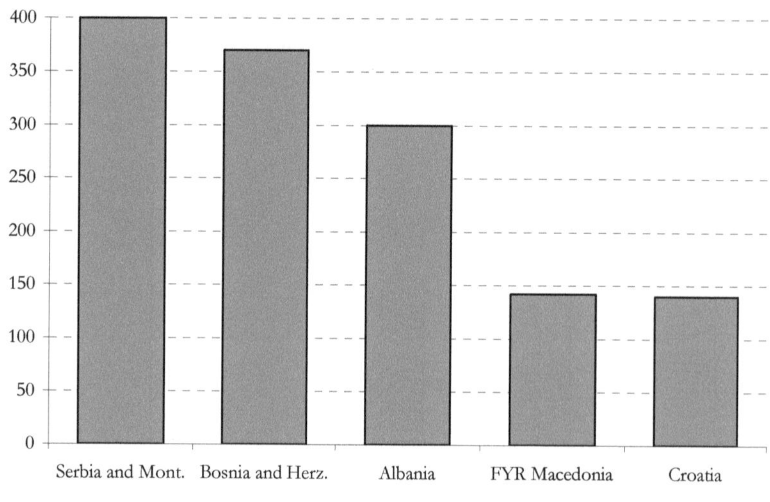

Note: Data on remittances have been taken from the IMF Balance of Payments Yearbook, unless otherwise stated.

Source: EBRD and IMF Balance of Payments Yearbook (2005).

III.8.3. Whereas the total amount of private remittances can only be estimated since large flows evade the banking sector and find direct ways to the beneficiaries, it is a bit less difficult to identify the main fields in which the money will be used. Overwhelmingly they finance private consumption. This spending pattern shows very different scales, however, ranging from everyday survival to luxury consumption. Most people need the transfers from relatives working abroad in order to have enough alleviate poverty and cover basic needs. This assumption is confirmed by the fact that, regularly monthly transfers to citizens amount to Euro 100 to 200 on average.

In Albania, where most citizens are beneficiaries of remittances, the average amount of private transfers annually is calculated to be about Euro 550. Since emigration was particularly strong from rural areas, households in rural areas register an annual average transfer income of Euro 800. For other reasons, Bosnia-Herzegovina reports figures in the magnitude of about Euro 250 a year. In more developed countries such as Croatia, Bulgaria and Romania that started to experience large-scale migration much later, only a smaller part of the population is involved directly in the "network of remittances". As a result, the average *per capita* inflow is much lower and ranges between Euro 100 and 150 a year. Since the transfers involve fewer people, in reality, the beneficiaries may have additional earnings closer to the Albanian figures.

There is no reliable data on the pattern of consumption financed by remittances. Based on the disposable domestic income and the price levels in Southeastern European countries, it can, however, be concluded that a relatively larger part is spent on covering costs of personal services than on the consumption of goods. In this context, construction of apartments and houses ranks at the top. The residential construction boom experienced in selected countries of the region (mainly in Albania, but also in Bosnia-Herzegovina, Bulgaria and Macedonia) could hardly be understood without external resources. Such activities may have three different goals. First, they can contribute to better housing conditions for relatives who remained in the home country. Second, they can create adequate housing conditions for migrants who, after a certain time, would like to return and continue their life in the home country. Third, investments in housing can also be done for reasons of speculation (see the booming housing market in most countries) or long-term savings.

Only a small part of remittances is used for personal cash savings.[98] The reason is twofold. On the one hand, most citizens do not have to the luxury to save, since remittances will be (almost) immediately spent on basic commodities and services. The culture of using such savings as an insurance against future income risks (*e.g.* unemployment) is not widespread in the region yet. The "savings (or dissavings) culture" goes just in the opposite direction. In recent years, foreign banks located in the SEE countries have started large-scale and – apparently – generous consump-

[98] Bulgaria seems to be an interesting exception, since private remittances helped increase the savings rate of the economy from 12.5 to 16% of GDP between 2003 and 2004. It has to be noted that this increase in savings maybe temporary, if it finances activities with delayed payments (*e.g.* housing sector or long-term credits).

tion-boosting credit programs that wiped out savings and turned a large part of the citizens into net-debtors. There are few signs that savings from remittances would be considered a guarantee to pay back credits in the future. On the other hand, some savings were based on the assumption that, in the foreseeable future, the national currency may be devalued. This value-conserving attitude can be found in countries with flexible exchange rate systems. Both previous experience with substantial devaluations (Romania) and the evidently overvalued exchange rate (mainly in Croatia, but also in other Western Balkan countries) that is not expected to be kept in the medium-term, are the underlying considerations.

An overall feature of private remittances in the SEE region is that only a small part (if any) of the money remains available for investments in business activities. Obviously, investments in housing or some durable consumer goods such as cars or computers can be considered of a dual nature, since they can appear both as private consumption and business expenses. However, common experience shows that such investments belong fundamentally to the category of private consumption. Looking at the huge investment needs and modernization tasks in Southeastern Europe, a much larger portion of private remittances should be directed into large-scale investment activities. However, private transfers (a large part of them evading the banking sector) cannot directly be rechannelled to such purposes. The decisions of the beneficiaries of transfers have to be motivated and influenced by favourable investment opportunities.

Micro-level initiatives should not be ignored in the process of building a functioning market economy. According to a study including three SEE countries (Albania, Bosnia-Herzegovina and Serbia-Montenegro) remittances do play an important role in covering the start-up costs of small enterprises (40% on average, including Moldova and Georgia, the two other countries involved in the survey). Interestingly, the role of remittances in covering start-up costs varies not only between countries but also according to the length of time the business have operated. In Serbia-Montenegro, with some tradition of business culture, most remittances support firms that have existed for about 10 years. In turn, new ventures (with a record of less than 5 years) were not able to attract meaningful financial resources from private transfers. In contrast, in late-starter Albania, new business activities can expect higher financial support from remittances.[99]

[99] The survey on the micro- and small enterprises relying to different degrees on remittances included 195 firms in Serbia-Montenegro, 151 firms in Albania and 122 firms in Bosnia-Herzegovina. 118, 103 and 81 valid answers, respectively, were produced. Out of these companies, 28 from Serbia-Montenegro, 25 from Albania and 20 in Bosnia-Herzegevina reported that they made use of financial resources linked to remittances (EBRD 2006a, pp. 6-7).

However, under the current conditions of globalization, economic policy-makers of the SEE have to be aware of the fact that successful economic performance cannot be imagined without large-scale investments for which, among others, sizeable potential domestic savings (represented by remittances) should be consciously collected.

The only and unwelcome exception in the use of remittances is money laundering. It is not at all impossible that part of the micro-level survey of the EBRD includes such activities that have been financed by private remittances coming from dubious sources and have been invested into small hotels, restaurants and other branches of the service industry (mainly in Albania, but, to a smaller extent, in other SEE countries as well). In addition, it has to be mentioned that some private transfers directly finance illegal or criminal activities.

III.8.4. Massive private transfers to the SEE countries have ambiguous effects. In the short run, the positive effects clearly prevail, but negative developments should not be ignored in the long run.

There is no doubt that such transfers can finance large trade deficits and keep the current account balanced or in a position of sustainable deficits (particularly if FDI and other revenues from services cover the remaining portion of the deficits). Moreover, they can stabilize the national currency. In turn, several negative consequences have to be mentioned as well. Too strong, *i.e.* appreciated national currencies favour imports and discourage exports. It is common experience that small and less-developed countries without significant raw materials or energy carriers can only break out of the vicious cycle of underdevelopment by an export-oriented growth. Not least, exchange rate policies are expected to support such a process. The strong (over)stabilizing role of private remittances on the exchange rate works in the opposite direction.

In addition, consumption financed by private remittances generally increases the demand for imported goods (and therefore it contributes to high trade deficits). This happens in two channels. First, in many countries adequate domestic goods are not available (either due to the disruption of previous production or as a result of imports squeezing out domestic commodities). Second, migrants (guest workers) gradually adapt to the commodities they consume during their stay in Western Europe (and overseas), and spread this consumption culture at home as well (both by transferring not only money but also consumption habits and preferences to the beneficiaries, and by their own consumption pattern once they return to their home country). As a result, growing dependency on imported goods (and partly services) develops. It is particularly strongly felt in Bosnia-Herzegovina and in Kosovo, where such patterns have been due to the sizeable international community that has a high share in total domestic consumption. An additional consequence of high amounts of

Euro in most SEE countries may lead to the "euroization" of the national economy, a clear trend already in Serbia.[100]

Another ambiguous economic impact of the massive private remittances lies in its volatility. On the one hand, this may be affected by the macroeconomic situation in the beneficiary country. Variable exchange and interest rates or even the security of transferring funds, including the (mis)functioning of the banking sector, can substantially alter the total amount of yearly flows. On the other hand, international experience proves that, except in special situations, the volume of remittances does not increase but will even out after some time. Or, even worse, it can start declining, as migrants tend to settle and establish their future life in the host country. In this case, their attention to relatives left behind tends to wane, as does their financial capacity, since they may need more money to establish their new life abroad. In a positive scenario, remittances may shrink as a result of high growth, more jobs, higher salaries and better living standards in the home country, so that relatives do not need as much financial support as before. Evident divergence from this trend only occurs if natural catastrophes or (civil) wars temporarily enhance transfer activities (this was the case in Serbia and Bosnia-Herzegovina in the post-war period). In sum, it is appropriate to launch programs that would encourage the redirection of remittances from consumption to investment and savings still in the peak years of transfers.

Finally, the almost non-existent impact of private remittances on domestic investment activities has to be mentioned. This also implies that such sources do not help to reduce uniquely high levels of unemployment and contribute to job creation. Just the opposite, unfortunately, large private transfers have created a gap between consumption and investment in several SEE countries at a time when sustainable economic development would have badly needed not only more investments but a clear path to growth fuelled by new investment. There is hardly any other domestic resource in the same magnitude that could (have) finance(d) large-scale domestic investments. The long-term consequence is either low investment activities resulting in low growth rates or a growing gap between domestic and foreign investments (provided that international direct capital finds competitive locational environment in selected SEE countries). The example of Central European new EU member countries

100 Similar developments can be identified in Bosnia-Herzegovina and Macedonia, while Montenegro and Kosovo already use the Euro as legal tender. Most probably, in structurally weak countries lacking the process of real convergence, this is a premature and highly costly adjustment to the European monetary system and the requirements of the Eurozone, with heavy consequences on exports and competitiveness of the given SEE economy, as well as on the slow inflow of FDI, a vital element of sustainable economic modernization.

indicates that, following the first stage of the massive inflow of foreign capital, further sustainable development (not only in economic terms) is vitally dependent on the interplay of large and medium- and small-sized firms, as well as multi-national and domestic companies. Until now, private remittances to the SEE countries have not contributed meaningfully to creating the domestic preconditions to build a "production and service network".[101]

The analysis would not be complete without a brief discussion of the non-economic consequences of private financial transfers. To some extent, their impact is stronger and lasts longer than the already mentioned economic effects.

First, it increases income inequality. Since all SEE countries have low income levels, the distortion is stronger than in high-income countries. More importantly, income inequalities do not result from different salaries or different quality of work, better or worse personal performance, but are almost fully separated from personal qualities and values. Those who are the beneficiaries of smaller or larger regular transfers generally show higher consumption and better living standards than others.

Second, income disparities can be further aggravated by the fact that better paid local citizens may get higher amounts of remittances.[102]

Third, it is not only the dissociation between income and employment that has to be highlighted but also a clear disincentive to find employment. Why should anybody put up with hard working conditions for a low salary if his or her living standard is guaranteed by transfers? It is likely that the high unemployment figures in the Western Balkan countries can partly be explained by a lack of motivation for the beneficiaries of transfers to find work. Also, regular remittances may stimulate temporary working activities and, thus, contribute to the further strengthening of the already strong grey and tax-evading economy.

Fourth, the "dependency symptom" undermines the work ethic and it is becoming the accepted attitude of a growing part of the citizens towards legal ways of earning a living and to sustain or raise their living standards as a result of their own efforts. A large rent-seeking social sector will result that leaves substantial resources for domestic economic

---

[101] The interesting survey conducted by the EBRD (2006a) and quoted in this sub-chapter reports initial steps. However, as of today, they lack convincing macroeconomic effects, let alone sustainable export- and investment-led growth path, fundamental structural changes or growing competitiveness reflected in the rapidly increasing export figures.

[102] A Serbian case study indicates that remittances generally go to families with above-average financial means. The sample shows that those getting remittances from abroad have a 15% higher income at home. Adding the remittances, the difference would increase to 34% (EBRD 2006a, p. 6).

growth unutilized. Moreover, it creates a highly restless social stratum that could destabilize the country at any moment the transfer payments decline or stop.

Fifth, the long-lasting "mental contamination" has to be pointed out. The more the private remittances dominate the economic prospects and living standards of people in the beneficiary country, the more immigrant workers will become symbols of a successful life. Two developments may follow from this attitude. First, social propensity to migration will be growing resulting in further large-scale migration in search of fortune or just a better life outside the home country. Second, defeatism, pessimism will spread at home as more and more citizens will consider the domestic situation hopeless, and the current state of underdevelopment as a "national plague or curse" that cannot be overcome. Needless to say, successful and sustainable modernization requires not only physical capital, high-quality administration and adequate human resources, but, maybe as an intrinsic part of the latter, a positive, future- and success-oriented, entrepreneurial attitude. This applies not only to the genuine business sector but also to the overwhelming part of the society as well. "Consolidation" or, even more, ossification of the pattern of consumption based on massive and lasting private remittances and the permanently deep-rooted rent seeking attitude may become one of the major barriers of breaking out of the vicious cycle of underdevelopment and poverty in the next years and decades.

III.8.5. In this context, active government policies are urgently needed. They should follow two main paths. On the one hand, the substantial gap between registered and actual transfers should be narrowed. At present, a large part of the remittances go right into the pocket of (mostly temporarily) returning emigrants and directly to the beneficiaries in the home country. High transfer costs, administrative and technical problems blocking easy accession to the money (particularly in rural areas without a convenient banking network) and deeply-rooted and hard-dying habits of "cash culture" can be mentioned as possible reasons.[103] On the other hand, the domestic environment has to be made more favourable to investments over consumption. This, of course, depends on the living standards of the beneficiaries as well, since citizens or families living in poverty or on the verge, cannot be expected to become savers (and, consequently direct or indirect investors). Nevertheless, part of the consumption could be diverted towards investments, without endangering a

[103] In Albania, for instance, "cash culture" is very characteristic. While more than 50% of the remittances by Albanian emigrants in Italy make use of the banking sector, this share drops to less than 20% on the Albanian side.

decent living standard. Just the opposite, it could foster to establish higher living standards in the future.

It is surprising how little SEE governments have done in this respect. Despite the remarkable volume of remittances, no country has developed a comprehensive plan to direct a part of the incoming transfers towards investments in line with the strategic economic goals of the beneficiary country. To be sure, it is not easy to divert private transfers towards savings and investments, particularly if a large part of the money changes hands in cash, avoiding the banking system. The government does not possess effective tools that can be applied here other than income, property or corporate taxes, with very uneven degrees of success and only in a few SEE countries. Since, however, these transfers represent the most important (if not the exclusive) source of potential private savings, real opportunities should be created for the beneficiaries to choose among different options to make use of the money.[104]

In a recent speech, the governor of the Bank of Albania formulated some policy instruments that could create a better registration of remittances and different options available to beneficiaries.[105] In the first case, high banking fees have to be reduced or completely abolished. Also, the use of credit cards should be promoted, as well as the option of cash payments reduced (*e.g.* payment of salaries, utilities, etc.). Furthermore, rural areas far away from banking services have to get a better financial infrastructure. As for investments and savings, small-business incentives should take into account such resources and offer favourable terms to potential investors. Another, government-led program could channel such resources into special funds that would finance large-scale investments (against bond issues, by encouraging forms of long-term savings at higher but economically still affordable interest rates). Moreover, emigrants who would like to set up a business in Albania, either by returning to the country or by just managing the firm, might get special advantages.[106] Of course, it has to be admitted that such advantages can hardly work if the general economic environment is unstable, the policy instruments constantly change and the socio-political climate is not conducive to longer-term investments, be they foreign-owned or financed by domestic capital.

---

[104] It has to be noted that the lack of different options in itself enhances the propensity to spend available financial resources for (immediate) consumption.

[105] Fullani (2006), pp. 2-4.

[106] One way could be to offer temporary tax advantages or exemptions to such investments (on the corporate or the personal income tax level, or both).

III.9. A Few Remarks on Poverty

III.9.1. SEE countries are generally considered not only poor in European comparison, but also characterized by widespread poverty. Of course, poverty can be measured in different ways, and by far not all official statistics can tell the (full) truth. In addition, economic indicators, even if they are reliable, cannot by themselves reflect the non-economic elements of poverty, including the social environment, the level of education, personal attitudes and mentality. All of them are factors of poverty, and, at the same time, they are also responsible to some extent for the prolongation or deepening of the poverty status.[107]

Economic and social statistics usually determine a so-called "poverty line" expressed in terms of *per capita* income. All those who do not reach this level are considered "poor" or people living in "poverty". Even in economic terms, such an approach can only be credible if we can correctly measure all financial and non-financial transfers (including those of goods and services without cash payments) among citizens of a given country and remittances and payments to citizens and institutions of other countries. Such statistics are not available For any country Still, lower levels of non-registered transfers provide more reliable statistics on poverty, while the high One example from the previous sub-chapter: those who can rely on regular and larger remittances from abroad are generally better off without earning their own income from employment than those who are employed and earn a low monthly salary but do not enjoy any transfer from abroad.[108]

---

107 Recently, the income and non-income dimensions of poverty have been differentiated. Income poverty can be expressed in *per capita* income figures below a predetermined average, mainly expressed in USD or Euro per adult equivalent per day). In turn, the non-income dimension of poverty includes illiteracy and the low level of education, high infant mortality, generally poor and deteriorating health conditions (disabilities, inherited or acquired illness, alcoholism, drug addiction, mental problems) and several other factors. Therefore, the Human Development Index (HDI) developed by the United Nations seems to be a better instrument to define poverty than just GDP *per capita* figures (let alone the difficulties attached to its "fair" measurement).

108 Even in economic terms, different levels of poverty can be identified. According to the World Bank, people at or below the absolute poverty line can hardly afford the basic necessities (enough food to survive and basic non-food necessities). Relative poverty is measured in comparison with the national average of welfare standards. All poverty calculations have to be made in terms of purchasing power parity (PPP), since national price levels vary from country to country. In addition, people with higher incomes in USD or Euro terms in more developed countries can be classified under the poverty line, while lower incomes in less developed countries may put respective citizens into a better category. In the categorization of the World Bank, absolute poverty line corresponds to a *per capita* of USD 2.15 at purchasing power parity, per day. (It is well known that a large part of the population in developing countries earn less than USD 2 per day.)

III.9.2. Poverty in SEE is not an absolutely new phenomenon. However, over decades, it was neither measured (due to the "socialist ideology" of ever increasing welfare for everybody) nor as widespread and as visible as it is today. Two key developments produced the dramatic change in the last one and a half decades.

The first is the systemic transformation that resulted in the collapse of the old economic, labour market and partly the social structure. Rapidly growing and long-term unemployment not only increased the number of poor people with no or minimal income (and without substantial savings in order to overcome difficult times) but made poverty also visible, by replacing in-door (workplace) un(der)employment by massive outdoor unemployment. In fact, ex-Yugoslavia only had experience with unemployment before 1990, but it became a new and previously largely unknown phenomenon in Bulgaria and Romania.

The second factor can be attributed to the wars and their consequences in the Western Balkan countries. Direct war damages were preceded, accompanied and aggravated by the disintegration of the Yugoslav Federation. Production broke down in many cases both as a result of the war and the loss of previous (domestic and partly foreign) markets. Delays in transformation, political and ideological opposition to genuine reforms have further exacerbated the situation. In fact, all SEE countries lost a substantial part of their previous GDP. However, the most important cuts were experienced in the ex-Yugoslav republics that, belonging to the Federation, were able to generate a certain level of welfare that, to some extent and until the end of the 1970s was an object of envy in Central and Eastern Europe. The unprecedented drop in living standards was particularly dramatic in those new countries that, for long decades, had been net beneficiaries of the intra-Yugoslav redistribution of income.[109] With the abolition of the Federation, this transfer mechanism stopped functioning.[110] Although the erosion of the system started well before the systemic transformation in Central and Eastern Europe, it acquired completely new dimensions after 1990. Today, there is hardly any household in Serbia-

---

[109] Even in Serbia-Montenegro, positioned in terms of development between "rich" Slovenia and "poor" Kosovo, absolute poverty doubled in the 1990s, living standards declined by at least 50% and GDP in 2000 stood at 46% of its level a decade ago (with the latter figure already showing a declining trend in comparison to the 1980s). According to Grecic (2004), one-third of the Serbian population lives in poverty (with a *per capita* income of less than Euro 30 a month), and another 10% can be classified as living below the poverty line (with monthly incomes of less than Euro 20).

[110] Transfers from the richer republics such as Slovenia and partly Croatia have boosted income levels in Macedonia, Bosnia-Herzegovina and particularly in Kosovo. Although the income differences could not be evened out, and transfers have not only had a positive impact (on a moderat scale, rent seeking mentality has its roots in this period), they did play a role in preventing or hiding poverty.

Montenegro, Bosnia-Herzegovina or Montenegro that has not suffered a dramatic collapse of its living standard. The masses of refugees and internally displaced persons deprived of their economic and social background and without any prospects of getting reintegrated into the new and still uncertain to volatile structures definitely aggravate, prolong and reproduce poverty.

III.9.3. According to the World Bank, absolute poverty affects more than half of the population of Moldova, followed by Kosovo (37%) and Romania (over 30%), Albania (over 20%) and Bosnia-Herzegovina (almost 20%). It is no surprise that these the countries have had the highest post-1990 immigration. Absolute poverty seems to be lowest in Croatia (less than 10%) and slightly higher in Bulgaria. As previously mentioned, these figures have to be considered with caution, not only because they may miss important factors that reduce or enhance the share of people living in poverty, but also because the picture can change rapidly: regrettably, mainly for the worse, as a result of macroeconomic developments (financial crises, exchange rate fluctuations or as a consequence of necessary and fundamental economic reforms leading to higher levels of unemployment or lower levels of social assistance).

In addition, different social groups are affected differently by poverty. Most vulnerable are the children, the elderly, the disabled, the long-term unemployed, precarious job holders, residents of depressed areas and ethnic minorities.

III.9.4. For answers on how under such conditions economic and political peace can be achieved, one has to look for additional sources of income and different strategies for survival and personal subsistence. No doubt the grey economy, as well as illegal activities have eased the poverty of many people (and enriched a small group). However, the long-term social and political costs of this development path are higher. Moreover, remittances by immigrants have had a substantial mitigating impact. According to Albanian surveys, such transfers have played a critical role in assisting many families living in poverty, particularly in rural areas. To some extent, they have even contributed to a less unequal distribution of income, at least between urban and rural areas (40% of the disposable income in rural areas stems from remittances, as compared to the national average of 33%) (Fullani, 2006, p. 1). Other countries' experience seem to go in the opposite direction, revealing increasing income inequalities. Despite the above figures, such a development maybe identified in Albania as well. Namely, only 27% of the total amount of private remittances reach poor people, while 60% goes to the middle income class (of course, at Albanian living standards).

Personal survival strategies included both a flight back to agriculture and massive migration to urban areas, depending on the individual country's specific situation (Romania is an example for the first, Albania for the second trend). Probably the most frequently used way to fight poverty has been emigration. In addition, a turn to illegal and criminal activities should not be ignored, either.

Concerning the future of Southeastern Europe in general and that of the Western Balkans in particular, the non-economic consequences of poverty may be more relevant than strictly economic developments. Once it reaches a critical level that has no precedent in international practice, poverty may leave substantial resources of economic development unused or distorted (by financing survival instead of investing scarce resources into development). More importantly, it could threaten political stability and social peace, particularly if not only the status quo but also the dynamics of the process is taken into account. An important factor that poses a great challenge to stability is the feeling of decline by many people who see no promising prospects for themselves in the future. Conflicts over the distribution of scarce resources – such as public employment – can easily assume ethnic dimensions and contribute to social disintegration (see in more detail Novák, 2005).

III.9.5. The potential risks of widening and deepening poverty may raise serious concerns about the low level of attention paid to this problem by politicians and policy-makers. Arguments that all countries have had to face many challenges that are perceived to be more urgent and more important than poverty-related issues can hardly be accepted without serious objections. In fact, the political elite everywhere has been inclined to formulate the public agenda with other issues, including narrow-minded political power games, the revival of history-related disputes with neighbouring countries, strengthening ethnic identity or, in the most positive case, with the managing of economic transformation and sustainable catching-up processes. Regrettably, it has been largely ignored that the objectives of catching up and future progress can hardly be achieved without finding the right (at least minimally required) strategies to fight poverty. The goals of sustainable political stability, both domestic and regional, as well as well-functioning institutions, success in combating criminality and illegal activities, or the political (and, in a longer term, the mental) settlement of ethnic issues cannot be achieved without stopping the rise of, and, in the medium-term, alleviating widespread poverty. The above issues, as basic components of sustainable political and economic conditions and key elements of successfully catching up with EU standards, will be addressed in the next part of the study.

III.B. Western Balkans-specific Issues

In the second part of this chapter some political and social issues will be addressed that seem to be indispensable to understand the situation in the Western Balkan countries and to formulate recommendations for the future both for the countries involved and the EU as well. Obviously, the selected areas chosen for analysis do not cover all relevant topics. Moreover, some issues to be addressed will be the subject of a more detailed analysis in the last chapter of this study, focusing on future scenarios. Here, the main goal is to highlight some of the developments that may have a long-term impact on the future of the region and on its relation to the European Union. The author is convinced that without considering these issues in the discussion of the future of the Western Balkans, no sustainable stability and meaningful economic progress can be achieved.

The forthcoming chapters covers only the Western Balkan countries, for this region was involved in a devastating war with serious questions yet to be resolved. Evidently, the war has affected the neighbouring countries as well, including Bulgaria and Romania. Some observations will be made about them as well, when necessary, but the main focus will remain on ex-Yugoslavia and Albania.

III.10. The Consequences of the Dissolution of the Yugoslav Federation and the Balkan Wars

III.10.1. Some of the professional literature on the Western Balkans tends to explain current developments and prospects on the basis of the wars in the 1990s. These experts seem to forget that the crisis in the territory of the ex-Yugoslav Federation had started several years earlier. A latent crisis could already be observed in the 1980s, following the death of Tito and the slowly but unambiguously changing conditions in Central (and Eastern) Europe, as well as in Gorbachev's Soviet Union.

Although the Yugoslav crisis became full blown after 1990, some preliminary signs were already apparent several years earlier. In fact, separatist movements were on the increase in Kosovo in the 1980s. In an effort to curb such movements, in 1988 Milosevic abolished the autonomy of Kosovo (along with the decades-long autonomy of Voivodina). Shortly after 1990, practically in less than a year, the Yugoslav Federation disintegrated and new "independent" "States" were established. On June 25, 1991, Slovenia and Croatia declared independence from the Yugoslav Federation. They were followed by Macedonia (December 19, 1991) and the Croat-Bosniak community of Bosnia-Herzegovina in February 1992. All of them were recognized by the international community as new independent states. The remaining part of Yugoslavia (practically Serbia-Montenegro, including Kosovo, with 40% of the territory and the same share of population of the previous Federation) has established the new Federal Republic of Yugoslavia that considered itself as the legal successor to the previous federation. As a direct consequence of the new situation, the new Yugoslav state headed by Milosevic launched military activities in order to unite Serbs living in the new independent countries within a "larger Serbia". The international response was immediate: in 1992 Yugoslavia was expelled from the United Nations (and its organizations) and a trade and financial embargo was imposed on Belgrade. Despite international sanctions, attacks by the Yugoslav National Army did not stop for several years, practically up to the signing of the Dayton Agreement (Balázs-Szalóki, 2006, p. 124). The military conflict only lasted a few days with Slovenia, but there was a bloody and lasting war between Serbia and Croatia. However, the most shocking events happened in Bosnia-Herzegovina, mainly as a result of the atrocities of the Serbian army. Thus, the two underlying components of the current situation in the Western Balkans: the dissolution of the Federation and the consequences of the war are inextricably related. They continue to be closely related when it comes to the political and economic agenda of long-term stabilization and the institutionalization of relations with the EU.

III.10.2. Political and socio-economic transformation that can rightly be considered as the major new achievement in post-World War II Europe, introducing unique and unprecedentedly rapid changes in Central Europe as well, and also, a few years later in Bulgaria and Romania, followed a completely different pattern in the ex-Yugoslav countries, with the exception Slovenia. This transformation was preceded by the break-up of the federation and years-long (civil) wars, before the fundamental issues of transformation could come into the limelight. Once these issues became manifest, the overall political, economic, social and mental environment in which transformation was expected to take place had already been heavily burdened with the legacy of the previous era. In contrast to Central Europe, where a democratic and market-economy-based transformation made quick progress and led to a strong and multi-level integration into the international political, economic and institutional networks, the post-Yugoslav region became dominated by nationalistic fragmentation. This (belated) nation-building process substituted for the post-communist revolutionary changes that were instituted in Central Europe, and gave way to the establishment of autocratic political regimes. Instead of concentrating on the swift and relatively smooth introduction of democracy and market economy, the governing elites in ex-Yugoslavia considered as their most important task the preservation and independence of their nation on the one hand (in the successor states) and the integrity of the state in Serbia, on the other, first by keeping together as much of the Federation as possible, and later by preventing any further territorial losses by what for years was called the Federation of Serbia and Montenegro. No less damaging for the successful transformation and European integration was the fact that the nation-building process was carried out everywhere on the basic principle of ethnicity, an outdated and, according to historical experience, extremely dangerous and destabilizing "guideline" to create new political structures (entities).

III.10.3. The "nation-building" process resulted in three subsequent developments.

First, ex-Yugoslavia was broken up into five independent states.[111] Slovenia rapidly dissociated itself from ex-Yugoslavia and in a historically short time became member of the EU. Croatia, Bosnia-Herzegovina and Serbia were mired in wars and civil wars for many years. The disintegration process did not end, however in the 1990s. In May 2006, Montenegro voted for independence from Serbia. In addition, the future status of Kosovo is likely to further strengthen the trend of dissociation from Serbia. Moreover, the future integrity of Bosnia-Herzegovina cannot be taken for granted, either. Recent developments that are interpreted by many Serbians as further undermining the "integrity" of Serbia (Montenegro and Kosovo) may encourage Serbs living in the Serbian Republic of Bosnia-Herzegovina to leave and (re)join Serbia, bringing with them, evidently, part of the territory of the current Bosnia-Herzegovina. Finally, again for ethnic reasons, the future of Macedonia is also in doubt due to the rapidly increasing Albanian population and the changing geopolitical environment of the country following the independence of Montenegro and the future status of Kosovo.

Second, it soon became clear that while it was relatively easy to leave the Yugoslav Federation, it was much more difficult (if at all possible) to build a new state, particularly, if the first years of the new-born entity suffers from wars and heavy economic and social losses. The viability of some countries in the Western Balkans is seriously questioned. Except for Slovenia, state-building seems to have reached the "stability level" only in Croatia. Bosnia-Herzegovina is an international protectorate without any clear prospects for survival on its own efforts and resources. Similarly, Macedonia's political stability and economic viability raise serious

---

111 In Central Europe, there was just one case of peaceful separation (Czechoslovakia was split into the Czech Republic and Slovakia). At the same time, there was also a peaceful reunification (between the Federal Republic of Germany and the German Democratic Republic). The territorial integrity and state borders determined by international treaties in the aftermath of the Second World War have not been questioned in any case. In turn, the ex-Soviet Union experienced a Yugoslav-type breakup but without open wars between the new countries and Russia (civil wars based on ethnicity, religion and, simply, driven by criminal activities could, however not been avoided).

concerns. Recently independent Montenegro and Kosovo (whatever the outcome of the current negotiations on its future will be) can also be added to the list of "failed states". Serbia's political stability may depend on the future of Kosovo and the capacity of the Serbian population to accept the fact and consequences of disintegration of Yugoslavia first, and of the remaining Serbia, second. In this context, not only the domestic stability of Serbia but that of the whole region may be at stake. In any case, the new geopolitical, economic, social and ethnic realities in the Western Balkans will continue to require a strong international presence in the foreseeable future order to avoid new open conflicts and, potentially, wars. This, however, will not be able to provide any credible answer to the challenge posed by the existence of failed (unviable) states. Maintaining apparent stability at increasing high economic costs is one thing, but to create new, stable and self-sustaining states in the region is a completely different issue.

Third, for most of the 20th century, ex-Yugoslavia, along with Romania, was the largest country in Southeastern Europe. Its territory could be compared to that of the pre-reunified Federal Republic of Germany. In population terms ex-Yugoslavia was at the top of the "medium-sized" European countries. As a consequence of the disintegration, Serbia, still the largest successor country, has a territory slightly larger than Bavaria, with a population of 10 mn (out of which 2 mn live in Kosovo of whom a vast majority belong to the Albanian ethnic community).[112] The new realities will have repercussions both on the international scene, related to the much lower bargaining power of the individual states (let alone the bargaining power of "failed states"), and on inter-state relations in the Western Balkans. New state borders have been drawn up as new States were born. Fortunately, until now the border question has not emerged as a major topic of potential conflicts. The only unsettled border issue is between Slovenia and Croatia, and, whatever its settlement, it will not have any impact on the stability of the Western Balkans. However, it cannot be taken for granted that future developments would leave the current borderlines unchanged. Danger looms in several aspects: the future of Kosovo, the position and political priorities of the Serbs (and Croats) in Bosnia-Herzegovina and, no less importantly, the rapidly growing Albanian population not only in Albania and Kosovo but also in Macedonia and, to some extent, in Montenegro may become serious

[112] In order to illustrate the new geopolitical realities, the changing "physical pattern" of Hungary can be quoted. For decades, Hungary was the smallest ex-socialist country in territory and the second smallest (after Bulgaria) in population. As a result of the disintegration of previous federations in the Central and Southeastern European region, today Hungary has the second largest territory and the second largest population (following Romania in both cases).

challenges not only for the countries of the region but also for the international community with a vested interest in the stability of Southeastern Europe.

III.10.4. The wars in the Western Balkans in the 1990s had unprecedented costs in physical, human, economic and political terms alike.

The direct costs of the war can be measured in the loss of people and property, disrupted production, damaged or devastated physical infrastructure. The indirect costs manifested in the displacement of millions, the prevailing problem of resettling refugees and returning persons as well as the reconstruction and restructuring of the economy are equally serious. Moreover, although many observers tend to forget it, the wars created a new social structure apart from the ethnic composition that may have a lasting impact on the pattern of economic modernization.

In human terms, several hundred thousands were killed either in war or due to ethnic cleansing, particularly in Bosnia-Herzegovina. In that country about 250,000 people died, more than a million left the country and another million became internal refugees. Human loss in Croatia (about 13 thousand killed and another 20 thousand permanently disabled people as well as those leaving the country) is estimated to amount to USD 12 bn.

In financial terms, the total cost of the wars can be put at tens of billions of USD. In Bosnia-Herzegovina, nearly half the capital stock was destroyed and one-third of the total housing stock was damaged or destroyed. In Croatia, houses and apartments suffered a loss of about USD 3.9 bn, while the loss of productive capacity amounts to USD 3 bn. As a percentage of GDP, total war damage has been estimated at 157% of the GDP in 1995.[113] It is telling that in one decade, the difference in *per capita* income between Slovenia and Croatia grew from 30% to 100%.

The management of the refugee issue has been quite complex, involving political, economic, social and human factors everywhere. Although to various degrees, no country in the Western Balkans was unaffected by this issue. Even more, most of them were affected both as "originating" and "receiving" countries. Figures on Bosnia-Herzegovina have already been quoted earlier in this study. Croatia experienced the exodus of 200,000 to 300,000 Serbs, while it admitted hundreds of thousands of Croats (and Bosniaks) both from Bosnia-Herzegovina and from Serbia. In turn, Serbian statistics report 340,000 refugees from Croatia (221,000) and from Bosnia-Herzegovina (119,000). It is still unknown how the

[113] This figure calculated by the Croatian Government Commission on war damages includes human loss (64% of 1995 GDP), houses and apartments (21%), budgetary costs (18%), loss of production capacity (16%), loss of public companies (13%), stolen goods (9%), etc. For details see: Lakatos, *Croatia country study*, 2005, p. 48.

break-up of the federation with Montenegro will affect the two-way flow of citizens. The future status of Kosovo could lead to another wave of refugees to Serbia. Although half of the refugees and internally displaced persons returned to their home country (but not necessarily to their original home town or village), the issue is not yet settled. According to an international agreement this should happen before the end of December 2006.

While, understandably, the direct and indirect costs of the war as well as the refugee issue represent the hot topics of domestic, regional and international discussions and policies, another long-term impact has been almost completely ignored. Namely, in contrast to the economic and social foundation and the players in the Central European transformation, the Western Balkan social and business structure has been built on a different kind of "entrepreneurs". One should remember that powerful interest groups benefitted from the wars, ethnic cleansing, embargoes, etc. In addition, most of them continue to benefit from special rents, pensions and other (budgetary and extra-budgetary) support. As a result, a powerful shadow economy and community were born engaged in different forms of rent seeking, distribution of international aid, all the way to criminality. These groups may still be interested in maintaining ethnic conflicts and sub-national ethnic communities. While even in late-coming Bulgaria and Romania, part of the former communist elite transformed itself into a business and managerial class, similar transformation in the Western Balkans was generated by cross-country and civil wars. As a consequence, the emerging business and managerial class is by far from being independent from the special networks run by war criminals and other wrongdoers (for more details, see Novák, 2005).

Although the Western Balkan countries involved in wars suffered most, conflicts and open hostilities did not leave the neighbouring countries unaffected, either. During the conflicts, over half a million ethnic Albanians fled from Kosovo to Albania and neighbouring Macedonia. However, they returned to their homes soon after. Bulgaria and Romania were spared from refugees but not from the economic costs associated with the main transfer routes of trade and the international embargo against Serbia-Montenegro, in a crucial stage of their domestic economic transformation.[114]

---

[114] As international capital generally takes decisions on the basis of regional considerations, the crisis and instability caused by the Western Balkan wars diverted business attention from all countries of SEE, irrespective of their level of economic development, domestic business conditions or national strategic plans. Trade reorientation towards Western Europe faced serious external barriers in Bulgaria, for which the natural export routes led through war-ridden Serbia which was under an embargo. As always, the embargo helped the emergence and spreading of unofficial, illegal and criminal

III.10.5. Several economic costs of the wars were mentioned earlier. It has, to be noted, however, that some of the costs are not directly linked to open hostilities.

First: a dramatic decline of trade began at the moment the Yugoslav Federation was broken up, as the successor states started to create their own "national economic space". The evident consequence was the disruption of production and trade relations developed over decades in a large(r) internal market. The former internal market fragmented into small (or very small) new domestic markets. One of the most serious issues of a successful transformation can be identified in the small size of the newly created domestic markets. Until now, bilateral free trade agreements between countries of SEE could not remedy this problem, since investment activities, if available, were directed to the new small national markets, previous networks were disrupted (except for the intensive activities of Slovenian companies in the region), physical infrastructure damaged. Moreover, new international border crossings were established within the territory of ex-Yugoslavia and visa policies unfavourable to business have been implemented (or imposed) by the EU.

Second: international direct capital has failed to start major investments in the region. In contrast to most Central European countries, FDI remained absent from the Western Balkans. However, this attitude can only partly be ascribed to the wars and regional instability. No less important have been the manifest barriers to FDI activities in practically all Western Balkan countries, including Croatia. International experience indicates other possible scenarios of FDI flows in post-war periods with great demand for reconstruction. In case of rapid transformation and swift liberalization, including the recreation of the ex-Yugoslav internal market just for economic activities, the Western Balkans could have been converted into a major new location of international business. However, mainly for domestic economic reasons as well as sustained cross-country hostility (or at least suspicion) this option did not prove realistic.

Third: In turn, the grey and black economies as well as criminal activities have seen rapid growth everywhere. Of course, such activities, to some extent, were present before the unprecedented changes of the last 15 years. However, its volume and share in total production were rapidly increasing in each country. According to unofficial estimates, the grey

---

activities. According to Bulgarian estimates, the Kosovo crisis caused a loss of 2.5% of the GDP, the growth of the negative fiscal balance by 1 percentage point of the GDP, one percentage point higher inflation and a deterioration of the current account balance by 1.25 percentage point of GDP (see: Petkovan, *Bulgaria country study*, 2006, p. 18). Negative effects of the wars, particularly of the intervention of NATO in the Kosovo crisis against Belgrade were also felt outside the region, *e.g.* in Hungary (both in the form of refugees and in economic terms).

and black economy may produce between 25 to over 50% of GDP. According the Transparency International Index, all countries earn low grades, even compared to Central European economies.

Difficulties and uncertainties related to the transformation, as well as much higher degrees of personal freedom and weak institutions have created a fertile ground for tax evasion, illegal and criminal activities. However, the wars in the Western Balkan lent a different character to such activities.

Accompanied by widespread corruption, these issues are high on the agenda of the EU when preparation for institutionalized relations, including full membership of the respective countries is assessed. No wonder that even in the two acceding countries, Bulgaria and Romania, these issues have always been highlighted by the Commission. The accession of both countries in 2007 largely depends on their progress in tightening their control on criminal activities and show a good track record in fighting corruption.

Bulgaria and Romania are important transit countries for illegal drugs, weapons (Bulgaria during the Balkan wars) and human trafficking (Romania) with an East-West direction. The final destination of these products and services in most cases is Western Europe (drugs, human trafficking), while Serbia and other Western Balkan states used to be the main destination of weapons. Cigarette smuggling is widespread in all these countries. A substantial part of forged euro notes comes from Bulgaria.

However, the highest level of criminal activities is attached to Albanian mafias. Its specific feature is that it operates well beyond the national boundaries. Networks have been established not only in neighbouring and Albanian-populated countries and regions, such as Macedonia or Kosovo but in many Western and Central European countries as well (Italy, the United Kingdom, the Czech Republic, Poland). (For a detailed recent study see Reuter, 2005a.)

Fourth: wars have resulted in an additional financial burden and had to be absorbed by the central budgets in most cases. Here, we do not mention the "usual" extra costs in the form of the reconstruction of production facilities, physical infrastructure or houses and apartments. We are referring to the war veterans in Croatia, Bosnia-Herzegovina (both Croats and Serbs) and Serbia who became the beneficiaries of special provisions and, despite several years of (apparent) peace and cooperation with The Hague international tribunal, keep enjoying this special status. Two examples, one from Croatia, the other from Serbia illustrate the ambiguous legal and mental situation of the policy-makers but also of the general public in the respective countries.

While about one-quarter of the Croatian population is made up of pensioners, this figure includes about 177,000 people (or almost 20% of all pensioners) who enjoy "merit pensions".[115] Most of them are registered as war veterans (including war criminals who are considered "national heroes"). The total amount of merit pension payments reaches more than 1% of the GDP (USD 400 mn) and 2% of total government expenditures in a country with an urgent need for (public) investments in many areas.

Serbia has not published budgetary figures on provisions paid to war participants. However, a system similar to Croatia is in place. The only officially published item comes from a statement by the International Court in The Hague. According to this, the Serbian leadership guarantees support to the families of war criminals delivered to The Hague until they return home.[116] It is clear that so-called high-ranking participants of the wars enjoy a generous support from the state budget.

III.10.6. The new geopolitical realities created by the dissolution of the Yugoslav Federation and the subsequent wars have not left unaffected the external and foreign policy orientation of the individual countries of SEE either. These developments can be identified in three areas:

- disruption of historical relations,
- search for new allies and
- the emergence of new tensions among the Western Balkan countries.

Historically, the individual republics of ex-Yugoslavia did not have a common foreign policy, since, as a federal issue, Yugoslavia (Belgrade) developed and represented a joint foreign policy. After the break-up of the Federation, each country started to develop its own foreign policy and quickly applied for membership in different international organizations. Similarly, traditional relations of other SEE countries such as Albania, Bulgaria and Romania to ex-Yugoslavia underwent substantial changes. Before 1990, both due to a "united" Yugoslavia and the geopolitical realities in Central and Eastern Europe (ranging from influence to domi-

---

115 Interestingly, the largest groups of "merit pensioners" are veterans of the Second World War (74,000), followed by members of the Croatian Homeland Army between 1941 and 1945 (35,000) and "Croatian defenders" (*i.e.* participants in the Western Balkan war) (31,000). Also, Croatian members in the previous Yugoslav National Army figure in the statistics with more than 16,000 members (Lakatos, *Croatia country study*, 2005, p. 40).

116 The overwhelming majority of the Serbian Parliament supported the draft law presented by the Radical Party that all Serbian military leaders charged with war crimes should be provided special assistance to be paid from the state budget. It includes the unchanged continuation of their salary or pension enjoyed in Serbia, the covering of all costs of legal assistance as well as travel and subsistence costs twice a month for two members of the family who want to visit the defendants (Reuter, 2005b).

nance by the Soviet Union), official relations were friendly and potential ethnic and border conflicts rooted in previous peace agreements (both after the First and the Second World War) remained suppressed or unknown to large part of the new generations in all societies. The events unfolding in the 1990s increased the instability in the entire region, even though war activities did not spread to all SEE countries. However, the consequences of the wars, including the bombing and the embargo against Serbia affected other countries much more than the indirect or psychological influences. Albania had to face the most critical situation, since the dissolution of Yugoslavia with which it had developed important economic relations as compared to the country's low level of dependence on foreign trade, produced a very different situation and challenged Albanian foreign policy. The emergence of Macedonia as a new independent State, as well as the unresolved status of Kosovo, with significant or majority Albanian populations respectively, gave rise to new challenges and conflictive situations.

Although with different intensity and with some delay, all countries of SEE redefined their foreign and security policy priorities. In the second wave of NATO enlargement, also as a reward for their solidarity in offering their air space and logistical support for the allied forces' military strikes against Serbia in 1999, Bulgaria and Romania became members of NATO, while some other countries have already applied for membership (Albania, Croatia and Macedonia). In political and economic terms, each country chose its future EU membership as its main strategic priority. Slovenia has already become a member in 2004, and Bulgaria and Romania joined the "club" in 2007. Croatia started official negotiations on accession, and Macedonia has submitted its application for membership. Other countries have reached different levels of institutionalized contacts with Brussels, but all of them nourish the hope of becoming full members in the first half of the next decade.

As a result of "solving" the dangerous conflict in Kosovo and preventing a further regional war by military operations carried out by the "allied forces", the United States became a key player in the region. Both Bulgaria and Romania have repeatedly proved their Atlanticist orientation (parallel to their quest for EU membership). However, Albania became the largest beneficiary of US policies, while Serbia's relations to Washington remained strained to frozen for several years. After 1990, Russia seemed to loosen its influence in the region. However, a few years later it became clear that long-term stability in the Balkans can hardly be created without the active participation of Russia. This is clearly manifested in the negotiations on the future of Kosovo. Both on the official political level and by the majority of the society, Russia is considered as a close ally of Serbia. A more detailed survey of the role of the major foreign players, both countries and international organizations, in the development of SEE, will be offered in chapter IV.

As for the future stability and potential development trends in SEE in general, and in the Western Balkans in particular, one should also be mindful of emerging political tensions, many of which were believed to have been a thing of the past. Just the opposite, and to the surprise of superficial observers, tensions fed by old historical grievances, including issues of "justice" and "injustice" have returned to the agenda of foreign and neighbourhood policy in practically all countries of the region. A short list of such tensions is sufficient to illustrate the potential sources of future risks and uncertainties.

Albania can be considered a crucial player in this regard. It recognizes the existence of the "Macedonian nation" (still questioned by Greece, a member of the EU and NATO), but points out that it does not belong exclusively to ethnic Macedonians, due to a large (and growing) Albanian population in that country. First, Macedonia's birth as a nation was welcomed by Albania as a potential counterweight to Serbia. From the mid-1990s on, the emphasis shifted more and more to the support of the Albanian minority, going as far as to demand the creation of a two-ethnic state. Evidently, bilateral relations have worsened significantly and Macedonia accused Albania of interfering in its domestic affairs. The crisis was temporarily eased (not necessarily solved) by accepting the Albanian representatives in the Macedonian Parliament and including them in the Government.

Albania's official relations to Serbia is a way to ensure good treatment of Albanians on Serbian territory, mainly in Kosovo, but also in Montenegro and in Presevo Valley (Southern Serbia). Until now, at least at the international and official political level, Albanian politicians have advocated closer political, economic and cultural ties among ethnic Albanians throughout the region but have resisted the temptation to call for border changes and create something like a "Great Albania".[117] Montenegro's independence and the future status of Kosovo will certainly have a rele-

[117] This position has not been shared by everybody in Albania and in the Albanian diaspora in Kosovo. From time to time, militant supporters of pan-Albanism make their appearance and weapons continue to flow from Albania (and Serbia) to Kosovo and Macedonia. Even a document of the Albanian Academy of Sciences insisted that the "rightful aspiration of all Albanians is the unification of all ethnic Albanian lands in a single national state". (For more details see: Mladenova, *Albania country study*, 2005, pp. 21-24.) Also, it has to be noted that Northern Albanian communities are in favour of unification with Kosovo, for they believe that their economic condition could be improved, since Kosovar Albanians apparently have higher living standard. Due to economic considerations but, even more importantly, based on cleavages rooted in history within the Albanian society, no unanimous public support can be expected for any kind of official priorities.

vant impact on shaping future foreign and neighbourhood policies in Tirana.

Another source of instability is the relations of multi-ethnic Bosnia-Herzegovina with Croatia and Serbia. Relations with Croatia have shown progress in the framework of the Inter-State Council. Bilateral agreements on the elimination of double taxation and on carrying out sentences in criminal cases have been signed. A document titled "Guidelines for Improvement of Relations between Bosnia-Herzegovina and Croatia has been signed. The Inter-State Border Commission has agreed on the demarcation of the border, but the agreement has not yet been ratified. Cooperation between the two border police has been negotiated and the agreement on dual citizenship has been signed. In turn, little progress can be reported on reaching an agreement on the port of Ploce and on settling property issues. Moreover, in March 2005, Bosnia-Herzegovina suspended part of its free trade agreement with Croatia. Many Croatians living in Bosnia-Herzegovina are increasingly treated as a minority by Bosnian Muslims. As a result, separatist ideas have emerged among Croatians, who, in contrast to the Serbs, do not enjoy "ethnic" autonomy in the country.

Relations between Bosnia-Herzegovina and Serbia remain strained, as long as influential political forces on both sides view the history of the last decade very differently. The war has left deep memories in the minds of the current generation and can hardly be eradicated without a generation change. The influential political forces share the view that war crimes can be justified as part of fighting for "freedom". Still, some significant progress has been made. Bilateral agreements on defence cooperation, establishment of border crossings and the facilitation of the flow of people and goods have been signed. In turn, the State border treaty still awaits signing and the (re)introduction of high import tariffs by Bosnia-Herzegovina on selected items (beer, flour) imported from Serbia have caused some problems. In addition, there is anecdotal evidence of Serbian authorities taxing lorries coming from Bosnia-Herzegovina, for the use of Serbian roads. The biggest friction, however, comes from the fact that Bosnia-Herzegovina's court officially accused Serbia and Montenegro at the International Court of Justice of alleged genocide.

On the surface, relations between Croatia and Serbia could be "normalized". However, the strong anti-Serbian (and, simultaneously, anti-communist) attitude of the Croatian population cannot be overlooked. This bias has repeatedly led to a discriminative, ethnicity-based selection of civil servants in Croatia, when Croatian and a Serbian citizens apply for the same job.

Serbia's regional and neighbourhood policy is dominated by the potential further dismemberment of the territory of the Serbian state. Montenegro voted for independence in May 2006. Originally, and according to opinion polls, this issue did not represent a major concern for the majority of the Serbian population, since, in most areas, Montenegro used to function as a separate state before the referendum. The only concern used to be the freedom of travel, since family contacts are widespread and many Serbian citizens have their second house or apartment at the Montenegrin seashore.

The Kosovo issue seems to be much more serious, since, depending on the modalities to be contained in the decision on the future of Kosovo, a massive flight of the (remaining) Serbian population of about 100,000 people could not be ruled out. (These topics will be dealt with more extensively in Chapter VI on future scenarios in the Western Balkans.)

III.11. Weak States with Distorted Institutions

III.11.1. According to historical and international experience, functioning states can hardly be "produced" as a result of international intervention or "support". Recent examples can be found not only in the Western Balkans (first of all in Bosnia-Herzegovina and Kosovo), but also in other parts of the world, from Afghanistan to East Timor. Even the unprecedented financial and military involvement in Iraq has been unable to establish a functioning state.[118] Another lesson to be learnt is that nation-building has generally happened in clear opposition to foreign powers and not with their collaboration. Moreover, such a painful and socially costly process was generated by their own efforts.[119] None of these features apply to the current situation and medium-term perspectives of some of the Western Balkan countries.

Problems do not end here. There is a Definite positive correlation between the strength or weakness of the State and the efficiency or inefficiency of public administration in most countries of the world. Weak states[120] are generally unable to create and sustain an efficient public administration. In turn, deficiencies in public administration impair the capacity of the State to act both in domestic and external/international affairs.

---

118 In Bosnia-Herzegovina, the international involvement cost about Euro 6.5 bn until the end of 2005. In turn, international operations in Iraq amounted to USD 250 bn. It clearly demonstrates that there is no direct and positive correlation between the success of state-building and the amount of money made available for such pursposes.

119 Buchsteiner (2006).

120 Gligorov (2002) describes the characteristics of weak States in three points. First, a weak State demonstrates weakness of political will. Second, it is unable to project the rule of law. Finally, it faces different kinds of periodic crises (p. 12).

This interdependence has acquired a new dimension at the beginning of the 21st century. In fact, public administration is to become one of the key elements of sustainable competitiveness in the coming decades. The previously decisive role of prices, quality or delivery time in shaping competitiveness both at the national and corporate levels are losing their primary importance and are getting accompanied by new, non-economic factors of competitiveness. Beyond the social cohesion and a future-oriented mentality, an outstanding role is already played by the quality of public administration at the national, regional and local levels alike.

III.11.2. As for institution-building, SEE countries seem to be far away from international trends and requirements. It is no accident that one of the recurring requirements in the country reports prepared by the Commission addresses the development and strengthening of public administration in each country of the region. It has to be added that one of the few areas where the new member countries were lagging behind in comparison with the level of preparation for membership in Spain and Portugal, was the efficiency of public administration.[121] However, the efficiency and structure of public administration as well as the speed of its transformation and adjustment in Central Europe cannot be compared with the current situation in Southeastern Europe. Despite the undeniable progress registered in recent years, even the Bulgarian and Romanian public administrations seem much less efficient than those of Central Europe. The really big gap, however, is evident when the situation in the Western Balkan countries is examined.

Moreover, it is increasingly recognized that the performance, and thus the (future) efficiency of the state are going through dramatic changes. In order to remain successful, a new balance has to be created between the old and new tasks to be assumed by the state. Evidently, its traditional role of redistributing part of the GDP according to (old-fashioned) social equity rules is diminishing. At the same time, in several cases, the state becomes an important player in generating additional output (GDP) by its increasingly future-oriented investment activities (mainly in human

[121] The Southwestern European Mediterranean countries could rely on their experience with and the existence of a well-developed public administration created during their colonial past. In addition, the reform of the public administration and its structural adjustment to EU requirements was also easier because changes of governments and coalitions did not lead to widespread restructuring and grass-root transformation of their public administration. Unfortunately, the opposite happened in Central, and even more in (South)eastern Europe following not only the 1989-1990 systemic transformation but changes in government as well.

resources, from education through research and development to the better health of the population).[122]

Beyond the obvious global (and European) challenges, all SEE countries have a very long way to go in order to be able to cope with such challenges.

III.11.3. Although each SEE country is characterized by the weakness or deficiencies in their public administration, basic differences can and have to be identified. In a first approach, the countries of the region can be classified into five groups (without considering the special case of Slovenia):[123]

Bulgaria and Romania (as well as Albania) had to face the transformation of their old public administration as part of the systemic change. Nevertheless, both of them (plus Albania) are clear-cut nation-states, with long national tradition. Moreover, their geographic territory has not changed after 1990. Their key task was to adjust the old administration to the requirements of the new one, and where necessary, develop new functions or abolish unnecessary old ones.

a) Croatia faced the problem of creating its national public administration as a result of independence. Still, the country could rely on some previous experience in the field. On the one hand, the idea and practice of the nation-state was not alien and could be based on historical traditions. On the other hand, many Croats used to work in the central public administration in Belgrade and could use their work experience in Zagreb. Finally, due to the federal structure of ex-Yugoslavia, part of the Croatia-related issues had been always managed by the local (Croatian) public administration. Thus, the

122 The (neo)liberal definition of the overall declining role of the State as a player that hinders private (investment) resources is not easy to prove in many cases. The fact of centralizing high shares of GDP in the state budget (high taxes) is not a clear indicator of efficiency. The fundamental question is: what are the basic objectives the centralized part of the GDP will be spent on. For an interesting comparison see the "Nordic model" harmonizing social welfare with the intensified global competitiveness with the continental European "welfare state model" (Buhigas Schubert and Martens, 2005).

123 Slovenia is not discussed here. Its example contradicts the general development of public administration in the (Western) Balkan countries. Despite the fact that it became independent only in 1991 and could not rely on any experience of the former nation-state, the Slovenian public administration achieved a high level of conformity with EU structures in an unprecedentedly short time. The "secret" can be found in the early recognition of the importance of efficient public administration both in EU negotiations and in managing a new and small state. In consequence, the Slovenian public administration has not been reshaped after each government change. Moreover, the general level of education of the society (both formal and informal) resembled the developed Western European region much more than Central or let alone Southeastern European countries.

new State could make use of these human and managerial resources.

b) The situation in Serbia is more complicated. Since the physical and human infrastructure of the federal public administration remained in Belgrade, it didn't need to be created from the ground up. The challenges originate, however, in how to restructure the previous administration and downsize it both in the number of institutions, the size of the staff, and most importantly, its mentality. The public administration in Belgrade was accustomed to manage federal issues in a relatively large and certainly influential country. The current tasks are, however, different. The everyday functioning of a much smaller and much less influential Serbia has to be ensured, to a large extent, with a public administration staff that, at least partially, is hardly able to think and act according to the requirements and constraints of the new reality.[124]

c) Macedonia had to establish its own public administration practically from scratch. It could not fall back on nation-state traditions (even if it attempts to create its own history). In addition, the representation of Macedonian experts in the central public administration in Belgrade used to be much lower than of either Slovenia or Croatia. Also, the rapidly growing Albanian population and the increasing Albanian claims of proper representation in different organs of public administration and decision-making institutions do not make the task of building an efficient (and impartial) public administration any easier. Newly independent Montenegro can be added to this category, since its public administration mostly dissociated itself from Belgrade several years ago and enjoyed "administrative freedom" well before the referendum that opted for secession from the Federation.

d) Finally, in Bosnia-Herzegovina, and even more in Kosovo, international institutions are either in executing position in relevant parts of the public administration or foreign experts are actively involved in different fields of the national administration. Their sudden departure from Bosnia-Herzegovina or Kosovo would create an administrative chaos or anarchy. Thus, risks to sustainable stability loom not only in the context of the withdrawal of the security and peace-keeping forces but, no less importantly, in the potential

124 Looking at the education and language background of the Serbian public administration, its capacity is certainly higher than in other Western Balkan countries and may be near the Croatian level (Martens, 2006c). However, its growing isolation from international networks in the last decade and its old-fashioned "nationalistic" mentality demonstrated repeatedly in EU-related documents and negotiations with Brussels represent a major handicap that cannot be compensated by higher level of education on paper.

> administrative "vacuum" as well. Therefore, some experts recommend that responsibilities assumed in the last few years by international organizations should not be transferred too early, at least not before two preconditions are considered fulfilled. One is an acceptable and sustainable government in the new country. The other underlines the importance of a politically neutral policy force and an independent judiciary formed according to unanimous criteria[125] (regardless whether those criteria are formulated by German, British, French, Austrian or American experts).

The establishment of a genuine and efficient public administration has been made more difficult by a number of constitutional failures. In an astonishingly self-critical approach, the international report, headed by former Italian Prime Minister Amato, mentions both such failures and some of their consequences (Amato, 2005, pp. 165-166). Between 1994 and 2002, and in a collaboration between international negotiators and local parties, several constitutional frameworks were created in the Western Balkan: in Bosnia-Herzegovina in 1994 and, as part of the Dayton Accord in 1995, changes for the Republika Srpska in 1996, Kosovo in 2001, Macedonia's constitutional framework based on the Ohrid Agreement in 2001, State Union of Serbia and Montenegro with direct engagement of the EU in 2002. Despite the above mentioned intense efforts, one is hard put to speak of lasting success. Future uncertainties and potential risks are rooted in the intrinsic deficiencies of negotiating such constitutional framework agreements.

First, the basic principle was not the enforcement of rights but power-sharing between international actors and influential local elites associated with or personally involved in the armed conflicts of the region. Thus, an end to the war as soon as possible and "at any price" enjoyed priority over a constitution based on a popular mandate.

Second, local groups that participated in the framing of the constitution were organized and driven by the principle of ethnicity. All multi-ethnic agreements (Bosnian constitution, Ohrid agreement, Kosovo constitutional framework) ensured specified quotas for various ethnic groups. In other words, ethnic differences have not only prevailed but became enshrined in international treaties. As a ticking time bomb, this structure can not only paralyze the (normal) functioning of central institutions but also undermines the power of the central (public) administration. Many experts have been aware of these dangers from the very beginning. However, the international community's absolute priority was to reach peace, which could have hardly been possible without giving special rights to the particular ethnic groups.

---

[125] *The Financial Times*, June 28, 2006.

Third, all constitutional frameworks exacerbated the already existent, inherent weakness of the central power. For several reasons, weak states are a common feature in most of the Western Balkans. As a result of agreements with strong decentralized entities between the different (ethnic) groups, the weakness of the central state became even more manifest and anticipated. Bosnia, or the defunct State Union of Serbia and Montenegro are obvious examples. These countries, as well as Kosovo, have "parallel structures that are wholly unaccountable to the constitutional frameworks... Intrusive international structures... have near monopolies of power which are nonetheless ill-defined in crucial state-building areas (for example, security in Bosnia and Kosovo)" (Amato, 2005, p. 166). All in all, state actors became much weaker, while powerful private actors representing political parties, oligarchs or just criminal mafias not only remained untouched but turned out to be increasingly influential in building and managing public the administration.

III.11.4. Distortions and deficiencies in public administration are, however, not only the consequence of political games. Internal problems play an equally important role. Some of them will be pointed out in the next paragraphs.

A strong public administration is characterized by a stable revenue basis. In other words, tax collection has to be efficient and at a level that ensures the normal functioning of the administration. This, however, is not the case in the SEE countries in general, and in the Western Balkans in particular. The traditional tax base had been seriously undermined in ex-Yugoslavia, due to the loss of jobs and the closure or destruction of many private and public enterprises. Declining consumption and massive return to agricultural self-subsistence have cut the VAT-basis significantly. Widespread smuggling deprives the state budget of revenues from customs duties. In addition, large-scale activities in the grey and black economy as well as in the criminal sphere are exempt from any taxation. The situation is most worrying in Albania, a country that before the changes did not have anything that would resemble a "normal" tax system in most European countries. Although some elements (corporate and personal income taxes) have been introduced in the meantime, tax revenues account for only about 20% of GDP. In turn, the size of the informal economy, including criminal activities, reaches more than one-third of GDP (or the double the average of the OECD countries).[126]

While budgetary income shrank dramatically, the structure of expenditures revealed a much lower degree of "flexibility" (downsizing). In fact, downsizing is hardly possible in some countries with very low centralization of the GDP. Albania's public spending is below 30% of the

[126] IMF estimates fluctuate between 30 and 60% of GDP.

GDP, in Romania is about 30% (both on the revenue and the expenditure side), while the corresponding figure for Macedonia remains below 40% of the GDP. In turn, other Western Balkan countries have much larger public sectors. In Croatia, Serbia-Montenegro, Bosnia-Herzegovina, social welfare payments lost a lot of their original value as did unemployment benefits. However, the rapidly increasing unemployment and social poverty did not allow substantial cuts in the volume of such expenditures. Additional burden is caused by the maintenance of an infrastructure that was created to support the needs of large-scale industries under the communist system but which is very expensive in the post-industrial period. Moreover, new expenditure targets emerged recently that seem to overburden not only the financial capacity of the budget but it also compromises the professional level of public administration. A part of the challenges stems from the fragmentation of the Yugoslav Federation and the emergence of a number of small domestic markets. In country after country, different value-added taxes, tariffs, customs and excise duties were introduced. Special levies on agricultural commodities, different service sector regulations, new national standards have been imposed. Border crossing procedures became more costly and complicated. Another challenge for the SEE countries comes from Brussels, since the establishment of EU conform administrative structures is an unprecedented task both from financial and human resources perspective. Moreover, the global and European legal and institutional framework has gone through further fundamental changes. Thus, in anticipation of a successful transformation, current efforts should be rooted in this upgraded environment revealing further dynamism in the coming years. In contrast to this international context, in many areas, the previous (still Yugoslav) regulations do not meet international requirements any more.[127] Another item that seriously burdens the budgetary expenditure is the payment to war veterans (both to "criminals" and "national heroes") in Serbia, Croatia and particularly in Bosnia-Herzegovina, where such payments make up the largest part of social welfare expenditure.

It is no surprise that, under such conditions, each country tries to increase budgetary revenues. However, due to the small taxpayer base, most of the additional burden has to be borne by those who could be registered by the tax authority. As a consequence, a smaller portion of the population is paying taxes for state services provided to a large number of those who do not pay taxes at all. High taxation necessarily leads to tax evasion and a growing number of enterprises and private persons to shift their activities to the grey market and the illegal sphere of the economy.

[127] It is symptomatic that Serbia stopped to be a member in many international organizations. Renewing membership, a key element of returning to the international community, would cost a lot of money and would require professional expertise.

Another consequence of the imbalance between budgetary revenues and expenditures is that high-cost government services (mainly for the physical infrastructure) will be increasingly neglected and their quality will deteriorate over years until a point when previously made and heavily financed investments become completely obsolete and unmaintainable. This budgetary situation has a double trap for the future. On the one hand, it builds up a huge investment need in public services. On the other hand, it does not leave any space for financial support for future-oriented and competitive (private and public) activities.

Another problem of public administration can be identified in its generally low quality. This qualification calls for some explanation. In some cases, the public administration staff is indeed not sufficiently trained. In other cases, however, the new problems pose new challenges to a differently trained staff. In addition, problems of quality can also be the result of inefficient coordination, outdated structures, outdated legislation. Even well-educated public administrators are unable to overcome such burdens. In the SEE countries, examples for all these cases can be found. In Albania, the old public administration was substantially downsized after the systemic change. However, the new system has remained over-politicized, non-transparent and with a poor record of implementing regulations. Also, public officials frequently have insufficient skills at all levels.[128] Low level of enforcement, lack of transparency and insufficient skills are the hotbed of widespread corruption.[129] In Bosnia-Herzegovina, the weak control of the government has to be underlined. The central authority has to take into account the existence and influence of competing institutions at the entity and cantonal levels. The country's parliament meets infrequently. Legislation is hampered by the slow input from the Council of Ministers. Many functions that should be carried out by different departments of the government come up to the level of the Prime Minister's office that is overburdened with administrative tasks. On top of all, ethnic division plays a relevant role in the everyday operation of the public administration (on different levels). The quality of the staff of public administration is certainly higher both in Serbia and in Croatia. However, no country could yet get rid of the legacy of the self-management system of former Yugoslavia. As a result, there is still a wide range of hybrid, semi-public institutions and agencies having de facto public management and regulatory power and leaving the citizens with no institutionalized control over their activities.

---

128 It's no wonder that more than two-thirds of the firms interviewed in Tirana are dissatisfied with the work of the public administration and the regulatory system. Even more, about 80% complain of the bureaucratic behaviour of public servants.

129 A good example is that about 70% of family houses and apartments in the country have been built illegally or at least without permit.

One of the distortions of the public administration appears in the contradiction between low quality work and overstaffed institutions. Except for Albania, where the old administration was downsized after 1990, all Western Balkan countries struggle with overstretched administrations. Meaningful public sector reforms have not been implemented in any country. The underlying consideration was not only the concern about hurting vested interests of influential people but also the rapidly growing unemployment in many sectors of the economy. Thus, public administration has become a preferred way to absorb some of the open unemployment and provide relatively safe survival to many people. The number of people employed in different fields of public administration amounts to 20 to 30% of the total of officially employed people. A small country like Macedonia, with less than half a million employed people registers almost 100,000 people engaged in public administration.

Another distortion is presented in the contradiction between the "high" wages[130] and low quality of public administration in ex-Yugoslav republics. This finding contrasts with the experience in Central European countries, as well as in Bulgaria and Romania, where, for a long time, private sector wages have increased much more dynamically than those in the public sector. In several cases, and among other factors, it has led to a counter-selection in human resources in the public administration. As of today, the situation seems to be different in the Western Balkan countries. Of course, several facts help explain this "strange" situation. First, public administration was already better paid in ex-Yugoslavia than in other socialist countries of Central and Eastern Europe. This payment system has been maintained in the successor states until today. Second, better payment conditions are a relative category. They appear to be better in comparison to income levels in other parts of the economy or, even more so, as compared to the declining real value of social assistance and unemployment benefits. However, it does not mean that these wages could escape the general trend of substantially falling purchasing power. Third, it is the widespread lack of foreign direct investments that make these wages appear high. In Central Europe, the massive inflow of FDI has generated substantial and quick wage increases in the private sector (dominated by multi-national corporations) with huge productivity reserves. As a consequence, public sector wages became relatively low and a new wage system became unavoidable (with a serious additional burden on the national budgets). SEE will be facing this tension in the coming years, provided that at least some countries of the region experience larger inflows of FDI (as is already the case in Romania and Bulgaria).

---

130 For instance, public sector wages in the Federation of Bosnia-Herzegovina are 35% higher than the average salary. In Republika Srpska, the difference amounts to 57%.

A further distortion is represented by the contradiction between "strong" and "weak" State. While most of the public sector activities are less than efficient and enforcement of new laws and regulations is unsatisfactory, the State presents itself as a competent (and "powerful") actor in many areas of civil (private) life (from tax collection to unpleasant border checking and traffic control on highways and roads). For the population (and for foreigners doing business or travelling in a Western Balkan country), the competence and power of the State appear as a compensation for the inadequate level of basic State-related activities.

Finally, the ambiguous impact of international players has to be mentioned. In institutional terms, the adjustment process to EU norms can be considered as a strong disciplinary element. As part of the deepening cooperation, a number of twinning programs can be listed. As a new element, the experts and expertise of the new (or candidate) countries are also involved in these programs.[131] It is another question to what extent the building of institutions are in harmony with the priority needs and adjustment capacity of the given economy and society. Also, as it happened in CEE, institutional adjustment to the EU can create two different levels of public administration, accompanied by different professional levels, wages, priorities, networks and, not least, by diverging "philosophies" of approaching key international, regional and domestic issues.

As for other international players, several shortcomings could be identified. The unclear definition of the authority of both the High Representative in Bosnia and the Special Representative of the Secretary General of the United Nations in Kosovo need to be mentioned here. Both institutions "have extraordinary power, including the authority to override local decisions" (Amato, 2005, p. 166). In Bosnia-Herzegovina ministers had to resign repeatedly at the initiative of the High Representative, making the otherwise difficult situation even more complicated. In financial terms, the presence of international players have produced large wage and income distortions. In fact, several administrative centers have been created in the last decade within Bosnia-Herzegovina, such as Sarajevo, Mostar or Banja Luka. The large differences in income, living standards and consumption patterns appear between those employed in international agencies and those who are not.

III.11.5. Fundamental reform of the national public administrations is indispensable in all Western Balkan countries. Bulgaria and Romania are in a better position since they started adjusting their national administra-

[131] As an example, French and Slovene experts try to help the preparation of Serbia-Montenegro. The fact that Macedonian experts were able to answer about 3,000 questions by Brussels in a record time, was partly due to the involvement of fresh Croatian experience gathered in the same exercise a short time before (Judah, 2006, pp. 5-6).

tion to EU requirements much earlier. Croatia has also made substantial progress. The "EU conformity gap" is, however still wide in the other republics of the region. Overall reform concepts have been formulated in some countries. However, their implementation, both in their content and in its timeframe, raises several doubts.

The Macedonian government established an inter-ministerial Committee on Public Administration Reform in 1998. The work of this committee resulted in a strategy that was adopted in 1999. Among others, it envisages the simplification of the public administration system, strengthening the democratic spirit, protecting (and not prohibiting!) public servants from political and interest group-activities, more citizen-oriented administration, decentralization, etc.[132] All of these objectives have been included in Macedonia's official strategy of preparing for EU membership.[133]

The Serbian situation is the most complicated, since a new administrative structure has to replace an old one based on different realities (of a large federation). Furthermore, for many years Serbia was excluded from the international community. The results can be summarized in two points. On the one hand, the establishment of a "modern" institutional system is in its initial stage, as indicated by examples taken from everyday business practices (weak contract enforcement by the courts, high costs of compliance with regulatory norms, deficient land registration and administration, barriers produced by still strong state ownership, inefficient and costly border crossing procedures, poor conditions for consumer and investor protection, etc.).[134] On the other hand, Serbia had become disintegrated from international organizations. It is not a member of the WTO and lacks membership in other important international business-related organizations. According to Serbian experts, the low record of export competitiveness has more to do with non-price than with price factors. Non-price factors definitely include participation in (or absence from) international organizations and business networks. Public sector reforms have to include a reduction and simultaneous restructuring of expenditures, cutting large-scale subsidies, structural reforms and strategic assistance to modern business enterprises. Moreover, and not least, a new wage policy in the public sector has to be introduced. Certainly, this could create additional tensions, as long as alternative income sources,

132 Similar tasks have been suggested by a World Bank study to Albania (see: Mladenova, *Albania country study*, 2005, pp. 17-18).

133 For more details see: Spassova, *Macedonia country study*, 2006, pp. 20-21.

134 At the same time, it has to be noted that in 2004 Serbia started to slash more red tape than any of the 154 countries involved in the World Bank's "Doing Business" report. Starting a business venture called for 51 days and USD 5,000 in 2003, and only 15 days and a deposit of USD 500 in January 2005.

mainly to be created by foreign direct investments will remain unavailable.

III.12. On Ethnic Issues

III.12.1. Ethnic issues in SEE differ from those defined and perceived in Western Europe in qualitative terms. Their historical roots, development process, complexity and potential management cannot be compared to classic Western European models. It is meaningful that the EU *acquis* does not mention anything about the collective rights of national minorities.[135] Such rights have always been classified as part of human rights. First in the set of accession criteria stipulated in Copenhagen in the summer of 1993, minority issues entered the conditionality list, but still as part of human rights. Special attention was paid to this requirement for the first time in the context of negotiating the Association Agreement with Slovakia. However, the interpretation of "minority rights" ended at the level of covering cultural autonomy, ignoring any kind of political or institutional autonomy.

Most old EU member countries consider themselves either ethnically homogeneous or societies that have integrated guest workers, asylum seekers and citizens of former colonies from Africa, Asia or the Antilles. There are only a few example for national minorities of the member countries living in neighbouring member states. Generally, this situation has not produced any major conflicts in recent decades (after the settlement of the Austrian minority in South Tyrol in Italy). Belgium and Spain organized minorities into a federal state structure, while Finland offered large-scale autonomy to the small Swedish community in its territory. Limited autonomy was granted to Scotland within the United Kingdom. Finally, the Roma minority, a largely unsolved issue in several SEE countries, has "disappeared" from the ethnic map of countries such as Spain.

In comparison with the current situation in the EU-15 it is understandable that the old member countries are concerned about importing any kind of minority-related instability into the framework of the enlarging EU. The first wave of Eastern enlargement brought into the Community largely ethnically homogeneous countries, similar to Western European standards. The issue of the (large) Russian minority in Estonia and Latvia has not been solved, but it has been considered to be no barrier to the accession of the Baltic countries. After some sanctions by Brussels for the

---

[135] Such an initiative carefully examined by Hungary concerning its large minority in Romania, did not become part of the official negotiations between Brussels and Bucharest and did not appear in any of the country reports on Romania. Only the obligation to observe minority rights was repeatedly mentioned.

Slovak government of Meciar for not respecting certain human and minority rights in the second half of the 1990s, the new government coalition that was formed in the late 1990s not only fulfilled EU demands but included the political representatives of the large Hungarian minority in the Government (similar to Romania now). In turn, the coming enlargements will be bringing countries into the EU that are associated with serious ethnic problems – either in the form of having large minorities of other countries in their territory, or by registering sizeable minorities of their own in neighbouring countries that, in most cases, are expected to join the EU as well. The utmost attention paid to the ethnic issue has another component, too. It cannot be overlooked that there are ethnically based "national" movements on the rise in selected old EU countries. Some of them are hostile toward foreigners living in an EU country. Another phenomenon is the separatist efforts by certain minorities, such as the Flemish community in Belgium, Scotland in the United Kingdom, or Catalonia and Valencia in Spain. All in all, ethnic tensions and conflicts may become a substantial hindrance on the way to EU membership, not only because of problems attributed to the applicant countries. The high level of public concern over further enlargement has also to be taken into account, since minority problems can always serve as an appropriate scapegoat in order to delay (or even derail) further enlargement. Moreover, growing nationalism in selected EU countries (both old and new) in general, and country-specific problems with different minorities in particular can become an additional obstacle to applicant and candidate countries on their way to accession to the EU.

III.12.2. In terms of future EU membership of the SEE countries, Brussels has formulated a very rigorous conditionality on the treatment of ethnic issues. At the same time, the EU has to understand the different nature of the ethnic problems in the Balkans when assessing the efficiency of policy instruments. In its centuries-long historical development, the Balkan region was always mixed ethnically, without well-established (modern) nation-states. Over centuries, the ethnically mixed population lived under foreign domination (Ottoman and Habsburg). The creation of new states on the ruins of the Ottoman empire, and even more, the new state borders determined after the First (and, with small modifications, reedited after the Second) World War, did not and could not take into consideration ethnic boundaries. The new borders crossed ethnic lines when the new multiethnic states were formed. The state-forming ethnic group had to deal with other ethnic groups in its territory, while part of the former became a minority in another state established by another ethnic group. Expulsion, flight or different kinds of ethnic cleansing (including "peaceful" bilateral exchange of ethnic groups) reaped small and temporary "successes" seen from the perspective of the state-building ethnic community. In addition, forced assimilation by different government measures made substantial progress over the decades, at least on the surface. In this context, the creation of a federal state structure in ex-Yugoslavia may serve as perhaps the best example.

The wars in the Western Balkans have brought the ethnic issue once again into the limelight. It turned out that different initiatives over decades, including deeply-rooted inter-ethnic family networks produced little resistance once Yugoslavia split. Mutual atrocities and ethnically-driven civil wars resulted in a massive flow of refugees and internally displaced persons. Many historical wounds opened up, while new and fresh wounds were struck on all sides. The "stabilization" of the Western Balkans imposed from outside had to be launched against this reality.

First, recent wars substantially modified the previous ethnic map of the Western Balkans. The number and size of multiethnic areas have dropped, and the position of the state-forming ethnic group became stronger in quantitative terms. Currently, most new nation states have an ethnic majority amounting to 80% or more of the total population. Albania, Croatia, Serbia (and Kosovo, if taken as a separate entity) report strong "national" majorities. Minorities reduced in size and number mainly live in compact regions of the respective country. As Amato states "we can talk perhaps about multiethnic regions but no longer so much about multiethnic countries" (Amato, 2005, pp. 179-180). In turn, Bosnia-Herzegovina, Macedonia and Montenegro remained multiethnic states.

Second, the process of ethnic concentration continues on the regional and municipal level. Most of the Croats in Bosnia as well as the Serbs in this country live in a social environment in which they form the majority. Similarly, Albanians in Macedonia or Southern Serbia, or Serbs in Kosovo are characterized by high regional concentration. Decentralized administrative structures further enhance the building of "ethnically clean regions" for groups that are in minority within a given state. One of the biggest challenges is the reconciliation of the "ethnically clean" local (municipal) level with the reality of living in a multiethnic state on the one hand, and in a minority position, on the other. Thus, the overwhelming principle of multiethnic societies, a basic component of sustainable peace and stability in the Western Balkans, clashes with the reality of the ethnic composition of selected regions within the same country.

Third, the imposed multiethnic principle cannot be based on strong social support or on a conscious and responsible civil society. For imminent security reasons and in order to stop the further destabilization in the Western Balkans, the decades-long practice of international "peace creation" has not followed the long and tiresome, at times controversial road to establish genuine multiethnic societies, but gave priority to a more or less balanced mixture of the interests represented by various ethnic groups.

III.12.3. Although to different degrees and in different ways, all SEE countries have national minority problems. In addition, due to demographic changes and the impact of large-scale migration, the ethnic composition of the domestic population has started to change to an extent that cannot be ignored any more if medium- and long-term developments in SEE are considered.

Albania is a special case for several reasons. First, ethnically Albania is the most homogeneous country of the Balkans, with almost 99% of Albanian citizens. Second, large and compact Albanian minorities can be found in Macedonia (between 25 and 40% of the population) and Montenegro, while in Kosovo Albanians have a 90% majority that could easily be increased, depending on the future status of the entity.[136] Third, Albania has the only (and rapidly) growing population in SEE with a high share of young and economically active people (based on the principles of international employment statistics). Fourth, despite the apparent ethnic homogeneity, Albanians are both historically and linguistically divided into two large groups (Tosks in the South and Gegs in the North).[137] They hold different views on the future of Albania and have developed different priorities concerning the Albanian communities outside the territory of the state. The internal balance between the two groups, until now controlled by domestic political leaders, can, however, change and result in destabilizing developments. On the one hand, Albanian politics in the Western Balkans can be affected (including, of course, the type of contacts to ethnic Albanians in neighbouring countries). On the other, serious intra-Albanian (domestic) conflicts can not be ruled out, either.

Bosnia-Herzegovina is a literally multiethnic country, with a weak (and largely foreign-managed) state administration, and consisting of two parts that enjoy a high level of local independence. However, while the Republika Srpska was founded on ethnic principles, the other part of the state tried to follow the genuine multiethnic principle by creating a joint Croat-Bosniak (Muslim) community. Thus, the creation of two separate administrations contributed to the deepening of the ethnic partition

[136] Other traditional Albanian communities can be found in Greece and Serbia. However, in terms of the future of the country, but also considering regional and European stability, the rapid and often organized spread of the migration-driven "Albanian network" (from job-seeking migrants to students to criminal mafia) in various European countries (from Italy through the Czech Republic to the United Kingdom) seems much more important.

[137] Tosks are considered to have a higher living standard and being further on the path towards creating a civil society in the modern sense of the word. In contrast, gegs still show several signs of a backward society based on clan-based hierarchies.

(Mintchev, 2001, p. 24). Administrative steps were followed by the decision of many displaced citizens and refugees to return to the community where they belonged to the ethnic majority. Sporadic, albeit in this case reliable, figures support this trend. Before the war, 44% of the Bosnian population were Muslim, 31% Serbian, 17% Croatian and 6% "Yugoslav". Following the war, the ethnic composition showed some interesting changes beyond the fact that the total population decreased. CIA Factbook figures indicate 48% Bosniaks (Muslims), 37% Serbs and only 14% Croats. The shift has been in favour of strengthening two ethnic communities (Muslims and Serbs) and leading to the exodus of many Croats to Croatia. Looking at the refugees and displaced persons, about a million of them returned to Bosnia-Herzegovina by the end of 2005 (442,000 from abroad and 569,000 from within the country). Nevertheless, less than half of them returned to places where they joined the ethnic minority. More than half of them opted for towns and villages where they belonged to the ethnic majority. As a result, the previous ethnic map of Bosnia-Herzegovina has changed substantially. About 12% of the total population decided to live in ethnic majority areas. While the multiethnic character of the country has not changed, there was a clear tendency of ethnic concentration within Bosnia-Herzegovina.

Croatia's population declined from almost 4.8 million in 1991 to 4.44 million in 2001. The largest drop could be observed among Serbians (from 582,000 to just 200,000 in a decade). Starting from a low level, the number of other citizens in most of the ex-Yugoslav republics shrank as well (Slovenians returned to Slovenia, Macedonians to Macedonia).[138] At the same time, more than 20,000 Bosniaks arrived, and also the number of Albanians increased to 15,000. However, the largest increase can be attributed to Croats, since more than 250,000 Croats from other parts of ex-Yugoslavia found their new home in Croatia. In consequence, Croatia also became an ethnically more homogeneous country. Before 1991, minority population accounted for 22% of the total population. A decade later, non-Croats only represented 8% of the (shrinking) population. Another feature of the ethnic map of Croatia is that the minorities are geographically dispersed. The small number of Hungarians or Italians living near the state borders (Baranja, Eastern and Western Slavonia, and Istria and Northern Dalmatia, respectively) cannot be reckoned with as minorities with significant influence. By far the largest minority of Serbs, 4.5% of the total population, lives in small communities across the country. In fact, and in contrast to Bosnia-Herzegovina or Macedonia, the establishment of an ethnically much more homogeneous country was not

[138] Similarly, the number of smaller ethnic groups living in Croatia have experienced a decline (Hungarians, Italians and Czechs).

accompanied in Croatia by the ethnic concentration of minorities at the local or regional level.

The future will tell how resistant Bosnia-Herzegovina's multiethnic pattern will turn out (under different options of international support and peace-keeping). Failures in Bosnia should be avoided when the future of Kosovo is at stake. Kosovo is an ethnically more homogeneous state (with more than 90% of Albanians), but with strong ethnic communities of Serbs. Moreover, for decades the Serb minority governed this region. Kosovo Albanians were driven to the periphery and became increasingly alienated from the state whose citizens they were (Mintchev, 2001, p. 23). Moreover, despite ethnic division, the population of Bosnia was united by the common language. Religious differences did not play an important role in distinguishing individual social (ethnic) groups, either. The situation is completely different in Kosovo where two ethnic communities are clearly separated by language, religion and by social values as well. (See for more detail Chapter VI on scenarios of future developments in the Western Balkans.)

To be sure, Western Balkan features do not characterize the two acceding countries, Bulgaria and Romania. Nevertheless, both have their own ethnic problems. They can be classified into two groups (national minorities and Romas).

On the one hand, both countries have in their territory sizeable national minorities, namely the Turks in Bulgaria and the Hungarians in Romania. The shared characteristic is that both of them could organize themselves into political parties and become members of consecutive coalition government.

Many Turks originally living in Bulgaria left the country in the "Bulgarization campaign" of the late 1980s[139] (few of them returned in the meantime). Still, Turks make up about 10% of the (shrinking) Bulgarian population. Moreover, they are well represented in business and nurture contacts with Turkey. Most importantly, however, the Turkish party (Movement for Rights and Freedom) is represented in the Parliament and became an unavoidable factor in creating coalition governments with a comfortable majority. According to many observers, they have a (much) higher influence in Bulgarian political and economic decisions than their share in the total population would justify. In fact, they dominate important ministries, also in terms of EU membership and the utilization of EU funds (agriculture, regional development and environment).[140]

---

[139] At that time, Turks living in Bulgaria were forced to take a Bulgarian name. Those who were not ready to do so left the country.

[140] Some complaints can also be heard concerning the "ethnicization" of ministries managed by ministers coming from the Turkish Party. According to reliable and inside

Ranking after the Roma population, Hungarians form the second largest minority in Romania (1.5 million, or about 7% of the total population). They partly live in large majority areas, but also dispersed throughout the country. In contrast to the Western Balkan countries, most of the Hungarian minority does not live in geographical proximity to Hungary, but several hundred kilometres to the east from the Hungarian-Romanian state border. Hungarians have been able to organize themselves into political parties,[141] and the Democratic Alliance of Hungarians in Romania (RMDSZ) became member of two Romanian governments. This development could be considered as an important step not only in Romania's road to the EU but also in overcoming centuries-old grievances, justified and unjustified stereotypes.

On the other hand, it has to be admitted that the most important ethnic challenge in both acceding countries can be identified in the treatment of the Roma population. Romas are numerous in Bulgaria and Romania (as well as in Slovakia and Hungary). In turn, they are not heavily represented in ex-Yugoslav republics.[142] According to unofficial estimates, there are about 2 to 2.5 million Romas in Romania and another 600,000 in Bulgaria (or 10-12 and 8-9% of total population, respectively). At least two demographic developments have crucial impact on the continuous increase of the Romas' share in total population. First, in contrast to the generally declining population, the Roma population is rapidly growing. Second, Bulgarians, Romanians, but also Hungarians in Romania show a high propensity to migrate to more developed European countries (or Hungarians from Romania to Hungary). This process generates automatic and continuous shifts in the ethnic composition of both countries.

III.12.4. SEE in general and the Western Balkans in particular have remained a multiethnic region. However, the last fifteen years, in many cases accompanied with extremely high costs of wars and civil wars, have witnessed the establishment of new countries mainly on an ethnic basis.

---

information, the composition of the public administration in the respective ministry led by a "Turkish" minister reflects Turkish majority, particularly in higher ranking positions.

141 There is no uniform representation of Hungarians in Romania, since two basic concepts on the desirable future development of the position of Hungarians in Romania clash. One is based on widespread cooperation with reasonable Romanian politicians, while the other is more "militant" and fights for territorial (and political) autonomy for Hungarians. Unfortunately, this cleavage is to a large extent rooted in and transferred to the Hungarians in Romania by the (irresponsible) polarization of the intra-Hungarian political map by some Hungarian "politicians".

142 For instance, Croatian statistics report about 10,000 Romas in the country. Certainly, there are more Romas in Bosnia and Serbia, but they have never attracted media attention or large public interest. Ethnic tensions have eclipsed any other kinds of concern, social injustice and personal emotions.

European history has a large number of unfortunate examples of creating ethnically "clean" states. From a historical perspective, we can state that the efforts to produce "homogeneous" nation-states are both dangerous and condemned to failure. Changes in the ethnic map of the Western Balkan did not only increase the share of the state-creating ethnic group in total population. At the same time, new ethnic islands with the majority of ethnic minorities were created within the given state. Part of the conflict potential has been shifted from the inter-country to the intra-country level, not excluding, of course, the firm support to the given minority by the neighbouring country, where the same ethnic group is in majority Therefore, despite strong international control and equally rigorous conditionalities set by Brussels, the revival of ethnic hostilities and open clashes cannot be ruled out in the future.

Such a development fundamentally contrasts with the basic and iron rules of globalization. Multi-ethnic structures and multi-culturalism are generally considered not as a potentially explosive disadvantage, but a substantial comparative advantage in global competition. In the global political and economic arena, Europe's (and particularly the EU's) strong cards could be designed, developed and used also in competition with the "homogenizing melting pot pattern" of the United States. Unfortunately, European developments, as experienced even in some of the key and traditional (founding) countries of the European integration, are not necessarily and directly heading this way. The final outcome is still unknown and fraught with a number of embarrassing questions and justified or unjustified concerns. To be sure, the ethnic dynamism of the Western Balkans (and the Roma issue in several other European countries, mostly members or almost-members of the EU) is not a closed case and does not make policy-making easier. It is, however, a hard and fundamental test of Europe's ability, willingness and maturity in choosing and shaping the pattern of its future development to a strong, multiethnic and multicultural global player or to a continent that is likely to return to its unholy and bloody past characterized by wars and widespread ethnicity-driven hostilities.

Thus, the way of settling and solving the ethnic problems in the Western Balkans, as a joint effort of the responsible political forces in the given countries and of the European Union (and other international players), with the growing support of the public opinion everywhere in Europe, can rightly be considered as one of the most important test cases of a Europe preparing to successfully face global challenges and become a more influential global player in coming decades.

CHAPTER IV

Southeastern Europe and its International Actors

IV.1. Introductory Remarks

IV.1.1. In assessing the future development of SEE, domestic and regional developments addressed in the previous chapter play an essential role. However, the activities and impact of the international community can hardly be ignored, either.

First, international actors, in different forms and quality, are widely present in the region. Kosovo is currently managed by the Mission of the United Nations, while in Bosnia-Herzegovina the High Representative of the European Union has key responsibility. In addition, although in a less open way, international organizations help keep the stability in Macedonia. In economic and financial terms, all countries, including Bulgaria and Romania, have developed intensive contacts with international financial organizations. Simultaneously, hundreds of non-profit and non-governmental organizations are working on strengthening stability and cementing a sustainable development all over the region.

Second, all countries are exposed to global developments, even if some of them would rather not face these challenges and are trying to protect themselves against opening up and liberalizing their economies instead of consciously preparing to meet these challenges efficiently.

Third, all SEE countries are small in terms of geographic size, population and, particularly, economic performance (in terms of GDP and GDP *per capita*). 55 million people (of which less than half, about 25 million, in the Western Balkans) certainly represent a promising market in the current global struggle for new business opportunities. But low *per capita* figures calculated at purchasing power parity substantially limit the purchasing capacity of this market. The cumulative purchasing power of SEE is not higher than that of the Czech Republic, Slovakia and Hungary combined. Moreover, the Western Balkan market of 25 million people has the same GDP (at purchasing power parity) as that of either the Czech Republic or of Hungary alone. There is no doubt that the development potential of the region is high, both due to post-war reconstruction requirements and the necessity of economic modernization. High growth rates, the promise of rapidly increasing investment and consumption have already started to attract substantial international business interest and foreign capital to Bulgaria and Romania. However, the sustainability of this process or, even more, the start of such a development in selected Western Balkan countries depends crucially on the opening up of the economy, the liberal treatment of foreign capital, straightforward, market-based privatization and a generally open social mentality towards external changes and international players.

IV.1.2. Barriers that used to hinder the way of selected SEE countries into international organizations in the 1990s has been largely overcome by now. The international isolation faced by countries involved in the Balkan wars, and the non-democratic regimes during and after the wars, such as those of Croatia and Serbia have been substantially eased or fully lifted. Croatia was the last European country to become a member of the Council of Europe (not counting Bosnia-Herzegovina and rump Yugoslavia). Economic isolation could only be broken when a new government came to power in 2000 (SAA with the EU, WTO membership). Serbia-Montenegro, as a new country, joined the United Nations, the OSCE, the Council of Europe and applied for NATO's Partnership for Peace initiative. In addition, it could renew its membership in such international institutions as the World Bank, the IMF and the EBRD after 2000. Also, its foreign debts became cleared along the lines of the so-called Naples terms.[1] In turn, WTO membership of the country had to be withdrawn and the redrafted version treating Serbia and Montenegro as two separate applicants was re-submitted in February 2005. The independence of Montenegro will have further implications on membership in those international organizations in which the State Union of the two countries was represented as one entity (*e.g.* United Nations and other political organizations). More restricted is the international membership of Bosnia-Herzegovina, due to its "protectorate" status. Furthermore, the international status, and therefore membership chances, of Kosovo have still to be negotiated.

Albania's incorporation into international organizations followed a completely different way, since, before the systemic change, the country stood out as a closed state with almost no international contacts. As of today, its international relations have changed fundamentally, with membership in international financial organizations from 1991, and membership in the WTO in 2000.[2]

1 Large part of the foreign debt could be written off both in the Paris and the London Club, while the remaining debt shall be repaid within the next two decades.

2 Other SEE countries, as Bulgaria, Romania (and Slovenia) have become full-fledged members in almost all international and European political and economic organizations (including the NATO and the EU).

IV.1.3. In the last decade, the European Union became the most important player in SEE. The most comprehensive approach has been the promise of full membership for all countries in the region, based on their domestic progress, adjustment to EU regulations and the fulfilment of a steadily widening list of conditionalities. In addition, the EU is directly involved in the everyday political and administrative life of Bosnia-Herzegovina. Furthermore, Brussels plays a decisive role in the negotiations on the future status of Kosovo. According to all political observers and analysts, the EU's role will continue to grow in Kosovo after completing the negotiations.

However, the EU is by far not the only external actor in SEE. Both the efficiency of EU efforts and the pattern of development of the individual countries are influenced by the behaviour, political and economic priorities and policy instruments applied by other international players. They can be classified in three major groups:

- other global players, most importantly the United States (but, in certain cases, Russia as well),
- regional players that have special traditional contacts, economic and social relations with the region, most of them neighbouring countries,
- international financial institutions with different but generally relevant impact on the shaping of economic structures and policies.[3]

All these actors can closely cooperate with the EU as key player in the region. However, they may also have different objectives and instruments or may see SEE opportunities and risks from a different aspect or in a different timeframe. As a result, a comprehensive and no less complicated network of cooperation and individual initiatives can be developed that is not exempt from controversial elements, either.

Finally, it has to be noted that the development of relations between the EU and the SEE countries is not a one-way street. Although bilateral relations are fundamentally shaped by a "policy-maker" status of the EU and the "policy-taker" status of the SEE countries, it does not mean that the latter countries would not have their special interests, objectives and concerns that should not fully harmonize with EU priorities in all cases. However, it has to be stressed that all of them consider the EU as the key anchor of their political and economic modernization and also as a significant player in fostering regional cooperation. Nevertheless, it does not mean that they were not interested in strengthening contacts with other global or regional players. Therefore, this element has to be taken into

---

[3] Despite the undeniable influence of a large number of non-governmental and non-profit organizations, their role will not be dealt with in this study.

account as well when the EU wants to formulate and implement a highly efficient strategy in the (Western) Balkans.

IV.2. Global Players Involved in the Development of Southeastern Europe

IV.2.1. The United States is the most important and the only player equal to the EU in Southeastern Europe. In the last decade, it had a crucial role in different events with lasting impact on the region, starting with the Dayton Agreement through the military intervention in 1999 and the Ohrid Agreement in 2001, all of them crucially shaping both the future of the (Western) Balkans and the manoeuvering room of Brussels. In several cases, the USA and the EU have cooperated, although not necessarily according to a pre-agreed common strategy. Cooperation was primarily the result of previous (and failed or ambiguous) experience with individual initiatives.

The roots of the different perceptions and later treatment modalities of the Western Balkan crises can be identified in the different basic approaches to conflicts by both major players. Rightly, the USA considered developments in the Balkans as European challenges to be faced and managed by Europe in general, and by the EU in particular. Washington has repeatedly criticized Brussels for its half-hearted position in crisis situations. On the one hand, the EU has always emphasized an equal footing with the USA on international political level. On the other hand, the willingness of being equal has not been accompanied by readiness to take concrete actions. The outbreak of the first Balkan war took Brussels by surprise, despite the embarrassing member state-level diplomacy that, missing new and fresh, and more importantly, EU-level ideas, seemed to return to pre-war-patterns of big-power attitude. Immediately after the outbreak of hostilities, each larger EU member country (starting with Germany, but France, the United Kingdom and even low-profile Italy as well) revealed its special interest in supporting or opposing one or an other country. After a short period of EU-level coordination consisting in the support of saving the integrity of Yugoslavia and condemning independence efforts in Slovenia and Croatia, France and Britain started to consider Serbian-dominated Yugoslavia as an efficient partner in containing the expansion of German influence in SEE. Instead of recognizing new realities in Central and Southeastern Europe and turning their attention to future tasks, both countries returned to their outdated historical instincts.[4] The independence of Slovenia and Croatia was soon recog-

[4] Moreover, Lord Carrington threatened with a weapon embargo against all Yugoslav republics, which, definitely, became the most important support to Serbia that was

nized by Germany, while France and the United Kingdom wished to support Serbia in maintaining the federation. Italy focused on Albania, not only because of historical ties but also due to the first and massive wave of Albanian immigration to Italy. Once again, in 1995, the EU failed to play a crisis prevention role. Either due to sufficient information on ethnic cleansing or a lack of conviction that it really was going on, or to underestimating both the extent and character of the conflicts, the EU remained inactive. Once it became aware of the seriousness of the problem, it had to state that the EU's intervention capacity and readiness seemed inadequate to risk a successful peace-restoring activity. Accordingly, the peace conference on the future of Bosnia-Herzegovina was planned and implemented by the USA in Dayton, and not somewhere in Europe. Finally, the EU did not venture a decisive pre-emptive intervention against the Serbian army in Kosovo. Again, albeit this time preventing massive ethnic suffering, it was the United States that, under the umbrella of NATO (allied forces) launched a military attack against Serbia and crushed any Serbian dreams of sustaining some part of the defunct federation under the unchallenged Serbian leadership.

Crisis management in the Western Balkan highlighted two basic differences with long-term implications between the USA and the EU.

First, it demonstrated that Europe still lacked the capacity to handle regional (European) problems on its own. To be sure, the USA would have never waited for any kind of European military intervention if a serious crisis had developed in its "backyard".[5] This European attitude, whether or not it will be demonstrated in future European conflicts, made a deep impression on the American leadership with respect to the intervention or crisis management capacity (and willingness) of the EU. The conclusion drawn was that the USA had to keep its positions in Europe, particularly in the Western Balkans, either directly or indirectly (*e.g.* through the United Nations Mission in Kosovo). This approach was further intensified by the spread of international terrorism, particularly in the light of September 11, 2001 not only on official US policies but even more on the public opinion and social mentality. As a consequence of the terrorist attacks in New York and Washington, D.C., US foreign and security policy was reshaped and selected regional tensions have been

---

militarily best prepared to lead a war against other republics, while, on the surface, "negotiations" were carried out. In detail see: Martens (2006b).

5 It is another question whether US interventionist policies could have resulted in better outcome than the potential achievements of other approaches. In the second half of the 1980s, it was the EU (but mostly by direct crisis management of the Socialist International) that could fundamentally contribute to the peace-creating process in Central America and to the "demilitarization" of Nicaragua and its guerillas operating almost in the entire region.

upgraded to potential global conflicts or conflicts in which American interests could be involved and damaged. The Western Balkans were considered as one such region, not only because of the history of violence for several years, but also due to the involvement of a Muslim (*e.g.* religious) dimension in the conflict. Interestingly, this issue caused more headache in Washington in the case of Bosnia-Herzegovina than in the much larger and potentially much more hazardous Albanian population.[6]

Second, not for the first and certainly not for the last time, the approach to crisis management has demonstrated the fundamental difference between the USA and the EU as to when and how to use military force. The Western Balkans was a telling example of the different philosophies of interest representation and implementation. Particularly in case of terrorist acts and the serious risk of conflict escalation, the USA opts for a preventive military action, even if the evidence is not clear or even non-existent (see Iraq). In turn, the EU believes that there is a much larger room for negotiations before any other coercive steps are necessary. Behind the two different approaches it is not difficult to discover the different theoretical roots of strategic thinking.[7] However, these strategic differences go back to different value systems. One of the EU's distinguished "export article" as a (would-be) global player is peace keeping, the high esteem of human values, tolerance, understanding the arguments and interests of others, openness, etc. American values were shaped by history somewhat differently. The Western Balkans were certainly not the first case in which different value systems clashed. However, most probably it was the first geopolitical terrain where these values were tried to be implemented side by side.

The "clash of values" within the same civilization[8] is not only a bilateral issue. In the last 15 years, transforming European countries in

---

6 First signs of a more flexible and more balanced US approach could be detected in the last rounds of negotiating the future of Kosovo in Vienna. The previously unilaterally Albania-favoured US position started to take into account the potential negative consequences of a one-sided pro-Albanian solution not only on Serbia but also on the entire region.

7 Based on historical "reflexes" certainly strengthened by the uniquely shocking experience of September 11, 2001, the USA holds that preemptive actions may cause less harm than post-event reactions. In turn, the EU believes that such a high price can be avoided by successful diplomacy. Thus, most and potential terrorist attacks can remain contained, anticipated and "diluted" (prevented) in the framework of diplomatic activities.

8 This point has nothing to do with Huntington's view on the "clash of civilizations". However, it reflects different approaches even within the fundamentally same, Christian-Jewish culture of democracy and human rights. Business people often mention that the more artificial obstacles are eliminated in transatlantic trade and capital flows,

general, and Western Balkan countries and societies in particular, have been confronted with the issue to favour or oppose one or the other approach. The local assessment has produced interesting results. Similar to some Central European countries (mainly Poland and the Baltics), the USA has a higher level of credibility than the EU in some SEE countries. This is particularly the case with Kosovo where Albanians clearly favour the USA that eliminated the Milosevic regime, ended the atrocities of the Yugoslav army and ethnic cleansing. Not surprisingly, Albania considers the USA as the representative of its interests concerning the future state of the entity. This position was further strengthened by US initiatives to solve the question of Kosovo. In fact, the negotiations could be continued on the basis of an American plan from May 2005 that was previously discussed with other major players. Nevertheless, the plan, both on the table and, more importantly, in the minds of Kosovar Albanians, appears as if the Balkans will be stabilized under American leadership (Reuter, 2005b, p. 394).

IV.2.2. At the moment, there is a wide gap between American the political and security-driven presence in the Balkans and the actual interests of the American business community. In Albania, the political engagement is obvious, but, as of yet, it has not been accompanied by the appearance of US business (both trade and investment flows are very modest).

The situation is similar in Bosnia-Herzegovina where the USA has significant activities through its influence in international financial organizations and through bilateral schemes (USAID). In addition, in November 2005 it reinforced its political leadership by getting the agreement of eight leading political parties on changing the Dayton constitution as an expected result of negotiations to be started in 2006.[9] Beyond coming to a sustainable stability, the US strategy in Bosnia-Herzegovina is focused on fighting international terrorism. In turn, capital investments in the economy are non-existent or conducted through selected European subsidiaries of US firms (Coca-Cola).

Although Croatia shows the most evident pro-EU position among all SEE countries, specific US activities in favour of Croatia are well remembered. Partly, the USA played an important role in effecting positive changes in the political attitude of the international community related to the war and the undemocratic regime in Croatia. And the US was also

---

the more different enterprise cultures become manifest. Mergers between US and European firms (*e.g.* Daimler-Chrysler) can certainly enrich this statement with a lot of interesting case stories.

9 This initiative is aware not only of the unsustainability of the current constitution but of some EU critics as well. Namely, Brussels, from the very beginning, has criticized the Dayton agreement and holds it (and the USA) "co-responsible" for the current situation (together with Bosnia-Herzegovina politicians of different ethnic origins).

involved in the process of peaceful reintegration of Eastern Slavonia to Croatia. Evidently, this friendly attitude cannot be dissociated from the lobby activities of hundred thousands of Croatians living in the USA. No less important is the firm commitment of Croatia to become part of the anti-terrorist coalition urged by the USA.

A further sign of the strong US presence in the Western Balkans can be seen in the fact that the US was among the first developed country that accorded diplomatic recognition to Macedonia (in November 2004) without any reservation. Despite Greek consternation, Washington officially accepted the denomination of "Republic of Macedonia".[10]

Among the Western Balkan countries, US relations with Serbia are the most strained. The US does not show any flexibility as long as Serbian war criminals are not delivered to The Hague and domestic politics do not indicate a major turn towards more democratization. Several concrete US actions verify this statement. In March 2004, the US stopped its financial support to Serbia-Montenegro. Also, by making use of its voting power, the USA has frozen a credit to be provided by the World Bank and the IMF to Serbia-Montenegro (in the amount of 500 to 700 million USD). At the same time, and in contrast with icy political relations, American business sees many promising opportunities for large-scale investments in this ex-Yugoslav republic. Once the political situation becomes more favourable, both in Serbia itself and in bilateral relations, large US-based transnational companies may be interested in investing in Serbia. Some of them used to make investments in the past, when the Yugoslav Federation was economically more liberalized and open than any of its Central or Eastern European neighbours. In addition, strong Serbian community in the US may support such activities.

US relations with Bulgaria and Romania are very good. Both countries were unambiguously supported by Washington in their process to membership in the NATO. American economic interests have been increasing in the last few years, partly based on former contacts with Romania (back in the 1970s), partly relying on new opportunities. Again, the political motive to reward both states for their positive attitude during the Kosovo war in 1999 should not be forgotten.[11] In some sectors, US firms are the leading producers (and exporters) in both countries (*e.g.* sanitary equipment and 30% of electricity production in a coal-fuelled plant in Bulgaria).

---

[10] It is known that Greece, an EU member country, still resists to accept the full independence of Macedonia for it considers large parts of the territories of the new Balkan country as its historical heritage. Therefore, Greece only was ready to accept the denomination of FYROM (Former Yugoslav Republic of Macedonia).

[11] Bulgaria and Romania opened up their airspace to military actions of the allied forces against Serbia and provided relevant logistic support as well.

IV.2.3. In recent years, it has not been clear what the (secondary) thoughts and priorities of the USA are in the (Western) Balkans. Does Washington consider the increasing management of the Balkan stabilization by the EU as a factor in increased competition in global affairs, with the prospect of more transatlantic frictions? Or is the deepening EU engagement in the Balkans seen as an instrument to weaken Europe(an integration) economically and embarrassing it politically? In the medium term, the – adequate or failed – answers have to be supplied by Brussels and through the required overdue deepening of the integration in many areas (including, of course, common foreign and security policies). Nevertheless, in the short run, sustaining stability in the Western Balkans has to be considered a common and mutually shared priority for both actors. Experience from the last decade demonstrates that a joint approach by both players, as was the case in Macedonia, can only prove successful. Cooperation and more coordinated actions in this region have to be in the interest of the USA and the EU not only because this seems to be the lowest-cost approach for both of them. It is a more important consideration that the perception of the lack of cooperation or mutual mistrust between these global players (and regional ones in relationship to the Balkans) could immediately give rise to the outburst of new hostilities between neighbours or even within the same country between different ethnic groups. Using the words of one of the outstanding experts of the region, "the Balkans is certainly capable of producing problems" (Gligorov, 2005, p. 13).

IV.2.4. Beside the EU and the USA, other relative or emerging global players, such as Russia or China, respectively, have a modest to very modest role in controlling, stabilizing and developing the (Western) Balkans. Still, the growing self-consciousness and self-assertiveness of Russia cannot be ignored. It is not directly linked to the Balkans, but the latter is certainly part of the global "self-appreciation" of Moscow reflected recently in many areas of global politics. Even more, Russia has become a member of the informal Balkan contact group at the moment of its establishment in 1994 (along with the USA, the United Kingdom, France, Germany and Italy). The group was created in order to stop the war in Bosnia-Herzegovina and was revitalized in 1997 in the context of the intensifying Kosovo crisis.

There is a rich historical record of Russia's friendly contacts with Serbia. Despite the temporary paralysis of Russian foreign policy in the 1990s, the break-up of the Yugoslav Federation saw the further strengthening of these relations, as other ex-Yugoslav countries turned more towards Western Europe (mainly Slovenia and Croatia). Russia clearly supports Serbia in finding an adequate solution of the Kosovo issue. Not so much in order to preserve key Serbian interests than to avoid any precedent that could be used by separatist forces in the territory of Russia or in the "near abroad" which are considered a continuous challenge to Russian domestic (and foreign) politics. According to some experts, Moscow may even be ready to use its veto to block Kosovo's independence in the Security Council. Others refer to developments that point to the loosening of strong ties between Moscow and Belgrade.[12] In principle, Russian politics towards the Western Balkans are driven by three interests. First, as a country geographically near the conflict region and economically interested in several businesses, including large-scale energy projects, Russia wants a stable region (even if in some of the modalities of how stability can be achieved and strengthened, the EU and Russian approaches may differ). Second, Russia is aware of the importance of good relations with the USA and the EU. Both essentially support key Russian foreign policy objectives since Russia wants to become a more powerful international actor and a cooperative partner in the fight against terrorism. Third, Moscow is deeply interested in not creating any ground for further separatism in its territory or in neighbouring regions. Therefore, it stresses that the future status of Kosovo is not only highly relevant from an international legal perspective but because of practical political and security interests as well. Therefore, the solution to the Kosovo issue should have a "universal character". Any arbitrary and one-sided decision that would deprive Serbia of part of its territory and would be taken without the consent of and in cooperation with Belgrade, could prove to be a precedent in critical areas in other countries in favour of secession (separatist forces in Transnistria in Moldova as well as in Abkhazia or Northern Ossetia part of the territory of Georgia, both friends of and supported by Moscow).[13] Additional arguments in favour of a "soft" final position of Russia include the fact that, in contrast with several other countries of the Western Balkans, Kosovo has never had strong ties to Russia. In fact, this territory does not offer any strategic political or economic advantage in order to justify any unilateral and confrontational attitude.

In contrast to a clear distinction between high political priorities and very modest (if any) business activities by the USA, Russia is more engaged in the economic development of the SEE countries. Some of them, such as Bulgaria but also Romania, were decade-long (junior) partners in the defunct "socialist integration". Certainly, the current

---

12 On the other hand, international observers do not exclude the possibility that the revitalizing global foreign policy of Moscow keeps open the Kosovo issue as a "topic for exchange" or a "bargain deal" and would be ready to join a less Serbia-friendly agreement if the required "price" were paid for it in any other issue of higher political relevance (*Frankfurter Allgemeine Zeitung*, December 16, 2005).

13 Martens (2006a).

situation is very different from that of two decades ago, since most state-owned companies have been privatized or have gone bankrupt, and the state administration of economic affairs has also undergone substantial changes. Nevertheless, some personal networks have survived and new mutual economic interests emerged. Russia is highly interested in increasing its influence and control in the energy market in the whole region, by buying petrol stations (Lukoil), refineries, storage capacities, but most of all, by developing a comprehensive energy network supplying Russian oil and gas for and through the territory of Southeastern European countries.

Russia is among the largest foreign investors in Bulgaria, particularly if money coming from Cyprus and from some tax paradises are added (some of these amounts have their original owner most probably among Russian companies or citizens). In addition, Russian (and Ukrainian) business has a high share in housing and vacation resort development in several parts of the country. Due to historical contacts, there is no hostility against Russians in Bulgaria, unlike in either Poland or the Baltic countries when it comes to potential Russian investments in the respective countries.

IV.2.5. The dramatically growing importance of China in world politics and economics is not yet reflected in the (Western) Balkans. Obviously, as a member of the Security Council, China has to consent to the document that will be negotiated and approved on the future status of Kosovo. Along with Russia, it can vote against the resolution. However, there are no clear Chinese interests in the Balkans. At present, it is not an area of political and economic interest of China. In addition, economic ties with the countries of the region are sporadic. Ties were much closer in the late 1980s with the Yugoslav Federation (particularly with Serbia). However, economic decline and war-ridden countries (let alone the unintentional bombing of the Chinese embassy in Belgrade with its psychological repercussions) convinced the Chinese to stop considering Yugoslavia (or Serbia) as a potential Eastern European gateway for further expansion in neighbouring countries and in the entire continent.[14] Every country would like to attract foreign investors from all over the world. In this context, no discrimination can be mentioned against potential investments coming from China (similar to other overseas countries such as Canada, Japan, etc.).[15]

---

[14] Chinese strategy towards Europe does include the establishment of such a regional headquarter. However, final political decision has not been taken or is not known as of yet. For its rapidly growing Chinese diaspora, and intensive trade (better to say, import) flows, Hungary can be one of the regional candidates.

[15] Meaningful Serbian minority engaged in business activities in Canada can upgrade Canadian investments in this country. Based on the experience with FDI from the Asian countries, the investment decision focused on just one flagship company could

IV.2.6. Finally, another potential factor of large-scale influence has to be pointed out. It is not linked to any large country with significant influence in world politics or economic relations. We mean the cross-country organization of protests or influence-building based on religion or shared values. Ethnic cleansing in Bosnia-Herzegovina has already provoked rage and protest in many Islamic countries. Taking into account that the Western Balkans have a substantial and rapidly growing Muslim population, ethnic conflicts or political "solutions" (apparently) violating or limiting the rights of Muslims could trigger widespread protests and lead to political and economic repercussions in the Islamic world. Based on the religious diversity of the (Western) Balkans, political decisions and long-term comprehensive strategies should not ignore this factor.

IV.3. Regional Actors in the Development Process of Southeastern Europe

IV.3.1. While the most important political questions have to be addressed with the active participation of global players such as the EU, the US and Russia (in some cases even China), essential contribution to the "fine-tuned development" of the Balkans is expected to be provided by neighbouring countries. Some of them also belong to the geographic area called the Balkans, such as Greece and Turkey. Others, like Austria, Italy, Hungary, the Czech Republic or Slovenia are located in Central Europe. All of them are already members of the enlarged EU. Thus, they can highlight their interests not only on the national level but they can call attention to SEE problems and suggest policy instruments and strategies in order to handle critical situations in the framework of the EU, a global player as well.[16]

The motives of why SEE is a high priority issue of the external relations of the Central and Southeastern European countries around the (Western) Balkans can be divided into different and interdependent categories. Certainly, security concerns form one important group. Any uncertainty or open conflict in the region could have direct and negative influences on the neighbours in the form of refugees, mass migration and disruption in or serious damage to the security environment of economic cooperation. Another group comprises economic interests. Examining

---

initiate the follow-up of several other firms. This, however, is more characteristic of Hungary and the Czech Republic than to be part of realistic short- and medium-term scenarios for the (Western) Balkans.

16 In fact, Austria, Hungary, Slovakia and Slovenia were pushing the EU to start official negotiations on accession with Croatia. Officially, all of them are supporters of the further enlargement of the EU towards the Western Balkans, even if most of them emphasize the importance of fulfilling hard conditions of entry before accession.

trade and capital flows, it is obvious that neighbouring countries (either more developed or equipped with higher economic potential) have a large share in the external trade and inward FDI flows in all SEE countries. In some of them they belong to the leading partners despite their modest economic strength as compared to the major trading and capital exporting countries of Europe (and the world). It is common among them (with the exception of Slovenia) that their share in total foreign capital stock in the individual countries is higher than their share in the total trade of the given country. Third, most neighbouring countries have substantial minorities in SEE that has led to two different approaches. One can be called "passive", *i.e.*, the protection and stabilization of the condition of the ethnic minority outside the state borders of the given country (Hungarians in Romania, Serbia and partly Croatia, Czechs and Italians in Croatia, Greeks in Macedonia, etc.). The other approach is more "active" since it openly wants to expand the influence in neighbouring countries, based not only on economic contribution but mainly on religious and social values. This is the case with the Turkish engagement in Bulgaria, Bosnia-Herzegovina and other parts of the Western Balkans. Finally, the surprising revival of historical ties has to be mentioned.[17] Here, again, two groups can be formed. The first is represented by Austria (as well as, on a lower level, by Hungary but also by the Czech Republic) that during the Austro-Hungarian Monarchy had a very important role in stabilizing and developing some parts of the Western Balkans. The second has a shorter history and is rooted in sustaining or reviving ex-Yugoslav contacts. In this context, Slovenia has made substantive progress and ultimately Croatia, due its uniquely European orientation,[18] also seems to have discovered the importance of the "close neighbourhood".

IV.3.2. Austria played a crucial role in starting negotiations with Croatia during the Luxembourg and British presidency. The Austrian presidency of the EU in the first half of 2006 offered further opportunities to speed up the process and separate the negotiations with those with Turkey. According to a public opinion poll by the Austrian Society for European Politics (ÖGfE) carried out in early 2006, the Austrian (and the Hungarian but not so much the Slovenian) population is much more

---

17 As an interesting evidence, Austria and Hungary have opened up a joint diplomatic service in Montenegro (as they had it over decades of the common foreign policy in the Monarchy). Such constructions had been discussing over more than a decade in the EU, with little result. Two small member countries, based on their historical contacts and experience, could implement such a pattern within a very short time.

18 As compared to all other SEE countries, including Bulgaria and Romania, as new member countries of the EU, Croatia shows an almost exclusive European orientation. The Government's program on international relations for the period 2003 to 2007 does not mention any non-European country directly. The only exception is the USA, but fundamentally in the context of NATO membership.

supportive of Croatia's entry into the EU than for Bulgaria and Romania (although, in both cases, the overwhelmingly positive attitude was demonstrated in the Hungarian poll, but much less in the Austrian and Slovenian one).

Austria has become one of the main investors in the region, based both on its historical relations and the experience gathered during 15 years of transformation in the Central European neighbouring countries (Czech Republic, Hungary, Slovakia and, to a lesser extent, in Slovenia). Investors from Austria, mainly in the banking sector and by (partly) state-owned public utility companies such as ÖMV, are among the top players in Bulgaria, Romania and Croatia. Slovenia has never broken its special relations to other ex-Yugoslav republics and could develop a relevant network of trade relations and establish good locations for Slovenian capital export into the region. Similarly, Czech investors appeared on the SEE market after 2004, with key interest in buying electricity companies (the first one in Bulgaria).

Some more details can be provided on the Hungarian strategy towards SEE. The region is considered as one of the country's foreign policy priorities, but no less important are economic contacts and perspectives. First, trade relations are characterized by a dramatic increase of exports in the last five years (more than doubling, and with a share in total exports increasing from 5.1% in 2001 to 7.5% in 2005, despite the definitely positive impact of EU membership on intra-EU trade and the liberalization of trade relations with the new member countries). Imports also doubled in the same period, however, their share in total imports only grew from 1.6 to 2.5%. Second, SEE countries are the most important trade-surplus generating economies of Hungary. In 2005, trade surplus reached almost Euro 2.5 bn, and could fully compensate for the trade deficit with Russia (mainly due to energy imports). Considering the substantial deficit of the overall Hungarian foreign trade, SEE countries play an important role in reducing this deficit. (For detailed figures see Appendix Tables IV.3.2/1, 2 and 3.) Third, Hungary, as a late-starter (and still "premature") capital exporter[19] is among the top ten foreign investors in the SEE countries, while having an overwhelming share in Macedonia and Montenegro through investments by its German-owned telephone company (MATÁV). A list of Hungarian FDI in the region can be found in Appendix Table IV.3.2/4.

Looking at the situation from the perspective of the SEE countries, Bosnia-Herzegovina has become an attractive investment location for Slovenian, Croatian and Serbian capital (the last two mainly in the respective ethnic majority areas). In addition, Slovenian and Hungarian

[19] In detail see Inotai (2005b).

interests can also be identified. (Still, the largest investor remains Lithuania with one single project in the manufacturing industry.)

Austria is the leading investor in Bulgaria, but also Hungary and the Czech Republic are present with some large projects in the banking sector and in public utilities.

Croatia considers itself a Central European country distinguishing itself from the – historically negative – attribute of belonging to the "Balkans". Accordingly, it puts heavy emphasis on strengthening economic contacts with Central Europe (mainly Austria and Hungary), even if some barriers to intensify capital flows have not yet been eliminated and substantial legal uncertainties have remained.

Trade relations with Central Europe are important for Serbia, too. About 10 to 12% of its total trade is carried out with the ten new EU members of 2004, with clear concentration on the five Central European countries. Bilateral free trade agreements have been signed with several neighbouring countries albeit with modest results until now (essentially due to the unstable political situation and macroeconomic environment).

IV.3.3. The systemic change in all of its northern neighbours opened up unique opportunities for Greek companies. In addition, the accession of Bulgaria to the EU will create the first direct continental border between Greece and Brussels (after 25 years of being geographically isolated from the European integration). Greek economic interests are particularly strong in Albania (along with Italy), Bulgaria and Macedonia. It is the second largest investor in Bulgaria (after Austria) and its presence includes a wide range of sectors (from telecommunications through financial activities to sizeable manufacturing investments). Relations with Macedonia are well developing in the economic field. However, they are eclipsed by a psychological factor that goes back to different interpretations of historical developments. Macedonia, once part of the Bulgarian state and the cradle of Bulgarian culture, has been divided among neighbouring countries several times in the region's turbulent history. Part of this historical territory belongs to Greece and has the official name "Makedonia". Therefore, Athens is not willing to accept the official name of its northern neighbour as "Republic of Macedonia" and threatens to veto Macedonia's EU membership once the issue may appear on the EU agenda.

IV.3.4. In the context of the neighbouring countries, Turkey is undoubtedly the most influential actor. It is economically larger than all Western Balkan countries combined, with a real regional economic core in and around Istanbul. In addition, it has a population of 70 mn that is 25% more than the total population of the SEE countries under review in this study. Moreover, it has the second largest national army under NATO command. Its geostrategic role can hardly be overestimated and is likely to be enhanced in the future, both as a result of growing Turkish economic performance and the upgrading of its strategic role in the EU's energy supply and within the framework of accession negotiations. At the same time, Turkey is a strong and reliable ally of the USA that supports the country's full membership in the EU on every international forum and in all bilateral discussions with Brussels.

With the accession of Bulgaria, the EU has got the largest joint continental border with Turkey. Apart from the "special contacts" between Greece and Turkey (and most recently, Cyprus), the EU may see many new developments as a result of having expanded the union to the Turkish border in 2007.

For some countries of SEE, Turkey is a major trading partner. Turkish expansion into the region is driven by trade and until recently not very much by direct capital flows. Turkish products are widely marketed in Romania, Bulgaria, Macedonia and Bosnia-Herzegovina. Few of them are produced locally by Turkish firms. Most of them are imported from Turkey, often within the framework of bilateral free trade agreements.

Bosnia-Herzegovina, with a free trade agreement with Turkey and a two million strong Bosnian-originated diaspora living in Istanbul, considers itself as Turkey's gateway to (Western) Europe and the EU's connection to the Middle East through Turkey. Although at present, both economic reasons and a missing modern physical infrastructure substantially dampen such exaggerated expectations, one should not forget about the overall Turkish sympathy for Bosnia's Muslim population. In addition, the Bosnian lobby in Istanbul represents a really powerful group in influencing official Turkish politics and the media.

Turkish influence in Bulgaria is obvious through the political party of the Turkish minority that is not only part of the government but holds key ministry positions connected with EU funds. Moreover, the party has direct daily contacts with Ankara. Business investments are sporadic and essentially concentrated in regions populated by Turks. Some important agricultural sectors are firmly dominated by regions with a clear Turkish majority (*e.g.* tobacco and some vegetables). Nevertheless, the largest green-field investment in Bulgaria (about USD 220 mn at its multi-stage completion) has been implemented by a Turkish firm (Sisecam in glass manufacturing, employing more than 1,000 people).

Serbia-Montenegro, in principle an interesting location for Turkish goods and capital, already feels abandoned by Turkish business, due to the latter's heavy expansion in neighbouring Bulgaria and Romania.

Unclear is the future of Albanian-Turkish relations, mainly based on the common religion. Until now, Turkey has not shown a major interest in developing economic and cultural ties with Tirana and did not participate in the high-level political maneuvering around the future status of Kosovo.

Current and future EU strategies concerning the stability and socio-economic development in SEE in general, and in the Western Balkans in particular cannot ignore Turkish presence in the region and Turkish interests related to SEE. Furthermore, the progress and outcome of accession negotiations are likely to have a major impact on the development pattern of SEE. There are both positive and negative arguments on a future Turkish membership in the EU. Much less attention has been paid to the potential repercussions of any of these scenarios (membership or less-than-membership option which would be seen as exclusion and isolation by the current Turkish leadership and by a large majority of the population) on future developments in the Balkans. It has to be added that not only the current EU but the population of the acceding and candidate countries of SEE have a split opinion on Turkish membership in the EU. Concerns, fears and uncertainties are particularly vivid in Bulgaria and Macedonia, countries that had to live under Ottoman occupation for five centuries. Such adverse emotions may be strengthened by the Bulgarian experience of coexisting with a significant Turkish minority that, for many citizens, seems to have a disproportionate political and economic influence as compared to its share of the total population. At the same time, other potential consequences of the Turkish role and its influence in SEE in the future with respect to the Islamic religion cannot be assessed on the basis of current developments. Certainly, the future of domestic developments in Turkey, its relations with the EU and prospective options in selected SEE countries (mainly in those with an overwhelming or large Muslim population) will effect the emerging pattern of relationship. It is a wide-open issue whether this pattern will contribute to the further stabilization of SEE or generate new challenges both for the region and the (expanding) EU.

IV.4. The Role of Selected International Organizations

IV.4.1. In the last 15 years, a large number of international organizations have started working in SEE. They have participated both in political stabilization and in creating the conditions for the process of sustainable economic development after the dramatic transformations and, in the Western Balkan, in the framework of economic reconstruction. In this short sub-chapter, the most influential actors will only be presented in the context of EU policies. International institutions closely linked to or functioning with the active participation of the EU will not be addressed, since they are considered as different EU agencies working in line with the official Brussels politics. Some others, such as the Stability Pact, were discussed earlier.

It is always a bit artificial to make a clear distinction between political and economic organizations. There is a double interdependence between the activities of both of them. On the one hand, political stability and economic development are correlated, since without stability no sustainable economic development can be achieved. In turn, sooner or later, the lack of economic development undermines political stability. On the other hand, political institutions have to take into account economic realities when designing political plans and instruments with which the desired objectives should be achieved. Similarly, and mainly in the background, decisions and policy-advising activities by international economic (and mainly financial) institutions have always been connected with political goals of the most influential members who have greater voting power in these bodies.

IV.4.2. The most important international political player are the United Nations that, through its Mission in Kosovo, for several years has been responsible for the stability of this part of ex-Yugoslavia while officially still belonging to Serbia. Less direct impact can be attached to the OSCE (Organization for Security and Cooperation in Europe) that has regularly made its presence in national elections throughout the region. It controlled the legitimacy of elections with meaningful consequences for local and regional stability and for the shifts in power relations of the domestic political scene (including the political representation of ethnic groups). In this context, Albania, Macedonia and, most recently, the referendum in Montenegro can be mentioned. Sometimes, the scope of actions of the OSCE is not limited to an observer and controller status. In Albania, it included legal assistance in the electoral process and, no less importantly, the organization was engaged in drafting laws on property restitution and compensation.[20]

IV.4.3. Extensive experience is available on the long-term activities and obvious "policy transfer" of the most important international financial institutions, namely the IMF and the World Bank (as well as the EBRD) in the different SEE countries. In order to underline the presence of these organizations in the economic life of SEE countries, both the IMF and the World Bank maintain resident representative offices in the respective capitals.

---

20 Such actions are generally of double-edge nature. In part, they may be very helpful in the process of democratization and institution-building. In part, however, they may be taken by some politicians and part of the public opinion as an open intervention into the domestic affairs of the given country.

IMF programs are currently in place in all countries. They have played a useful role in the macroeconomic stabilization of several countries. As a result, the (apparently) more advanced countries started to reconsider the contents of traditional framework agreements with the IMF. Bulgaria has substantially loosened its dependence on IMF programs, while Romania did not conclude the second and third part of the Stand-By Agreement, due to the distance between the appropriate economic policy line represented by the IMF and the position and priorities of the Romanian government. The key dilemma and disputed priority used to be a too quick and strict fiscal consolidation required by the IMF and a larger budgetary manoeuvring room in order to keep political and social stability and give more room to structural reforms considered vital by the target countries. It is no surprise that conflicting positions have been presented by Bulgaria, Croatia and Romania, the more developed countries with imminent or realistic EU accession. In turn, consensus on top priorities was relatively easy in Bosnia-Herzegovina where the IMF conditions were in line with EU requirements. (The latter contained some additional elements with political impact, such as customs and tax reforms.)

The World Bank focuses on providing technical and financial assistance with a wide array of structural adjustment programs.[21] The main recommendations and guidelines are summarized in Country Assistance Strategies (CAS) published regularly. Most recently, social projects have also become part of the World Bank agenda. In the poorest countries of the region such as Albania, Bosnia-Herzegovina and Serbia-Montenegro, economic programs are closely linked to a poverty reduction strategy. In "richer" Croatia and not necessarily "richer" Macedonia, social programs are carried out in the framework of the SAA concluded with the EU. Although cooperation with the World Bank is considered "easier" and has a lower level of conditionality as opposed to having to negotiate and work with the IMF, missing objectives laid out in the CAS can lead (and, in fact, has already led) to the postponement of funding.

Both the World Bank and the EBRD are coordinating their technical and financial support with the EU.[22] As countries of the region reach higher levels of EU conformity, reflected in the agreement with Brussels,

21 Between 1999 and 2003, World Bank support to the region amounted to USD 3.9 bn (including planned but already approved projects). Considering the whole period of decades of cooperation between the World Bank and Romania, in this country only the World Bank built a portfolio of over 30 projects, with accumulated disbursements exceeding USD 4 bn until mid-2004.

22 A case in point is the coordinating role of the Stability Pact that brings together potential donors, including the World Bank and the EU. For instance, the donor conferences on supporting Serbia's economic reconstruction, offered between 2000 and 2003 altogether USD 3.16 bn, of which one-third was contributed by the EU.

more and more assistance tasks are taken over by the EU from other international financial organizations and become integrated into the Community's external assistance program.

Moreover, the EBRD shows an appropriate level of flexibility. According to its main mission, the London-based bank should give priority to private sector development. Since, however, the private sector is still underdeveloped, both due to the low level of economic performance and to unfavourable economic, legal and institutional conditions (a legacy of the Yugoslav economic model), EBRD loans can be used to develop the public sector as well (notably in Serbia-Montenegro and Bosnia-Herzegovina).

IV.4.4. Despite several attempts to coordinate Balkan-related financial assistance of major international players, some frictions have remained. They may have two negative results. First, the efficiency of the assistance is likely to be impaired. Second, since all SEE countries are "policy-takers", the (enforced) acceptance of different development approaches and accompanying conditions can easily create an embarrassing situation in which elements of different "imported models" contradict each other. The situation is made worse if foreign policy makers compete to sell their own models. Even more, external competition can lead to internal competition represented by different domestic power groups that happen to have special contacts to one or the other external actor.[23]

The major problems that are automatically imported by the SEE countries as a result of their contacts with international financial institutions and the EU are threefold. On the one hand, the type of governance is different in the EU and in the World Bank approach. Second, different levels of flexibility have to be pointed out. Third, and associated with the flexibility issue, expectations related to the applied policies differ.

Concerning the first, the EU approach, including its conditionalities, is driven by "enlargement governance". For all countries of the region to become full-fledged members of the EU, they have to comply with a rapidly developing *acquis communautaire*. As a result, economic and social policies are mainly motivated and determined by how to comply with EU requirements as soon as possible, even if the internal logic of

---

[23] The most advanced transforming countries of Central Europe have experienced this "model competition" in the first years of the systemic change. The EU and its key members wanted to sell the social market economy model, while the USA tried to convince domestic policy-makers of the advantage of a more liberal approach. Finally, at the beginning also Japan made some efforts in order to let accepted some important components of its development model. In most cases, the emerging development pattern of the Central European countries will represent a mixture of the Western European and the Anglo-Saxon (American) model, with predominance of the former (just due to EU membership and the adjustment to the *acquis communautaire*).

transformation (and economic reconstruction) would indicate a different option, both in terms of the policy mix to be applied, and the sequencing of reform and adjustment steps.

In turn, the IMF/World Bank approach emphasizes the key role of "development governance" in the current stage of economic development of the SEE countries. To be sure, this approach is not exempt from elements of an imported pattern, either (namely the neoliberal position of the international financial institutions). Nevertheless, it is based on the real economic and social development needs of the respective countries (Bartlett, 2005, pp. 11-12).

The differences are particularly clear in the different emphases on competitiveness, privatization, deregulation and the declining direct role of the State by the World Bank, and on employment protection, social welfare, equitable development and state-level intervention that characterizes the EU practice and is anchored in basic EU documents and legal acts.

The second difference is manifested in the flexibility of domestic decision-makers when negotiating with international actors. Negotiations on accession to the EU only leave a very modest bargaining room to the candidate/applicant country. The *acquis communautaire* has to be adopted, and no opting-out is allowed. It is a clear process of "take it or leave it". Certainly, neither negotiations with the IMF nor with the World Bank are free from strict conditionalities, some of them being stricter in the short-term than the EU legislation that, to some extent, has to be fully applied right after accession. However, the specific development needs of the respective country can be taken more into account when agreeing on the final structure of the project to be financed. In addition, IMF and World Bank programs can start within a short time period and are often accompanied by direct and rapidly felt painful consequences and adjustment costs. In turn, the EU accession process may last for a decade, with difficulties and adjustment costs spread over a longer period. However, a reversed example of flexibility can also be mentioned. International financial institutions have advised the SEE countries repeatedly to adopt a fixed exchange regime, including currency board arrangements. In fact, Bosnia-Herzegovina and Bulgaria have opted for this system, while Kosovo and Montenegro have unilaterally introduced the euro as their legal tender. Against creating this monetary and structural inflexibility, the EU's view on how would-be member countries should approach the monetary union is different, since it is based on a slow and more flexible process of real convergence (Gligorov, 2002, pp. 9-10).

Finally, the adoption of the EU *acquis* is expected not only to bring the SEE countries in line with the EU structure but, at the same time, to support a harmonization of domestic economic policies among the Balkan (and previously, among the Central European and Baltic) countries. However, many cases indicate that the "adjustment capacity" of individual countries is rather different. Therefore, even by trying to reach the one-size-fits-all goals and instruments determined by an external actor[24] (now by the EU), the outcome may be quite uneven (or, in some cases, even chaotic and highly counterproductive). In contrast, although by far not always, the international financial institutions formulate more country-specific recommendations or the target countries can choose among different approaches (particularly if they can convincingly argue in official and informal discussions) instead of automatically accepting a uniform model offered by the World Bank.[25]

24 Such programs are regularly supported by specific EU funds.

25 This is what happened to the recommended three-pillar pension reform that was not accepted by various Western Balkan countries. The exercise resulted in heterogeneous approaches and practices (Bartlett, 2005, pp. 12-13).

CHAPTER V

Evaluation of the Key EU Approach to Southeastern Europe

The Politics of Conditionality

Similar to several other bilateral relations of the EU with other countries or regions of the world, the pattern of Brussels' relations with Southeastern Europe can be described as a classic "policy-maker" and "policy-taker" pattern. One pillar of this pattern is the widely different political and economic weight and influence the two actors represent. The other pillar is rooted in the fundamental behaviour and negotiation strategy of a dominant club, namely the (enlarging) EU that sets clear conditions for the entry of any potential new member. This position significantly widens the existing gap between the bargaining power of the policy-maker and the policy-taker(s).

Still, during the negotiations the policy-taker is never fully deprived of some room to manoeuver. Its passive or active approach to the given topics affects both the achievements during the negotiation period and much more in managing the consequences of the agreement in order to get the best possible conditions. Since membership in the EU has a large number of short- and long-term consequences, its economic and social benefits and costs can sometimes be influenced and modified substantially depending on the active or passive strategy of the policy-taker country.[1]

This chapter is structured the following way. First, based on theoretical and practical experience, a general assessment on the efficiency of policy transfers will be provided. The second part goes into details of the conditionality policy of the EU. The next two parts devote special attention to the policy-taker side, namely the SEE countries. On the one hand, the reaction of the SEE countries to EU policies and conditionalities will be briefly described. On the other hand, the social and behavioural framework of the policy-taker countries will be surveyed, since the active

[1] Of course, the same holds for the internal distribution of costs and benefits between potential and real winners and losers. In few cases only we can speak of an unavoidable predestination (predetermination) of the distribution of positive and negative effects.

and passive attitude of the subject of the transfer (and conditionality) policy as well as the overall public opinion can be considered as important elements of the functioning and the degree of efficiency of the policy transfer. The special mixture stemming from inherited values, attitude and mentality as well as of new, imported (and many times imposed) priorities and instruments can largely be modified by the behaviour of the policy taker country (including its social groups, institutions or even individual citizens).

V.1. Evaluation of Policy Transfers: Some General Remarks

V.1.1. In a deeply interdependent world such as our global community, many policy transfers take place each day. Most of them, however, do not have an institutionalized or contractual form. They are "just" part of the high level of internationalization in which most States and national economies participate, although at different degrees and with highly different mixtures of policy-maker and policy-taker components. The rules of international trade and capital flows, financial markets and exchange rate developments influence our everyday life as much as technological standards and progress or consumption preferences.

In turn, professional literature understands policy transfer as the flow of policies from one country (or group of countries) to another country (or group of countries), based on institutionalized relations. Evidently, such relations can be of a very different nature and define the cooperative (voluntary) or coercive role of policy transfers. The most one-sided and imposed form of policy transfer could be experienced by countries that, in their history, have lost wars (see the strong US presence in shaping the West German and Japanese societies after 1945). Over centuries, colonial rules imposed by Western European countries largely determined the development pattern of most African and Asian countries. The EU, with its *acquis communautaire*, trade and aid policies follows a much more peaceful and cooperative way, even if the objective, namely the acceptance of its special values by the policy taker, may be similar. The means, however, with which the enforcement of special values is expected to be reached have nothing to do with military intervention. The main channels of transaction are political and economic contacts, special agreements and cooperation at the level of institutions, non-governmental organizations and citizens. In the case of Central, Eastern and Southeastern European countries, we can speak of a high level of voluntary transfer, since all of them have emphasized for a long time the strategic importance of the process of "Europeanization" which practically means adjustment to and membership in the EU, considered as the anchor of their sustainable security and development.

V.1.2. The result of policy transfers is generally measured by its efficiency. However, "efficiency" is a rather vague and relative concept. A policy transfer may be considered effective for the policy maker (the country that transmits policies) but not necessarily to the policy taker (the destination of transfer). Furthermore, the priority objectives to be achieved by policy transfers may differ widely, starting from the prevention of armed conflicts to political stabilization to narrowing the gap in economic development. In addition, the materialization and perception of advantages or disadvantages of policy transfers are highly time-dependent. Some results appear in the short term, while others, sometimes contradicting the short-term outcome, need much more time. Also, time-dependent discrepancies may emerge between policy maker and policy taker countries. Thus, the efficiency of a policy transfer can be seen in view of converging or diverging developments in the countries involved.

The EU's main objective in the Western Balkans differs from its priorities in the Central European transforming countries. Whereas policy transfer to Central Europe (as well as to Bulgaria and Romania) has been driven by guaranteeing a smooth and quick transition towards democracy and market economy structures, policies towards the Western Balkans have focused on conflict prevention and immediate control of dangerous and destabilizing ethnic and other hostilities. As of today, the efficiency of policy transfer can be measured by how successfully further hostilities and ethnic cleansing could be stopped. However, it does not imply by any means that the roots of potential conflicts have been irrevocably contained or eradicated.

Favourable economic conditions, including free access to the EU market and upgraded EU financial assistance may contribute to high growth rates and economic modernization. Nevertheless, such instruments can hardly accelerate the process of (desperately needed) nation-building. Simply, the instruments and the time required to achieve such different goals are highly divergent.

Another important element of "efficient" policy transfer is the flexible treatment and openness of the value package offered. Elements of the package should be in conformity with the real needs of the policy-taker country (or community), or at least leave some room for their partial contribution to the final package. It would be a very short-sighted and mistaken approach if the EU wanted to stabilize the Western Balkans only because it would not like to have wars and ethnic problems at its doorstep. In order to avoid the trap of "footloose stability", more has to be done, including some rewarding elements for the policy takers (such as the clear perspective of EU membership). Moreover, the "export" of the values of a policy-maker country or community can only be successful if a receptive mindset and the sufficient critical mass of absorption capacity are available in the target country. The fact that EU policies have proven more or less successful in country after country in Europe can be explained by the different levels of adjustment capacity and willingness of the individual policy takers.[2] The roots in the Western Balkans can be found not only in the historical legacy such as delayed nation-building or long-lasting foreign occupations. In the future it is no less important to take into account the emergence of weak or failed states that are hardly able to contribute to the efficiency of policy transfer. Just the opposite, their artificial survival supported by short-term Western European security interests aggravates the problem since they are fully exposed to the objectives of policy makers in the region, without any noticeable capacity to create a more appropriate "policy mix" for their adjustment.

V.1.3. Many attempts at transferring special values, policies and instruments have ended in complete failure, with serious consequences for all participants involved. It is a general experience that unilaterally imposed policies do not work even if they have a carrot and stick approach. However, if the carrot is not tailored to the immediate needs of the policy taker, they tend to be of little help. Free trade agreements among the SEE countries or costly and unpopular adjustment to the EU *acquis*, with, for instance, comprehensive visa restrictions are certainly not in line with the most important priorities of the policy taker societies.

Another problem arises when the policy maker does not define the instruments to reach its objectives with the transfer, or they applied differently in different countries. It contradicts not only the principle of "equal treatment" but seriously questions the accountability of the policy maker country as well.

Moreover, the passive or even opposing role of the target countries can be reckoned as a major source of failed policy transfers. On the one hand, justified criticism has been often expressed that policy packages to be transferred do not satisfy the genuine interests of the "beneficiary" countries. On the other hand, it has to be acknowledged that in many cases the latter are either uninterested or unable to develop an active attitude in negotiations with the policy makers and/or prepare for the consequences of the transfer. In some cases, like in Serbia, one can even find open opposition to adjustment to EU rules. It is the all the more surprising since the Yugoslav Federation used to be considered by many as the most "European" in the Eastern part of the divided continent. Now, it seems that decades of political neutrality and more contacts with West-

[2] Such a difference does not only characterize the new and future member countries. 25 years of Greek membership in the EU is the most telling example of a highly inefficient adjustment, despite the transfer of huge amounts of financial resources. In turn, less money worked a "miracle" in Ireland and generate the fundamental economic and social modernization in Spain and Portugal.

ern Europe have not necessarily strengthened the European character of that society, rather it was the temporary result of the Cold War. This, however, is a completely different adjustment pattern from the one required by today's realities.

Finally, failures can be ascribed to the lack of experience and direct contacts of policy-transferring politicians and experts with local conditions in the target countries. In this context, the EU's personal decisions in different areas of Brussels' Balkan politics can hardly be described as "great" choices.

V.2. EU Conditionality: Facts and Impact

V.2.1. From the very beginning of its existence, the European integration formulated conditions for admission to the club. The Rome Treaty (1957) already stipulated two basic conditions, one geographic and another political (system-related). Accordingly, countries applying for admission had to be European countries and democratic states.[3] During the long process of almost 40 years, no new conditions were created, although four rounds of enlargement took place (without considering the membership of the ex-GDR in the framework of German reunification).

However, with the manifest aspirations of the transforming Central and Eastern European countries, Brussels (and politicians of the member countries) came to the conclusion that new barriers to accession have to be established. This initiative was driven by doubts concerning the stability of Europe's transforming region going through dramatic political and economic changes. In addition, the EU did not have any clear strategy for the case of this unprecedented (and, in fact, largely unexpected) political sea change. It was believed that the establishment of new conditions may prolong the politically unstoppable process of "Eastern" enlargement and the "old" EU may buy additional time for its own and necessary adjustment. As a result, the Copenhagen criteria were formulated that included five points. Four of them are related to the status and adjustment process of the candidates and address one political, two economic and one legal-institutional requirements. The fifth condition, however, had nothing to do with the level of preparation and EU-maturity of the would-be members, but pointed to the ability of the EU to admit new countries. While the last criteria became part of the first comprehensive EU strategy on enlargement to the East (Agenda 2000), its state and progress were not analyzed in the regular country reports that started to assess the annual progress of the candidates from 1997 on. These reports were strictly

[3] It was not necessary to point out the market economy requirement separately since it was understood that democratic states must have a market economy. Democracy and market economy mutually suppose each other.

based on four (instead of all five) Copenhagen criteria. This approach was complemented by one or more monitoring reports following the signing of the Accession Treaties in order to control the process of further adjustment in the period between the Accession Treaty and the date of accession.[4] The possibility to introduce safeguard clauses after accession in case of non-fulfilment of commitments laid out in the Accession Treaty can be interpreted as another hidden conditionality. This may gain special significance if the monitoring report postpones the accession date. While the "threat" to introduce safeguard clauses was faced by the first-wave of "Eastern" members as well,[5] the date of accession was not "either-or" but fixed on May 01, 2004. For Bulgaria and Romania, the time span of accession, in rigorous reading of the text, lasted from January 01, 2007 to December 31, 2008. In fact, no new conditions were introduced, since the two-year period seemed to be an excellent opportunity to keep the instrument of conditionality alive. In addition, the monitoring process was sustained after accession.

V.2.2. The situation in the Western Balkan countries (and, not least, Turkey) is remarkably different. Some of the differences can be explained by the internal development of the EU. First, the more members the Union has, the more special interests and suggestions (or "threats") have to be taken into account. Second, each round of enlargement brings new experience that Brussels wants to incorporate into its next negotiation agenda. Third, the EU is constantly changing and new areas of community-level policies are involved in the everyday practice of the integration. Evidently, the constantly enriching *acquis communautaire* forms a part of the negotiation agenda.[6] The later a country starts negotiating, the more

---

4 The time lapse between the two events was less than one year in case of the enlargement in 1995, but increased to one year in case of the first wave of "Eastern" enlargement and to more than 20 months for Bulgaria and Romania (in the case of the optimistic scenario of joining as of January 2007). The difference can be explained by technical reasons, for the enlarged EU needs more time for ratification by each of the national parliaments of the member countries (plus the European Parliament).

5 While all countries got some yellow and even red cards in the monitoring reports, no safeguard clause was applied after May 01, 2004. Whether all countries have made such successful progress just in the last months before membership can be doubted. Therefore, either some of the warnings were not fully justified or waiving safeguard clauses followed the political logic of equal footing from the very beginning of membership (except, of course, the transitional measures that form part of the Accession Treaty).

6 Portugal and Spain had to negotiate about 40,000 pages of *acquis commmunautaire*, mainly concerning agricultural issues. The Central European countries were faced with an *acquis* of more than 80,000 pages covering a large number of new community policy areas that had not existed at all two decades ago.

chapters it has to negotiate on.[7] Fourth, negotiations do not occur in a vacuum but are constantly influenced by the overall political and economic environment in the EU, including trends in the public opinion of the (leading) member countries. In a domestic political and socio-economic situation that is not favourable to further enlargement, politicians can hardly resist growing domestic pressures that demand the continuous tightening of conditions for further enlargement (or even to stop the process). Thus, the package of conditionalities may be "enriched" by an important domestic (intra-EU) factor as well.

Nevertheless, Western Balkan countries face a serious challenge by a number of additional conditionalities mainly deriving from their history of the last 15 years. They have been built into the different Copenhagen criteria, and form a part of the enlarged set of political, economic and institutional requirements. Some of them are closely related to the institutionalized framework of cooperation (SAP and SAA), others are linked to specific areas of financial assistance. The largest part, however, stems from the key political agreements that have been expected to stabilize the region (UN resolution on Kosovo, Dayton, Ohrid, the State Union between Serbia and Montenegro).[8]

Indeed, the annual country reports are drafted similar to previous reports on Central European candidates. However, the contents are more extensive and the emphasis is more on the special (new) conditions. This study does not intend to make a comprehensive comparison of the annual reports, neither between countries, nor in terms development over a period (progress made by the given country within a period of several years according to Brussels' view). We will not discuss the interesting monitoring reports on Bulgaria and Romania, either. We will concentrate on the new conditions that can be divided into four parts.

V.2.3. Political conditions have been significantly tightened and enlarged, due to the general political situation in the region, including the consequences of wars. Strengthening political stability in weak states, cooperation with international organizations, meaningful progress in establishing reliable and politically neutral legislation and judiciary systems, the creation of a conscious and influential civil society and fight against crime and widespread corruption take up a large part of each country report. Some requirements have to be met as a precondition of membership. Some others, however, will not disappear with membership (not even within five to ten years, when most Western Balkan countries

7 While the Central European countries as well as Bulgaria and Romania had 31 chapters on the negotiation agenda, this number increased to 35 for Croatia and Turkey. This is partly due to new topics and partly to the restructuring (splitting) of previous chapters.

8 For a detailed analysis see Altmann (2005, pp. 205-206).

may have realistic prospects to join the EU). For instance, it is naive to think that corruption can fully be eradicated before membership.[9]

The really new elements can be found in three areas: ethnic and minority issues, the treatment of refugees (including their resettlement) and cooperation with the Hague tribunal. Concerning the minority question, the EU is characterized by the contradiction between the absence of an adequate legal framework (*acquis*) and the practical implementation of this conditionality. In the absence of an *acquis communautaire* on minorities, it can deal with this question only in the framework of general international obligations addressed by the Council of Europe in Strasbourg. This limitation notwithstanding, the minority issue already emerged as a topic regarding the political conditions in the renegotiation of the Association Agreement with Slovakia after the split of Czechoslovakia. It became a regular issue in the next decade with respect to the countries of the first-wave of EU enlargement.[10] However, due to the ethnic conflicts in the Western Balkans, the issue acquired a completely new dimension. The ethnic map of the region has undergone substantial changes in the last decade and small states based on ethnic principle have been created. The multi-ethnic character has changed, either because of the declining share of non-majority population or due to the shift from the country level to the level of specific regions and communities within the individual countries. Still, the multi-ethnic character prevailed at the state level both in Bosnia-Herzegovina and Macedonia (in the latter, with substantial contribution by the EU). Moreover, with the independence of Montenegro another multiethnic state has appeared on the Balkan map. The treatment of ethnic problems will not be facilitated by the agreement on the future of Kosovo either, whatever the solution may be. All these factors explain the utmost attention the EU is devotes to the minority issue.

The resettlement of refugees and internally displaced persons is a common element of all SAPs and SAAs. It emerges in its most developed legal and practical form in Croatia. Previous laws based on ethnic principles and automatically discriminating against non-Croats concerning accommodation, job and other issues, have been changed in conformity

---

9 Schwarz (2006).

10 The European Parliament's support for Romania's EU membership puts a clear emphasis on the importance of meeting the commitments concerning the minority rights of the Hungarians (including the financing of Hungarian-language higher education, the return of Church property and the approval of a comprehensive law on minorities in line with the principles of subsidiarity and self-governance). Still, an appropriate law on minorities has not yet been approved by the Romanian Parliament. Restitution covers only 3% of previously confiscated (nationalized) property and obvious deficiencies remain in the field of Hungarian-language education.

with EU rules. This can be attributed to the high number of refugees (from Bosnia) and displaced persons (from Serbia), but also to the most advanced stage of institutionalized relations with the EU. Without solving this problem in a clear legal manner, Croatia could have hardly started official negotiations on accession.

Cooperation with the Hague is one of the hottest conditionalities formulated by the EU. Upgrading of the EU-related status of a given Western Balkan country crucially depends on its willingness to cooperate with the Hague tribunal. Croatia has extradited several (alleged) war criminals before the key person, Gotovina could be found. In March 2005, negotiations on accession could not start because Zagreb's cooperation was not considered sufficient. The EU itself was split on this topic, since some of the member states argued for starting negotiations without fulfilling this condition, while others, the majority, wanted to show a clear precedent for strict EU conditionality (Kusic and Claudia Gruppe, 2005, pp. 230-231). Then, in October 2005 negotiations started, although Gotovina was not yet delivered to the Hague, but reliable information has already identified his place of residence. In turn, Serbia could not or was not willing to find Mladic and Karadzic. Although, starting in November 2004, lower-ranking Serbian generals (from Serbia and Bosnia) have gone voluntarily to The Hague,[11] it did not impress Brussels. In consequence, negotiations on a lower level of cooperation have been frozen.

V.2.4. According to the Copenhagen criteria, economic conditions include the establishment of a functioning market economy and restructuring in order to cope with external competition. Individual country reports indicate that SEE countries are on different levels of reaching the above goals. Even Romania got the qualification of "functioning market economy" shortly before concluding negotiations. At present, with the exception of Croatia that is considered as a functioning market economy (but not yet a competitive one), none of the Western Balkan countries meets the two economic conditions. The process of economic restructuring, including the closing of uncompetitive state-owned firms, market-conform privatization, liberalization of activities for FDI, shows a highly differentiated picture. In addition, in most countries the reshaping of social networks is in its initial stage.

One special country-related economic requirement has been formulated in the 1999 annual report on Bulgaria. It concerns the closure of the Kozhloduy nuclear plant since it was considered ineligible to meet the EU

[11] It is interesting and contrary to the Croatian practice, that they were not handed over by the Serbian government. The voluntary act of "true patriots" was chosen in order to save the country from material loss and international isolation (Reuter, 2005b, p. 402).

level of safety.[12] Bulgaria was obliged to follow EU conditions if it wanted to start negotiations. Therefore, it signed a memorandum on decommissioning the plant in November 1999, shortly before the positive decision of the Helsinki summit on opening the way to official negotiations. However, this condition created substantial uneasiness and even open opposition in domestic political and professional circles and, in the best scenario, generated "mixed feelings" in large segments of the society.

The truly new element of economic conditionality was the implementation of regional free trade before opening accession negotiations. It was thought that the "common economic space" could compensate for the costs stemming from the disintegration of Yugoslavia and the establishment of small and partly economically unviable states in the region (Amato, 2005, p. 178). Such a request by Brussels was also incorporated into the Association Agreements with the Central European countries as well. However, regional cooperation and free trade (that, by the way, had not become reality up to the very moment of accession) did not become a strict precondition of negotiations (not even a condition for concluding accession talks).[13]

V.2.5. At first glance, legal and institutional conditions have not changed, except for the continuous growth of the *acquis communautaire* to be adopted and enforced. However, a closer look shows that some important but largely neglected "technical" details contain additional conditionalities. One is the voting procedure linked to Romania's accession. The general EU rule is that following the signing of the Accession Treaty, membership can only be impeded by the unanimous rejection of all member countries. In turn, originally, in case of non-compliance with EU requirements, Romania's membership could have been delayed until 2008 by the negative vote of a two-third majority of the member countries. This condition was created when in 2004 it turned out that Romania was substantially lagging behind Bulgaria in many areas. Based on the positive experience of the last two years, this conditionality was lifted in May 2006. It has to be underlined that such a conditionality has never been formulated *vis-à-vis* Bulgaria, so that, in fact, the EU created a provisionally differentiated treatment between the two countries.

Three additional conditions have been introduced into the negotiation process with Croatia (and Turkey). The most important change is that the applicant country has to show an adjustment record in several cases

12 Similar requirements were part of the EU conditionality list in case of Lithuania, Slovakia (and partly the Czech Republic) as well. Lithuania's Igmalina plant is not allowed to continue its operations, while the Slovak and Czech plants (including those constructed recently) do not have to stop generating nuclear energy.

13 A detailed analysis of free trade agreements among the SEE countries dealing with their advantages and deficiencies can be found in Chapter III.2.

before starting negotiations on the *acquis* of the respective chapter. In previous negotiations, such a condition was not set or was only required in order to close the chapter. Another difference from previous negotiations lies in the possibility of a Commission decision that in its report to the Council (practically the position paper of the Commission) the opening or the temporary closing of negotiations (or both) on a given chapter can be linked to the fulfilment of special conditions. The third new element already stressed by Brussels in the early stage of negotiations with Turkey is that the Commission can reopen any temporarily closed chapter at any time and at any stage of the negotiations if specific conditions are considered unfulfilled. In principle, the possibility of reopening chapters was a part of previous negotiations as well. However, such an action was strictly considered in technical terms, if, for instance, similar topics or overlaps appeared in two or more chapters or the development of the EU *acquis* during the negotiations would have made the reopening inevitable. In effect, the new condition (or the new interpretation of the general rule) can prove a "useful" instrument to delay or stop negotiations at any moment.

Another seemingly technical issue has to be mentioned that may substantially influence the speed of negotiations as well as the general perception of how much progress has been achieved. In contrast to the road map followed in earlier negotiations and based on starting with "easy" chapters in order to report on the success of the negotiation process, Croatia and Turkey (and other would-be candidates) have to face a mixture of "easy" and highly complicated chapters already in the early stage of negotiations.[14]

V.2.6. The condition that the EU has to be willing and open to accept new members is part of the Copenhagen criteria. However, it has never been emphasized in the process of previous enlargements. More importantly, a more exact definition of how to interpret the EU's readiness to enlarge has never been created. However, following the big bang enlargement in 2004 (and its completion by Bulgaria and Romania in 2007 or 2008), politicians and the public opinion strongly voice their doubts about the viability of the integration in case of further territorial expansion. Based on the argument of "enlargement fatigue", the ability and willingness of the EU to keep the promise of the enlargement process

[14] To be sure, the Commission has a wide arsenal to slow down or even stop negotiations without "discovering" new conditions. The delayed preparation of reports and position papers by the Commission is a well-known instrument. Between October 2005 and April 2006, in half a year of negotiations with Croatia, the screening of only four chapters could be accomplished, but in two of them the EU has not yet produced the corresponding report. In addition, Zagreb was requested to present just one position paper out of four.

alive is seriously questioned. Evidently, the "fatigue" or the growing uneasiness and mounting domestic problems have nothing to do with the enlargement in 2004. On the contrary, even according to the official statement of the Commission, this seems to be the most successful enlargement that has not entailed any disruption in the normal functioning of the EU institutions. The problems are partly represented by global challenges for which many EU countries and societies have not been sufficiently prepared. Moreover, politicians and societies are increasingly experiencing the difficulties and potential social tensions of implementing fundamental growth-oriented reforms and of making the labour market more flexible in key member countries. Also, the obstacles to further integration in crucial areas of traditionally strong national competence have to be added (creating a full-fledged internal market for energy, transportation and financial services, let alone the development and implementation of common initiatives in the field of foreign and security policy, justice and home affairs, migration, etc.).

Still, whatever the roots of the growing opposition are to further enlargement, the fact is obvious. Thus, all Western Balkan countries have to be prepared to deal with a more reluctant EU and, no less importantly, to face a less enthusiastic public opinion in several member countries. Fortunately, there is a new promise that the list of conditionalities will not be further expanded. In this context, the summit concluding the Austrian presidency in June 2006 agreed on two basic points. First, the enlargement ability of the EU has to be taken into account when designing the road map for the accession of new member countries. Second, and more important, the "absorption capacity" of the EU, whatever its definition would be, shall not be determined as a new and additional condition for accession of current and future candidates.

V.2.7 Conditions formulated by the EU have a mixed track record. In many cases, the apparent success is obvious, while in others the EU had to suffer a setback.

Without any doubt, the biggest and most comprehensive success was achieved in the substantial speeding up of the preparations for membership by Bulgaria and Romania. Despite still existing deficiencies (partly marked by a "red card" in the latest monitoring reports) both countries achieved great progress. Concerning their level of preparation for accession, although having been in some areas significantly behind the new member countries, they were clearly ahead of Croatia, let alone Turkey. According to the annual surveys of Deka-Bank in Frankfurt, on a scale from 0 to 100, in the last two years Bulgaria could improve its rating from

59 to 65 and Romania at an astonishing speed from 41 to 63 points.[15] Certainly, the new member country with the previously poorest progress record, Lithuania earned 74 points, while Croatia's rating stood at 59 (and Turkey's at 49).[16] The development confirms the positive impact of conditionality, as previously experienced with countries in the first wave of "Eastern" enlargement. In the latter case, Slovakia's delayed catching up was a spectacular success of EU conditionality, but also other new member countries benefited from the "benign imposition" of external conditions.

Concerning the Western Balkans, the political achievements have to be highlighted.

First, transparent EU presence and the clear message of Thessaloniki in 2003, namely that all countries of the region may become members of the EU once they fulfil the conditions, has had a relevant stabilization impact in the whole area, particularly in the most turbulent conflict regions. After 1999, certainly not independently from the experience with the military intervention of the allied forces, further wars in the region could be prevented. Even more, the possibility of new armed conflicts has been substantially reduced (if not yet fully eliminated).

Second, the preventive role of the EU has to be acknowledged. It is well demonstrated by the role played in the Ohrid agreement on the status of Macedonia and the prevention of potential ethnic conflicts between Macedonians and Albanians. The appeasement process in other parts of the Western Balkans also showed clear progress. Again, the quality of institutional relations with Brussels, and, more precisely, the proximity of negotiations (and future membership) have played a crucial role.

Third, and most important, Croatia made a strategic decision that accession to the EU was considered more important than creating a "greater Croatia". (Serbian, and partly Albanian, leaders still have a long way to come to this conclusion.) Although the firmness of the decision is yet to be proven against potential future "ethnic storms", in the Croatian case the EU conditionality policy could break the overruling principle of ethnicity. This happened for the first time in the modern history of the Western Balkans. The conditionality-driven improvement of the situation in Macedonia is far less stable. Nevertheless, the Ohrid agreement can rightly be considered as an anchor to keep Macedonia's territorial integrity.

---

15 It was partly due to the new government that considered the timely EU accession of the country their absolute top priority, not only in political declarations but also in everyday activities. Thus, it produced a "To do list" in 2004 comprising the main tasks in accordance with the EU requirements.

16 For more detail see Appendix Table V.2.7.1.

Finally, the success achieved in the extradition of supposed war criminals has to be mentioned, mainly by Croatia, but, partially, also by Serbia (and Bosnia). In this context, however, we have to note that the rules of the cooperation between Brussels and the International Criminal Tribunal in The Hague are not sufficiently clear. One has the feeling that The Hague is sometimes stricter and less flexible than Brussels. Are the EU-related decisions on this issue really made in Brussels or are they transferred from The Hague and automatically adopted and applied by Brussels? In any case, this conditionality only partly comes from the EU, even if it is Brussels that has to" "instrumentalize" this objective.

In the economic framework, all bilateral free trade agreements have been signed. Thus, at least on paper, one of the conditions of starting negotiations with the EU can be declared accomplished. The future will show to what extent the letter and spirit of the agreements will be observed. In addition, it has to be seen how much these agreements (and their upgraded version of a multilateral free trade scheme) will not only be implemented but interpreted by the participating countries as a substantial instrument toward socio-economic growth and increasing economic interdependence with mutual benefits.

Not surprisingly, progress in the transposition of EU legislation, institution-building and absorption capacity was the most pronounced in Bulgaria and Romania. Enhanced initiatives were not only driven by compliance with EU norms but also by getting access to the largest part of the pre-accession fund from EU budgetary sources for economic, social and institutional development.[17] Western Balkan countries will need much more time to adjust to the EU *acquis*.[18]

Finally, it has to be noted that EU conditionality has started to shape public opinion as well. Successful adjustment to the EU cannot be limited to meeting political and economic conditions. Its sustainability badly needs the support by the majority of the society. This, however, can hardly happen without a simultaneous adjustment of the citizen (although not at the same speed). The successful transformation and integration of Central Europe but also the advanced stage reached in Bulgaria and

---

17 For example, Bulgaria completed its plan to manage national funds in the SAPARD framework (earlier than most of the new member countries). According to a multi-annual plan, SAPARD staff, which is expected to efficiently manage all money coming from the Common Agricultural Policy (including direct payments) from the moment of accession, will be increased by 450 people that started training in 2004.

18 As the example of the new member countries shows, transitional agreements with reasonable time limits can be negotiated (*e.g.* in the costly application of selected environmental rules). However, based on their current situation and level of development, time for adjustment needed for most of the Western Balkan countries is well beyond the "reasonable" limits.

Romania could not have been achieved without profound changes in social behaviour and mentality. This process has hardly started in the Western Balkans, due both to their historical legacy and, in several cases, the existence of weak states.

V.2.8. For a balanced picture, several shortcomings and setbacks of the EU conditionality policy have to be discussed as well. Some of the problems come from discrepancies (target conflicts) between the essence of EU conditionality and the priorities of the reconstruction and transformation process in the Western Balkans.[19] Others can be attributed to the much lower support to painful but necessary domestic reforms both by a majority of the political elite and, despite pressing poverty, dominant public opinion. These "externalities" should, however, not hide the mistakes that the EU has committed and those it may commit in the future, unless some approaches, both in content and form, are revised and adjusted to real conditions.

In political terms, several examples can be mentioned. In the early 1990s the EU supported a united Yugoslavia. Later, the independent republics of the ex-Federation were not recognized by all member countries simultaneously. In the mid-1990s Brussels did not intervene in the wars that caused the death of hundreds of thousands of people. The EU's position on Milosevic was equally controversial (by first negotiating with him, including him in the Dayton agreement and then bringing him to trial in The Hague). Moreover, the EU (along with other important external players) has completely misunderstood the fall of Milosevic in Belgrade in 2000. It was emphasized that a new era may start without bloodshed. As a matter of fact, however, all that happened was that they preserved the old regime without Milosevic but with the most influential politicians, generals, policemen and security chiefs under the Milosevic system (Reuter, 2005b, pp. 379-380). The imposition of a State Union on Montenegro in the spring of 2003, in order to keep at least part of ex-Yugoslavia together, proved a major failure. This artificial structure has never functioned and created a lot of (hidden) conflicts, particularly in Montenegro. The referendum in May 2006 put an end to "Solania" (the project named by its most fervent supporter, Javier Solana, the EU's special commissioner). The mistake was aggravated by creating an absolutely undemocratic rule (another but extremely dubious EU condition) of requiring 55% of votes for a valid decision in favour of independence. (For more details on Montenegro as one of the future challenges to the EU, see Chapter VI.) Finally, the floating of the future status of Kosovo

[19] Evidently, there was no full harmony between the two priorities in the new member countries either. However, the gap was narrower, conflicting areas were fewer and the political and social support to continue both processes, despite eventually higher economic and social costs, was stronger.

over several years has to be pointed out. Initially supported by the United States, Brussels did not want to address this issue. However, reluctance, delay (and ignorance) nourished Serbian (nationalist) hopes that this area may forever belong to Serbia. One can only hope that big political failures will not be repeated once the Kosovo negotiations enter their decisive stage and the outcome will very much depend on the position of the EU (which, at the moment, is as vague as ever).

Both in political and economic terms, the biggest mistake would have been to delay accession by Bulgaria and Romania by one year.[20] In this context, the enlargement fatigue and narrow-minded domestic political considerations of some (Western) European leaders clashed with the paramount task of bringing the two countries into the EU in January 2007. The potential application of some safeguard clauses would not have changed the general situation. The argument that the two countries could have gained one more year for better preparation was both hypocritical and counterproductive. First, the coercive side of conditionality can much better work once a country is a full member and feels the daily pressure of further adjustment than in case of an "outsider" and highly disappointed country. Second, postponement would not improve either the economic performance or the institutional capacity. On the contrary, it could have discouraged foreign (and domestic) investors and made the public administration either lazy or far too "innovative" to immediately find several new priority areas instead of concentrating on successful adjustment to the (costly and complicated or contradictory) EU requirements. Moreover, coalition governments that had been formed to demonstrate political stability in the crucial pre-accession period could have been easily dissolved and a domestic political crisis and lasting institutional instability might have followed. Finally, it is very difficult to anticipate the negative impact on the respective societies. To be sure, anti-EU sentiments would have been on the increase propagated by demagogic and populist politicians (who are, unfortunately, numerous in almost all EU member countries as well).

The application of the regionality principle (beyond free trade) seems to conflict with the original goals of this conditionality. More progress in EU-related adjustment is rewarded by more financial funds, assistance, incentives and, not least, by the upgrading of institutionalized contacts with Brussels. As a result, the Western Balkans, instead of converging, is on the way to increased divergence and a widening gap in development. This hits unfinished states especially hard, with an obvious negative impact on regional stability (Van Meurs and Weiss, 2005, pp. 10. and 12).

---

[20] For more detail see Inotai (2006).

One of the most important and alarming setbacks can be seen in abandoning the original and correct conditionality of "standards before status" developed by Michael Steiner, the previous head of the UN Mission in Kosovo. Based on the Kosovo conditions, he wisely formulated that no status talks on the future of Kosovo can be started until selected key norms of democracy are efficiently enforced. This principle was then transferred to the desired treatment of other Western Balkan countries as well. It meant that before talking about the status of relations with Brussels, all countries have to fulfil a list of requirements (called standards). However, this conditionality was first diluted by reducing the number and lowering the required quality of standards. Most recently, the interrelation of the two elements showed a complete reversal. Even more regrettably, the current situation cannot be interpreted either as "status before standards" but much more as "status without standards". Croatia convinced Brussels that its EU-related institutional status needs upgrading in order to meet some standards that would be difficult to be achieved due to domestic political and social resistance. Albania's unexpected signing of an SAA could only happen in the context of this harmful change, since a number of basic conditionalities (key standards) have certainly not been fulfilled.[21] It is clear, that other (failed) countries such as Bosnia-Herzegovina and Kosovo are also demanding changes and getting higher status without offering anything in exchange.[22]

In contrast to the clear but abandoned principle of "standards before status", many other conditionalities set by Brussels lack clarity and enforcement capacity. In the annual country reports, Brussels reserves the right to differentiate among various stages of fulfilling requirements, but without defining the criteria of assessment (Calic, 2005, p. 9). Several conditions are vaguely formulated, so that nobody knows whether or not the steps taken or the reforms implemented reach the required level. It is not less problematic for the EU to evaluate the real progress made by the

21 After (!) finishing SAA negotiations with Albania, Brussels asked Tirana to speed up administrative and economic reforms, to ensure freedom of press, to fight efficiently against corruption and organized crime and to establish conditions to the independent status of the judiciary. As if these requirements had not been among the basic demands well before any substantive negotiation.

22 The situation is perfectly described in the following way: "Kosovo has successfully argued that it can only fulfil Steiner's catalogue of standards once it has independent status. Bosnia has persuaded the EU to give it SAA status although serious deficits on basic criteria remain. Once it had been given SAA status, Croatia convinced Brussels that its progress towards EU standards actually required the instruments and incentives of candidate status to produce further results. The conflict between the vicious circle of "no standards without status" and the virtuous circle of "status after standards" cannot be resolved as long as the stabilization of the region and its entities or states is not pushed with a targeted and relevant menu of conditions and incentives" (Van Meurs and Weiss, 2005, p. 13).

individual countries and make realistic comparisons on the basis of which transparent and viable strategies could be developed. Even lacking objectivity, such reports automatically generate competition among the Western Balkan countries that is further exacerbated by the characteristically bilateral treatment of the individual countries.[23]

In principle, the regatta rule could be very useful in establishing benchmarks that should be reached by all countries. In this context, differentiated positions do not necessarily mean growing divergence but a good opportunity to catch up and redouble adjustment efforts. However, the same principle also envisages the goal of keeping the region together. This means that any progress made in one country has to be accompanied by a similar (or some) progress in another country, irrespective of the actual achievements. For instance, Croatia's start of official negotiations cannot be separated from the negotiations on the future of Kosovo or the signing of an SAA with Albania and the launch of SAA talks with Belgrade (that were interrupted in May 2006 because of the non-fulfilment of a key political conditionality). As can be seen from the above cases, the EU record of conditionality is rather uneven and unpredictable. Some cases demonstrate that conditionality is "melting down", while in other cases, suddenly, it will be applied in full strength. It creates a different situation for the decision-makers of all countries involved in this "conditionality network". The picture becomes even more embarrassing when it turns out that the evidence of "strength" of the other side is a particularly convenient instrument to dilute EU conditionality. In effect, this is what happened in Kosovo where public disorder, street demonstrations and criminal acts (including the plundering of holy Serbian monasteries) can, at the end of the day, be rewarded by the status of independence. What really has happened and is happening can be described as the fact that the EU "accepts threats and potential eruption of violence as a legitimate instrument of politics." (Martens, 2005b)

The widespread use of double standards can also be mentioned in this type of failures. They can be widely found between old and new member countries and are certainly not helpful in strengthening the social and political trust in the EU at a critical stage of post-accession adjustment. However, the adverse impact is no less harmful in the Western Balkans. Before the freezing of SAA negotiations with Serbia, there were periods when Croatia was evaluated differently from Serbia in the case of the extradition of war criminals. The rules were applied in a much stricter form for Croatia. When Zagreb complained in Brussels about the unequal

[23] It has to be noted that all accession negotiations of the EU have been carried out on a strictly bilateral level. In this way, the originally given dominant policy maker position could be further strengthened *vis-à-vis* a policy taker country that was not allowed to join modest forces of other countries in the same position.

treatment, Rehn, the enlargement commissioner answered that a candidate country has to be treated stricter than a country that is still far from this status.[24]

In sum, the conditionality issue, accompanied by the above mentioned merits and deficiencies, has wider implications than its everyday history in the Western Balkans. Three elements have to be highlighted.

First, the transparency and objectivity of the use and implementation of the conditionality principle indicates the quality of cooperation between Brussels and the member states. Any kind of member state "Alleingang", be it direct or through the Council, may undermine the reliability of this important EU instrument.[25]

Second, double standards, the country-specific application of conditionalities designed for the entire region, including bilateral diluting or different interpretations from country to country, are likely to question the anchor role of the EU in the Western Balkan, including its ability to keep peace, order and contribute to sustainable development. As a consequence, such a situation would enhance the efforts of each country to imitate its "more fortunate" or "less coerced" neighbours and further dilute EU power.

Third, the EU's ability to create stability and prevent conflicts in the Western Balkans has a global message as well. In many crisis-ridden parts of the world Brussels is considered as an honest broker able to achieve objectives with peaceful means and in cooperation with local communities. Thus, success or failure of the EU's policies in the Western Balkans has global implications by influencing the acceptance of the European integration as a leading (peace-keeping and peace-spreading) power.

V.3. EU-related Policies in Southeastern European Countries

V.3.1. Despite various critics, the overwhelming view on the role of the EU in the SEE region is positive. All countries emphasize the positive impact of better access to EU markets. Also, Brussels' financial transfers and the EU's favourable role in economic restructuring and institution-building are acknowledged. The emphasis on the advantages of coopera-

---

24 Kusic and Claudia-Gruppe (2005), p. 240.

25 According to a Bertelsmann discussion paper, the lack of coordination between the Commission and the SAP on the one hand, and the activities of Solana and the Council (representing the member countries) on the other hand, have "substantially reduced the leverage of Europe and the consistency of EU leadership in the region" (Van Meurs and Weiss, 2005, p. 13).

tion with Brussels is stronger in those countries that, either based on historical experience or on the current state of their country, do not believe that they are able to make the necessary changes without this external anchor.

Nevertheless, the sustainability of success largely depends on the active policies of the SEE countries. In this chapter a short overview is offered about those areas where the respective countries started to formulate and implement active policies and not only fulfil what the EU has prescribed as conditionality for current and future relations. In the Western Balkans, Croatia, Macedonia and Serbia-Montenegro have approved national strategies concerning their process of adapting to the EU and/or have designed target-oriented action plans in order to eliminate the deficiencies mentioned in the SAP reports.

In the next paragraphs, the political, institutional and economic actions will be reviewed, followed by a summary that describes some of the frequent problems and shortcomings.

V.3.2. Political contacts among the SEE countries in general, and within the Western Balkan group in particular have intensified substantially in the last few years. Certainly, the Stability Pact assumed a crucial role in the beginning, but genuine bi- and multilateral relations started to develop as well. Countries involved in ethnic hostilities and were both the generators and victims of massive refugee flows and internal dislocation of many people have set up adequate agencies and reshaped and harmonized their legislation in line with EU requirements in order to ensure a relatively quick and peaceful solution to the problems. The post-Tudjman government of Croatia introduced significant modifications in its refugee policy, including issues of citizenship and residence, property repossession, reconstruction, occupancy rights, security, war crime arrests and amnesty and economic conditions.[26] Interestingly, also the Roma minority got adequate attention (and some money for the implementation of selected projects), although, in this respect, Croatia does not face the same kinds of problems as some other Central and Southeastern European countries. Following the open ethnic conflicts in Macedonia (carried out mainly by Albanian gangs), the government asked the EU to help in the professional training of their police force. Moreover, Croatia tries to settle its border conflict with Slovenia in line with international standards for dispute settlement.[27] Finally, the cooperation with the Hague tribunal can

[26] For more details see: Lakatos, *Croatia country study*, 2005, pp. 31-32.

[27] On its part, Slovenia has warned Croatia that any dispute about the Piran bay and the common sea border could lead to a Slovenian veto on Croatia's membership or already opposition during the official accession negotiations. Experience shows that such national warnings, particularly if they come from small countries, will be settled within

be mentioned. In this context, the record is ambiguous. For a long time, government institutions did not show the required readiness to cooperate. On the contrary, they seemed to work together with wanted war criminals instead of delivering them to the tribunal. Once the pressure of EU conditionality was felt, the attitude started to change. Croatia has implemented most of the measures that were required, while Serbia's cooperation remains fundamentally in doubt.

V.3.3. Activities in institution-building included the reform of the judiciary, legal harmonization and the restructuring of public administration according to the preparatory tasks to adopt EU structures.

Commission reports have repeatedly pointed out the weakness of the judiciary reform in several countries, not least in the acceding ones, since its adequate state is considered a basic precondition for membership. Bulgaria, in particular, was repeatedly warned, including red cards contained in the last monitoring report. The government developed a four-year program that did not satisfy the EU (looking at the potential accession date of 2007). Therefore, the process had been speeded up and most of the corresponding laws have been approved by the Parliament shortly before joining the EU in January 2007. The package included such important elements as the implementation of the new penal code, structural changes guaranteeing the checks and balances between separate powers, greater responsibility of the judicial bodies, clear separation of the prerogatives of courts of justice and the Prosecution Office, faster procedures and quicker and a more efficient professional and administrative operation of the courts and the introduction of an Integrated Information System for Combating Crime. No doubt the new government became much more active in the last minute, when the accession date of 2007 was seriously questioned by some EU officers.

As far as the Western Balkan countries are concerned, substantial progress can be registered in their legal harmonization. Bosnia-Herzegovina has received a long list of tasks to be carried out.[28] Several requirements have been met in recent years. Still, the implementation (enforcement) of these measures is significantly lagging behind in many fields. Macedonia is aware of the importance of successful legal harmonization, since many of its products and services can only reach EU markets once some basic adjustments have been made. However, until now, in spite of enjoying a candidate status, not much has happened. Serbia has created a mechanism (similar to that applied in the new member countries in the same period of preparation) in which every draft bill must be accompanied by a state-

the EU before they could create bigger damage (see the Austrian protest against the construction of a Czech nuclear plant near to the Austrian border).

28 See: Bassa, *Bosnia-Herzegovina country study*, 2005, pp. 7-9.

ment on compliance with the EU *acquis*. Even more, Montenegro, with its separate (and recently independent) public administration, requires a mandatory statement on compatibility of draft bills with EU standards.

The perspective of EU membership, including the challenge of several stages of this long process, has convinced most countries relatively early that successful adjustment is not realistic without substantive reforms in the traditional and (generally highly) ineffective system of public administration. In the first stage, decision was taken on the highest level of competences: *i.e.*, who should be in charge of coordinating EU-related politics. A few countries have created a special ministry for European integration, others made it the responsibility of the Prime Minister's office, yet in other countries it is the Ministry of Foreign Affairs that is entitled to exercise most of the coordinating functions. Irrespective of the character of the highest level, in all countries most ministries had to establish special departments dealing with EU issues.

Bulgaria quickly realized that restructuring and functional separation, even in their perfect form, do not automatically create an efficient and EU-conform public administration. Therefore, intensive professional courses (including language and computer skills) have been introduced to train public servants. Originally, the project was implemented in nine pilot administration units and was introduced on all public administration levels at the beginning of 2006. Understandably, special attention was paid to the development of administrative capacities in areas directly related to EU funds. In Bulgaria, it was not only the utilisation ratio of the EU pre-accession fund that created problems (until the end of August 2005 only 45% of the available funds was contracted[29]) but the efficient monitoring of how to use resources as well. Therefore, a new body within the Council of Ministers was established in order to supervise projects funded by the EU budget.

V.3.4. Active economic efforts concentrated on trade liberalization, structural modernization and agriculture. The EU's uniform and Autonomous Trade Mechanisms (ATMs) provide duty- and quota-free access to the export of most manufactured goods from the SEE countries, but particularly from the Western Balkan economies.[30] It is easy to see why all SEE countries made serious efforts to create improved conditions for foreign trade. First, they wanted to make the best use of the opportunities

---

29 Unfortunately, the current record, including one more year of EU resources, only shows a utilization rate of about 20%.

30 According to experts, this scheme is more generous than the much advertised EU program of "everything but arms" offered to the least developed countries, let alone the asymmetric (but, at the end of the day, reciprocal) preferences provided under the Europe Agreements to Central and Eastern European countries (Michalopoulos, 2001, p. 9).

offered in Western European markets. Second, although not everybody was convinced of the high economic importance of regional free trade, all of them signed bilateral free trade agreements as a precondition for upgrading institutional relations with Brussels.

Competitive pressure, legal harmonization and the urgent tasks of domestic economic transformation generated large-scale structural transformations in Bulgaria and Romania, even if the process was not smooth and several difficulties had to be overcome. Relative to the inherited structure, meaningful changes have also taken place in Albania. In turn, the ex-Yugoslav republics, including Croatia in many areas, remained rather reluctant with regard to privatization and economic liberalization.

Finally, one shouldn't ignore the negative phenomena either. It may be surprising but unfortunately true that most countries did not put special emphasis on agriculture. Several factors, such as the high level of employment in this sector, its capacity of self-subsistence in critical periods, its inherent comparative advantages and better export possibilities have been either ignored or overlooked. Neither were the potential dangers of free trade and EU membership for an outdated and uncompetitive agricultural sector seriously reckoned with.[31] As a result, none of the SEE countries has designed a comprehensive agricultural strategy. Their own activities only included legal and institutional adjustment to EU requirements but nothing happened to the real economy, without which all kinds of "perfect" accommodation to EU rules remain nice legislative documents without any tangible economic benefits. Progress to accommodate EU standards was measured in setting up SAPARD agencies (important, if there is any productive activity to be financed), in preparing for the Integrated Administration and Control System (provided that there is an output to be administered and controlled), in managing common market organizations and rural development activities (a difficult issue without sizeable agricultural production).

V.3.5. In order to arrive at a balanced evaluation of their efforts, difficulties in the process of developing and sustaining their own initiatives should be kept in mind. Some of them have been certainly "home-made", but EU policy failures also had an impact.

On the domestic level, an overall deficiency can be identified in the missing linkage between domestic and EU-related policies. In the early stage of relations with Brussels, the SEE countries did not understand that the transfer of EU legislation, standards, norms and expectations (condi-

[31] For instance, according to the latest agricultural census carried out in Bulgaria in 2003, almost 680,000 units are available for agricultural activities. However, only about 50,000 of them reach the lowest level that can be defined as "agricultural holdings". The situation is certainly not better in Romania and in most Western Balkan countries.

tionalities) cannot be considered as a package without a direct and manifold impact on most areas of the domestic economy (and politics). It is impossible to manage two policies, economies and administrations at two different and separate levels, and based on two (highly) diverging requirements. In turn, successful institutional adjustment should mean that the EU becomes part and parcel of the everyday work of the whole public administration (and, increasingly, a large part of society as well).[32] No less importantly, often it was not understood that successful preparation and efficient negotiation and implementation require a high level of consensus among different political groupings on the domestic scene. Conflicts may remain in many areas, but open disagreement on EU-related issues only harms the position of the SEE country or, in the "best" case, does not allow the utilisation of the potential benefits offered by Brussels. In some cases, as in Bosnia-Herzegovina, domestic political short-sightedness was aggravated by "ethnic short-sightedness".

Future-oriented activities were frequently hampered or blocked by status-quo oriented lobbies, particularly in the Western Balkan countries. Preventing promising privatization deals, keeping traditional but outdated structures functioning (financed by state budget subsidies), expressing fears of liberalization and opening up have created substantial barriers to launch and foster viable initiatives. It is symptomatic that in countries like Serbia or Macedonia (but partly also in Croatia), complaints on possible disadvantages could be heard much more often than positive attitudes about how to make use of the opportunities. Macedonia repeatedly made reference to the negative impact of opening its tiny market. Even worse, a long list of disadvantages can easily be put together by using negative Serbian statements.[33]

Last but not least, the deficiencies of the public administration have to be addressed. Even in those countries that not only started restructuring their administrative system but also "replenish" it with new, fresh, young, talented, ambitious and well-trained people, mainly in the first years, the efficiency of administrative reforms remained modest (see the case of the

---

32 This "mental harmonization" needs more time, as the example of the new member countries shows. One of the fundamental deficiencies in EU-related communication is the differentiation between "they" (*i.e.* Brussels) and "us" (*i.e.* politicians, institutions, business leaders or citizens of the given new member country). It has to be understood that, from the very moment of membership, Brussels are "we" (together with the other member countries and the EU institutions).

33 Just a first-glance selection from the discouraging messages. Membership will not be able to narrow the development gap and if such a thing happened, it would happen despite (or just instead of) membership. EU subsidies end up in lower competitiveness. EU membership does not promise any acceleration of FDI inflow. EU enlargement turns Serbia into a collector country for illegal immigrants (due to the extension of the Schengen system to Serbia's borders).

competences of the Integration Ministry in Belgrade). On the one hand, and at best, institutions with clear EU competences remained an island in the overall administrative structure. In a worse version, they became the "common enemy" of the traditional administration (both because of their higher level education, knowledge of foreign languages, travel opportunities and, in some cases, also higher wages). On the other hand, sustainable new EU-conform structures do not only require fundamental restructuring of the public administration but also a lot more money and the constant supply of well-educated public administrators.

On the EU side, two embarrassing factors can be pointed out. One is the already mentioned conflict between the priority of EU conditionality and the priority of structural reforms. For all countries started from the conviction that the EU is their ultimate saviour, overall politics, and even more administrative structures were built on meeting this requirement. Evidently, such an approach generates attitudes different from the development and implementation of a genuine, "home-grown" but open development strategy. The continuous pressure to comply with "imposed conditionalities" results in short-term (*ad hoc*) reactions, thus in generally passive or one-sidedly adaptive behaviour. Active, self-confident policies, naturally based on the acceptance of external realities, would develop different political attitudes and administrative structures.

The other factor is rooted in the perception that, at the end of the day, all decisions on enlargement/accession have a deeply political character. Integration is perceived as a decision taken in Brussels, and not the result of the respective country's own efforts and level of preparation. Therefore, although it is not openly voiced it automatically follows from this position that it is not so important to develop their own initiatives after all, since everything depends on Brussels' political decision. This view was clearly reflected in an Albanian public opinion survey.[34] However, most probably, a similar mentality can be found in other countries of the region as well.

Two conclusions follow. First: the EU has to improve its communication strategy towards the region and even more to emphasize the importance of the countries' own efforts in different stages of preparing for membership.[35] Second: the impact of EU conditionality, including the chances of successful or failed preparation for membership, cannot be correctly assessed without a detailed survey of the social and mental situation as well as the dominant trends in the public opinion in the SEE

---

34 See: Mladenova, *Albania country study*, 2005, pp. 6-7.

35 Most probably such activities have to be extended throughout the first and critical years after accession as well. Experience acquired by the new Central European member countries seems to support this suggestion.

countries. This was exactly the underlying idea of including the following subchapter.

V.4. Social Attitudes, Mentality and Public Opinion in the SEE Countries with Respect to Relations to the EU

V.4.1. It is impossible to understand the actions and reactions of any country in the world without studying the factors that essentially shaped its history. More importantly, no strategy aimed at creating the political, economic, institutional and social (human) conditions for sustainable development can ignore the values rooted in history, endeavours, expectations but also perceptions, fears and concerns. This general statement holds especially true for Southeastern Europe with a difficult history embedded in a complicated and many times from indifferent to hostile international environment. For different reasons, the involvement of the region in the historically unprecedented process of European integration have highlighted many of these historical components. Most of the analysis that follows in the next paragraphs concerns the Western Balkans, although some features are true to the situation in Bulgaria and Romania as well.

This subchapter starts with the identification of the basic features that have shaped the region and the attitude and mentality of people living there. Next, the impact of the dissolution of the Yugoslav Federation and the subsequent wars on social behaviour and mentality will be demonstrated. Then the other destiny-shaping factor, the EU will be discussed from the perspective of public opinion in SEE. In the last sections, fears, dangers and tasks will be summarized.

V.4.2. Social attitude and mentality in the Balkans and even more in most parts of the Western Balkans have been molded by three basic developments:

- historical experience, mainly shaped by foreign domination, repeated efforts of liberation (often with foreign support and intervention) and struggle for political independence,
- belated process of nation-building, often assisted, directed or distorted by different big power interests,
- the experience with a federally structured Yugoslav state.

It is needless to say that the above elements are closely interrelated. Foreign domination and belated nation-building are directly linked. Similarly, the incapacity to build a strong nation had negative repercussions on sustainable independence. Moreover, several features of the Yugoslav Federation are connected with the two other components. A high-level independence (manoeuvring room) was created by suppressing the authentic process of nation-building in the individual republics of the Federation. At the same time, this same federation offered real chances to resist foreign influence and achieve a higher degree of independence on the federal level. Constant fight for independence could not be coordinated with creating more democracy according to Western European values, since it required the concentration of forces on the most important priority. Also, (several times) belated nation-building was a more urgent task than the introduction of democratic values with a high level of decentralized (shared) power. In this context, the Yugoslav Federation did not contribute very much to the dissemination of democratic principles.

Endeavours to reach national sovereignty were generally linked to the creation of weak states. Therefore, it was often possible to fight foreign domination without sustainable success efficiently but only provisionally. Only strong nation-states can resist foreign domination long term. Physical and human resources may have sufficed to withstand or ease foreign domination, but they failed (or lacked the will) when it came to focus on the meticulous and time consuming task of nation-building. Moreover, nation-building was always a self-definition against others,[36] be they foreign powers that used to dominate the region or against the international environment that, maybe a bit simplified, but used to be considered as hostile or at least unsympathetic of the priorities of "nation-builders".

Concerns started once a weak, emerging nation faced long-standing nation-states with strong competences, deeply-rooted values and a large variety of instruments to implement specific goals. Two basic reactions were generated by such situations. On the one hand, a very mixed perception of admiration and anxiety *vis-à-vis* the foreign actor was evident. The more developed foreign state is admired for its wealth, discipline, clear goals, stable structures that should be realized in the weak states, too, in order to overcome underdevelopment and weakness. However, envy usually did not result in concentrated efforts to build stronger structures by using the experience of others. On the contrary, envy generated fear, resistance and attitudes to show that "we are different". Such historically rare situations, instead of concentrating on the future, fell back on the historical reactions of fear and opposition to outside domination and "foreign values". It is also true that often there was no sufficient time to realize original plans for the emerging nation fell victim to yet another foreign attack before becoming sufficiently strong. Delays and failures, aggravated by repeated foreign interference have led to an exaggerated (overheated) and distorted feeling of nationalism. Today, its most evident

---

[36] In fact, nation-building in other parts of the world have often been understood and carried out as an action against others (foreign occupants, dominant or just chaotic neighbours). In very few cases the process was built on a positive approach of creating and stabilizing traditional values without fighting others.

manifestation can be seen in Serbia. In a recent article it was described by the fairly correct phrase of "armoured nationalism" ("*verpanzerter Nationalismus*").[37] Delayed nation-building, based particularly on ethnic principles in Europe in the early 21st century is in itself an anachronism and an extremely dangerous source of further instability. It is, however, an even bigger risk when the explosive nature of this development is further fuelled by unrestricted, unbridled and volatile nationalism. Therefore, the strong linkage between nationalism and independence on the one hand, and openness and foreign domination on the other hand, has to be broken above all.[38] Such correlations have never worked, but they are extremely devastating and counterproductive in the age of globalization. It is more than symptomatic, that after the very first attempts to restore Serbia's formal position in international institutions and organizations, political opponents to international integration started to appear. They immediately declared an ideological struggle between "mondialists and patriots".[39]

A further distorting factor is the still alive in the "Yugoslav economic model" based on workers' self-management that crucially hinders any reform, not least market-conform privatization. In this section, however, it is not the economic costs that are addressed. A much more important and lasting impact can be observed in the social attitude of people in all Western Balkan countries (including Croatia). This is a fundamental barrier to sweeping reforms. The problem lies not so much in the implementation of concrete plans but the absence of such initiatives. The attitude inherited from ex-Yugoslavia results in the lack of real commitment to reforms both on the political level and in large parts of the society. The risks of such a "muddling through" without any clear goals and instruments are certainly enhanced by the fact that all countries of the Western Balkans reflect an apparent macroeconomic stability based on private consumption mainly financed by remittances and international donors. In such a situation, the need for reforms is not felt as an urgent task. Thus, the Yugoslav heritage and artificially sustained consumption strengthen each other, despite the rapidly growing poverty and lagging behind neighbouring countries, let alone from global developments.

---

37 Wiedemann and Flottau (2006), p. 99.

38 The example of several Central European countries including Hungary shows that real progress could only be made when efforts to enhance "national independence" were accompanied by openness to the international community. The struggle between "guards of national independence" and supporters of economic modernization characterized most of the 19th-century history of Hungary. Regrettably, the first clear signs of this conflict have made their reappearance in several SEE countries, not least as a reaction to EU membership.

39 See: Hernádi, *Serbia-Montenegro country study*, 2006, p. 26.

Inflexibility and inability to act are further supported by the distorted concept of individual performance and protection by the state. All Western Balkan countries still have a long way to go to achieve the level of individual freedom and full-fledged observation of human rights as it is common in European democracies, including in the new member countries of the EU. Still, more freedom as compared to previous periods, has not led to more intensive and more responsible private activities and the conscious self-separation from the "father state". On the contrary, a very curious and distorted individual behaviour started to emerge. It consists of more individual freedom without individual responsibility.[40] Freedom is particularly enjoyed in higher personal consumption (of goods, services and "intellectual" products) but not in starting (legal) business activities. At the same time, most responsibilities remain with the state and it is the state's duty to help everybody, including irresponsible citizens.

A special Yugoslav heritage is linked to the former role and influence of the Federation that has been completely lost by now. At first glance, the amazing discrepancy between the former and the current situation seems to be absorbed and managed easier in the new nation-states than in Serbia that considers itself as the legitimate successor to the Yugoslav Federation. For a certain time, the "glamour" of the new nation-state may eclipse the wide gap between the global and regional influence of Yugoslavia for decades and the current bargaining power of the emerging small and failed states. The intellectual and emotional legacy is much more difficult to handle in Serbia. For many people it is still unbelievable how a regionally enviable and, indeed envied country of the 1970s (and partly 1980s) could become the poor house of Europe within a very short period of time. How could it happen that Central and Eastern Europeans (even

---

40 The same problem can be found in other transforming countries, too. One of the biggest failures by leading politicians at the beginning of systemic transformation was that they did not explain to the citizens the fundamental interaction between rights and responsibilities (either due to ignorance, political short-sightedness or fear of losing supporters). However, it was clear that the transformation has definitely disrupted the artificial connection of rights and responsibilities imposed on Central and Eastern European societies after the Second World War and under Soviet domination. The imposed linkage of rights and responsibilities was based on the deprivation of citizens of their individual and human rights in exchange for the state's all-around responsibility (from subsidized food and apartment through a series of state-provided assistance to full employment). This imposed pattern was broken in 1989-1990 when citizens of these countries regained their individual rights. However, if one key element of the model stops functioning (due to almost unanimous social approval and support), the other cannot remain unchanged either. Nobody tried to explain that more individual freedom would be accompanied by more individual responsibility and (much) less direct support and protection by the state. Part of this imbalance is still alive in the minds and attitudes of citizens of the new member countries. (It is no "consolation" that such behaviour can widely be found in Western Europe as well.)

Bulgaria and Romania) that admired Yugoslavia in general and Yugoslav citizens in particular due to their (relative) intellectual freedom, right to travel in the world, opportunity to work in Western Europe and, not least, the (relative) material welfare today enjoy more freedom and have a (substantially) higher living standard? No less importantly, the Yugoslav Federation was an important international actor, due to its political neutrality, geopolitical situation and clever leadership characterized by a balanced foreign strategy. Nothing of this legacy has survived. Citizens experience just the opposite. Instead of actively participating in international forums that used to set a precedent for other countries around the world, all ex-Yugoslav states became the unilateral (one-way) policy takers of external conditionalities imposed either by the United Nations, the US or, more importantly, by the EU. It is obvious that politicians and citizens are fundamentally challenged by the new reality. In the longer term it is perhaps easier to come to terms with the new (and disappointing) economic situation. However, the "past glory" of active and internationally esteemed participation of Yugoslavia in important global, European and regional political affairs will not be easily forgotten, even if currently both politicians and citizens are fully committed to solve or mitigate pressing everyday problems. If this unique hidden risk is not taken seriously and the help particularly to Serbia in order to digest the loss of its "glorious" past will be either ignored or managed inappropriately form, the ongoing and automatic generation of more and more nationalistic attitudes will be difficult to be reduced or even kept under control.

V.4.3. The behavioural and mental basis shaped by history, as described in the previous paragraph, was further burdened and distorted by the Balkan wars and its consequences as well as the repeatedly delayed and until now (in the best case) half-hearted initiatives at economic and social reforms. In all cases when transformation was associated with potential foreign participation (liberalization of the flow of goods, services and capital, privatization, etc.) nationalist and anti-foreign behaviour made the way of transformation bumpier.

The Balkan wars definitely nourished national emotions and produced concrete actions to define national mentality (and statehood) against the neighbours. This process developed both in the cross-nation framework and in ethnic determination and separation. Armed conflicts were differently perceived on both sides. In Serbia, commander of the Yugoslav National Army, the main objective was in preserving as much of ex-Yugoslavia as possible. In turn, in countries that wanted to get rid of "Serbian supremacy" and the previous federation, all efforts were understood as part of a justified struggle for national independence.[41] No less importantly, there is a huge confusion concerning the interpretation of the role of leading politicians and generals deeply involved in war and ethnic cleansing. Although some of them have been handed over to the Hague tribunal, it has not changed their public assessment. On the contrary, it deepened the "perception gap" in the individual Western Balkan societies. Statements by incumbent politicians further contaminated the mentality. For instance, Kostunica, the Serbian Prime Minister described the Hague tribunal repeatedly as an "anti-Serbian installation". To put the whole issue into a clear perspective: those who are accused of different kinds of crimes (including genocide) committed during the wars according to international law, are largely admired as national heroes at home. Zagreb's willingness to find, arrest and transport Gotovina to the Hague could open the way to official negotiations on accession to the EU but could not necessarily convert Croats into better Europeans. Just the opposite happened when, as a form of massive popular reaction, spontaneous demonstrations took place in favour of Gotovina, "the hero of Zadar and Split" in different Croatian towns. Similarly, Mladic and Karadzic are not only national heroes in the eyes of large parts of Serbian society, but they have a large influence on domestic politics and public opinion. As a small but telling example: Karadzic's book is widely available in many bookshops in Belgrade. Certainly, the intervention of the Allied Forces against Serbia and the long isolation of the country from normal international activities (including the suspension of its rights to participate in basic international organizations) struck additional wounds on the Serbian soul and could easily be put into the service of the strengthening of defiant and stubborn nationalism. In addition, it increased the popular belief that Serbia was an "innocent" country that fell victim to an international conspiracy. Therefore, international environment and foreign actors can always be blamed for any kind of domestic failures and deficiencies. Even more, it spreads the feeling and attitude that it does not make any sense to become more active and self-reliant, for everything will be decided by others.

It is not surprising that several aspects of the transformation process that directly or indirectly may involve foreign partners (and interests) are seen with utmost reservation, suspicion and mistrust. The privatization of "national assets" should be not allowed to be sold because it would mean the "selling-out" of the country to foreign business (and politics). Preparation for EU membership is costly and does not bring advantages. It is much better to stay with the small but highly lucrative and often illegal

---

41 Moreover, a significant part of the Croatian society considers any discrimination against the Serbian minority justifiable, since the armed conflict at the beginning of the 1990s was a direct consequence of Serb aggression.

(or criminal) business that could be established during or in connection with the wars. In addition, even reform-minded politicians and experts have very difficult tasks when they try to strike a balance between the size of potential reforms and their social costs in war-ridden countries with substantial physical and human devastation. The costs of reforms are frequently considered too high as compared to the already existing costs inherited from previous decades and the burden-taking capacity of the society. Most recently, resistance to reforms has been accompanied by growing disillusion with politics in several countries. Political and social passivity, however, automatically supports nationalist and extremist movements and political parties. The danger that such political forces could come to power in one or more countries of the Western Balkans is far from impossible.

While future-oriented activities are scarce and weak, mental contamination by nationalistic ideologies is booming everywhere and on different fronts. In this context, special attention should be devoted to formal education on the primary and secondary level. History books are highly distorted[42] emphasizing the glory of the given country, its special "national values" that differentiate it from the neighbours and, frequently, the fixed idea of having been repeatedly victimized in history. In formally multi-ethnic Bosnia-Herzegovina, schools remain ethnically divided (one ethnic group studies in the morning the other one in the afternoon). One group learns about the positive impact and religious tolerance of Ottoman presence in the Balkans that had liberated the population from the atrocities and yoke of local landlords. In contrast, the other group hears each day that the centuries-long Turkish occupation is to be blamed for the underdevelopment of the whole region.[43]

Even the smallest success of the neighbour is accompanied by openly malicious remarks (gloating, *Schadenfreude*). The old tradition of Eastern, Southern and partly Central Europe that the most important issue is not my progress but the bankruptcy, failure and defeat of my neighbour, seems to be more alive than in previous decades. There seems to be a rather long way until politicians and societies of the region will understand that their personal fortune and development are closely linked to the successful modernization and sustainable development of the neighbour-

---

42 A small but symptomatic fact is that the statue of Jellasic, the Croatian national hero who, commissioned by Austria to defeat the Hungarian war of independence from the Monarchy in 1848, has changed direction. Originally, the general on the back of a horse pointed with his finger in the northeastern direction, namely towards Budapest. Now, as part of reinterpreting history, it has been turned to the East, namely to Belgrade.

43 Martens (2006d), p. 1. The journalist correctly notes that the "so-called ethnic cleansing should be followed by cleaning the history books".

ing countries. This process should (have) start(ed) with identifying and admitting all crimes and failures that have been committed by citizens of all Western Balkan countries (but mainly Croats and Serbs). It should (have) continue(d) by a process of genuine national and ethnic reconciliation[44] the signs of which are hardly evident compared to the nationalistic propaganda and distorted self-confidence (again defined against the neighbour and not in the global or European context). This is (would be) the right way towards the "European dream", of which different stages of institutionalized contacts with Brussels, including potential full membership, are just an external form of expression.

V.4.4. The above objective is largely absent in the public opinion that enthusiastically wants to join the EU. Of course, it is understandable that all countries look at the EU as their anchor for stabilization and modernization. Although the original level of unreserved and borderless "love" and hopes has become somewhat more modest, all opinion polls keep indicating pro-EU attitudes of the majority of the population.

Even in Western Balkans comparison, Albania belongs to the countries with the highest support and (often exaggerated) expectations. Still, this public attitude enabled the government(s) to introduce reforms that would have been hardly swallowed without reference to the adjustment needs to EU rules. Moreover, a campaign has been started to tell people that accommodation to the "European rules of the game" is not only a precondition of enhanced cooperation but it is in the best interest of the Albanian society as well. Bulgaria expects mainly economic and social benefits, a better infrastructure, more FDI and more manoeuvering room in a globalized world. In turn, security considerations are overwhelmingly associated with NATO. The majority of Macedonian citizens are convinced that EU membership is the most important goal of the country. The EU is expected to ensure higher living standards and prosperity. It is interesting that EU-related goals are widely shared both by Macedonians and the Albanians living in the country. Most citizens expect a higher level of stability and political and social integrity. For many Serbs, the EU has become the "last resort".

Digging deeper into expectations and comparing them with the reality, wide discrepancies and, in several cases, fundamental misunderstanding of the functioning, ability and willingness of Brussels (and the member countries) can be identified. Some symptomatic examples will be taken only from the country studies to support this statement. Many Albanians

---

44 The long road to reconciliation between France and Germany can provide many helpful points and instruments on how to reach this objective. To be sure, the work should start with the prohibition of any kind of literature or documents that are connected with war criminals.

look at the EU as a region where they can travel and do (frequently illegal) business without any restrictions. Even more, free movement should be guaranteed from the moment of the ratification of the SAA, and should not be linked to further negotiations. Great popular support in most countries, *e.g.* in Serbia, is based on weak foundations, due to the rather scarce knowledge of the EU. Montenegro has high hopes that its newly gained independence will substantially speed up the process of EU integration.[45] Expectations linked to quick membership are an obvious evidence of not understanding how the European integration works. For some time, Croatia nourished hopes to become an EU member state along with Bulgaria and Romania. Expectations were based on the by far not always justified conviction that Croatia's living standard is higher than that of Bulgaria and Romania. In addition, it considers itself a Central European country and, indeed, has received substantial political, diplomatic and psychological support from Austria, Bavaria, Hungary and some other countries of the region. Thus, the distorted impression emerged in which the country was more advanced in economic, political and social terms. The barriers to real socio-economic transformation that adversely affect the country's real convergence to EU standards were largely neglected. As, however, the preparation became more intensive and more detailed, many shortcomings emerged that may slow down the accession process, even if political support from some EU members and an adequate external climate were anticipated. More interesting is the Serbian case. In November 2004, the newly established European Integration Secretariat in Belgrade presented a strategic paper on the country's preparation for EU accession. In the first pages several reasonable arguments were summarized why the EU is the key partner of Serbia and why integration brings clear advantages to the country. However, in the following sections that surveyed the most important elements of EU legislation and compared them with the Serbian reality, huge differences were identified. In several cases, the conclusion was not what kind of reforms should be undertaken by Belgrade in order to accommodate EU standards, but simply and bluntly: this and that EU *acquis* were not acceptable to Serbia. This approach conveyed the view that the *acquis* could be modified by an applicant country. In addition, the document was prepared by a professional body (and not a political body) that, most probably had to know how little is the manoeuvring room of a policy taker (small) country in EU negotiations. The conclusion is not only that some experts still do not, or do not want to, understand the basic character and rules of

45 Some politicians from the Western Balkans openly stated that they expect quick accession to the EU. Thus, in documents made public in the first years of the new millennium, Serbia-Montenegro produced an accession date of 2007, while Bosnia-Herzegovina wanted to join no later than 2009 (Altmann, 2005, p. 185).

the game of European integration. The underlying mentality is much more problematic, for it suggests that everything (or most of the goals) can be achieved, if one is tough enough and has a high level of self-confidence (let alone to consider and "sell" himself as a victim of history and conspiracy).

Exaggerated hopes and unfounded expectations may produce two negative consequences. First, optimism can rapidly turn into pessimism and disappointment[46] that would not only reduce the popular support for European integration but could fundamentally constrain the government's room for action at a time when reforms with high social costs should be implemented with reference to Brussels and the "promising prospect" of membership. Second, while facing growing problems in more intensive everyday contacts with Brussels (either in official negotiations or in fulfilling conditionalities) intolerance may be rising. This could provide good reasons for aggressive and populist politicians to enhance their political influence in wider circles of the society and/or consolidate their position in the domestic power constellation.

In spite of a (still overwhelmingly) favourable attitude to the EU, anti-EU emotions and positions should not be ignored. Their outstanding representatives mainly come from Serbia. The political elite of that country has not yet followed the Croatian mental and strategic transformation. While the new Croatian leadership recognized that the country's priority is Brussels and not the creation of a "larger and ethnically clean" Croatia, Serbia is still hostage to the issue of Kosovo. The official political line that enjoys large popular support is that keeping Serbia together (which means that Kosovo remains a territory of Serbia) has higher priority than relations to Brussels and, consequently, it shall not be "sacrificed" to pave the way for EU accession.

EU activities and EU-related policies of the SEE countries has not left either the political life or the society unaffected. In some cases, a more or less acceptable position could be achieved, while in some other cases the gap between supporters and opponents of (the modalities of) integration remained wide or became wider. It was certainly not easily accepted by Bulgarian society that the nuclear plant in Kozhloduy, the most important electricity-producing factory with relevant and manifold impact on a rather "poor" and catching-up economy was closed upon EU conditionality.[47] More problematic is the impact of EU-related politics on the shifts

---

46 To quote Vasilev, a Bulgarian journalist, "EU integration is a long process that starts with euphoria and ends in pessimism".

47 Many citizens believe that the conditionality to close the four units until the end of 2006, misses convincing arguments, because the power plant is safe. In turn, most people see in this conditionality the interests of Western European electricity companies that could conquer the Bulgarian and regional markets, since Kozhloduy used to

in domestic power relations. Growing anti-EU sentiments and attitudes have already radicalized the Serbian political landscape. According to the latest opinion polls, the pro-European Serbian party (G17Plus) will have a hard time getting into the national parliament if election were held now.[48] Even more concern is generated by the fact that, again recently, the extreme pro-Mladic Radical Party became Serbia's most popular political group with an almost two-fifth support of the population.[49] The political disagreement on the EU strategy of Serbia that is at least partly responsible for the non-extradition of Mladic and Karadzic on the one hand, and the subsequent interruption of official negotiations between Brussels and Belgrade, did not escape high-level experts either. Thus, the head of the Serbian negotiating team, Miroljub Labus resigned and blamed his own country's politicians for breach of promise. For the time being, the Serbian society is increasingly polarized both concerning the assessment of its previous generals (whether they were war criminals or national heroes), the way and speed of socio-economic transformation (remaining in "not-so-splendid" isolation or opening up the economy) or the EU strategy (we do not need the EU or the EU is our "last resort" for economic development but also the key instrument to avoid further nationalistic radicalization).[50]

V.4.5. Beyond the overall public perception of the EU that has been showing a positive general attitude, there are some specific and critical points in which public awareness and political concerns can be identified as more "to the point".

First: the fear that adjustment to the EU rules and EU membership can impair national sovereignty is not very evident. This may seem paradoxical since most countries of the region acquired national sovereignty just in the last decade, or are still fighting for it or for the consolidation of weak national structures. This attitude seems to be in line with the behaviour of the new member countries that were also supposed to develop more resistance to transferring traditional national competences to Brussels only a few years after achieving "independence". Usually, small (and less developed) states are more inclined to share sovereignty with Brus-

---

be a large regional exporter of electricity as well. Nevertheless, this issue has not eroded the positive attitude to the EU.

48 Martens (2006e).

49 *The Economist*, May 06, 2006, p. 28.

50 It has to be added that, in the last time, public media became more balanced and try to influence public opinion in a more positive way. For instance, the previous terminology that differentiated between "patriotic" and "non-patriotic" attitudes according to the assessment of the generals and the way Serbia should follow in its contacts with Brussels, started to disappear and gave more room to arguments why cooperation with the Hague is important and in the interest of the country.

sels in order to have better economic chances in exchange, higher protection and a larger room for bargaining as members of the influential club. Old-fashioned national patterns could only be found in Poland (some of them had been on the increase in the last period) and, among the SEE countries, Serbia and partly Croatia. In the meantime, Croatia implemented a strategic turnover by opting unambiguously for the Brussels priority. Such a change has not happened in Serbia. Worse, recent developments point to the strengthening of traditional and isolationist nationalism.

Second: many more concerns are associated with the EU's attitude on the future roadmap of enlargement. In the last period, statements and reports multiplied indicating a rapidly declining readiness of the member states to let further countries join. Looking at the "enlargement fatigue" in more than one member country, the increasing domestic pressure to introduce substantive reforms and the deadlock in critical areas of deepening the process of integration, there are justified doubts that the EU will not be able or willing to keep its promise made in Thessaloniki in 2003. Except for Bulgaria and Romania, which have got a clear promise of membership in 2007 or 2008 the latest, and, in fact, became members at the earliest date promised, no SEE country can take membership for granted. The larger the institutional gap between Brussels and the respective countries of the Western Balkans are, the deeper the doubts.

Third: for different reasons, for some years, neither Bulgaria nor Romania could sit back and feel safe. The Commission kept their membership date "floating" as long as October 2006, when the next monitoring report recommended their membership as of January 2007. As discussed in one of the previous paragraphs, there were no credible arguments in favour of postponing membership, since the damage caused by the delay would have been much higher and widespread than the unlikely "disciplinary impact" of such a step.[51]

Fourth: in the medium term, the existing discrepancy and, potentially, the further growing gap between priorities of a sustainable socio-economic development on the one hand, and preparation for EU membership on the other can produce new tensions. The longer the period of preparation lasts, the higher the risk of such "target conflicts". It cannot be ruled out that in some cases the process enters a stage in which short-term but urgent priorities will divert efforts from the EU path and threaten to derail integration.

Fifth: longer waiting periods for membership are associated in several countries with the drying up of EU financial transfers. Even Bulgaria and Romania were concerned that in case of delayed membership (in 2008)

---

51 Inotai (2006).

financial resources would become less and less substantial, although the financial framework for the two newcomers was firmly established at least for the first half of the new budgetary framework covering the period between 2007 and 2013. More realistic was the fear that, in case of delayed membership, substantial amounts of money earmarked for Bulgaria and Romania could be lost, since the current pre-accession rules would be automatically prolonged. This, of course, would have been a serious loss in financial (and development) terms. No wonder that the financial argument was widely used in order to avoid any postponement of the accession date. In turn, the budget-related concerns of the Western Balkan countries are completely justified. First, there is no supplemental budget in case they join within the next financial period, *i.e.* before 2013. At the moment, such a move seems unlikely except in the case of Croatia. However, Croatia does not have a separate allotment in the coming budget, either.[52]

Sixth: the most delicate and politically explosive component of the "sovereignty" discussion is the purchase of agricultural land by foreigners. Despite clear and mutually accepted regulation enshrined in the Accession Treaty (seven-year transition period from the moment of accession), the topic keeps turning up in statements of populist politicians (see Hungary, *par excellence*). Similarly, Bulgarian and Croatian fears could be detected, while Romania seems to follow a more relaxed attitude, including the already existing practice of selling high-quality agricultural land to foreigners (mainly to Italians in the Banat, Southwestern Romania). In fact, the real problem today in Bulgaria is not who is the owner, but that there is no owner or at least nobody who would cultivate the land. This creates enormous losses in production and exports, higher (rural) unemployment, widespread underdevelopment in vast areas and economic, social and environmental degradation. Therefore, the very real point of discussion should not be about fears of a foreign takeover, but the establishment of normal conditions for agricultural ownership and ventures. Otherwise, the fear of "losing" agricultural land to foreigners is all the more justified the less development the domestic agriculture can generate in the transitional period. Weak, unmodernised, fragmented agriculture without strong market channels that definitely need high-level cooperation with other market actors would be largely exposed to the willingness of foreign (EU) buyers at extremely low prices. In fact, this

---

52 This difficulty can, however, be overcome by minimal regrouping of the resources, since Croatia's membership would not dramatically increase the budget. Much more restructuring was needed in the previous enlargement when the budget approved in 1999 was planned for six member countries only, with accession in 2002 and without any direct payment to farmers.

would be a "selling-out" for which the national government and the farmers of the given country would have to take all responsibilities.

V.4.6. Also some real dangers that shape social attitudes, public opinion and mentality have to be addressed.

First: inactivity, the lack of true national strategies concerning preparation for the EU and traditional expectation that somebody else, in this case Brussels, will do the homework of the SEE countries can be grouped in one package. In fact, too much foreign influence, as seen both in Bosnia-Herzegovina and Kosovo, may result in such an attitude of domestic policy makers and large social groups. Similar influences can be attributed to regular and large-scale private remittances from abroad to local people. Most societies have been "trained for centuries not to take decisions". They gladly accept somebody from outside (either a person or an institution) who would assume responsibility and, if things go wrong for local citizens, they can be readily blamed. The experience of the previous high representative of the EU in Bosnia, Lord Ashdown, can be briefly summarized. On the one hand, after a while it became clear that Bosnia's problems are far more rooted in the distant past than in the recent war and its consequences. On the other hand, most Bosnians are pleased to have a new "pasha" who gives orders and his subordinates will have to follow his instructions.[53] If this basic attitude cannot be markedly changed, one of the most important risks for the region's stability, namely deference and passivity, will prevail.

Second: influences and challenges to all countries regularly come from very different sources. Therefore, it is imperative to distinguish between domestic problems, EU-related issues and global developments. Certainly, in our increasingly interdependent world it is not always easy to create clear categories for problems. However, it has to be avoided that in case of failures or problematic situations politicians, different interest groups or citizens get accustomed to blame each other but themselves. In order to create a realistic picture of European integration, including the attached benefits and costs, the EU's role has to be clearly defined and conveyed to society. No case in which the EU plays a role, either positive or negative, should be kept confidential or concealed. However, no domestic policy mistakes should be interpreted as if Brussels were responsible for them. Again, global developments may produce critical challenges that cannot be fully met by the available domestic or EU-level instruments. Still, people have to be aware of the fact that membership in the EU offers a much more efficient protection against negative external effects than the best available national set of policy instruments.

---

[53] In detail see: *The Economist*, November 26, 2005, p. 38.

Third: EU-related national communication strategies should refrain from one-sided and (over)optimistic messages that enhance expectations that cannot be met. Realism, balanced information and the constant awareness of advantages and costs have to become an integral part of everyday information dissemination. No less importantly, communication should not be limited to critical periods of negotiations, important changes in the attitude of Brussels or of the candidate/applicant country or only when the public has to be prepared for a referendum. Mental and behavioural preparation for EU membership has to become a regular, everyday task. This is the best evidence that the given country takes EU relations seriously.

Fourth: along with the clear advantages and benefits, the costs of the preparatory stages for membership have to be calculated and communicated to the society as well. Politicians and policy-makers should not have any fear that honest communication and open discussion would result in declining for membership. On the contrary, this is the way of creating balanced expectations, of mobilizing a country's own resources and enter the EU with self-confidence and responsibility. (There are plenty of lessons to be learned from the rather different and not very successful communication policies of the new member countries.)

Fifth: the EU has to support the formation of healthy, balanced and responsible mentality of politicians (it is sometimes rather difficult) and of the civil societies (which, hopefully, is a bit easier). Therefore, it must avoid any situation which would raise the issue of double standards and individual treatment. Each country and society is rather sensitive to this issue. Western Balkan countries on different levels of EU relations and facing new uncertainties about their promised membership are, understandably, even more sensitive. Moreover, EU officials and experts have to refrain from creating even the temporary impression of "second-class membership" in selected policy areas. Evidently, transitional agreements do not belong to this category, because they have a clear deadline when those will be lifted. Experts dealing with SEE in general, and the Western Balkans in particular, need a fundamental understanding of the attitudes and mentality formed for centuries in this region and became exacerbated in the ex-Yugoslav states as a consequence of recent deplorable developments.

V.4.7. Some of the priority tasks can be summarized in a few points:

- develop a balanced information system,
- keep the positive picture of the EU over a longer time, if membership in the EU is considered the highest national priority,
- identify domestic and EU-related tasks clearly and ensure a well-functioning interface between the two sides,

- differentiate domestic, EU-related and global challenges both in policy-making activities and in communication to the wider public,
- develop a set of measures to create a proactive society and business with clear ideas, self-confidence and responsibility,
- enhance the quality of public administration and the media by preventing or at least slowing brain drain and involve highly-skilled emigrés in several EU-related activities (independently, whether they return lastingly or remain outside the country but in constant contact with policy-makers and public opinion-shapers),
- immediately stop mental contamination in general, and the generation of ethnic hatred (or differentiation) in particular, both in formal education and in the wider information policy,
- enhance the development of 21st century national consciousness (which has nothing to do with 19th century nationalism).[54]

Needless to say, the above tasks are in many cases interrelated and they influence the individual policy measures' efficiency. In addition, they cannot be carried out in a uniform timetable. Some of them will show results earlier than others. This, however, must not be used as an excuse. On the contrary, starting or redoubling activities does not tolerate any delay.

54 In this context, an interesting initiative is the project to promote the Bulgarian national identity. It includes special measures for the development and presentation of Bulgarian culture in the EU, active participation in European cultural initiatives and programs, development of regional cooperation in culture and encouragement of private investments in Bulgarian culture and traditions (See: Petkova, *Bulgaria country study*, 2006, p. 6).

CHAPTER VI

Agenda for the Future and Recommendations

VI.1. Introductory Remarks

VI.1.1. At the turn of the 21st century the EU substantially stepped up its efforts in Southeastern Europe. It invited Bulgaria and Romania to start negotiations in early 2000, took direct responsibility for stabilizing Bosnia-Herzegovina and actively participated in the negotiation of the Ohrid agreement in 2001. Half a decade later, significant progress can be registered. Bulgaria and Romania have not only completed official negotiations in 2004 and signed the Accession Treaties, but became full members in January 2007. Peace and stability in the Western Balkans could be preserved and threatening ethnic conflicts in Macedonia prevented. In addition, during the Thessaloniki summit meeting the EU made it clear that each of the Balkan countries has the European perspective. In other words, all of them have an open door to join the EU once conditions have been fulfilled. As a first step, accession negotiations with Croatia (and Turkey) started.

VI.1.2. Compared to the manifest enlargement dynamics of the last years, the prospects for the Western Balkan countrys seem to have deteriorated most recently. The number of conditions to be met to qualify for a higher stage of institutionalized relations has grown and some hidden conditions have also been applied. "Enlargement fatigue", but frankly speaking, growing domestic problems of some key member countries have diverted attention from enlargement in general and from the Western Balkans in particular. Moreover, public opinion in Western Europe has become much less receptive and open to further enlargement. At the same time, politicians want to consolidate the integration after its big bang enlargement (and its second stage involving Bulgaria and Romania) before the EU would expand to new countries. The changing political and psychological climate is accurately represented by the fact that influential politicians and experts started to discuss both the "tolerable" critical mass of expansion in geographic, economic and financial terms and the timetable of potential further accessions. Even the idea of privileged partnerships, junior membership and other forms of partial or second-class integration reappeared on the agenda as a substitute for full-fledged membership on equal footing. In turn, officially Brussels still insists on its strategy of offering full membership conditions to each of the Balkan countries. In conformity with this strategy, the 2005 report of the International Commission on the Balkans chaired by the previous Italian Prime Minister, Amato underlines not only the importance of keeping the promise of full membership but make this offer more credible by an accession road map in 2006 (Amato, 2005, p. 164). This would last for about one decade so that all Western Balkan countries could work for achieving the target date of 2014/2015[1] or any time sooner. Thus, the whole Balkan region could become a full member of the EU shortly before or together with the highly disputed and increasingly open issue of Turkey's entry.

There are, however, some open or hidden traps on this road, even if a roadmap is accepted. First, the possibility of new conditions for accession is not ruled out despite the promise of Brussels. Second, public opinion in member countries is increasingly skeptical and does not support any further commitment to potential new applicants. Third, the latest data on development in selected Western Balkan countries indicate that they may need a longer period to achieve the required quality of institutions, governance, rule of law, and to put their economies on the path of sustainable development with noticeable real convergence. Fourth, the new geographic map involving an independent Montenegro, a Kosovo with changing status and potential Serbian reactions along with all calculable consequences and incalculable risks entails several factors that could have a significant impact on any enlargement agenda related to the conditions of admission, the number of new member countries and, not least, the timeframe to be followed.

VI.1.3. In sum, the future of the Western Balkans' road to Brussels essentially depends on three different and dynamic (constantly shifting) elements: the political and institutional element, and the "preparation dynamism". Each of these factors has one pillar in the Western Balkan region and in the individual countries, while the other pillar is in Brussels and the member countries. The fact that all of them are in constant flux does not imply that either the direction or the speed of developments around both pillars overlap each other. In a fortunate scenario, the individual processes are likely to strengthen each other and favourable results in one dynamic area may positively affect the dynamism in another area (either by providing additional dynamism or by moving things in the same direction in both pillars).

---

1 The referred Amato report ends with the following paragraph: "2014 is the year and Sarajevo is the place where the European Union can proudly announce the arrival of the European century" (Amato, 2005, p. 184).

VI.1.4. Some sections of this chapter address selected outstanding issues that are assumed to have a major impact on the future of the Western Balkans and its relations with the EU. In this context, a general overview of the current situation and short-term prospects will be presented. It will be followed by three new features of the Western Balkans' political and power constellation map. Separate sections deal with Montenegro, Kosovo and the potential Serb reactions. In the second part of the final analytical chapter the basic dilemmas of the EU will be surveyed. The last section sets out to formulate recommendations for future policy-making (and policy-shaping).

VI.2. Current Situation and Short-term Prospects of EU-SEE Relations

VI.2.1. On January 27, 2006 the European Commission presented its Western Balkans program. It includes the following main points:

- free trade area among the countries in the region,
- easing of import regulations of the EU to facilitate exports of Western Balkan products,
- the EU's Western Balkan politics has to embrace the objectives of economic modernization, as stipulated in the Lisbon Agenda,
- facilitation of travel of Western Balkan citizens into EU countries,
- increasing the number of fellowships for students from the Western Balkans (once the renewed EU education program becomes operational in 2007),
- prolongation of the European Charter on small- and medium-sized companies in the region.

The current picture of institutionalized relations between Brussels and the individual SEE countries is highly differentiated. There are two countries that can rightly consider themselves as full members in a very short term. Next we find Croatia that started negotiations. It is followed by Macedonia that submitted its application for membership. The next level of the institutional pyramid is represented by Albania, followed by Bosnia-Herzegovina and Serbia at the bottom. Moreover, institutionalized relations are yet to be established with the newly independent Montenegro and with Kosovo whose current status is most likely to be changed.

VI.2.2. The fact that Bulgaria and Romania successfully finished negotiations, signed the Accession Treaties and held an accession-supporting referendum brought both countries to the threshold of membership in 2006. After last-minute ratification of the accession treaty by the parliaments of some member countries, the EU was able to finish the second round of "Eastern" enlargement in January 2007. Obviously, it would not have been difficult to find some points to prove that Bulgaria and Romania have not met EU requirements (beyond, of course, the transitional measures stipulated in the official accession documents). Such weaknesses could have also been easily identified at the level of preparation of Central European and Baltic countries. Still, in both cases, the political logic proved to be the overriding factor. Nevertheless, inadequate preparation in selected areas can and, in fact, has produced some safeguard clauses to be implemented upon accession. More importantly, the "preparation gap" can manifest itself in the smaller degree and the potentially lower level of efficiency of available financial resources, in barriers to exports and, generally, in only partial benefits deriving from membership.

Accession of Bulgaria and Romania is not hindered by budgetary constraints. In contrast to the previous enlargement, the new financial framework determines the financial contribution of the EU available to each of the two countries. In turn, the figures have not been calculated until the end of the financial perspective (2013), but only for the first three years until the end of 2009. In this period, Romania is entitled to have access to Euro 8.9 bn, while Bulgaria may get a maximum of Euro 6.4 bn.[2]

VI.2.3. Half a year later than scheduled, Croatia started negotiations in October 2005 along with Turkey. In the first phase, 35 chapters had to be screened. "Real" negotiations can only start on chapters that have already been screened. Croatia's efforts are characterized by two priorities.

First, the country wanted to start effective negotiations as soon as possible. However, previous expectations that negotiations can be finished in less than two years and Croatia may become a full member by 2009 seems to be unlikely.[3]

Second, and successfully, Croatia did everything to dissociate itself, as early as possible, from Turkey with which it started negotiations simultaneously. This is an understandable effort and has already had partial results (some chapters were screened without Turkey). The underlying motives are twofold. On the one hand, technical linkage to Turkey does not allow speeding up negotiations. If the situation of parallel negotiations prevailed, Croatia could hardly become a member of the EU before Turkey. On the other hand, Croatia would like to get rid of the ambiguous image Turkey, or more precisely, Turkish accession to the EU has had in the majority of European public opinion. Any lasting linkage could have

---

2 For the seven-year period, Bulgaria expects about Euro 11 bn from Brussel (excluding direct payments for the farmers).

3 In a recent statement, Olli Rehn, the enlargement commissioner said that Croatia will not be able to join the EU before 2010 as the earliest. EurActiv, June 09, 2006.

easily taken Croatia hostage of the outcome of negotiations with Turkey (including interruption, suspension of talks or denying full membership at the end of the day).

However, successful separation from Turkey would not automatically make Croatia's way to the EU easier. There are at least three formidable barriers to overcome.

First, the growing resistance to further enlargement in several countries must be emphasized.

Second, more detailed surveys required by Brussels as well as the "deepening" of the preparatory work in Zagreb have shown that Croatia overestimated its adjustment level (and probably its capacity as well) to meet EU requirements soon. In several areas, there is a wider gap both in economic performance and legal accommodation between Zagreb and Brussels than it was the case at the beginning of negotiations with the Central European applicants. Among the main shortcomings the sluggish reform of the judiciary, the delayed implementation of the program on the return of refugees, the absence of guarantees to free press and electronic media without political interference, substantial economic reforms in order to reduce the high budgetary and current account deficits, transparent legislation on real estate purchase, guaranteeing the free circulation of services or the appropriate institutional preparation to absorb SAPARD funds can be mentioned. Moreover, according to the current EU *acquis* accepted in Nice (and not changed, due to the rejection of the Constitutional Treaty by France and the Netherlands) the EU cannot have more than 27 members. The changing of this rule requires a revision on the highest level of EU decision-making, namely by the Council. It is too early to take a position in this question, since whether or not it will be carried out, this modification may depend substantially on the domestic political and economic situation in key member countries and also on the general state of European integration.

Third, technical issues make the process of negotiations more difficult and prolonged than in the case of previous enlargements. Most professional surveys underline the difference in the number of chapters to be negotiated. The fact that the new members had to come to terms with Brussels in 31 chapters altogether, and Croatia and Turkey have 35 chapters on the negotiation table, can easily be explained by the growing *acquis communautaire* that countries acceding later have to observe. The real problem is in the large number of stages to be negotiated in each chapter.

The real problem is in the large number of stages to be negotiated in each chapter. In this context, the introduction of benchmarks deserves special attention, Such conditions were included into the negotiation process in two stages. On the one hand, the fulfilling of selected benchmark criteria is a precondition of opening the respective chapter. On the other hand, also the temporary closure of the chapter is made conditional on the implementation of other benchmarks.

Needless to say, the technical procedure offers a lot of opportunities, arguments and excuses to Brussels (or any of the member states) to block, or, more likely, to slow down the negotiation process. Special conditions to be fulfilled as a requirement to open or close a chapter may further prolong the duration of the accession path.

Table VI.1. offers a comprehensive "progress report" and the current stage of negotiations at the end of the German Presidency (end June 2007). It can be seen that the negotiation process consists of not less than twelve stages before the country can successfully report on the provisional closing of the given chapter. These stages are:

a) Explanatory stage of screening,
b) Bilateral screening with Croatia (not necessarily at the same time as with Turkey),
c) Screening report to be prepared by the Commission,
d) Council's working group for enlargement discusses the screening report,
e) Benchmarks to open a chapter are identified and have to be fulfilled by Croatia (so-called opening benchmarks),
f) Croatia prepares and delivers its negotiating position to the Commission,
g) The Commission prepares the draft of the common EU position,
h) Council's working group for enlargement discusses the draft common position,
i) The Council adopts the EU's common position for the opening of negotiations (in fact, this is the stage where negotiations on the given chapter start),
j) Croatia meets further benchmark criteria set by the EU in order to provisionally close the chapter (so-called closing benchmarks),
k) Provisional closing of the chapter at the Accession Conference.

The table shows some significant progress but only as a result of opening up six new chapters at the end of June 2007. In more general terms, the picture is less encouraging. In fact, almost two years after starting official negotiations, one-third only of the 35 chapters have been opened. Out of them two "easy" chapters could be provisionally closed (science and research as well as education and culture). All other ten chapters already opened contain one to six benchmarks each to be met before the given chapter can provisionally be closed (the total number of closing benchmarks amounts at the moment to 32). In another ten chapters opening benchmarks have been determined (altogether 20 special requirements). An illustrative list of some closing benchmarks can be found in Appendix Table VI.2.3/1.

In sum, as compared to the process of negotiations with the Luxembourg and, later, with the Helsinki group of Central and Southeastern European countries, the Croatian negotiation is likely to last longer[4], even if optimistic views repeatedly keep on projecting an accelerated procedure from the very beginning of official negotiations.

VI.2.4. Macedonia disposes of a functioning SAA and, encouraged by this agreement, has submitted its application for membership in the spring of 2004. After carrying out the usual examination in the framework of the "avis" procedure that contained 3,000 questions and was answered within record time by Macedonia, the European Council granted candidate status to Macedonia in December 2005. However, this step was not accompanied by any concrete time offer on when negotiations may actually start. More precisely, the official document states that "negotiations will start once sufficient progress with complying with the Copenhagen criteria and the Stabilization and Association Agreement has been achieved" (European Commission, 2006). Obligations not yet met include telecom liberalization and the protectionof the intellectual property. The procedure and the explanation call for some critical remarks. First, looking back at the overall roadmap of the accession process completed by several countries, there used to be a fairly strong correlation between the date of finalizing the "avis" and the announcement of the date of starting negotiations. This is definitely not the case with Macedonia. Second, the official explanation clearly reflects a fundamental structural failure of the EU's Western Balkan conditionality politics. If relevant elements of the Copenhagen criteria and, even more, basic conditions of signing an SAA were not met, how could Macedonia sign an SAA? In turn, if conditions are fulfilled, it is difficult to interpret the remaining objections. Third, the only possible

4 There were just a few weeks between the presentation of the avis and the Luxembourg summit that recommended the Council to start negotiations with six applicant countries in 1998.

interpretation of the quoted explanation can be that the fulfilment of all criteria has several stages. Accordingly, there must be a critical level that has to be achieved in case of each criterion in order to get upgraded in the EU's institutional pyramid. However, the lines between or among different levels of requirements are completely unknown and are at Brussels' discretion.

The outcome of the recent elections will not necessarily make it easier for Macedonia to start accession negotiations. The elections on July 05, 2006 were won by the previous opposition party headed by Gruevski.[5] However, it needed the support of one of the two Albanian parties that also reached the parliamentary threshold. On the surface, nothing has changed, since the previous government consisted of a coalition with Albanians as well. However, the new leading party did not want to enter a coalition with the same Albanian party representing 60% of the Albanian population but with the other one – instead that it has won fewer votes. As a consequence, the Albanian party with more votes wanted to impede the new coalition and has boycotted Parliament from its first meeting in July 2006. Fortunately, until now the decision did not produce special intra-ethnic problems among supporters of both Albanian parties in the country. The picture becomes even more complicated if we are aware of the fact that the smaller Albanian party, with which the winning Macedonian party entered a coalition, is headed by Xhaferi, a politician who used to demand the unification of Kosovo with Albania. At the moment of Kosovo's separation from Serbia, the border issue between Kosovo and Macedonia may come to the fore (it is about 1,200 hectares). Kosovo's Prime Minister, Ceku has never recognized the current border reconfirmed in an agreement signed by Belgrade and Skopje in 2001. Still, the government's five-year program includes preparation for NATO and EU membership by 2010 and meeting EU membership criteria by the same date.

VI.2.5. With a ratified SAA, it is an open question whether and when Albania will follow Croatia and Macedonia and will apply for membership status in Brussels. According to common practice, it can happen any time, and should be followed by the mandate to prepare an avis on all political, economic, social and other aspects of Albania's development level, preparation for EU requirements and "negotiation maturity". How-

---

5 The conservative party (VMRO-DPMNE) got 55 of the altogether 120 seats in the parliament, while the previously governing socialist party obtained 32 seats. In addition, two Albanian parties got sufficient votes to become part of the new parliament. The larger party (DUI) led by Ahmeti was the ally of the socialists in the previous government. However, also the second and smaller Albanian party (DPA) headed by Xhaferi got sufficient votes to join the winning conservative party in a coalition with more or less convenient majority (at least, according to Western European democratic rules).

ever, serious problems could emerge if the expansionist efforts of some Albanian politicians continued let alone intensify as a consequence of the new status of Kosovo.

VI.2.6. Bosnia-Herzegovina, Montenegro and Serbia (let alone Kosovo) represent the bottom of the institutional pyramid. SAA negotiations with Serbia-Montenegro, although started, were frozen in early May 2006, after the repeated non-fulfilment of the EU's demand to find and hand two key war criminals over to the Hague Tribunal, Mladic and Karadzic. After more than one year of interruption, official negotiations were reopened in June 2007. Some experts underline that Serbia may reach SAA status within one year. Despite official refusals, it it clear that this path will closely be connected to the ongoing international and bilateral negotiations on the future status of Kosovo.

Newly independent Montenegro started SAA negotiations in September 2006 and could practically finish them within half a year. However, ratification is pending on some conditions Montenegro still has to fulfill, but the country's SAA status is realistically expected in the autumn of 2007.

Unlike in Montenegro, the path to SAA by Bosnia-Herzegovina may hide unexpected hurdles. First, the finalization of an SAA was linked to some constitutional changes. After several months of uncertainties and domestic political struggles, in late April 2006 the Bosnian parliament failed to ratify the required constitutional changes. Second, progress in SAA negotiations was made dependent on the outcome of general elections in October 2006. Both the election process and the building of a new government occurred in an atmosphere of stability and indicated a certain level of political maturity. Still, the police reform, the last but inevitable condition to be fulfilled before signing the SAA was blocked by Bosnian Serb leaders. They are not ready to give up the entity's "independent" police and oppose any move to allow Bosnian police to cross the inter-entity borders. The Prime Minister of the Republika Srpska has repeatedly indicated that he would rather see Bosnia-Herzegovina lose the opportunity to join the EU than agree to abolish the entity police force.[6] As a result, the several times prolonged deadline to sign the SAA (from October 2006 to March 2007) is again "floating". Furthermore, and not least, the situation may turn out to be even more complicated since, based on the recommendation of the international commission led by Amato, ten years after the Dayton agreement, the Office of the High Representative (a kind of international governor)[7] should be closed in June 2007.

---

6 *Southeast European Times*, February 23, 2007.

7 From 1996 to the present, the position of the High Commissioner was filled by well-known diplomats, such as Bildt, previous Prime Minister of Sweden, Westendorp, ex-

According to current plans, some of the functions will be handed over to Bosnian institutions and to local representatives elected in October 2006. At the same time, the international control will be managed directly by the Commission in Brussels and in person by the commissioner responsible for enlargement (Rehn at the moment). The consequences, if any, for Bosnian stability and domestic politics are difficult to assess. However, it should not be overlooked that this change is scheduled to occur at a time when Montenegro's independence and the status question of Kosovo are changing the political and statehood map of the Western Balkans. Therefore, some experts suggest to prolong the current institutional framework for some more time. This will, however, hardly change the similarly wide gap as experienced in the case of Montenegro and Kosovo, between expectations and realities. This gap, a fertile basis for future widespread disappointment and even new hostilities, seems to be much more of a qualitative character in Bosnia-Herzegovina than in other parts of the Western Balkans, since a "glorious" past for a never before existing new country was invented and widely publicized.[8]

VI.3. Reflections on the Future of Montenegro

VI.3.1. The referendum on the separation of Montenegro from the State Union of Serbia-Montenegro and the declaration of its independence on May 21, 2006 resulted in the creation of a new mini-state in Europe. With a territory of 14,000 km² and a population of about 630,000, it is the smallest ex-Yugoslav country and among the smallest in Europe. This is particularly true to its economic performance if Montenegro is compared to other mini-states in Europe which, although small, all have high living standards and, most of them, specific advantages (financial centre, banking, transportation, tax system) as well.[9]

VI.3.2. Montenegro is proud of its 1,000-year history because it was the only Balkan territory that was never under lasting Turkish occupation. For the first time in history, Montenegro became independent in 1878 by a decision at the Berlin Congress on how to restructure parts of the previous Ottoman Empire in the Balkans. In 1910, it was converted into a

---

foreign minister of Spain, Petritsch, an Austrian high-level diplomat, the British opposition leader Ashdorf, and, at the moment (until the planned handing over of most authorities to Bosnian politicians and institutions) Schwarz-Schilling from Germany, and post minister of the Kohl government.

8 Some amateurs state that they have found much older and larger pyramids in Bosnia thant hose in Egypt dated back to 12,500 years. Thus, Bosnia would "rewrite the history of the world". Not less importantly, this will be the most convincing argument to experience a quick path to EU membership (!!). *The Economist*, August 12, 2006, p. 24.

9 For a comparison see Appendix Table VI.3.1.1.

kingdom. In 1918, the Serb majority in the Podgorica legislation opted for joining the Serb-Croat-Slovene kingdom and Montenegro became part of Yugoslavia. After the Second World War, Montenegro remained part of Tito's Yugoslavia but achieved a higher level of self-determination in the newly created federal structure. The overwhelming majority supported Milosevic's rise to power and, in the 1992 referendum 96% of the population decided in favour of remaining part of Milosevic's rump-Yugoslavia. The political break with Serbia happened in 1997, when Djukanovic won the elections. His main priority was to squeeze Serbian politicians out of Montenegro's power structure. As an important element in the growing independence from Belgrade, an independent economic policy was designed and implemented. The Yugoslav dinar was replaced first by the German mark, and later by the Euro and an independent fiscal and customs policy was introduced.[10] Moreover, important national symbols were created as a sign of distinction from Serbia (new national flag and anthem, new date of the national day).

Nevertheless, after the end of the Kosovo war, Montenegro was not allowed to become an independent state but was obliged by the Western powers to enter a forced State Union with Belgrade. This initiative largely came from the EU and from Solana, in particular. With some cynicism, the new formation was called "Solania", a structure invented by the highest ranking foreign policy representative of the EU. Fortunately, the agreement contained a paragraph saying that after three years a new referendum may be held on independence or sticking with Serbia and head to Brussels together. This legal possibility was made use of in May 2006. Most Montenegrins see in independence a historical continuation of what started in 1878.

VI.3.3. Also, Montenegro emphasizes a positive feature namely that as a multi-ethnic country it was the only ex-Yugoslav republic whose territory remained exempt from war and ethnic hostilities. On the contrary, the country took in several waves of refugees at times amounting to about 20% of its total population. The ethnic composition shows a rather balanced proportion of Montenegrins and Serbs (although they are hard to distinguished since they speak the same language and most of them have the same orthodox catholic religion), with 40% each.[11] Larger minorities include Albanians, Croats and Bosniaks. Interestingly, it was still the ethnic composition that seemed to play a decisive role in the pro-

[10] Montenegro did not participate in Serbia's bilateral trade deals either. For instance, the agreement with Brussels on better access of Serbian textile and clothing articles to EU markets does not include similar products from Montenegro.

[11] In the 1991 census, 62% of the population admitted to be Montenegrins, followed by Muslims (15%), Serbs (9%) and Albanians (7%). Certainly, the question of staying with Belgrade or voting for independence has largely polarized the society.

independence outcome of the referendum. Taking Montenegrins and Serbs alone, most probably the State Union would have been maintained, since most Serbs voted for keeping the status quo. However, ethnic minorities, primarily Albanians and Bosniaks, voted almost unanimously for independence and, of course, against Serbia. The overall outcome of more than 55% in favour of independence hides the strong geographic concentration of different ethnic groups. In most areas either Serbs or Montenegrins formed an overwhelming majority (above 80% of the votes). Regions mainly populated by Albanians overwhelmingly voted in line with the Montenegrins.

VI.3.4. The legal framework of the referendum was unique, since, according to the relevant regulations only those were entitled to vote who had been living in the territory of Montenegro for at least two years prior to the referendum. Montenegrins working abroad or living in Serbia as well as Serbs with Montenegrin roots but living outside the country were not allowed to participate in the referendum. Calculations made on this legal basis suggested that the majority (50% plus one vote) can be reached by the pro-independence voters. The other precondition of valid referendum, namely the 50% participation of those entitled to vote has never been questioned. Since, however, the EU did not like a new independent state in the Balkans and did not want to humiliate Serbia any further, a unique and highly undemocratic condition was created. Solana imposed a rule on the leadership in Podgorica according to which independence required a 55% share of total votes. If this condition had not been accepted, the EU would not have recognized Montenegro's independence even if a simple majority favoured independence. Obviously, this highly undemocratic and unprecedented procedure did not increase the EU's popularity. Still, at least for the time being, the appeasing and reassuring majority of almost 56% (against 44%) let the pro-independence voters (and the politicians) forget about the EU's behaviour. Brussels seemed to be relieved as well, once the results became public.

VI.3.5. The real challenges are, however, still ahead of the youngest multi-ethnic nation-state in Europe. It is correctly noted in a comment prepared shortly after the referendum, that national sovereignty is not a goal in itself. It is a framework that may still to prove a success or failure.[12]

First: it is widely believed that separation from Serbia will substantially speed up Montenegro's way to the EU. It does not have to remain a "junior partner" of Belgrade and wait until Serbia is ready to comply with different EU requirements. It is interesting that, according to the president

[12] Tupy (2006), p. 13,

of the Republic, Montenegrin national identity would have been much more at risk in case of joining the EU in a union with Serbia than as a small but independent country.[13] At the moment, nobody is dealing with the new reality. Namely, Montenegro as a sovereign state has to start negotiations with the EU from scratch, since the agreements reached in negotiations between Serbia-Montenegro and Brussels cannot be transferred to Podgorica.[14] Nevertheless, experts hope that the results already achieved in previous joint negotiations between Belgrade and Brussels will be automatically acknowledged and the negotiations can be accelerated. One problem could be the lack of EU experts in the new country, since all official contacts with Brussels were managed by Serbian administrators. In spite of the above mentioned potential handicaps Montenegro emphasizes the fundamental advantage of having ridded itself of one of the most serious barriers to streamlining negotiations with the EU. In fact, the EU conditionality of handing over war criminals has nothing to do with Montenegro, while, in a State Union, Podgorica would have remained hostage to Belgrade's political opposition to EU demands.

Second: there are comprehensive plans to revitalize the economy. There are some exaggerated claims that Montenegro might become the "Liechtenstein of the Balkans" in the medium-term. This and other optimistic attitudes have little in common with the quite serious challenges stemming from everyday reality. There is a wide gap between nominal and real convergence of the economy. In fact, Montenegro uses the euro as official currency and has low inflation (1.8% in 2005), a balanced budget (well within the 3% margin of GDP) and a low level of public debt (42.5% of GDP). However, the fulfilment of the Maastricht criteria does not automatically mean real convergence. The economy has few productive sectors. Official unemployment is over 20%, real unemployment is much higher. The average monthly salary is about Euro 200, foreign direct investment is modest and competitiveness of goods is insufficient. Only about 20% of the territory is cultivable (not necessarily also cultivated) agricultural land. In turn, smuggling and corruption are widespread. Short- and medium-term pillars of sustained economic growth cannot be identified without the sole exception of tourism. However, here again, the high-flying hopes seem to be largely unfounded. First, despite the unique natural beauty, one sector can hardly put the economy on a solid and lasting growth path. Second, natural beauty is far from sufficient, if adequate tourist facilities are either unavailable or on a quality level that would call for immediate and large-scale investments.

---

[13] Djukanovic (2006), p. 13.

[14] The same happened when Czechoslovakia was split and the Association Agreement still negotiated and signed with this country (in December 1991), had to be renegotiated with both successor countries (in 1993).

Third, more than half of the tourists used to come from Serbia, since many Serbs own houses and apartments on the seashore.[15] It is highly uncertain whether this flow will continue and what would happen to property owners if they happen to be Serbian citizens. Still, it has to be admitted that the government has spoken of quick and decisive economic decisions in order to create the most favourable conditions to business in the Western Balkans. Accordingly, corporate tax rate is just 9% and will be abolished in coming years. Four days and three documents are needed to register a company. No less important, the country would like to introduce English as one of the official languages.

Third: the weak economy coexists with a(n extremely) weak public administration. This can prove a barrier to sign relevant agreements with the EU, since the latter requires an administrative capacity capable of implementing and enforcing commitments. Evidence of limits to the government's competence are provided by the low level of judiciary reform, the modest record of combating organized crime and the inefficient fight against corruption.

Fourth: separation from Serbia has several political, social and technical consequences. The few common issues that were managed by the State Union, have to be split (*e.g.* foreign policy, embassies, representation in international organizations). More difficulties may arise from the settlement of properties of Montenegrins in Serbia, since about 400,000 "Montenegrins" (Serbians and Montenegrins) live currently on Serbian territory. What about visa policies? Will two neighbouring Western Balkan countries mutually introduce visa restrictions or can "double citizenship" be introduced? Finally, what will happen to a historically evolved special region called Sandzak that will be split by the Montenegrin-Serbian state border?[16]

Fifth: independence is likely to generate major and pressing social and economic problems. According to available data, there are several hundred thousands of Montenegrin citizens living, working and studying in

---

15 In 2005, about 820,000 tourists came to Montenegro, or at least 25% more than the total population of the country. However, the large majority, about 550,000 persons arrived from the ex-Yugoslav republics, mainly from Serbia. The tourist sector is by far the largest employer, since every sixth employee finds a job, directly or indirectly, in this sector. The decline of tourism would further increase unemployment and make prospects for development, survival or even staying in the country uncertain. For details see: *Frankfurter Allgemeine Zeitung*, May 23, 2006, p. 8.

16 Sandzak is located between Serbia, Montenegro, Bosnia and Kosovo. Following the Berlin Congress in 1878 the region remained under Osman administration but Austria-Hungary got the right to have military units there. Sandzak registers 11 towns and villages, out of which 6 belong to Serbia and 5 to Montenegro. Large part of the population (above 60%) are Bosniak Moslems and the demographic map is rapidly shifting in favour of Moslems. See in detail: Martens (2006f), p. 6.

Serbia. They may become foreigners very soon and face rather difficult times. About 10,000 students will have to stop studying under the current conditions. As foreigners, the will have to pay higher tuition fees (if they can afford to). Many of them do not have the real option to return to Podgorica, since the Montenegrin higher education does not offer as many choices in higher education as Serbia. Public servants lose all of their privileges they enjoyed in a State Union. Already prior to the referendum about 6,000 Montenegrin citizens employed in education and public health have been dismissed in Serbia. Many more will be followed. For skilled and unskilled workers, special work permit may be needed to keep their job in Serbia. The Montenegrin economy and public administration can hardly absorb a potential massive inflow of citizens. Most of them would add to the already high number (and share) of unemployed people. Thus, the day may come soon when the majority of people will not only enjoy the symbolic importance of independence but also bear the high economic costs of "sovereignty". Moreover, in the future it will be impossible to blame Belgrade for all domestic problems. Comparisons between Serbia and Montenegro based on obvious advantages and much more progress made in Montenegro can become more balanced and not always point to real advantages of a small country. In this context, the next country report of the Commission that will deal with Serbia and Montenegro in separate documents can provide some sobering and disappointing remarks on the state of affairs and the realistic foundation of EU-related hopes for Montenegro.

VI.3.6. Brussels has acknowledged the result of the referendum and, together with all EU member countries, established diplomatic relations with the new state. Also the new diplomatic position of Montenegro could be smoothly arranged. It has been recognized by the large majority of the international community. In addition, the country became the 192nd member of the Untied Nations, and asked for membership in the Council of Europe (expected in June 2007).

Facing a new situation, in September 2006 the Commission got the mandate to start negotiations on a SAA. In this context it has to be underlined that, from the very beginning, Brussels did not want to face the reality of another small state in the highly unstable Western Balkan region, let alone one that has common borders with Kosovo and Bosnia, two hot spots of potential conflicts. By imposing on Montenegro the State Union with Serbia in 2002, the EU believed this instrument was effective to avoid further destabilization. The independence of Montenegro was thought to be a vehicle of independence of Kosovo with unpredictable impact both on the whole region and on Serbian domestic and regional politics. However, separation could not be prevented and it came at a critical moment of negotiations on the future status of Kosovo. To be sure, the independence of Montenegro is not expected to generate a domino effect in the Western Balkans (or, as a potential reference point, elsewhere, *e.g.* in the crisis regions of Russia). Nevertheless, the danger should not be underestimated, let alone ignored, that the simultaneity of Montenegrin developments with essential changes in Kosovo and reactions to the changes in Serbia can produce a spark with immeasurable adversities. More importantly, such a scenario should not be overlooked when the coincidence of major events happens in a region characterized by weak (or failed) states, inefficient institutions, high and growing economic problems and only apparently and superficially "controlled" ethnic tensions.

VI.3.7. On its part and at first glance, Serbia has accepted Montenegro's decision for separation with calm. Certainly, it is by far not as sensitive an issue as the future of Kosovo. Also, everyday reality of the State Union was anything but "union". In most vital economic and domestic political areas the two parts of the Union became separate years ago and the creation of the artificial "Solania" could not check this process either. Furthermore, Serbia had stopped its financial support to Montenegro several years ago.

Still, the new situation produced new realities and, accordingly, some recent reactions as well. First, as a consequence of Montenegro's independence, Serbia has lost its last direct access to the Adriatic Sea. Yugoslavia used to have a long and highly variable seashore (with thousands of islands and unique tourist attractions), the new Serbia became a landlocked country, similar to several other Central European countries such as Austria, Czech Republic, Slovakia, Hungary, Switzerland. Changes that happen instantly in the geographic map need much more time to be absorbed and processed in people's minds, in terms of economic planning and social attitude. In various fields, the consequences are yet to be felt. Second, the economic and social segregation between "Serbs" and "Montenegrins" living in the territory of Serbia has already started before the referendum. As a result of independence, however, this development will substantially intensify. One can only hope that it will not end in latent or open hostilities. Third, as it could be expected, the Serbian Parliament reacted in less than two weeks to the independence of Montenegro by passing a law on considering the Republic of Serbia as the legal successor of Serbia-Montenegro. Therefore, in all international organizations Serbia will keep the previous place of Serbia-Montenegro, while Montenegro, as a new state, has to wait for diplomatic recognition and apply for a new place in all international institutions. Fourth, the result of the referendum has further burdened the already complicated and cloudy relations between Belgrade and Brussels. Fully in line with the "conspiracy theory", Kostunica accused Brussels of generating anti-Serbian sentiments in

Montenegro before the referendum, when official negotiations on the SAA were frozen. When Solana offered its support to the coming negotiations between Serbia and Montenegro on settling and separating outstanding agreements, the Serbian reaction was that Belgrade did not want any kind of help "à la Solana".[17]

VI.4. The Challenge of Kosovo

VI.4.1. The solution for the future status of Kosovo is crucial not only for the stability of the Western Balkans but also in the context of the EU's development as a European (and global) political player. For several reasons, Kosovo is not Montenegro. It cannot look back to its own national history, let alone statehood. It has always been an internationally recognized integral part of Serbia (and Yugoslavia). Its population is three times higher than that of Montenegro. Moreover, it is not based on a multi-ethnic cooperative culture as Montenegro which has successfully managed such a situation over centuries, including the last and very critical decade. More than 90% of the population consists of Albanians, with a small and shrinking Serbian minority. Finally, Kosovo is controlled by security forces from the United Nations (UNMIK). Right to the point, some observers call it "Unmikistan".

VI.4.2. Kosovo has been under Serbian sovereignty since 1912. In the federal structure of Yugoslavia it enjoyed a high level of autonomy from 1973 to the early 1990s. Although it belonged to Serbia, as one (and the strongest) constituent part of the federation, but with substantial self-determination (similar to the other autonomous area within Serbia, Voivodina). However, the qualitative legal difference was that while "the people" of each of the states forming the federation had the right to secede, the two autonomous regions were firmly anchored legally in Serbia. This structure was based on the differentiation between "people" ("narod") and "nationality" (narodnost). The former got their own republic, while nationalities were not given the right to self-determination. The official argument was that these nationalities (namely Albanians and Hungarians) have their nation-state outside Yugoslavia.[18] Milosevic abolished this system of limited autonomy and created a "unified" Serbia.

Kosovo was heavily involved in the Balkan wars. The wars were used by the Yugoslav (Serbian) army to strengthen its presence in Kosovo that was already overwhelmingly populated by Albanians with very low participation in the management of the region (which was firmly controlled by the Serbian administration). After the failure of the Kosovo

17 Martens (2006c), p. 5.

18 Martens (2005b).

conference in March 1999, NATO launched air attacks against Serbian targets. In turn, Belgrade intensified its land campaign to expel Albanians from Kosovo. Hostilities ended on June 10, 1999 with a resolution (No. 1244) of the Security Council of the United Nations, an standard reference from then on to all kinds of efforts to create sustainable stability in and around Kosovo. The UN mission in Kosovo (UNMIK) can be considered one of the most ambitious and largest endeavours of the United Nations. It is led by a special representative of the UN (first Steiner from Germany, after 2004 Jessen-Petersen from Denmark). According to the UN resolution, the main objective of the international governance is to cement stability and build up a viable administration with the incorporation of the "people of Kosovo" (Albanians and Serbs alike), by giving them "substantive autonomy within the Federal Republic of Yugoslavia". Thus, the document does not question (does not even mention) the territorial integrity of Yugoslavia.

As an important step believed to stabilize Kosovo and help establish democratic political structures was the approval of a provisional constitution in May 2001. In November of that same year, elections were held in order to elect members of a provisional parliament in Prishtina. Since, following recommendation from Belgrade, the Serb population did not attend the elections, Albanian parties, including those supporting full the independence of Kosovo even by armed force, achieved a landslide victory. Supported by the election results, almost all government positions have been taken by Albanians, and Serbian administrators were "squeezed out" of their jobs.[19] Simultaneously, domestic pressure for independence was growing further.

However, the predominance of Albanians in all areas was not only the result of a certainly much larger population than that of the Serbs. The UN resolution explicitly stated that appropriate conditions have to be secured for refugees and displaced persons to return to their former homes. Within a few weeks, hundreds of thousands of Albanians returned, and expelled Serbs from their homes. In addition, many Serbs did not see their personal safety guaranteed in a predominantly Albanian community. Their fears became reality in 2004, when Albanians rioted in Kosovo and destroyed not only Serbian homes but also some of the most sacred Serbian churches and monasteries. The allied forces were unable to prevent the outbreak of Albanian atrocities and could "stabilize" the situation only several days later, after serious damage, both physical and psychological, had already been done. The capacity to keep the situation

---

19 For instance, the electricity company, being the largest company in Kosovo, previously had as many Serb as Albanian employees. At present, practically no Serb staff has remained.

in Kosovo under control would have needed the (limited) presence of Serbian soldiers (or policemen). The UN resolution permitted the return of a previously agreed number of military and police personal in order to clean up minefields as well as to safeguard historical buildings and border crossings. However, this possibility remained on paper. In sum, Kosovo became more and more an ethnically almost "clean" country. It became more and more difficult to live with the everyday and obvious contradiction that a region almost devoid of Serbs still belonged to Serbia politically.

VI.4.3. Fully aware of the explosive situation in Kosovo and the rapidly growing support for full independence without any guarantee for a normally functioning administration and for "ethnic stability", the high representative of the UN, Steiner has formulated the basic principle that should have been observed concerning the future status of Kosovo. "Standards before status" meant that status issues can only be seriously discussed once several fundamental standards of stability and sustainability have been achieved. The riots in 2004 proved that, despite the large UN role, Kosovo was absolutely unable to achieve such standards. Still, the status issue remained on the agenda and rapidly started to break its linkage (conditionality) to standards. Since nobody was able to contain the political dynamic, negotiations on the status issue could not be avoided any more, albeit without any kind of conditionalities in the spirit of the Steiner principle. Evidently, conditionalities, or more precisely, some key framework conditions remained, but they were incorporated into the political negotiations and had nothing to do with stabilizing the situation before seriously thinking of any concrete talks on the future of Kosovo.

VI.4.4. In its 2005 report, the Balkan Commission chaired by Amato came to the conclusion that the official negotiations on the future status of Kosovo cannot be delayed any further. Certainly, the independence of Kosovo would by far not solve all problems but any other option, including the artificial maintenance of the current situation seems to be worse. Therefore, a four-stage recommendation was formulated. First, overwriting the UN resolution No. 1,244, Kosovo will separate itself from Serbia. Second, Kosovo will get "independence without full sovereignty" (in contrast to the Serbian preference of "more than autonomy but less than independence"). It implies that the political responsibility will be transferred to domestic political groups and institutions. However, the international community reserves the right to intervene any time the government does not observe the Copenhagen criteria or does not keep previously made and binding commitments. Special emphasis is laid on the observation of human and minority rights. In this phase, Kosovo formally remains a UN protectorate but the leading political role will be taken by the

EU. At the same time, the international forces under NATO's auspices will remain in Kosovo. In order to keep peace, the northern part of Kosovo (Mitrovica) where most Serbs live shall enjoy a special status and the protection of the allied forces, along with the remaining orthodox churches. This stage also foresees the establishment of a decentralized structure, with Serbian self-governance in areas with a Serbian majority population. Moreover, for better cooperation between Albanians and Serbs, the EU should develop special incentives for companies that are ready to employ citizens belonging to the respective ethnic minority. The third stage is labelled "guided sovereignty". Here, Kosovo would be recognized as an EU candidate country and negotiations with Brussels may be opened. However, a precondition is the sovereignty of Kosovo, for the EU does not have the mandate to negotiate with one of its protectorates. Therefore, EU influence has to be converted from a direct to an indirect one. The situation in Kosovo will be controlled by the well-known conditionalities of Brussels. Negotiations can be interrupted any time if basic conditions are not fulfilled. However, whatever happens in Kosovo, the EU will not have the direct instruments to intervene, as it is available in the first and second stage of Kosovo's future path as laid out in the Amato document. Finally, the fourth stage called "full and shared sovereignty" will represent the incorporation of Kosovo into EU structures and policies, including full membership in institutional and legal terms (Amato, 2005, pp. 170-172).

VI.4.5. Based on the above recommendations, official negotiations between the international Contact Group chaired by Ahtisaari, as well as the representatives of Belgrade and Prishtina started in February 2006 in Vienna. For a period of almost one year, several meetings have been held without any tangible or acceptable results to all parties involved. The forum was considered to be an opportunity to put forward Serbian and Kosovar arguments as if they represented an important factor in a future decision on the status of Kosovo. These so-called negotiations were more like saving face in order to show the Serb and the Kosovar society that their respective leaders "are fighting hard". The basic Serb position is that Kosovo is historically a Serbian territory (practically the location where the Serb state/nation was born[20]). Therefore, the argument that there are living more than 2 million Albanians, cannot provide a legal basis for separating itself from Serbia. Some extremists even hold that the Kosovo

---

20 In itself, it is more than interesting that the birth of a country/nation is linked to a momentous and historically far-reaching defeat and not to a victory. For almost five centuries, independence was lost in 1389 in Kosovo Polje (Amselfeld) in a decisive battle against the Osman Empire. Still, it was this event that helped keep national identity over several centuries, despite the fact that the first mythical legends on this tragic event appeared a century later.

question can best be solved by ignoring any autonomy to the region and bring it back firmly under Serbian rule and authority. In turn, Prishtina cannot imagine any other solution than full-fledged independence. There is a large – and for many experts in the neighbouring countries but also in the EU frightening – majority that sees in the independence a decisive step towards creating "Great Albania".[21] In fact, the Serbian and the Kosovar position reflect two different aspects of international law. Serbia rightly refers to "territorial integrity", while Kosovo emphasizes the "right to self-determination" (Judah, 2006, p. 2).

The third and probably decisive party, the EU hesitated for a long time about how to shape the future of Kosovo. Recently, the position seems to prevail that Kosovo has to become independent but with several restrictions and conditionalities (more than autonomy but less than full-fledged independence). However, it does not mean that all EU member countries fully share this view.[22] There is, however, a consensus at least in two issues. First, no option should lead to border changes that could generate a domino effect in other parts of the Western Balkans (first of all in Bosnia-Herzegovina) and could be interpreted as a precedent far away from Southeastern Europe as well. Therefore, the possibility to attach Kosovo regions with Serbian majority to Serbia and create an ethnically even "cleaner" Albanian Kosovo by guaranteeing stability through dividing borders has not been seriously considered. Second, Kosovo's independence does not have any linkage, not even in the distant future, to the creation of a "Great(er) Albania".

Some weeks later than originally planned, the chief negotiator Ahtisaari presented his plan of the future of Kosovo in early February 2007, very well being aware that the official position of Belgrade and Prishtina remained unchanged.[23] One has the impression that the Vienna talks were a "meeting of autists". Negotiations on decentralization of the public administration in Kosovo, property rights, the number and status of Serbian communities in Kosovo with a changed status ended without any result. Only small progress was made in recognizing the special status of

---

21 Rugova, Kosovo's late president belonged to the moderate politicians in Prishtina. But even he stated that independence can only be considered as a compromise between the current status and unification with Albania which, accordingly, would be the optimal solution (Van Meurs and Weiss, 2005, p. 5).

22 For instance and probably based on their personal and successful experience, the Czechs and Slovaks are definitely for full independence. Evidently, what could work in some cases, is not necessarily functioning in other situations. Just to mention one "small" difference consisting in the capacity of the political structure and public administration to manage the given country.

23 The negotiations were correctly characterized by a Bertelsmann Foundation document as "negotiating the non-negotiable" (Van Meurs and Weiss, 2005, p. 3).

the Serbian monasteries on Kosovo's territory (free access for pilgrims and the sovereignty of the Orthodox Church and the patriarch in Belgrade).[24] Another stumbling block is the person of Agim Ceku, the new Kosovo Prime Minister, who was appointed by the new president, Fatmir Sejdiu after the death of Ibrahim Rugova. Ceku was an Albanian guerrilla leader during years of hostilities but, interestingly, not accused by the Hague tribunal of war crimes as his Serbian (and Croatian) counterparts. Still, and understandably, he cannot be accepted by the Serbs as a negotiation partner. In consequence, status negotiations are unlikely to produce any progress and may end in a deadlock, while the political dynamism is working unstoppably.

However, two recent developments deserve mention. One can be seen in Serbian minority circles in Kosovo that started to prepare themselves for the new situation of living in an independent Kosovo and organize their activities accordingly.[25] The other shift is apparent in Belgrade. Most (but by far not all) politicians had to admit that Kosovo cannot be kept within Serbian territory any more. Therefore, two parallel efforts have been designed.

On the one hand, a list of Serbian demands was drawn up concerning the future rights of the Serb minority in Kosovo. As a starting position for negotiations, it includes all conceivable forms of autonomy (individual, collective, territorial, economic, judiciary and educational) (Van Meurs and Weiss, 2005, p. 8). Certainly, it is obvious already that by far not all of them and not in full scope will remain in the final text of an eventual agreement. Even more important is that Belgrade and the EU (as demonstrated in various documents and statements) may have different interpretations of observing minority rights. Apparently, Serbia wants full-fledged autonomy for its minority in Kosovo that would create a closed ethnic region and a part of a "federal" Kosovo, similar to the Bosnian structure. In contrast, the international community has a different idea to protect the Serb minority by offering full-scale integration into the new status. Instead of creating new and highly dangerous "ethnic islands", opportunities and instruments for inter-ethnic cooperation have to be significantly fostered.[26]

---

24 Martens (2006j).

25 However, different Serb communities may need different survival patterns. Areas geographically connected with Serbia (*e.g.* Mitrovitza) cannot be put on the same level as smaller Serbian settlements surrounded by Albanian majority population (*e.g.* Lipljan that has about 800 Serbs with 6,500 Albanians in the direct neighbourhood). *The Economist*, July 22, 2006, p. 35.

26 The negative experience with the Bosnian Federation and its internal partition are obviously influencing the negotiating position of the EU (less that of the USA that is ready to accept the negotiations as an "open process").

The second and parallel approach is a bargaining process behind closed doors about what Serbia may get in exchange from Brussels (and the USA), if it gives up its original position and shows a certain degree of flexibility. It is difficult to assess where the limits are to the flexibility of the EU (and the USA), since it is not Serbia but the international community led by the EU that is in a rather strong policy-maker position. Namely, Serbia cannot bloc or veto any international agreement on changing the status of Kosovo. It has to accept the new situation. The international parties, however, have to take into account that the decision should not produce further damage, destabilization or open crisis either in Serbia or in the entire Western Balkans.

VI.4.6. Whatever agreement (decision) will be negotiated (imposed) on the future status of Kosovo, the implementation will not depend only on the efficiency of international control. To a large extent, the question is to what extent Kosovo is prepared for any kind of (more) independence? The fundamental concerns and uncertainties start at this point. It is obvious that Kosovo will become the most artificial "state creation" in the Balkans. It will add to the list of failed states or protectorates controlled by another big power(s). Newly founded statehood, extremely weak domestic administration and completely unjustified hopes by the Albanian population contrast with the demand to implement hopefully rigorous (and not diluted) international conditions concerning democracy, the rule of law, minority rights on the one hand, and the bleak economic reality, on the other.

As described in the previous subchapter, the contrast between expectations and reality is enormous in Montenegro. Compared to the Montenegro situation, Kosovo is in a much worse shape. In fact, it is literally the "Balkan suburb of utopia".[27] Nevertheless, it would like to become the "Bahrain of Europe",[28] based on the only natural resource it has, low-quality lignite. Despite some reconstruction of roads, houses and schools after the 1999 war, the economy lacks any meaningful resource to start sustainable economic development. Despite being the (almost) only European "country" with a rapidly increasing population, the human resource potential is absolutely inadequate for the requirements of the 21st century (half the adults only completed primary education and 6% are illiterate). The current level of GDP *per capita* of less than Euro 1,600 is the lowest in the Western Balkans. Decades-long difficulties of catching up are illustrated by the fact that Kosovo used to get huge amounts of financial transfer in ex-Yugoslavia in order to narrow the significant development gap between more developed parts of the country and its

[27] Martens (2006g), p. 7.
[28] Martens (2006k), p. 5.

economic poor house.[29] Still, convergence, based on the financial resources, that should have been started could hardly be supported by facts. After the Yugoslavia's collapse, transfer payments were unilaterally provided by Belgrade, again without any visible result.

In contrast to most other SEE countries, economic growth shows big fluctuations, with high growth based on imminent reconstruction in 2000-2001 and negative growth rates in the following years. As a geographic disadvantage, the country is landlocked, with the nearest port in Thessaloniki, since there is no connection to the Albanian port of Durres. Agriculture, a potential source of development, is based on self-subsistence without any competitive advantage (not even in the neighbouring markets). Economic activities are concentrated on small-scale import-based trade and services and only in very few cases on domestic production. In spite of the massive inflow of capital, both private remittances and international transfers, the economy does not show any signs of sustainable revival. Growth, if any, is fully based on consumption that mainly consists of consumption financed from private remittances or the consumption by the massive presence of the representatives of the international community living in Kosovo (several thousands of administrative staff and a 17,000-strong military force). In just a few years, UNMIK spent about Euro 2.6 bn on commodities, services and personal costs.[30] Trade practically means one-sided imports, since exports are almost non-existent (Euro 43 mn in 2005, against imports for more than Euro 1 bn). Deficit of trade and service flows amounts close to 70% of GDP. Unemployment is between 30 and 45%, but is at least 70% among young people. As the only European country with a high birth rate and positive domestic demographic trends, about 20,000 young people enter the (imaginary) labour market annually. Most of the labour force is unskilled and inactive, due to the demoralizing impact of transfers from abroad and partly to longstanding historical traditions. The discrepancy between high expectations for becoming a "magnet for foreign direct investments" and the desolate state of the environment (streets, parks, public places and lighting) is striking. Needless to say, creating normal living conditions is not a question of money but one of mentality and discipline. The latter is fully absent since everybody can do what he or she wants, without any

---

29 By the end of the 1970s, the golden age of ex-Yugoslavia, the *per capita* GDP amounted to USD 5,315 in Slovenia as compared to USD 795 in Kosovo, being the Yugoslav average USD 2,635. See Martens (2006h), p. 10.

30 Even if only some (according to some estimates, a quarter) of this money remains in Kosovo, its positive impacts should have already been felt. The only feasible consequence, however, is the employment of several thousands of Kosovar citizens with wages that are substantially higher than the average wage of people employed outside the UNMIK.

legal consequences. According to conservative estimates, at least 70% of the houses and apartments have been built without a permit. Many people simply don't paying for electricity and other utilities. Consequences – although very much contrary to those what could be expected in a "normal" country – follow only when somebody tries to introduce measures against individual irresponsibility, undisciplined attitude or the constant violation of laws.[31]

There is widespread optimism that independence would generate massive capital inflows and would develop Kosovo as a magnet for foreign investors. However, one needs extremely vivid imagination as to from where, into which sectors and why capital should come. There is no plan known from any country and any investor who is eager to invest in Kosovo. Except for lignite, the country lacks natural resources. According to estimates, an electrical power station based on domestic lignite could not only stabilize the domestic electricity supply but become the largest export sector of the country (up to 17% of the GDP). In contrast to high hopes, the current situation is characterized by regular breakdowns of the electricity supply. Another unanswered question is why foreign capital should come into a country with a (theoretically massive) supply of unskilled and undisciplined labour? But, above all, investors, both (serious) domestic and foreign ones, need order, transparency, a well functioning public administration, a low crime rate. None of them is available at the moment in Kosovo.

While it is highly unlikely that separation from Serbia will attract more investments and speed up privatization to interested foreigners, the negative impact will be clearly felt from the very beginning of the new status. First, Belgrade will stop transferring money to the new state (as it used to do so until it was its territory). Second, part of the foreign debt of Serbia may be "reallocated" to Prishtina with a negative impact on the balance of payments. Third, Kosovar citizens regularly working in Serbian enterprises will be fired or will need special permission to keep on working there. The already unprecedented level of unemployment will keep on rising. Since, officially, the Western European market remains closed to Kosovar Albanians,[32] the domestic pressure on the labour market will further grow. The straightforward consequence is even higher

---

[31] The head of the city planning office tried to reduce the predominant disorder in the housing market. The disorder survived, the man was shot on the street.

[32] In the medium term, and disregarding large-scale international financial support, the only way to sustain the economy would be remittances generated by exporting more and more (unskilled) labour. For more than one reason, however, this option seems to be extremely limited.

criminality and a potential springboard of international terrorism in a region that used to belong to the hot spots of instability and crime.[33]

In sum, the final and most urgent question is who will pay the bill for independence, and who will substitute the money previously transferred by Belgrade? In addition, international transfers are also likely to be reduced in the future. Before trying to answer this question, one additional remark has to be made. The issue of financial transfers once again emerges in a society that had been accustomed to rent seeking over decades (first in the Yugoslav period, later under international governance). For Kosovar Albanians, the answer is evident: it is the responsibility of the international community and in no way the duty of the citizens of the country that is waiting for "independence". In no other European country had the rights and responsibilities, personal freedom and responsible behaviour been as much separated from one another as in Kosovo.

VI.4.7. On February 02, 2007 Ahtisaari presented his plan for the future of Kosovo. A delicately balanced approach suggests sovereignty for Kosovo under substantial international control. Extensive measures to safeguard the future of all communities living in Kosovo, especially the Kosovo Serbs are included in the package. Since, however, neither the Albanians nor the Serbs were satisfied with the plan, the negotiation period was extended and intensive consultations are expected to be running in the first half of 2007. Even in the best case, voting in the UN Security Council is unlikely before the autumn of 2007.

Despite the current uncertainties, some conclusions already seem to be "carved in stone" for the future of Kosovo. First, the need for continuing international military presence is non-negotiable.[34] Second, the Serbian minority has to get strong legal guarantees and acquire some role in the new, "independent" government (not least in the field of judiciary). Third, the international presence has to remain at least on the level it has achieved in recent years. Within the international governance a (much) larger EU role cannot and should not be avoided. The key question is not whether the EU will assume a larger responsibility for Kosovo but to what extent is it prepared to carry out this unprecedented task in a transparent, reliable and efficient way. Instead of speculating on tentative answers and different scenarios, it is sufficient to underline that the future status of Kosovo and the EU's growing liability to the region will not reduce the number of dilemmas the European integration is facing in the next period.

---

[33] One of the Serb arguments in favour of keeping Kosovo within the territory of Serbia was that criminality can be controlled easier and more efficiently in the framework of a larger state with more adequate instruments. Jansson and MacDonald (2006), pp. 1-2.

[34] *International Herald Tribune*, August 19-20, 2006, p. 4.

VI.5. The Serbian Factor

VI.5.1. Seemingly, Serbia has been a full-fledged participant of the Vienna conference on the future status of Kosovo. However, a closer look makes it obvious that its scope of activity was very limited when we start from the fundamental difference between the original Belgrade position on the future of Kosovo and what most likely will be the result of an international agreement (or decision). Most likely, Serbia has no chance to keep Kosovo within its territory. The "independence" of Kosovo based on EU (and American) plans cannot be prevented. It took a long time until responsible Serbian politicians (by far not all of those who had been influencing domestic politics and "washing the brains" of the Serbian society) recognized that the original Serbian position on Kosovo, namely the prolongation of territorial integrity by keeping Kosovo within the boundaries of Serbia, cannot be maintained. After gradually becoming aware of the new realities of policy-maker vs. policy-taker power relations, two important shifts has emerged in the Serbian practice (not necessarily in the communication policy towards the population that kept following the hard line of no compromise). On the one hand, negotiating experts tried to get the best conditions out of the changing status of Kosovo with respect to the protection of the rights of the Serbian minority and Serbian cultural sites in the entity. Second, and simultaneously, negotiations behind closed doors were initiated on the potential "reward" Belgrade may get in exchange of facilitating[35] the process of giving Kosovo a new status, both from the EU (integration-related issues) and from the USA (NATO-related issues).

While the EU (and the US) have firmly rejected all Serbian approaches to leave Kosovo's status unchanged (*i.e.* within the territory of Serbia), they are aware of the potential destabilizing impact in case of a decision that would negatively affect the Serbian population both in Serbia and in Kosovo. Therefore, the EU started looking for different forms and modalities that could "sweeten" the especially bitter pill of Kosovo's separation from Serbia not only by responsible politicians but by a largely nationalistically-minded and "educated" society.

VI.5.2. This task may become more difficult than many Western European politicians believe. In effect, the current Serbian society is in a uniquely difficult situation with the failed experience of several experiments (from monarchy to a federal structure of the statehood; from communist to neutral orientation in foreign policy and from the orthodox to self-managed approach in the economy). All initiatives have failed,

[35] The word "guaranteeing" would be inconvenient and misleading, because Belgrade does not dispose of any instrument to block any decision of the international conference or prevent decisions from implementation.

similar to all interventions in which the Yugoslav National Army was involved in the last 15 years. No wonder that as a result of repeated failures and the loss of the privileged situation of the past in political, social and economic terms, a general atmosphere of disappointment, pessimism but also intolerance and aggressiveness has arisen. At present, a large part of Serbian society is characterized by overheated sensitivity, distorted historical judgment and the inability to face and digest most recent catastrophic events. The dominant impression or even conviction often communicated by leading politicians is that Serbia had repeatedly fallen victim to a conspiracy led by foreign actors. In addition, reconciliation with its own recent past by facing the personal responsibility for war crimes and ethnic cleansing has not begun at all.[36] Often, there is not even a nuanced differentiation between war crimes and heroic national actions. If a society in this situation experiences further failures whose causes are not sought in the country's own mistakes but are seen as the outcome of yet another international conspiracy, the critical mass of tolerance may easily be overstrained. In a positive scenario it could generate a breakthrough from the past to the future, the start of a new life based on the recognition of realities. However, the other outcome seems more likely, a return to the "glorious" past and a growing hostility against everything which is alien, foreign and international, be it people, ideas, values, proposals or opportunities for cooperation.

VI.5.3. Unfortunately, the current Serbian situation carries an additional and unique burden. This is the continuous and unstoppable disintegration of a united Western Balkans under Serb nationalist leadership. Even well-informed politicians and well-informed observers of the situation find it difficult to understand the Serbian case. Irrespective of the half-truth of every comparison, the current state of Serbia, both on the political and the socio-psychological level shows the "Trianon syndrome" Hungary experienced after the First World War. The Hungarian state emerging from the ruins of the Monarchy lost as much territory as Serbia as a consequence of the dissolution of the Federation and with much more Hungarian speaking people. Similar to Serbia, it became isolated, it was considered responsible for the outbreak of the world war (even if the last spark was produced in Sarajevo that, a few years later became part of the Yugoslav Kingdom). Another similarity is that it had lost some of its "sacred national sites". In turn, there was a significant difference concerning the timeframe of the process. While Hungary had to face a new reality practically overnight, the process of dissolution lasted one and a half decades for Serbia. Montenegro and particularly Kosovo represent the last nails in the coffin. Another difference can be identified in the com-

---

36 This is in sharp contrast to the overall mental development that started after the Second World War in Western Germany.

pletely changed European and global framework. The post-1918 period brought the renaissance of the nation-state, particularly in Central and Southeastern Europe. This can hardly be a viable solution to the burning problems of the 21st century. The consequences of Trianon on the Hungarian attitude can be still felt and some irresponsible politicians still play this card to collect more votes. Fortunately, their efforts were not followed by the majority of the population. Still, one cannot state that the Hungarian mind has already fully absorbed and processed the Trianon trauma after almost 90 years after what happened in 1918-1920. Will Serbia need as much time to come to terms with the new realities? Or even longer? Will it fall back into extreme nationalism as a "remedy" and, as a result, remain a constant destabilizing factor in the region? Or will it find a quick way to the future of Europe? These questions cannot be answered today. It is, however obvious that beyond its own substantial efforts the attitude of the EU (and the USA) to Serbia will also influence political choices and public reactions.

VI.5.4. In a negative scenario, two possibilities can be analyzed that do not exclude each other at all. One is the impact of the loss of Kosovo on the domestic political situation in Serbia. The other is the potential reaction of the Serbian leadership in the Western Balkan region.

There is widely-felt concern in part of the political elite that the independence of Kosovo would further boost the influence of (ultra)nationalist politicians and seriously endanger the preservation (and further strengthening) of democratic structures. Although parliamentary elections resulted in a coalition building of moderate to progressive parties, it should not be forgotten that most votes were won by the nationalistic Serbian Radical Party. To be sure, and based on huge international pressure, the "winning" party could not form a new government, but the current coalition building seems to be unable to create a government. Therefore, accordign to the constitution, new elections may be held in May. Such a situation is most unlikely to create domestic stability and a comfortable environment of accepting Ahtisaari's plan. Just the opposite is already happening. Growing support to radical nationlistic forces could already be observed during the last year. Some politicians have tried to make reference to this danger in order to prevent Kosovo's new status.[37] No wonder that the international plan to Kosovo's new status has been fiercely criticized in Belgrade. One should not forget that, as a preventive step and surprisingly without any serious warning or retaliation by the international community in general and by the EU in particular, in the autumn of 2006 Serbia approved its new constitution. It clearly states that

[37] Kostunica has repeatedly made use of the argument that a Serbia without Kosovo cannot remain democratic.

"the province of Kosovo-Metohija is an integral part of the territory of Serbia… the territory of the Republic of Serbia is inseparable and indivisible" and the borders are "inviolable". Furthermore, "the National Assembly of the Republic of Serbia would proclaim and imposed solution of the Kosovo Metohija future status illegitimate, illegal and void".[38] The Serb Radical Party goes as far that, in case of a Security Council decision on the future status of Kosovo it suggests reconsideration of Serbia's membership in the United Nations and call off efforts to join the EU.[39] Growing political resistance would have adverse consequences on domestic reforms such as the speeding up of privatization or trade and capital liberalization may become hostage to nationalist and isolationist policies. In an extreme case, normal contacts with much of the (developed and democratic) world could be further reduced or cut and cooperation with anti-Western powers and terrorist groups intensified. An alliance of the partly still intact military and security apparatus and ultra-national political forces is not at all ruled out both due to apparent ideological similarities and based on the identification of common enemies. Such a constellation could certainly make its impact outside the state borders of Serbia, too.

The most likely regional reaction could lie in launching new initiatives to be compensated for the loss of Kosovo through the "return" of the Bosnian Serb Republic into the "fatherland". Such a move could easily destabilize the "Dayton-created Bosnia" and reignite open ethnic hostilities by changing already fixed state borders along ethnic lines. As an indirect and opposite impact of Kosovo's independence, the growing concerns of Macedonia(ns) cannot be ignored, either. They are related to manifest (although not official) Albanian efforts to use Kosovo's independence as an excellent opportunity to create a large and unified Albania, including Albanians in Macedonia in the medium term (or even sooner). This could hardly happen without redrawing state borders within the Western Balkans, and would be a flagrant violation of one of the strictest principles of the Vienna negotiations on the future status of Kosovo (the guaranteed stability of current state borders).

Finally, the potential impact of the independence of Kosovo on the future (autonomy) status of the Voivodina has to be kept in mind. This issue can once again occupy a relevant place in the domestic (and international) political agenda. Although the ethnic situation in Voivodina is very different from that of Kosovo, ethnic tensions cannot be ruled out, particularly if an ultranationalist leadership happens to take power in Bel-

---

38 *SEE Online*, February 13, 2007.

39 *Southeast European Times*, February 25, 2007.

grade. The massive flight of Serbs from Kosovo into the northern part of Serbia could generate additional tensions as well.[40]

Obviously, there are more optimistic projections as well. They point to the positive elements of Kosovo's independence on Serbian politics. Their main argument is that the loss of Kosovo would clearly prove the misguided path Serbian politicians have been following in the last 15 years. Thus, the only real option for Serbia's modernization and catching up to European patterns (and living standards later) is a full-fledged democratization of the country that includes the elimination or essential debilitation of the power centres of the "old guard", the introduction of comprehensive economic reforms and the start of a historical reconciliation and coming to terms with the past (*Vergangenheitsbewältigung*). Regrettably, the latest opinion polls do not seem to support the likelihood of this alternative, at least not in the difficult weeks and months following the resolution or agreement of the Vienna conference. Still, the international community in general, and the EU in particular could do a lot in both directions. On the one hand, external actors should be prepared for the potential risks and uncertainties as a consequence of possible Serb reactions in the Western Balkans. On the other hand, a clear European perspective could shorten the eventual return to ultranationalist and anti-democratic patterns and substantially strengthen the position and the public support of those who want to put Serbia on the path toward modern Europe.

VI.6. Dilemmas in Future EU Policies in Southeastern Europe

VI.6.1. At the moment, EU policy towards SEE in general, and towards the Western Balkans in particular has arrived at a crossroads. The current situation is characterized by a number of positive but also negative influences on the substantive decades-long involvement of the EU in the development process(es) in the region. At the same time, also the target countries offer a rather different or differentiated record in restructuring, transformation, modernization and adjustment to the EU. Moreover, and once again, the geographic, political and institutional map of SEE is going through historic changes. First: the EU has been enlarged by two SEE countries and has now more direct and long continental borders

40 It has to be remembered that the major source of previous ethnic hostilities in the Voivodina between Hungarians and Serbs was the settlement of Serbs coming from other regions, mainly from the southern part of ex-Yugoslavia. There were few problems between native citizens of the Voivodina who used to work and live together in peaceful terms. Moreover, tensions emerged among the Serbian population as well, since the attitude and values of the citizens in the northern part of the country differ from those in the southern regions.

with the Western Balkans and with Turkey, After a quarter of century of membership, Greece got its first continental EU border. Second: hopefully the last territorial changes related to state- or nation-building efforts have occurred (Montenegro in 2006) or are likely to occur in the near future (Kosovo in 2007). Third: the EU conditionality policy towards the Western Balkan countries, the key element of the current EU strategy to the region, needs fundamental reappraisal.

Based on the above changes and driven by the permanently high dynamism of domestic and regional politics in the Balkans, it is easy to summarize the basic dilemmas the EU is facing in shaping and implementing policies in this region. Although fully aware of the incorporation of EU policies into the global framework, the identification of challenges follows more a European and regional approach. Some global implications will be dealt with in the concluding chapter VII. In turn, at least some of the challenges go far beyond the evaluation of special EU policies. Some dilemmas challenge widespread and well-known political and economic theories as well. In addition, the success of EU policies is dependent not only on identifying the most important issues and on developing the most appropriate policies. The attitude of the target countries fundamentally affects the quality, intensity (deepness) and sometimes even the main direction of the implementation of the respective policies.

VI.6.2. From the very beginning of the dissolution of the Yugoslav Federation, the Western Balkan countries have been facing three parallel state-building processes. First: they have to build a (modern and functioning nation-) state, which, in most cases and rather regrettably, is based on the ethnicity principle of the 19th century. The achievements are highly uneven. There are functioning states (Croatia), rump states with no clear orientation at the moment (Serbia), weak states (Albania and Macedonia) and international protectorates that show the characteristics of failed states (Bosnia-Herzegovina). An "independent" Kosovo will most likely join the last category, while the future of Montenegro is open. Second: state-building is connected with the building of transforming states. To varying degrees, all Western Balkan countries are still hostage to ex-Yugoslavia, both in economic terms and in social attitudes. State-building concentrated on differentiation from others and seeking instruments of self-strengthening in closed, inward-looking and autocratic policies that would lead to a complete fiasco. Third: adjustment to EU requirements produces a process of member-state building. Can membership-building as the highest priority, be considered an adequate instrument to support state-building and transformation? Or should these countries achieve a certain level of normal functioning as a state before membership building becomes the top priority? Is a top-down or a bottom-up process more promising? Or should both go on simultaneously hoping that history, favourable developments or genuine and responsible government policies can create the interface where, at one point in the future, the two processes meet and fuse smoothly? Since (nation-)state-building is generally a process that lasts several decades and not without domestic and external (regional) tensions, and the Western Balkan political dynamism is much quicker, Brussels has hardly any other alternative than to support membership-building as the instrument to foster regional stability. The question, however, of in what capacity the Western Balkan countries, as member states, would function in a further enlarged EU, is something one can only speculate on. Without offering the opportunity of member-state-building, for several reasons diverging (nation-)state building processes would undermine stability in the respective countries and in the region, with uniquely adverse consequences for Europe at a time when it would like to define itself as a global player in the first quarter of the 21st century.

VI.6.3. Another set of dilemmas arises around the EU's regatta principle. One can only agree that the individual countries have to be evaluated and "rewarded" on the basis of their political, legal, economic performance and the quality and speed of their adjustment process to EU standards. However, since the EU has a regional approach, different timetables and adjustment records should not threaten the cohesive nature of the Western Balkan strategy and should not lead to fragmentation. The promise of membership to all countries seems to provide an appropriate framework if intra-EU developments do not raise serious and justified doubts about the capacity of Brussels to keep this promise. If, however, the latter is not the case (or if it becomes uncertain), trends to fragmentation, also driven by the individual Western Balkan states as a form of fierce competition, start to dominate reality. The regatta principle works as long as it is considered an instrument to encourage poorly performing countries to do better. However, particularly in a region with the historic heritage of mutual suspicion and envy, the better performing countries are not always looked at as examples to follow but as neighbours that should be pulled down to the lower level of the others. In addition, wide gaps in performance can easily create the impression of backwardness, failure, incapacity that may generate old-fashioned and outdated answers. They are not only unable to mobilize societies for the future but can generate disappointment and create dangerous sources for domestic and regional conflicts. The EU's strategy of gradual development of institutionalized relations (from the SAP through the SAA towards different stations of the accession process) was based on the positive demonstration impact of this scheme. It did not take into account that the adjustment capacity of the individual countries is widely varied. In contrast to the countries that became members in 2004, Western Balkan countries have been burdened with unique difficulties rooted in weak (or failed) states, lower levels of economic development, the lack of genuine transformation, huge loss of human resources, negative and far-reaching experience of wars and ethnic hostilities. Obvious and prevailing differences among the new member countries did not jeopardize the big bang enlargement and did not create large performance gaps when EU conditionalities had to be met. In addition, the eventual exclusion of any acceding country was not expected to create huge stability risks (in fact, Bulgaria and Romania were not taken at the same time, and it did not generate any destabilization in these countries and in their region). However, stability in the Western Balkans is much more fragile. Wide gaps in the EU-related roadmap can easily produce vacuums and black holes. Therefore, the dilemma about the principle of rewarding or punishing "individual performance" by different qualities of institutional relations on the one hand, and the understandable concern about the cohesion and (apparent) stability of the whole region was only possible to "solve" if each country, almost irrespective of its performance, was given some reward, when the best performing country/countries upgraded their relations to Brussels. Most likely, however, the opposite strategy of keeping the better and quicker adjusting countries waiting that, in some cases under significant domestic pressure, met hard EU conditions (*e.g.* the extradition of Gotovina by Croatia), would have produced more and immediate tensions. Due to the absolute priority of preserving stability, standards had to give way to status considerations. If the new or promised status position will be rapidly cemented by fulfilling the required standards, the balance can be restored. This, however, is in no case granted. Just the opposite, the discrepancy between status and standards can create a very bad example that could be repeated in the future without serious consequences. At the end of the day, the EU may become hostage to its Western Balkan politics. Thus, the basic dilemma remains on how to create a policy mix that contains the critical mass of cohesion and differentiation. Moreover, such a mix has to be constantly restructured and adjusted to (rapidly) changing regional and country-specific conditions, tasks and conflict sources.

VI.6.4. Further dilemmas are raised by the application of the conditionality principle. To be sure, the larger number of conditions for the Western Balkans on their road to the EU should not be objectionable. They contain requirements that have to be fulfilled in order to become members of the club. However, not all countries involved in the "promise package of Thessaloniki" can cope with them simultaneously. Thus, a serious dilemma emerges between keeping the negotiation process open and, at the same time, not letting the conditionality package be diluted by individual states or "state-like entities".[41] Another conditionality-related dilemma can be identified in the contradiction between strict insistence on conditions on the one hand, and the pressure to produce visible results, on the other. The preference given to the latter in many cases with respect to keep stability and appease less- or non-performing countries, has already diluted some basic conditionalities (see the latest SAA agreement with Albania). Such an approach may avoid immediate local or bilateral tensions between the respective country and Brussels but, in the longer run, it undermines EU credibility and sets a precedent, if other countries think it necessary or even desirable. No less importantly, the critical connection between the tolerance level of the target countries and the timeframe laid out in the roadmap (if there is any) has to be addressed. Perspectives do mobilize domestic players to make the required changes, including political and social transformation, if the goal is transparent, rewarding and the road to it is free from further unexpected and incalculable barriers (namely new conditionalities) and is reasonably short and reliable (*i.e.* not floating). However, it is hardly possible to set the same conditions for each country, since their starting position, adjustment capacity and, most importantly, social tolerance vary. What is a mobilizing factor for one country may turn out to be frustrating for another country. Passivity, and even more, demobilization, disappointment and frustration of any country on the way to the EU due to the disequilibrium between the promised reward and the limits to domestic transformation and adjustment within the given timeframe and under the given conditions can produce a dramatic turnaround into the blind-alley of nationalism and isolationism and strengthen the historically heavy burden of constant failures whatever attempt had been initiated by (or imposed on) the countries of the region over several centuries. Therefore it would be a mistake if the non-compliance or untimely compliance of a country were considered as a factor in its exclusion from "Europe". It is not necessarily the country that is "incapable of becoming European" (provided the standards of the EU are considered to be "European") but, in some cases, it is the conditions and the expected timeframe that can be blamed for failures. It has to be underlined that none of the acceding countries is protected from the temptation that too big commitments will be assumed to reach membership earlier. If, in this case due to a self-imposed adjustment process, membership may be reached but at the expense of huge domestic economic and social problems, the priority principle of (regional) stability will be defied. In other words, the additional stability supposed to be imported by membership can, in the negative sense, be easily defeated by the domestic instability due to commitments that overstretch the economic and social texture of the new (or would-be)

41 Auswaertiges Amt – CAP – Bertelsmann Stiftung (2002), p. 15.

member country. According to international experience, imposed transformation, let alone imposed state-building can only work if domestic conditions, resources and willingness are available.[42] Thus, the real challenge for the redrafted or refined Balkan strategy of Brussels lies in how to preserve a cohesive plan of prospective membership on the one hand, and develop country-specific instruments that would facilitate the adjustment process in the individual and, in many aspects, highly different countries, on the other hand.

VI.6.5. The sometimes rather contradictory interdependence and sequencing of stability and integration represents another strategic issue. To what extent can the approach from stability to integration work? How much stability can be expected of the way towards integration? And where is the turning point when effective integration has to be considered as the convenient instrument to further stabilization? This question can be answered easier in case of normal and functioning (nation-) states. The specific problem in the Western Balkans stems precisely from the non-existent or failed states or from "state-like" formations. Brussels cannot abandon these entities and wait for their hopefully successful state-formation. It is not unlikely that the dilemma will be eliminated by extending the EU to the protectorates and not only to "independent" and functioning states.[43]

VI.6.6. Furthermore, the sustainable regional stability and the treatment of ethnic issues are closely interrelated. The dilemma is the choice between a relatively easy, short-term solution and a more complicated one that, hopefully, offers better conditions in the longer term. Evidently, the quick-success-scenario lies in creating stability in multiethnic regions and states by separating ethnic groups in geographic terms, and if possible, also in institutional aspects as well. Thus, ethnic communities should join the mother country with or without border changes or enjoy far-reaching autonomy within a state with different ethnic groups. As the example of Bosnia-Herzegovina shows, this pattern may work for a while and under strict international control. According to the current situation, the viability of a sovereign Bosnia-Herzegovina without international supervision and facing the revival of ethnic hostilities or the strong desire to secede from this state to the ethnic mother state could be seriously

---

42 Although the Western Balkans is not Afghanistan, the example of the failure of trying to help this country (and many others) can be summarized in the following way: "Once again, we wanted to stand up – but we were forced to run. Now, we are again falling". Buchsteiner (2006).

43 In this context, legal, political, institutional and economic conditions of the membership of selected overseas territories of France, Portugal and Spain should be studied. Obviously, some similarities and experience applicable to some Western Balkan entities can be found.

questioned. The other way is more cumbersome but not without hopes for lasting success. It is the creation of multi-ethnic states by facilitating increasing cooperation between and among ethnic groups with the help of a wide range of encouraging instruments. Macedonia and, hopefully, Kosovo can be cited as working examples, while Montenegro is already the best example for peaceful multiethnic coexistence. Thus, the EU has participated in the creation of both patterns (Bosnia-Herzegovina vs. Macedonia), without being able to develop a clear stance in this basic dilemma.[44]

VI.6.7. Several dilemmas have been produced by finding the most suitable economic approach to the Western Balkans. Three of them have to be addressed briefly.

First: as already mentioned in earlier chapters, there is a dilemma between the priorities of development-driven and enlargement-driven strategies. Although several conditions set by the EU in its enlargement documents coincide with key issues of sustainable development. Still, the EU-related adjustment process is mainly based on institution-building and legal harmonization, both of them being necessary framework factors of sustainable economic development and modernization. However, without genuine economic progress these framework conditions remain a dubious achievement, a façade without substance on which real cooperation in the "club" could hardly be based. The literal interpretation of nominal convergence to the EU cannot replace real convergence.[45] No less importantly, real convergence based on a development strategy should come first and support nominal convergence, including the provision of the necessary financial resources to implement EU legislation and meet conditionalities. At the moment, there is a huge gap between the effective performance of the Western Balkan economies (including partly even Croatia) and the already introduced or to be introduced legal framework and required institution-building.

Second: it is not only a dilemma but, in many cases, a misconception to start from the assumption that trade integration with the EU can replace comprehensive development cooperation between countries on different levels of economic development. Certainly, particularly in the case of small and export-oriented countries, free access to key external markets is a crucial element of growth, structural change and employment. However, the historically existing development gap cannot be overcome just

[44] In effect, most probably there is no clear answer to this problem. The approach depends fundamentally on the concrete situation and the power relation not only between external policy-makers and domestic policy-takers but, sometimes more importantly, also among different policy-makers involved in the process.

[45] With the words of Gligorov: "...the process of enlargement has not revealed itself as a substitute for or even as a complement of development policy" (Gligorov, 2002, p. 14).

by trade integration, even if it is understood as an asymmetric but, at the end of the day, reciprocal process. Short transitional periods as applied in the Association Agreements to the new member countries in the 1990s were in most cases inadequate to provide sufficient time to the evolution of competitive domestic small- and medium-sized industries and service activities. Still, it has to be admitted that in the era of globalization there is hardly any other instrument that has the potential for success. The Western Balkan countries do not only face the development gap characteristic to Central Europe. Their economies are less developed, much weaker, still facing most of the fundamental structural changes and without the critical mass of international productive investments. Thus, the evolution of the positive role of free trade is not supported by the rapid increase of output that could be exported to liberalized markets. The lack of output is tangible both in the insufficient volume of exports and in the insufficient level of competitiveness. Therefore, trade liberalization is a necessary and favourable instrument that can contribute to economic development. However, for the sustainable economic development of the Western Balkan countries, it is far from being a satisfactory external contribution.

Third: a similar gap is revealed between expectations (conditionality) and the reality of regional free trade agreements. There is no question that in principle regional trade liberalization can contribute to economic growth, cross-country specialization and increased attraction of foreign (and regional) investors. However, it cannot act as a substitute for trade with the largest partners that are usually located outside the regional free trade zone. Moreover, even the potential positive impact can be limited by bilateral protectionism (despite the text and spirit of the respective free trade agreement), similar production, export and import structures, administrative barriers (customs, taxes, etc.), the state of the physical infrastructure (including border crossing) and the disruption or lack of regional business networks.

The current problems and development dilemmas can only be solved if the obviously positive and necessary steps taken in the field of trade policy will be complemented by other development-oriented policies.

VI.6.8. In this context, the importance of the EU's financial contribution has to be underlined. It is unnecessary to discuss the obvious gap between available financial resources of the EU and the volume of international assistance needed for reconstruction, restructuring and sustainable economic modernization in the Western Balkan countries. Such a decision is taken in the much larger framework of the EU's multi-annual financial perspective. The latter is the outcome of a delicate balance among multiple interests, pressures, resistance and bargaining. Two other aspects, however, can be mentioned.

First: the conditions of having access to financial resources of the EU have to be substantially improved. Long bureaucratic processes should be avoided and the absolutely necessary paperwork has to be adjusted to the available institutional capacity of the individual countries. In addition, objectives that are allowed to be financed from EU resources should be identified in line with the urgent priorities of the respective beneficiary country. Namely, the efficiency of financial (and other) resources as well as the so-called "financial absorption capacity" of the potential beneficiary depends significantly on the availability of funds.

Second: the current practice of positive correlation between progress made in the adjustment agenda and the volume of financial resources has to be reconsidered. According to current logic, countries that make more progress are rewarded by higher amounts of money, while countries lagging behind are punished by getting much less. As a result, a vicious cycle might be established, since quicker adjustment is hampered, among others, by the lack of resources. Therefore, the financial support to those Western Balkan countries (and entities) that are at or near the "bottom of the institutional pyramid" should be substantially enhanced.[46] (Of course, it does not mean that funds available to more developed countries have to be necessarily cut. The overall urgent task of channelling more resources to the Western Balkan can hardly be ignored.)

VI.6.9. A further important and supportive instrument to achieve higher stability could be the reconsideration and substantial liberalization of the EU's visa policy *vis-à-vis* the Western Balkan countries. The basic dilemma lies in the fact that the EU wants to help the countries of the region but keeps people away from "Europe". Visa policy is not an economic issue but an important element of overall stability, including human resource development, institution building, higher conformity with EU standards, the free flow of social values that influence personal and group attitudes, etc. Another contradiction exists between the market opportunities available on paper and visa-related difficulties to make use of business opportunities offered by free trade (both in EU and regional markets).

---

[46] In this context, it is instructive to point to the general rules of the Marshall Aid as compared to the EU practice of financial assistance (both to less developed member and non-member countries). The important difference in our case is between the front-loaded vs. phasing-in approach. The Marshall Aid, scheduled for a period of four years and amounting, on the yearly average, to 1.2% of the US GDP at that time (or more than the share of the total community budget in the EU's GDP), started with a massive help reaching 2% of US GDP in the first year and declining to 0.5% in the concluding year. In contrast, the EU opted for a phasing-in pattern which, in the first years of membership, adversely differentiated between old and new member countries benefitting from EU funds. More visible is the difference between financing member and non-member acceding, candidate and applicant countries.

At present, the EU's visa policy is as heterogeneous as its pyramid of institutional relations with individual SEE countries. Before the systemic transformation in Central and Southeastern Europe, Yugoslav citizens generally were allowed to travel free to and within Western Europe. However, fundamental restrictions were introduced later, both as a consequence of the coming to power of undemocratic regimes, the growing regional instability and, above all, the wars in the 1990s. In turn, other SEE countries that previously needed entry visas were exempted from this requirement. Bulgaria came first, followed by Romania. Visa liberalization occurred not at the beginning of the accession negotiations but at a later stage of the process or, as in the case of Romania, at the very end of negotiations. A different procedure was applied to Croatia. It started to enjoy visa-free travel before beginning negotiations and became a point of reference of Brussels' double standard politics.[47] In addition, visa liberalization was not linked to the fulfilment of such conditions that were strictly observed in case of negotiations (*e.g.* the arrest and extradition of Gotovina to The Hague). To make the picture more complex, Slovenia, with its early statehood and exemption from Western Balkan wars, could continue the ex-Yugoslav status and did not face visa restrictions even temporarily.[48] On the other hand, the citizens of other Western Balkan countries all need a visa when travelling to EU countries.[49] Moreover, Brussels' visa policy had to be accepted by the new member countries that, in the past, did not need visas either to ex-Yugoslavia or to the successor states of the Federation.

The EU visa policy towards the Western Balkan countries has been explained by Franco Frattini, the Commissioner responsible for Justice, Freedom and Security with the following arguments:

---

47 The other Western Balkan candidate country, Macedonia did not reach any alleviation from travel restrictions. This, however could be attributed to the grave mistake of the Macedonian negotiation team, when, in official talks with Brussels, it proudly declared that Macedonia was not interested in any special facilitation but only in the complete elimination of the visa obligation (which, evidently, was not provided by Brussels). (Martens, 2006i).

48 Even more, Slovenia is the only country in Central and Eastern Europe, the citizens of which can freely travel to the United States. (Even the citizens of Greece, with a quarter-century of EU membership need US visa). Despite repeated efforts both on the national and on the EU level, the USA has only been ready to consider a more flexible visa policy, but not to provide visa free traffic for CEE citizens. In turn, US citizens can travel to all CEE countries without needing visa.

49 Following the guidelines of the Amsterdam Treaty, the European Council adopted a regulation in 2001 that puts all other Western Balkan countries (Albania, Bosnia-Herzegovina, Macedonia and Serbia-Montenegro) on the list of third countries subject to visa requirement. As long as this regulation remains in force, only negotiations on a bilateral basis (*i.e.* between the respective country and Brussels) are possible (Amato, 2005, p. 181).

- after the wars, a massive flow of refugees and asylum-seekers[50] took place towards Western Europe that needed to develop an asylum and return policy after the hostilities,
- for several reasons, including work and family ties, there is a strong current migration from and through the Western Balkans to the EU,
- much of organized crime, mainly trafficking in human beings (according to EU data, about half a million of women per year), is coming from or through this region,
- finally, the Paris riots in the summer of 2005 substantially increased the sensitivity of the public opinion to illegal immigration (Frattini, 2005, pp. 3-5), even if Western Balkan citizens had nothing to do with that event.

The legitimacy of the security needs of the EU can hardly be denied. In turn, other aspects of sustainable stability should also be taken into account.

First, as experience shows, criminal activities can hardly be stopped by visa regulations at the border. All restrictions mainly affect the vast majority of citizens who want to travel to other countries due to family contacts, tourism, business or education. Irrespective of the strictness of any measure, criminals will be the first in overcoming all kinds of barriers, both because they have money ("corruption propensity") and networks.

Second, and based on the simplest market laws, intensive trafficking in people (women) and drugs requires two sides, supply and demand. Supply can only work if demand is available. However, this demand does not exist in the Western Balkans but in the EU countries. It is not only ineffective but highly unfair to restrict the supply side of the market without doing the same on the demand side. Western European market interests should not question or undermine European and regional stability. Therefore, the only efficient way of combating many types of criminal activities is a two-way strategy, both on the supply and the demand side. This, however, and very regrettably, does not figure in any of the EU documents related to the Western Balkans (and other countries of origin of criminal or illegal activities).

Third, while normal "civilized" and "civilizing" contacts, both personal, business, cultural and others, are hit, criminal activities are forced to increase. In order to get a visa, more and more people are assumed to establish contacts with criminal networks that can help them overcome this "technical barrier".

---

50 Between 2003 and the first half of 2005, with almost 50,000 applications, Serbia-Montenegro placed second on the EU list of countries of origin of asylum seekers.

Fourth, the current restrictions have a particularly negative impact on younger generations. The young people are the ones who are expected to change the past- and hostility-oriented history of the Western Balkans, since they have not been direct participants (victims and offenders) of wars and ethnic cleansing. However, restrictions that are applied against them can only foster nationalism, extremism, isolationism and develop an extremely narrow-minded but highly dangerous attitude against the outside world that they cannot get to know and understand. Therefore, a resistance against anything that comes from outside is the absolutely "normal" response. It is more than surprising and probably foreboding with respect to the future of the region that less than 20% of young Serbian citizens have a personal encounter with the "developed Europe".

Fifth, the negative repercussions can be seen in other population segments as well. Many Western Balkan citizens who used to be accustomed to freedom of travel for decades now have to put up with a lot of restrictions. This not only impairs their mobility but, more importantly, it deepens the impression of being excluded from Europe (and the world) and punished for something they do not understand and have hardly digested (whether they were direct participants of the atrocities or just let them happen, whether or not driven by "nationalist enthusiasm").

The EU's basic dilemma concerning visa policy is how to apply it as a positive, encouraging incentive to prepare the Western Balkan countries for EU membership, and even more importantly, for EU-conform behaviour and mentality, while, at the same time, achieve the highest level of effectiveness in combating crime and illegal migration. At the moment, the emphasis is definitely on the second pillar, while the first one became a victim to the current visa policy. Thus, without changing the emphasis and starting from the much more positive impacts of free travel, Brussels will keep on experimenting with in-between solutions. It tries to single out different groups and activities that should enjoy quick access to short-term visas. Better opportunities have to be created for professors, students, researchers, businessmen, media representatives not only for short-term stays in the EU but also for longer working contracts. This, however, is again a double-edged approach. On the one hand, it can produce an artificial division in society between those who can travel without difficulty, and those who can't. On the other hand, it can become an instrument that deprives the Western Balkan societies of the still remaining human resource potential, an indispensable precondition for substantial socio-economic and mental transformation and successful adjustment to EU requirements. Attracting highly-skilled and mobile young people due to short-term and narrow-minded interests of several EU countries can hardly be considered an adequate instrument to create sustainable stability in the Western Balkans. What in this case can be achieved is a vacuum that will probably not explode but implode. The long-term costs and consequences of an economic and social implosion would certainly not be less than those of a potential explosion.

The ambiguity of the visa policy of the EU got another component in May 2006. Based on a French initiative, the visa fee would be increased from Euro 35 to Euro 60,[51] which is an obvious discrimination against most third-country citizens subject to the visa requirement. Not least citizens of the Western Balkan countries will be affected, since most of them can hardly afford to pay Euro 60 for a visa. In turn, criminals can easily cope with the new regulation. It is symptomatic that in the first stage of negotiating the above draft, many EU countries were against the French proposal (Poland, the Baltic States, Greece, Hungary, partly the Czech Republic and Slovakia, and as an "external supporter", Sweden). Thus, they could form a blocking minority. However, this group became much smaller in the final stage of negotiations, so that Greece, Hungary[52] and Sweden became isolated and unable to prevent the introduction of the new regulation. Therefore, in the new situation the efforts of the latter countries were concentrated on how to achieve certain alleviations or exceptions for selected citizens coming from countries with visa obligation. They will include exemption from visa fee for students, professors, researchers and up to 6 years-old children.[53] One additional contradiction of the visa-related regulation is that while the EU makes a clear difference between countries with membership perspective and countries that are part of the EU's Eastern and Mediterranean neighbourhood policy (as well as other third countries included into the external activities of Brussels), the visa policy is uniform. Thus, although Western Balkan countries are considered prospective members, they are not differentiated from other third countries in the EU's visa policy.

This is a situation that can hardly be sustained for a long time without serious consequences. In diplomatic circles the possibility of a special agreement with the Western Balkan countries has been mentioned. According to this speculation, Western Balkan countries may be exempted from paying the visa fee if they sign an agreement containing two conditions. First, progress in reforms in relevant areas, including border man-

---

51 The official argument behind the drastic increase of the fee was the rapid rise of the costs of producing a visa (due to the necessity of biometric identification marks). However, an additional and important underlying reason was certainly the growing hostility to foreigners in several EU countries, particularly in France but also in the Netherlands.

52 Hungary is not obliged to introduce the new EU regulation before becoming full member of the Schengen area (the earliest date is end-2007).

53 Sweden failed with its initiative to grant exemptions from the visa fee to all citizens less than 18 years old.

agement, has to be reached. Second, and more important, they have to sign a readmission agreement with the EU on taking back everyone who migrated to the EU illegally from their territories. This new conditionality would not make the entry into the EU free for Western Balkan citizens, since the visa obligation (without paying for the visa) would remain. In turn, some Western Balkan countries that are transit regions to illegal migration originating in Turkey, Caucasus, Pakistan, Sri Lanka and several Middle Eastern countries, would have to take on the burden of dealing with these people in their countries (without having bilateral agreements with the countries of origin on sending them back to the real source of migration). It does not take a vivid imagination to imagine the significant destabilizing impact of such a situation on the Western Balkans, including the substantial strengthening of already existing or emerging new criminal networks, again in contact with "specified" Western European "markets".

Some of the consequences of the current EU visa policy can already be observed in the neighbouring countries that have become full members of the EU recently. Since citizens of Hungary, Bulgaria, Croatia and Romania can freely travel to all EU countries, large national minorities of these countries living in the neighbouring Western Balkan states started to apply for citizenship en masse (with or without the intention of changing their place of residence). Tens of thousands of Macedonians (suddenly) found evidence of their Bulgarian origin, and even more citizens of Moldova applied for Romanian citizenship. Hungarians in the Voivodina have already had a long history in this respect. Most probably, an increasing number of Croats living in Bosnia (or sporadically in Serbia) will follow the same path. This development is likely to create additional tensions within the individual Western Balkan countries and could generate new ethnic conflicts (between the "visa-free" and the "non-visa-free" citizens). Even more, if the visa-free status drives more and more "visa-free" people to change residence and find a new home in Bulgaria, Romania, Croatia or Hungary, regional stability may be further undermined by two developments. First, if cross-country migration happens in larger numbers, the new home country (actually the – newly discovered – "fatherland") will have to take care of the immigrants. Second, any future migration would generate further shifts in the ethnic composition of such multiethnic countries as Bosnia-Herzegovina or Macedonia. Both developments are likely to have a negative impact on stability both on the country and regional level.

A special issue is the present and future of visa policies within SEE. The free movement of people is not only a key goal in the EU framework but also in the regional context. It is hardly possible to deliver convincing arguments in favour of regional stability, more trade, economic cooperation, mutual understanding, if, as a consequence of visa regulations, individual countries of the SEE region will be separated from each other. And this is exactly what is happening. New member countries of the EU have already had to follow Brussels' common visa policy and could hardly receive special treatment.[54] For instance, Bulgaria and Romania will have to require visas from Serbian citizens. More importantly, acceding countries have to change their current national visa policies and adjust them to EU requirements. As a result, Romania has to introduce a visa requirement to Moldova, with an overwhelmingly Romanian speaking population and with very close family contacts. Similarly, Bulgaria has to apply the EU policies *vis-à-vis* Macedonia, again with a large Bulgarian "minority".[55] At a given moment in the accession negotiations, Croatia will not be able to avoid this situation, either. Sooner or later it will have to introduce a visa requirement for all Western Balkan countries at a lower level of institutional contacts with the EU.

Three embarrassing developments may result. On the one hand, countries of the Western Balkans that have not started official negotiations, and have only a long-term promise of membership, will fall into the group of countries with visa obligation and, thus, become part of a "Balkan ghetto". Second, Western Balkan countries may extend visa policies in all or most bilateral relations within the region as well. Third, a highly imbalanced network may emerge as a result of liberal visa policies of the Western Balkan countries towards third-country citizens (certainly towards all those coming from an expanding EU) and a much more restrictive policy applied by the partners.

As of today, EU citizens generally do not need a visa to enter Western Balkan countries, while the opposite is true if a Macedonian, Albanian or Serbian citizen wants to travel to any of the EU countries.

For instance, Albanian citizens need a visa if they want to travel to most countries. In turn, the citizens of all EU member countries plus those of Bulgaria, Romania and Croatia are allowed to go to Albania without a visa.[56] Citizens of Bosnia-Herzegovina require a visa to the EU

---

54 For instance, Hungarian citizens do not need a visa to Bosnia-Herzegovina and Macedonia in parts of the calendar year. In turn, citizens of these countries need a valid visa if they want to enter the territory of Hungary. It is the same asymmetric treatment Hungary, and other CEE countries have to "swallow" in their visa relations with the USA.

55 No wonder that many Moldavian and Macedonian citizens applied for Romanian and Bulgarian citizenship.

56 A further slight differentiation is that Czech and Polish citizens may enter without paying the entry tax of Euro 10 (but no other EU citizen!).

and to most SEE countries except Croatia, Macedonia and Serbia.[57] However, the regulation is not uniform for tourists, diplomats or holders of service passport. Holders of the latter two can enter Albania or Hungary without a visa, while this condition does not apply for other EU countries. In respect, even the EU common policy may contain country-specific differences. At the moment, Bulgaria does not require a visa of anyone coming from the SEE region if he or she holds a diplomatic or service passport. Holders of regular passports, however, need a visa if they come from Albania, Bosnia-Herzegovina (as well as Turkey and Moldova). In turn, Bulgarian citizens need a tourist visa only when entering Bosnia-Herzegovina (and Moldova). Macedonian citizens can travel visa-free to the Western Balkan countries and Bulgaria, but not to Romania and Albania. In many cases, the visa regulation is extremely complicated and very different conditions apply when travelling to different countries of the world, including the type of passport, the time of stay abroad or the fee to be paid for the visa). Until accession to the EU the Romanian visa policy acknowledges five different types of entry visa, with a stay from 30 to 90 days in the country. Bulgarian citizens did not need a visa but only could stay in an EU country for 30 days. In turn, EU citizens (including Slovenia and Hungary) are allowed to remain in Romania for 90 days. The same applies to Moldova at the moment, but this special regulation has to be adjusted to EU policies before accession. Western Balkan countries are treated rather differently. Croatian citizens enjoy the same situation as their Bulgarian counterparts. Citizens of Bosnia-Herzegovina and Macedonia can only enter Romania without a visa if they possess a diplomatic or service passport. The circle of Serbian citizens also includes citizens with an official passport. Moreover, under such conditions, Bosnian citizens are allowed to stay for a period of 30 days, while Macedonian and Serbian citizens can remain in Romania for 90 days. Albanian citizens can only enter Romania without visa if they possess a diplomatic passport (for a duration of 90 days). Serbia provides visa-free entry to citizens from a large number of countries (often including those who would need a visa if travelling to the EU). All ex-Yugoslav countries are included in this list, however, Albania is handled separately (and more strictly). The already complicated picture may become even more so as a result of Montenegro's own visa policy, let alone the consequences arising from the future status of Kosovo. As one of the latest developments, and with future implications, Albania announced in August 2006 that it would abolish visas for Macedonia (due to the free travel of the large Albanian ethnic population living in that country). In contrast,

57 In turn, Bosnian citizens are exempt from the visa requirement when they enter such countries as Malaysia, Singapore, Tunisia, Turkey or several island countries in the Caribbean and the Pacific.

Macedonia cannot take the same decision, since, at the level of its relations with Brussels, it feels obligated to observe EU requirements in order not to jeopardize its (desired) roadmap to accession negotiations. As a tentative approach, the following table tries to give a general picture of visa requirements of selected SEE countries, without considering the many special features that some of them covered in the above paragraph.

Table VI.2
Visa policies of the SEE countries towards foreign citizens (visas needed or not needed)

Citizens of SEE to: / Citizens of country to SEE:	Albania	Bosnia-Herzegovina	Bulgaria	Croatia	Macedonia	Romania	Serbia-Montenegro (b)
Albania		Needed	Needed	Needed	Needed(a)	Needed	
Bosnia-Herzegovina	Needed		Needed	ID card only	Not	Needed	Not
Bulgaria(c)	Not	Needed		Not	Not	Not	Not
Croatia	Not	ID card only	Not		Not	Not	Not
Macedonia	Needed	Not	Not	Not		Needed	Not
Romania(c)	Not	Needed	Not	Not	Needed		
Serbia-Montenegro(b)	Needed	Not	Not	Not	Not		

(a) visa requirement to be lifted according to an amended decision of the Council of Ministers as of August 04, 2006 (No. 439).

(b) after the secession of Montenegro, different visa policies cannot be ruled out.

(c) as a precondition of EU membership and participation in the EU's community policies, Bulgaria and Romania have to apply EU visa regulations. Citizens of all countries that need visa to enter the EU will have to have it also when travelling to Bulgaria and Romania.

Source: own composition based on information from the SEE countries.

Under such conditions it is very difficult and to a large extent, controversial or irresponsible, to press SEE countries for more regional economic cooperation and mutual understanding, let alone expect substantive results from free trade agreements.

VI.6.10. The sometimes apparent, sometimes very real contradiction between national (state) sovereignty and EU integration presents another dilemma. It was widely assumed that Central, Eastern and Southeastern European countries, on regaining their national independence would be more reluctant to join an EU which requires the giving up of some crucial features of national "sovereignty". Overall experience shows that it has not created significant problems in any of the new member countries.

Namely, two things were clear from the very beginning of adjustment process to the EU. First: a clear strategic decision was taken in favour of EU membership and orientation towards "Western" values. This approach has never been questioned by influential political forces. No serious attempt was made to replace the EU by "independent" national or regional initiatives.[58] Second: membership in the EU was considered to compensate abundantly for sacrificing some of the "national sovereignty" by offering a larger space to implement or protect "national interests" in the framework of a large, globally influential Union and enjoying the new opportunities offered in the framework of "shared sovereignty". For several reasons detailed in previous chapters, this process encounters more difficulties in the Western Balkans. Some of the problems originate in the complicated process of state-building. In other cases, ethnic considerations seem to be more important than EU integration. On the official political level, Croatia could break with this pattern, while Serbia is still hostage to the old-fashioned approach. Latest developments, such as the freezing of SAA negotiations without fixing a date for its resumption, the independence of Montenegro and the future status of Kosovo can easily strengthen the nationalist attitude and further widen the gap between Serbia and the EU.[59]

Moreover, the choice is not only between "sovereign" (nation-) state-building and EU integration. Much sooner than EU integration, Western Balkan countries, as well as connected EU policies may be facing another pressing dilemma of what is more important: to build a "sovereign" state or a functioning state.[60] No doubt the EU is primarily interested in supporting the latter. No relevant negotiations can take place with a weak state with chronic shortcomings in the most important functions of the state. No commitment can be taken seriously if any partner country of the EU disposes of a non-functioning state, whatever its official status of "sovereignty" is.

VI.6.11. Dilemmas also emerge concerning the "tactical" issues of negotiations and prospective membership. On the one hand, various alternatives to full-fledged membership have returned to the agenda recently. Internal difficulties of the EU and of some member countries, the lack of a clear roadmap as well as the slow and contradictory progress

---

58 Of course, some (irresponsible) political statements could be heard concerning the possibility of "life outside the EU" (the head of the FIDESZ party, Orbán in Hungary) or several nationalistic opinions expressed regularly by some Polish politicians.

59 Such a development also represents a barrier to future-oriented socio-economic transformation. As rightly stated, "...socio-economic transformation makes limited inroads as long as issues of state sovereignty and inter-ethnic power games dominate the regional and national agendas" (Van Meurs and Weiss, 2005, p. 10).

60 Auswaertiges Amt – CAP – Bertelsmann Stiftung (2002), p. 11.

of potential members in adjusting their economies, legislation and institutions to the EU have resulted in suggestions to find an interim-solution that could take into account the consequences of the political dynamism in the Western Balkans (and later in Turkey and probably also in the Ukraine) and, at the same time, fit into the multi-stage institutional framework of European integration. However, it is hardly believable that in the current situation any country that was offered the membership perspective was ready to give up this option voluntarily.[61]

The other "technical" dilemma lies in the utility and effectiveness of making use of the instrument of delayed membership. In previous chapters this study argued against applying this instrument, since, according to all estimates, its calculable costs heavily outweigh the benefits attributed to it by some experts.[62] Still, this option should not be ignored, since the EU had been prolonging the deadline of announcing its readiness to open its doors to Bulgaria and Romania in January 2007 until the very last minute (autumn of 2006). In addition, special delaying tactics can slow down the accession process of the Western Balkan countries if Brussels and some influential member states believed that a narrow-minded balancing between EU enlargement promise, domestic problems and negative public perception of the ongoing enlargement process were suitable for some members. Macedonia is already a case in point, since it has a candidate status without any date of starting negotiations. Although the linkage of official negotiations with Croatia and Turkey seems to be broken, negotiations with the former country will not be automatically speeded up.

VI.6.12. The dilemmas presented above do not constitute a full list, they are representative, instead. In the end, the answer to most of them depends on how the EU imagines its future role and function in South-eastern Europe. The real choice is either enlargement or empire, a stable structure based on partnership or a return to the well-known European experience of neo-colonialism (Amato, 2005, p. 162). To make the answer more difficult, it has to be added that the choice does not only depend on Brussels' intentions or strategic options. Without elaborating here on global developments, at least two additional and basic factors

---

61 This option is even less likely to be accepted if the EU offer consisted in participation in the "benefits of a common institutional framework" without "political integration with large transfers" (Hammermann and Schweickert, 2005, p. 17).

62 The Croatian argument according to which the postponement of the starting of negotiations should be taken as a good chance to get better prepared for negotiations, can only be understood as a pretext to divert attention from the obvious failure of EU-related Croatian politics (Kusic and Claudia Gruppe, 2005, p. 237). The statement misses even more sense, if it is compared with exaggerated hopes of Croatia for joining quickly the EU.

shape the climate in which decisions have to be taken without a long waiting period.

First, the option will be crucially influenced by the future of the EU. A revitalized, reformed, more competitive and globally active and respected EU would probably opt for the partnership-based enlargement. An EU with substantial domestic problems and (self-)deprived of dynamic growth will be inclined towards relations based on neo-colonial attitudes, including lasting protectorate structures.

Second, developments in the Western Balkan countries are no less decisive in the shaping of the pattern of future institutionalized relations. Successful state-building and socio-economic modernization, as well as tangible results in the consolidation of inter-ethnic relations enhance the probability of the first version (equal-footing membership). If, however, past and partially current problems survive and regional stability will be seriously threatened (whether by nationalism, ethnic tensions, economic backwardness, failed and non-functioning states, etc.), there is no other alternative than to incorporate the region into a neo-colonial network. This option is likely even if the EU moves along the optimistic scenario but the Western Balkan produces the pessimistic version. Most probably, the EU, supported by other global players, mainly the USA, will be neither ready nor able to reconsider the absolute priority of imposed stability in this part of the continent, even if it proved to be obvious but still manageable.

VI.7. Recommendations

VI.7.1. For several reasons, Europe has reached a turning point in the last years. Certainly, developments in SEE in general, and in the Western Balkans in particular are only one segment of the comprehensive picture. Still, this region presents a unique challenge to the future of the continent on three levels. First, conditions of the approximation of the Western Balkan countries to the European integration have to be determined. Second, whatever the EU's option to SEE would be, the choice will have a fundamental impact on the future of community-level policies in many areas of the integration. Third, the management of progress and setback in the Western Balkans will influence the EU's global position as well. In consequence, the EU's "Balkan strategy" should not be separated from the global approach of the integration but form an integral part of it, instead. After years of specific treatments and special instruments, SEE has to become part of the general strategy of European integration, both on the European and on the wider, global (cross-regional) levels. While the strategic perspective of full membership has to be maintained, new instruments have to be identified in order to improve the effectiveness of cooperation on the one hand, and enhance the adjustment capacity of the respective countries (including that of the EU and of its member states) on the other.

This subchapter intends to summarize briefly some of the basic tasks. They cover areas of security, justice and stability, as well as economic and financial issues. Institutional developments in the EU's approach to SEE are indispensable as well, along with the definition of clear forms of future cooperation.

VI.7.2. Brussels has to remain aware of its key security and stabilization role in the region. In the coming period, its responsibility will not be reduced in Bosnia-Herzegovina (even if local authorities will take over most of the functions of the High Representative). At the same time, the EU will have to assume a much more influential position in Kosovo following the new status of the "entity". In addition, all other countries of the region, from Albania to Serbia, may experience a domestic and regional development in which Brussels cannot remain absent or neutral.

Security and stabilization can hardly be successful without building new and functioning states in the Western Balkans. The question of working together with healthy nation-states, functioning states without (ethnic) nation-building or failed states (established both on ethnic and multi-ethnic principles) has not yet been solved. Most probably, the EU has to develop viable strategies for all options, since SEE will not produce just one pattern. Some countries will present themselves as functioning nation-states, while others are likely to continue to struggle with the process of state-building, and without a clear decision on the priority of building a functioning state or an ethnic state. However, some preconditions apply for all cases, such as the development of a functioning state administration and more intensive regional cooperation (far beyond bilateral free trade agreements). No less importantly, a basic document on freedom, security and justice affairs should be accepted and enforced in all countries of the region. This seems to be more important in the current situation than a similar document on adjustment to the EU's single market. Namely, successful implementation of the accession process has to be based on the rule of law, transparency and a priority for key issues of justice and home affairs (Amato, 2005, p. 178). In this context, special attention has to be devoted to minority issues and the problems of marginalized people (who generally are of different ethnic origins). This task may become more relevant in the new EU member countries, Bulgaria and Romania, than in other Western Balkan states in the coming years since both current developments and the potential differentiation impact of membership in the first years after accession can widen the economic and social gap between different groups of the society.

More attention should be paid to a region-wide reconciliation. The strict conditionality of delivering war criminals to The Hague is far from sufficient. Just the opposite, if it is not accompanied by more positive developments in the Western Balkans, it can keep or even exacerbate ethnic and other hostilities. Therefore, the EU has to urge all countries to examine "the causes and consequences of their troubled past" (Amato, 2005, p. 182) as well as their own responsibility. In addition, education and public opinion-shaping have to be put into the service of tolerance and reconciliation.

Furthermore, the reform and loosening of EU visa policies towards the countries of the region is a major factor of stability. There are, however, two opposing views on stability. Most of the EU countries believe that any improvement in the conditions of entering the EU might reduce the security level in the respective EU countries. In turn, Western Balkan countries argue that it is exactly the barriers to travel that endanger stability in their societies. Even more, restrictive visa policies do not only create a "Balkan ghetto" but prompt the affected countries to introduce the same restrictive conditions to the neighbouring countries as well. The obligation of the EU *acquis* that all member countries have to follow the community line and introduce a visa obligation to all countries from which the EU demands an entry visa, may, apparently, create greater security within the enlarged/enlarging EU, but at a very high cost of increasing insecurity at the new borders of the integration. As a result, external insecurity (either in the form of domestic or regional instability or manifested in growing political, economic and social pressure) can become a more important factor than the expected gain in additional and mostly apparent security. Third country policies of the EU have to clearly distinguish between visa obligations imposed on citizens coming from distant countries and those from close neighbour countries that have confirmed prospects for full membership in the club.[63]

Finally, the EU's steady and deepening engagement in the Western Balkans will necessarily raise obvious demands to create a genuine European foreign and security policy, including a European army. The problem is that this challenge may become manifest sooner than the EU would be prepared to assume such a task. At the moment, one of the most dangerous developments can be identified between the fundamentally

[63] The new (and still changing) external borders of the EU have to be secured, even if it requires much larger financial resources. However, such an approach does not automatically guarantee a higher level of security within the EU. First, terrorist gangs, as it has been often seen, can always cross even the best secured networks. Second, domestic and intra-EU stability cannot be separated from developments in the immediate neighbourhood. In a globalized world, intra-EU stability and neighbourhood instability cannot coexist in the long term.

different intensity of conflict-creation in the Western Balkans and the slowly enhancing crisis management capacity of the integration. It cannot be ruled out that, without taking fundamental steps urgently, the divergent developments in the EU and in the Western Balkans may end in a huge gap with dramatic consequences.

VI.7.3. In the economic context, Brussels has to modify its approach in several aspects. First, without giving up the conditionality of approximation to EU rules, legislation and institution building, the new approach should put more emphasis on the requirements of short-term economic development in the SEE countries in general, and in the Western Balkans in particular.

Second, and in line with the shifting emphasis on development policies, sector-oriented priorities have to be identified. Of course, general support to overall economic development is helpful, but sustainable growth cannot ignore a clear development strategy based on driving forces (both economic factors of growth, different sectors and key players). First of all, a clear support should be provided to comprehensive plans to upgrade the level of human resources. This is not only a global requirement to all countries of the international economy and to all citizens who want to improve their living conditions. In SEE, at least three additional factors have to be considered. On the one hand, the high levels of unemployment can hardly be reduced without fundamental upgrading of human capital (supported by business that has to develop the demand side of the labour market). On the other, the massive outflow of skilled and young people can only be restricted (and later reversed), once a favourable environment for higher-skilled human resources has been created (it is far from being only a question of income but, much more, a function of general political, social and human conditions). Finally, the general level of education has to be increased in several Western Balkan countries, where large parts of the young generation only has primary education, and ever more young citizens belong to the category of "modern illiteracy".

Another field of special attention includes selected economic sectors. Two of them seem to be crucial for longer term and sustainable growth. One is the comprehensive development of physical infrastructure, not only as a consequence or war damages but much more as a legacy of underdevelopment over centuries. Without an efficient physical infrastructure network of SEE, both linking the region to the most important Western European markets and ensuring low-cost transportation within the region (from the Adriatic Sea to the Black Sea), sustainable modernization can not be carried out. Similarly, utmost attention has to be paid to the future of agriculture in the SEE countries. Agriculture is a key sector of GDP and employment, as well as an instrument to fight poverty. In addition, in all countries it is almost a potential source of export-oriented development if free market access to the EU is guaranteed. However, in the current situation, the real danger is that agricultural products originating in the EU countries could flood the local markets. The reasons range from low level productivity in the SEE countries, to trade policy barriers to the import-based consumption pattern of international personnel mainly in Bosnia-Herzegovina and Kosovo.

The EU's economic development-related projects should embrace local businesses more. Also, Brussels' financial assistance should focus more on small and medium-sized domestic companies and take into account the special features and development level of these firms instead of trying to automatically transfer the general experience and rules of the game of much more developed countries.

Finally, the EU's financial assistance needs revision since the requirements by individual countries are expected to grow as they enter new stages of transformation and a costly path to adjustment to EU regulations. In addition, some of the international support is likely to diminish in the future, particularly in Bosnia-Herzegovina (in line with handing over some or all their power to local authorities) and in Serbia (following the post-war reconstruction period). Most probably, the financial commitment to Kosovo must be kept on a high or even higher level than up to now. Beyond the quantitative changes, a further shift in the origin of transfers can be expected, since the international community considers the EU as the key player in the region. This, of course, would entail a much greater financial contribution by Brussels as well. The first signs of the changes can be traced in the financial framework approved for the period between 2007 and 2013, in which Euro 11.5 bn is earmarked to non-member Western Balkan countries (and Turkey). However, the efficient and timely utilization of the funds would call for fewer bureaucratic rules, less administration and more manoeuvering room for the would-be beneficiary states to influence decisions on priority projects. In addition, the role of the cohesion policy should be upgraded, since local and regional administrations are in most cases not sufficiently developed to make use of the structural funds (Calic, 2005, p. 32).[64]

VI.7.4. It is obvious that not all domestic and regional developments in the Western Balkans can be influenced from outside. Nevertheless, the EU's position on the future of the region, including keeping the promise

64 For several reasons, some new member countries also face this problem. However, they were able to negotiate better terms of using EU money, both by shifting the proportions from structural to cohesion funds and by reducing the share of cofinancing. In itself, cohesion money requires a substantially lower level of national cofinancing than the utilization of structural funds (10 to 15% as compared to 50%).

of full membership can be considered as a crucial impact factor. In this context, the following recommendations can be formulated.

First, the temptation of developing new and in-between forms of institutionalized relations between the Western Balkan countries and Brussels should be avoided. None of the Western Balkan countries (and Turkey) will be satisfied with "less than full membership" offers. Conditions of full-fledged accession should remain strict and unambiguous, in some cases even leading to a long process of adjustment before membership can be achieved. This pattern is still less discouraging, demobilizing and frustrating than any other offer of "junior" or "partial" membership (let alone a "privileged partnership"). Instead of developing interim "solutions", efforts should be concentrated on how the way of the Western Balkan countries towards full membership could be facilitated. This multiple-stage process can, of course, contain new and modified forms of institutionalized relations based on the adjustment record of the applicant (candidate) country and the prevailing political, economic and social situation in the EU. However, none of these stages should lose sight of the final goal of full membership or be considered as a substitute for full-fledged accession.

Second, the negotiations with Turkey have to be clearly separated not only from negotiations with Croatia but also the potential negotiations with all other Western Balkan countries. The impression has to be avoided that various Western Balkan countries may join the EU only after Turkish accession.

Third, the EU has to create a fundamental consensus among the member countries concerning its future enlargement strategy. It is well known that some members favour enlargement more than others, while some countries would like to stop the process for an indefinite time. Beyond this task, threats of a national veto have to be prevented not only in old but sometimes even in new member countries.[65]

Finally, many more politicians and experts coming from the new member countries have to be involved into the development and implementation of the EU's Western Balkan strategy. Such an initiative would certainly strengthen the consensus culture of the EU in the new member countries. However, and more importantly, the special experience, networks and "psychological surplus" of politicians, experts and business people coming from the new member countries could substantially improve the effectiveness and enhance the credibility of the EU's objectives in this part of Europe.

---

65 See the special requests and conditions set by Slovenia to Brussels' negotiations with Croatia.

CHAPTER VII

Conclusions

VII.1. In the last decade, several years have been mentioned as the critical period of developments in European integration, in the (Western) Balkans and in bilateral relations between Brussels and SEE. The last prediction put a special emphasis on the year 2006. However, most developments seem to point towards the year 2007 as the breaking (or failing) point both in the future destiny of the Western Balkans and the new international role of the EU.

First, the geographic and political restructuring of ex-Yugoslavia may end with the future status of Kosovo. However, several factors seem to indicate that the history of the Western Balkans is far from entering calmer waters. The reactions in Serbia are largely unknown. Second, Bosnia-Herzegovina should take its future into its own hands with a much smaller and indirect role to be played by international (mainly EU) actors. Whether it will be able to do so, even if with some delay, depends on a number of developments in the "post-Kosovo status" situation. Third, Bulgaria and Romania became members of the EU in this very year. Fourth, the Union's absorption capacity, both in economic, technical and psychological terms, is likely to face additional challenges, as long as the integration process is unable to generate fundamental reforms. As a result, the widely shared assumption is that a more active and pro-accession role of the EU may be tested in two aspects. On the one hand, new challenges may make evident the limits of the stabilization capacity of the European integration. On the other, internal developments in the EU, including the consequences of the so-called "enlargement fatigue", can reduce the positive impact and favourable image the Western Balkan countries expect from European integration. In a worse-case scenario, critical regional developments may overlap with the reduced commitment by Brussels, or at least the appearance thereof.

VII.2. Several official and professional opinions that have been formulated recently have indicated changes in the EU's accession strategy. Having given the green light to Bulgaria and Romania in 2007 does not modify the general process. Just the opposite, it could be considered as the final stage of the "Eastern" enlargement that may be followed by a different type of integration pattern in an uncertain timeframe. Obviously, the promise of accession given to all Western Balkan countries in 2003 will not be withdrawn. However, it may be accompanied by ever new conditions to be fulfilled. No less importantly, it may lack any clear roadmap, as it is already demonstrated in the negotiations with Croatia and in the delay to fix a starting date for negotiations with Macedonia.

Any further steps in the Western Balkans-related accession process will be affected by a number of crucial developments in the EU. Most probably, a more positive general environment for further accession would require a much more dynamic EU, with growth levels catching up to the United States (and other growth centres), substantially lower levels of unemployment and renewed dynamism in key integration-related policies. In this context, the ambitious deepening of the integration in several areas seems to play a leading role. Full-fledged liberalization of the internal market, the elimination of national veto rights in most areas and a more coordinated foreign and security policy definitely belong to this package of requirements. Reluctance toward basic national and community-level reforms has to be broken. Most societies have to be prepared for the new challenges instead of blaming different external developments for their incapacity to change. Until most recently, the enlargement in 2004 did not cause any meaningful problems in the normal functioning of the community's institutions and in the decision-making process. Therefore, reference to "enlargement fatigue" was not appropriate in the first years of membership of the CEE countries. However, more recent domestic political developments in Poland, the Czech Republic, Slovakia and, ultimately, also in Hungary can, in fact, create such a situation. Furthermore, Bulgarian and Romanian accession can add to the rising tide of enlargement fatigue. Thus, each of the ten new member countries should be fully aware of its responsibility in shaping the future of the EU, with respect to deepening and widening the integration. As *The Economist* has warned, Central Europe's risks may become a "bad advertisement" for the further expansion of the EU.[1] Adverse developments in the Western Balkan countries, including the incapacity of the EU to keep the region's stability at least on the current level, could dramatically increase the inward-looking mentality of the public opinion that has become less and less enthusiastic about letting more countries join in the foreseeable future. The balance between the integration maturity of the candidates and the EU's readiness to expand has clearly shifted towards the negative. More and more, the emphasis is on the latter, even if a candidate country already happened to fulfil all requirements for membership.[2]

---

1 *The Economist*, July 22, 2006, p. 33.

2 Bildt, the previous Prime Minister of Sweden characterized the new situation in the following way: "Previously Brussels used to stress that we will be ready, once you, candidates are ready. Now, the general position is that the EU does not know whether

VII.3. However, some developments may change the EU's current general attitude. One factor can be identified in the ongoing and sometimes accelerating internal political dynamism of the Western Balkan region. This element played an important role in the second half of the 1990s in the process of starting negotiations with the CEE countries. Another component may be a growing need for "surface stabilization" in the region after the new status of Kosovo. Finally, it cannot be ruled out that it is the new level of political (and ethnic) volatility in the Western Balkans that will force the EU to intensify its role in the region's stabilization. In a positive scenario, this pressure could represent the critical mass of deepening community-level activities, at least in the area of foreign and security policy.

VII.4. As of today, the EU only has a partial Western Balkan strategy. This includes the promise of membership, but without any clear roadmap. The number of conditions to be fulfilled has been gradually growing, and the establishment of new conditions is not ruled out Shifting and repeatedly modified targets have not exactly made the "stabilization anchor" in the region more reliable. Moreover, differently applied conditions have created double standards. The spectacular failure of a clear concept based on "standards before status" has not inspired confidence either. However, dramatic developments in the Western Balkans do not rule out a much stronger role by the EU to manage critical situations (indeed, not all of them seem to be manageable at the moment). However, European integration can only fill the power vacuum and become a reliable stability anchor in security, political and economic terms if the EU is able to make qualitative progress in several areas. First, the EU has to define its mission both around the world and in SEE by developing a clear vision of its role in the coming decades. Second, European integration badly needs clear leadership. Third, no meaningful expansion can be imagined without fundamental deepening the integration process in critical areas. Deepening and widening have characterized European integration for decades. The 2004 enlargement was the first one that missed this simultaneity. Thus, the gap that developed between large-scale widening and the freezing (blocking) of the deepening process has to be bridged as soon as possible. The right answer is evidently not enlargement fatigue but willingness and readiness for adequate reforms. Unfortunately, at the moment the member countries' interests are far from the real possibility of harmonization or coordination in more than one crucial area. Different national attitudes to the accession of the Western Balkan countries (and, of course, Turkey) are just one of such policy fields.

---

it will be ready once the candidates may be ready" (Martens, 2006e). Some politicians even question whether the EU wants any new member or if the integration process should be finished as it stands with the completion of the "Eastern" enlargement.

VII.5. In a realistic approach, enlargement towards the Western Balkans contains numerous risk factors. At the same time, it is no less important to emphasize that non-enlargement is definitely not the right answer. as this entails serious risks as well.

Three basic risk factors can be identified in European integration. First, and understandably, the EU would not want to import instability, *i.e.*, admit countries that fail to comply with the most important norms of a functioning (and democratic) state. Second, insufficiently prepared new member states are believed to slow down or block the normal functioning of EU institutions. Instead of generating additional energy or pressure to deepen the integration process and shape a future-oriented Europe, even the traditional mechanisms could be undermined in several areas. The debate on the optimal number of countries in a community is related to this issue. Third, the geographic boundaries of the EU represent a topical issue. Several experts consider the overstretching of the integration as the most important risk factor.

At the same time, it should not be forgotten that accession is not without risk factors for the new members, either. If they are not well prepared for membership, they may easily slide back to "second class membership" with adverse political, economic, social and emotional consequences. No less importantly, stability resulting from joining the club might turn out to be illusory in a relatively short period. Namely, it is one thing to fulfil all (or most) accession criteria on paper, and another to withstand the almost unlimited competition by other member countries while complying with the *acquis communautaire*. It is perhaps a paradox, but domestic instabilities can easily appear soon after importing stability through membership.[3] They can be aggravated by an incompetent public administration, the bureaucratic mechanisms of the EU and, not least, by exaggerated short-term expectations of large parts of the society in the new member country.

As mentioned earlier, risks cannot be reduced or eliminated by ignoring the Western Balkan countries. Any EU attitude that would abandon this crisis region could immediately threaten the stability of the EU itself (not only as a result of well-organized international criminal gangs). The idea of creating a "quarantine" with the aim of sealing off this part of Europe from other parts of the continent would not work, either.

VII.6. In this respect, the most pressing challenge for the EU is what kind of presence would promise the best results in the Western Balkans? There is no disagreement among the member countries that the EU must stay in the region. The tough question is which are the most appropriate

---

3 It has to be underlined that the political crises in the Central European new members are mainly rooted in non-EU-related factors.

instruments to create sustainable stability and, at the same time, reconcile regional expectations with internal EU possibilities of new stages of institutionalized relations.

VII.6.1. Either the withdrawal of the EU from the region (as a consequence of pressing domestic problems of the integration related to previous enlargements), or the necessity of deepening (stemming from a more volatile situation in the Western Balkans emerging after the "settlement" of the status of Kosovo) would, however, cause incalculable and high-level sources of threat for the stability of the continent. Furthermore, abandoning the tight control in Bosnia-Herzegovina could produce new dangers as well. stabilization in a new (or destroyed or failed) country takes a long time. The EU presence must not end with confidence in the success of apparent stabilization. Nation-building has to be based on a long process of creating functioning institutions and a cooperative, responsible society. Only once these conditions have been established can direct foreign presence be phased out. No doubt, neither Bosnia-Herzegovina nor Macedonia has reached this level, let alone a future Kosovo or its potential effects on Albania and Serbia. Therefore, the EU can only play a real stabilizing role in the region if it reconsiders its withdrawal plan in Bosnia-Herzegovina, keeps its "soft control" in Macedonia and will be able to assume fully its new responsibilities in Kosovo. These tasks, if adequately performed, will necessarily have a sizeable impact on the future of related EU policies not only in the given region, but they are likely to become an integral part of deepening community-level activities as well.

Still, the fundamental question whether, as a result of long and direct EU presence in the Western Balkans, the region will be able to become part of a comprehensive and dynamic enlargement process or will turn out to be an disliked/unpreferred but inevitable part of a new "European empire" cannot be clearly answered (Amato, 2005, p. 162). Not all the cards that may influence this decision are in the hands of the EU. However, those that the EU and the larger international community seem to possess should be made full use of.

One basic conclusion is that the current pattern of surface stabilization hardly offers any long-term solution. Managing the status quo (that may produce dramatic changes after the decision on Kosovo's new status) is insufficient and inadequate. All available instruments to promote a fundamental and deeply-rooted transformation have to be applied. In this regard it is crucial to understand that surface stabilization, as a mostly inevitable first step, has to be followed by genuine economic and social modernization. Only this strategy holds the promise of sustainable stability and catching up to the EU anchor, not just in economic terms of *per capita* GDP, but, no less importantly, in competitiveness, structural change and social behaviour.

It is needless to underline that Western Balkan stabilization needs close cooperation between the EU and the United States. Even if the EU emerges as the main external actor in the region, it can only become successful if the transatlantic relations in general, and the USA-EU relations concerning the future of the Western Balkans in particular, function smoothly.

VII.6.2. Lasting success, however, also depends on internal developments in the target countries (and region). Two risk sources deserve special attention.

One is rooted in the current economic and social situation in most countries, characterized by (extremely) high levels of unemployment, structural rigidities, a lack of meaningful privatization (mainly in the two largest countries, Croatia and Serbia) and, most importantly, the growing dependence on international and private remittances. As a result, a highly distorted socio-economic structure is already in the making. The main problem is not so much the growing inequalities between those who can rely on such external sources (either directly or indirectly, due to the fact of being employed by foreign institutions located in the given country) or those who can't. More dangerous for future adjustment is the spread of a job-avoiding mentality, the growing gap between people's own efforts and financial assets and the private consumption-oriented utilization of remittances (from housing to criminal activities). Currently, primarily two key processes indicate opposite developments. On the one hand, each country strives to upgrade its institutional relations with the EU with the ultimate aim of joining the European integration. In contrast, economic and social developments can create attitudes within society may lead the Western Balkan countries away from "normal" European standards. Thus, any strategy for economic modernization has to tackle this issue with utmost urgency.

The other risk factor lies in the unknown and delayed impact of imposed imported (external) rules. Historical examples of successful socio-economic and institutional modernization call attention to the existence of an "interface" between imported rules and values on the one hand, and genuine home-grown domestic development on the other hand. The transfer and application of benchmark examples is believed to be part of future success stories all over the globalized and interconnected world. This should be even more applicable to countries that are falling behind but would like to catch up in political, economic and other terms to more stable and more developed countries. Stabilization of the Western Balkan countries needs foreign support, while their future membership in the EU requires the application of basic European values and standards. However, in the medium-term, an overflow of imposed imported values can result in a situation in which this interface does not develop, either because quick stabilization does not allow the emergence of a certain "harmony" (co-development) between domestic and imported values, or because there is a large initial gap between the perception of a country's "own" and "foreign" values. In both cases there is a real danger that "overkill" (experienced also in the hasty and superficial overtaking of EU *acquis* with the only aim of showing "EU maturity") produces a serious backlash at a later stage of surface stabilization. As proven in several cases, the time factor plays an important role in this regard, since rapid political stabilization and even improved economic performance cannot be taken as a guarantee against adverse social and mental attitudes that need more time to become manifest than short-term political or economic results. The danger of the missing interface can only be substantially reduced if domestic and imported values can find a common platform and their "interlinking process" takes place in a relatively long period. This requirement, however, seems to contradict the political will and social expectation of the Western Balkan countries to become full members of the EU as soon as possible.

VII.7. Without fundamental reasons the EU can hardly withdraw its membership promise given to the countries of the region. Negotiations with Turkey further limit Brussels' manoeuvering room. Thus, the only option is to strengthen the criteria of membership and continue to float the definition of a concrete road map for the region in general and for the individual countries in particular. After the collapse of the "standards before status" conditionality, the EU has formulated its new strategy based on "three Cs", namely consolidation, conditionality and communication. In January 2006, the EU published its new Western Balkan program that contains traditional and new elements. In the first category we can find regional free trade among all countries of the region, the facilitation of import rules affecting commodities produced in the respective countries and the prolongation of the European Charter for Small and Medium-Sized Enterprises. The second group includes easing the visa regime for Western Balkan citizens, more fellowships to students from this region, as well as the incorporation of the Lisbon Agenda into the Western Balkan policy of Brussels. Some of the new goals are contradictory. Better educational and training possibilities can be welcome, if the students are ready to return to their respective countries after finishing their studies. This option, however, does not only depend on the student's willingness but mainly on the political and economic situation in their native countries within the next few years. This fact underlines the importance of relevant socio-economic reforms in the Western Balkan countries. In turn, the Lisbon Agenda can also be interpreted as a further and difficult conditionality on the road to accession.

Accession perspectives are largely influenced by the pattern of development that the countries of the region are likely to implement. In this context, three main scenarios have been outlined. The pessimistic scenario is based on a dramatic economic downturn accompanied by enhanced intra-regional rivalry and increasing international isolation. Without questioning the key role of the EU in the region, it could become a powerful argument against further enlargement of the integration. The optimistic scenario projects a progressive path of integration, consisting of successful domestic transformation and rapidly growing regional stability hand-in-hand with clear perspectives of membership in the EU. Finally, the in-between (more realistic) scenario reckons with gradual progress not exempt from smaller setbacks, but generally increasing stability and country-specific fulfilment of the EU conditionalities (Balázs-Szalóki, 2006).

Beyond a massive physical presence in critical countries of the region (mainly Kosovo and Bosnia-Herzegovina) Brussels should pay much more attention to the creation of basic elements of sustainable economic development. This, however, would substantially increase the community's financial engagement in the area. While, as a result of putting financial assistance into one new fund (IPA) the organizational changes in providing EU funds to the Western Balkans seem to be appropriate, the amount offered may prove to be quite modest in relation to the tasks to be performed. The EU's commitment to the stability and sustainable modernization of the region has to be manifest not only in political speeches and a growing physical presence in the region but also in its financial contribution, accompanied by clear and transparent rules and priorities on how to utilize these resources.

If there is any possibility to move back from the membership promise, or at least to delay further enlargement of the EU, it has to be accompanied by a new quality of cooperation. "Strategic partnership" does not work in itself, since it would be considered by the countries waiting for membership as a clear retreat from the original goal. Delayed membership, however, may work, if the prolonged period of preparation and adjustment is based on a new quality of cooperation that includes at least three key issues: a substantially higher financial commitment, relevant progress in the visa regime, and clear examples of abandoning the practice of double standards. As for the last element, the EU could improve its credibility if its repeated claims of combating criminality and corruption were strictly applied not only in the Western Balkan countries but also in various EU member countries in which such criminal gangs are active. Policies that combat illegal activities such as drugs dealing, money laundering, and the trafficking of human beings can only work if supply and demand are reduced simultaneously. Evidently, one may produce or transport the above mentioned goods and services. However, if there is no demand for them, the "business" cannot work. It is ineffective and unjust to blame exclusively the supply side for criminal activities. Most of these operations could be substantially reduced if the demand side were as strictly controlled and prosecuted in key Western European countries, as required by the supply sources. It is hardly believable that British, French, German or Dutch internal security forces had no idea about the widespread operation of Western Balkan criminal gangs (mostly intertwined with domestic groups) in general, or the "Albanian mafia", in particular. Of course, a new strategy is needed to manage the consequences of the collapse of such chains, since many people in the Western Balkans have integrated such activities and revenues into their daily survival or into longer-term individual or family-level life strategies.

VII.8. For several reasons, European integration has arrived at a critical juncture. Its commitment to the Western Balkans and the strategy to be developed and implemented is, however, only one, albeit crucial, element of its future. First of all, Europe has to redefine itself at the beginning of the 21st century. Its own values have to be reassessed, while a new mission has to be developed under a clear leadership. This is a precondition for facing global challenges successfully, implementing a fundamental deepening of the integration and enabling it to admit new members. It is this set of requirements that could offer a transparent and reliable roadmap for the Western Balkan countries. The EU's capacity to manage new emerging situations in the region will have a crucial impact not only on the future of Europe in general and the process of European integration in particular, but it would largely shape the image of Europe in the world characterized by traditional and emerging global players. Europe's influence in the global arena will not remain unaffected by the success or failure of creating sustainable stability in the Balkans. What makes these challenges even more difficult is the fact that the success of a strategy for sustained stability in the Balkans has to incorporate instruments to foster coexistence among different values, religions and ethnic groups. The EU has to be prepared for the emergence and consequences of global religious solidarity, an area in which the Western Balkan can prove to be a relevant "testing ground".

The EU is under a tremendous time pressure. This should always be kept in mind, even if some of the Western Balkan countries seem to be "surface-stabilized". The fact that Europe can no longer be split into different groups of countries, with some of them isolated for a longer time, has been demonstrated more than once in the last decade. Neither stability, social peace nor economic abundance is possible in one part of the continent, with failed institutions, distorted social behaviour, poverty and a 19th century ethnic mentality in the direct neighbourhood of the enlarged EU, just a few (hundred) kilometres from the centres of stability and affluence. If the EU refuses to commit itself in a qualitatively new way to the Western Balkans, the region nonetheless will increase its influence in the EU. The adverse consequences of political destabilization andsocial disintegration are incalculable, but they certainly much higher than even the total cost of the most "generous" common strategy based on nothing else but the "enlightened self-interest" of the EU. As the latest Amato report concludes: "The real referendum on the future of Europe will take place in the Balkans".

Appendix: Tables, Graphs and Maps

Appendix Table I.2.5/1
Annual foreign aid inflow and share of total by sector, 1999-2004 (amounts are in thousands of Euro)

Sector	Spent-1999	Spent-2000	Spent-2001	Spent-2002	Spent-2003	Spent-2004	Total spent during 1999-2004	Share of total (%)
Public utilities	16,854	127,693.6	193,210.4	94,099.7	91,703.3	54,029.1	557,621	25.92
Housing	26,895	155,530.7	90,831.7	67,572.9	14,107.0	6,888.3	361,825	16.25
Trade and industry	124.44	56,570.5	42,263.5	27,061.9	29,189.8	21,034.1	176,244	7.90
Education and science	43,256	74,503.0	65,671.8	49,493.0	31,092.8	19,908.2	283,926	12.74
Infrastructure	202	50,183.7	48,295	20,968.2	12,807.0	1,955.7	134,411	6.03
Agriculture	125.05	17,736.8	34,377.4	17,565.3	15,880.4	4,514.9	90,200	4.05
Environment	85	184.64	633.62	1,097.2	3,471.4	1,063.8	6,536	0.29
Technical assistance, capacity building and others	89,976	124,979.1	117,917.6	120,758.5	90,113.4	54,035.8	597,780	26.82
Total	143,991	273,974	260,863	215,975	169,747	100,556	2,228,511	100.00

Appendix Table I.2.5/2
The European Commission's financial commitment to Bulgaria and Romania between 2007 and 2009 (Euro mn)

Main objectives	2007	2008	2009	Total
Agriculture of which:	1,141	1,990	2,342	5,473
– market intervention				1,120
– direct payments				1,312
– rural development				3,041
Structural instruments	1,938	2,731	3,605	8,273
Internal policies	440	434	426	1,304
Administrative expenditure	96	125	125	346
Total financial commitment	3,619	5,279	6,498	15,396

Source: European Commission. Financial Framework for the period between 2007 and 2013 (preliminary).

Appendix Table II.6.3/1
Legislative Institutions in Non-EU Europe, 2004

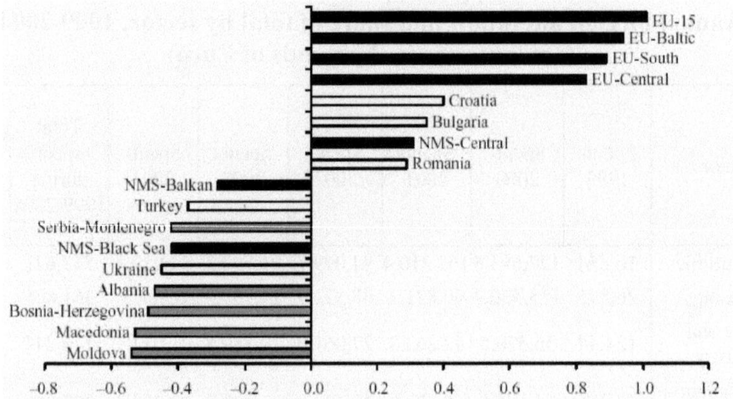

Source: Kaufmann *et al.* (2005); own calculations.

Appendix Table II.6.3/2
Administrative Institutions in Non-EU Europe, 2004

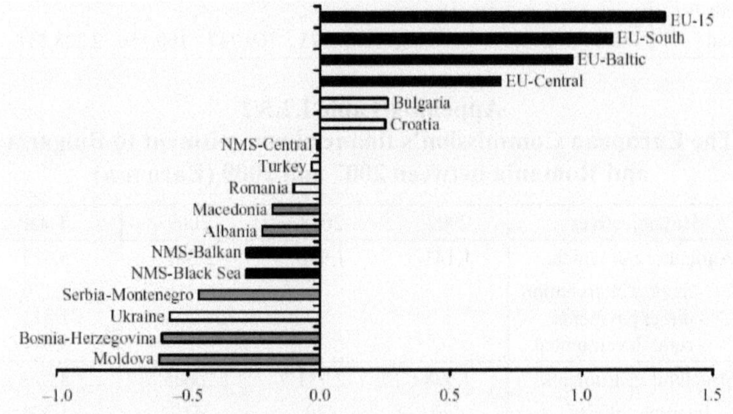

Source: Kaufmann *et al.* (2005); own calculations.

Appendix Table II.6.3/3
Judicative Institutions in Non-EU Europe, 2004

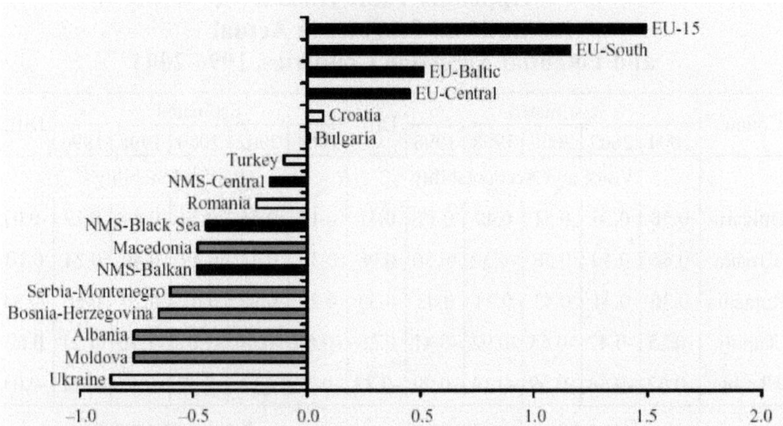

Source: Kaufmann *et al.* (2005); own calculations.

Appendix Table II.6.3/4
Overall Institutions in Non-EU Europe, 2004

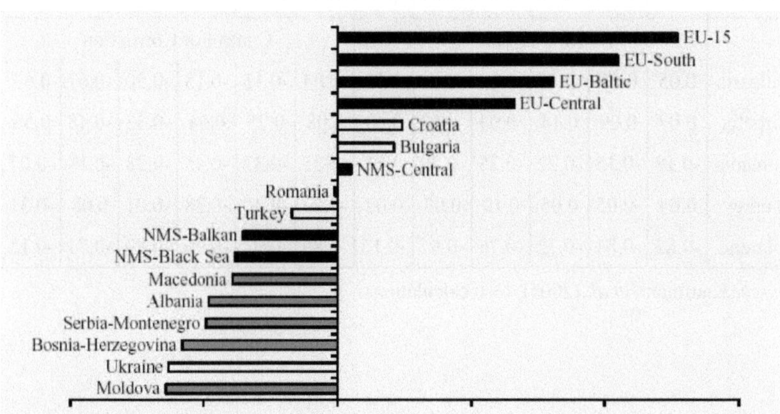

Source: Kaufmann *et al.* (2005); own calculations.

Appendix Table II.6.3/5
Institutional Progress in Actual and Potential Accession Countries, 1996-2004

Country	Estimated					Diff.	Estimated					Diff.
	2004	2002	2000	1998	1996		2004	2002	2000	1998	1996	
	Voice and Accountability						Political Stability					
Bulgaria	0.58	0.56	0.51	0.40	0.17	0.41	0.13	0.56	0.30	0.44	0.19	-0.07
Croatia	0.46	0.49	0.38	-0.30	-0.50	0.96	0.35	0.48	0.49	0.46	0.24	0.10
Romania	0.36	0.41	0.43	0.24	0.03	0.33	0.22	0.34	0.01	0.20	0.56	-0.34
Turkey	-0.15	-0.47	-0.65	-0.92	-0.41	0.26	-0.60	-0.66	-1.01	-1.10	-1.21	0.62
Ukraine	-0.62	-0.64	-0.39	-0.14	-0.39	-0.23	-0.27	0.12	-0.48	-0.19	-0.22	-0.05
	Government Effectiveness						Regulatory Quality					
Bulgaria	-0.08	-0.02	-0.16	-0.94	-0.45	0.38	0.60	0.62	0.22	0.47	-0.08	0.68
Croatia	0.32	0.23	0.15	0.30	-0.17	0.50	0.19	0.19	0.31	0.34	-0.08	0.26
Romania	-0.15	-0.30	-0.59	-0.61	-0.55	0.41	-0.06	0.04	-0.27	0.30	-0.43	0.38
Turkey	0.01	-0.16	-0.07	-0.31	0.01	0.00	-0.07	0.05	0.24	0.86	0.51	-0.59
Ukraine	-0.67	-0.76	-0.78	-0.97	-0.61	-0.06	-0.48	-0.62	-1.22	-0.89	-0.59	0.12
	Rule of Law						Control of Corruption					
Bulgaria	0.05	0.01	-0.13	-0.22	-0.09	0.15	-0.04	-0.15	-0.13	-0.50	-0.67	0.63
Croatia	0.07	0.09	0.14	-0.04	-0.53	0.60	0.08	0.25	0.04	-0.33	-0.48	0.56
Romania	-0.18	-0.15	-0.22	-0.25	-0.29	0.11	-0.25	-0.32	-0.45	-0.38	-0.18	-0.07
Turkey	0.04	-0.05	0.05	0.19	0.03	0.02	-0.23	-0.40	-0.28	-0.01	0.08	-0.31
Ukraine	-0.83	-0.84	-0.72	-0.76	-0.67	-0.15	-0.89	-0.97	-0.96	-0.89	-0.74	-0.15

Source: Kaufmann *et al.* (2005); own calculations.

Appendix Table III.3.11/1
Comparison of selected operational costs of FDI in SEE countries (in Euro)

Country	Wage Monthly (a)	Electri-city (kwh)	Phone call (b)	Broad-band Internet monthly	Office space Monthly rent per m²	Industrial space Monthly rent per m²	Shipping costs (c)
Albania	191	0.08	1.62	140	23.5	2.5	2,260
Bosnia-Herzegovina	381	0.03	3.00	150	12.5	3.0	.
Bulgaria	326	0.07	1.33	48	5.5	2.0	1,400
Croatia	841	0.15	0.92	66	12.0	2.5	1,000
Macedonia	356	0.05	1.45	65	2.5	.	2,800
Romania	303	.	0.57	.	17.0	6.25	1,300
Serbia	308	0.04	1.22	.	18.96	16.21	1,600
SEE average	330	0.07	1.39	.	15.87	4.78	1,726
CEE benchmark	591 Poland	0.06 Slovakia	0.22 Hungary	56 Poland	12.0 Hungary	3.5 Hungary	900 Hungary

(a) average gross wage.

(b) based on a 3-minute call to Germany.

(c) shipping a 40 ton truck from the respective capital city to Germany.

Source: OECD (2006) based on data provided by ICEG Consultants.

Appendix Table III.5.2/1
Changing structure of transportation in the SEE countries (as a percentage share of total transportation, excluding air and sea traffic)

Country	Passenger transportation				Cargo transportation			
	Railway		Road		Railway		Road	
	1990	2002	1990	2002	1990	2002	1990	2002
Albania	26.7	1.2	73.3	98.4	34.0	6.0	62.0	94.0
Bosnia-Herzegovina	30.0	8.0	70.0	92.0	47.0	12.0	50.0	86.0
Bulgaria	20.4	11.0	79.6	89.0	46.8	48.9	45.8	41.5
Croatia	26.2	17.1	73.8	82.9	45.0	19.0	32.0	66.0
Macedonia	20.9	9.0	79.1	91.0	21.0	10.0	79.0	90.0
Romania	49.1	32.9	50.9	67.1	81.2	51.6	7.5	32.4
Serbia-Montenegro	15.0	6.5	85.0	93.5	24.3	33.3	42.0	46.8
Memorandum items:								
Greece	10.0	7.0	90.0	93.0	4.6	3.3	95.4	96.7
Slovenia	10.0	8.0	90.0	92.0	46.1	40.3	53.9	59.7

Source: Erdősi (2005, pp. 62-63), based on national and international statistics (Trends in the Transport Sector. European Conference of Ministers of Transport, 2004).

Appendix Table III.5.2/2
Composition of the road network of the SEE countries (in km)

Country	Year	Total road network	Of which: highways	Road density (2000, in km per 1,000 km²)
Albania	1990	17,400	-	
	2000	18,000	-(a)	219
Bulgaria	1990	36,922	273	
	2000	37,301	324	336
Croatia	1990	32,796	291	
	2000	28,534	411	492
Macedonia	1990	10,591	83	
	2000	12,666	144	338
Romania	1990	68,316	113	
	2000	72,907	113	308
Serbia-Montenegro	1990	46,019	374	
	2000	45,387	374	319
Memorandum item:				
Slovenia	1990	39,553	228	773
	2000	38,403	427	

(a) there is a 2x2 lane motorway between Tirana and Durres that has not been registered in the primary statistical source.

Source: Erdősi (2005), based on Central Statistical Office of Hungary, International Statistical Yearbook 2002.

Appendix Map III.5.2./3.
The oil and gas networks in the region
Energy – OIL AND GAS transmission pipelines

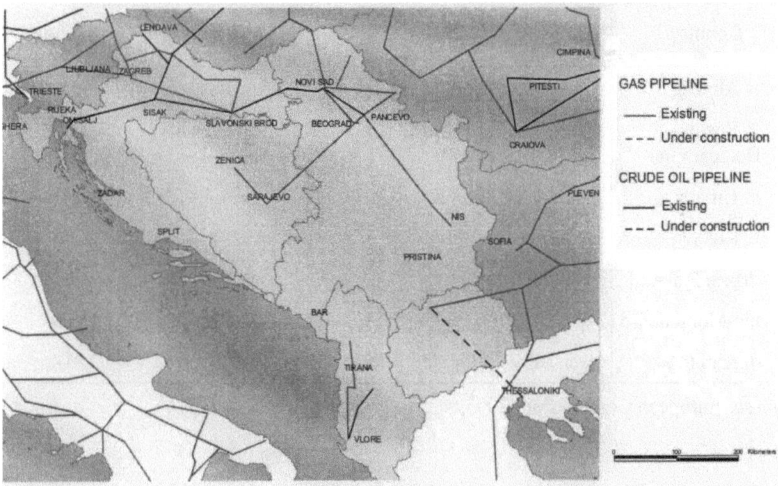

Source: Erdősi (2005).

Appendix Map III.5.2./4.
The electricity network in the region
Energy – Electricity lines (400kV)

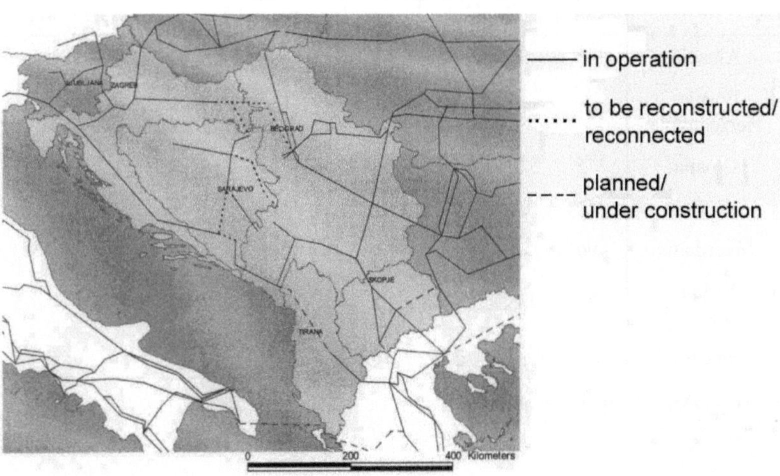

Source: Erdősi (2005).

Appendix Table III.5.3/5
Distribution of investment costs by country and project status
(in Euro mn)

Country	Committed projects	Ongoing projects	New projects	Grand total
Albania	123	66	366	555
Bosnia-Herzegovina	0	254	277	531
Croatia	126	291	564	981
Kosovo	0	6	98	105
Macedonia	97	81	304	482
Serbia-Montenegro	333	163	669	1,165
Grand total	679	862	2,277	3,818

Source: European Commission (2003).

Appendix Table III.5.3/6
Distribution of investment costs by country and transport mode
(in Euro mn)

Country	Road	Rail	Airport	Sea port	Inland waterways	Multi Modal	Border crossing	Grand total
Albania	480	0	67	8	0	0	0	555
Bosnia-Herzegovina	401	114	4	0	0	0	12	531
Croatia	275	520	36	146	0	1	4	981
Kosovo	70	10	21	0	0	0	4	105
Macedonia	406	52	21	0	0	0	3	482
Serbia-Montenegro	533	465	126	8	6	0	27	1,165
Grand total	2165	1160	275	162	6	1	50	3,818

Source: European Commission (2003).

Appendix Table III.5.3/7
List of Regional Transport Infrastructure and Facilitation Projects under Implementation (as of June 30, 2003)
Sector: Transport/Roads

Title:	Implemented in:	Lead Agency:	Costs
Road Maintenance Project	Albania	WB	USD 24 mn
Fier-Vlore Road	Albania	EIB	Euro 23 mn
Tepelene-Gjirokaster Road	Albania	EIB/EC	Euro 22 mn
Elbansan-Librazdh Road	Albania	EBRD	Euro 25.66 mn
Emergency Road Repiar	Albania	WB	USD 14.46 mn
Main roads and bridges	Bosnia-Herzegovina	EIB	Euro 120 mn
Bridge reconstruction	Bosnia-Herzegovina	EC	Euro 17.50 mn
Autocesta Rijeka-Zagreb	Croatia	EBRD/EIB	Euro 100 mn
Croatia Motorway rehabilitation project	Croatia	EIB/EBRD	Euro 125 mn
Skopje Bypass	Former Yugoslav Republic of Macedonia	EIB/EBRD	Euro 50 mn
Finalising the upgrading of the E 75 road (Corridor X) section Negotino-Demir Kapija (Phase III)	Former Yugoslav Republic of Macedonia	EC	Euro 11 mn
Blace Border Crossing	Former Yugoslav Republic of Macedonia	EC	Euro 8.50 mn
Demir Kapija-Gevgelija (Greek border)	Former Yugoslav Republic of Macedonia	EIB	Euro 32 mn
Transport Rehabilitation	Serbia-Montenegro	EIB/EBRD	Euro 132 mn
Transport Rehabilitation programme	Serbia-Montenegro	EIB	Euro 14.15 mn
Urgent Road – Emergency Road rehabilitation	Kosovo, Serbia-Montenegro	WB	USD 60.00 mn

Source: www.seerecon.org.

Sector: Transport/Railway

Title:	Implemented in:	Lead Agency:	Cost:
Railways Recovery Project	Bosnia-Herzegovina	EIB/EBRD	Euro 80.00 M
Railway – sections of corridor VC	Croatia	EIB	Euro 22.00 M
Yugoslav Railways Reconstruction Project (Serbian/ Montenegro	Serbia-Montenegro	EBRD/EIB	Euro 170.00 M.

Source: www.seerecon.org.

Sector: Transport/Ports and Waterways

Title:	Implemented in:	Lead Agency:	Cost:
Port of Durres rehabilitation and modernization	Albania	EIB/WB	Euro 34.00 M

Source: www.seerecon.org.

Sector: Transport/Airports

Title:	Implemented in:	Lead Agency:	Cost:
Zagreb Air Traffic Control	Croatia	EIB/EBRD	Euro 55.00 M
Civil aviation upgrading project	Former Yugoslav Republic of Macedonia	EBRD	Euro 11.20 M
Yugoslavian Air Navigation	Serbia and Montenegro	EIB/EBRD	Euro 130.0 M

Source: www.seerecon.org.
27 projects, total cost 1,140,426 M Euro (1,509,230 M USD).
1 Euro = 1.0748 USD.

Sector: Cross Border/Trade Facilitation

Title:	Implemented in:	Lead Agency:	Cost:
Border Crossings between Croatia and Slovenia, and Croatia and Serbia-Montenegro	Region	EC	Euro 7.75 M
Border Crossings between BiH and Croatia, and BiH and Serbia-Montenegro	Region	EC	Euro 7.50 M
Border-Crossing at HORGOS on Corridor X, between Belgrade and Budapest	Region	EC	Euro 5.00 M
Trade and Transport Facilitation Program fro Southeast Europe (TTFSE)	Region	World Bank	USD 117.6 M

Source: www.seerecon.org.

Appendix Table III.8.1/1
Financial transfers of migrant workers in 2004(a)

The largest recipient countries(b)	USD bn	The most transfer-dependent countries	In % of GDP
India	21.7	Tonga	31.1
China	21.3	Moldova	27.1
Mexico	18.1	Lesotho	25.8
France	12.7	Haiti	24.8
Philippines	11.6	Bosnia-Herzegovina	22.5
Spain	6.9	Jordan	20.4
Belgium	6.8	Jamaica	17.4
Germany	6.5	Serbia-Montenegro	17.2
Great Britain	6.4	El Salvador	16.2
Morocco	4.2	Honduras	15.5
Serbia-Montenegro	4.1	Philippines	13.5
Pakistan	3.9	Dominican Republic	13.2
Brazil	3.6	Lebanon	12.4
Bangladesh	3.4	Samoa	12.4
Egypt	3.3	Tadshikistan	12.1
Portugal	3.2	Nicaragua	11.9
Vietnam	3.2	Albania	11.7
Colombia	3.2	Nepal	11.7
USA	3.0	Kiribati	11.3
Nigeria	2.8	Yemen	10.0

(a) in many cases rough estimates.

(b) the first 20 countries indicated above account for 66.4% of total financial transfers of migrant workers.

Source: United Nations. International Migration and Development. New York, May 2006 (fundamentally based on original figures calculated by The World Bank).

Appendix Table III.8.2/1
Private remittances to selected Southeastern European countries (based on balance-of-payment statistics, in USD mn)

Country	1998	1999	2000	2001	2002	2003	2004
Albania	452	357	531	615	643	778	.
Bosnia-Herzegovina	1,144	1,099	950	919	956	1,143	1,312
Croatia	520	454	534	583	67	797	851
Macedonia	63	76	80	68	92	146	161
Memorandum items:							
Hungary	26	26	53	51	39	39	26
Poland	938	698	1,534	1,802	1,725	2,288	2,347

Source: IMF. Balance of Payments Statistics. Yearbook 2005. Washington D.C. 2005.

Appendix Table IV.3.2/1
Hungary's exports to the countries of Southeastern Europe (Euro mn and growth rates)

Country	1995	2001	2003	2004	2005	Growth rates	
						2005 1995=100	2005 2001=100
Albania	4	10	11	16	26	650	260
Bosnia-Herzegovina	30	237	251	218	232	773	98
Bulgaria	29	118	141	223	325	1,121	275
Croatia	131	255	379	570	717	547	281
Macedonia	22	41	44	59	63	286	154
Romania	210	854	987	1,413	1,867	889	219
Serbia-Montenegro	30	218	281	409	499	1,663	229
Total	456	1,733	2,094	2,908	3,729	818	215
In total exports (%)	3.5	5.1	5.5	6.6	7.5		

Source: Central Statistical Office and Ministry of Economy and Transportation of Hungary and own calculations.

Appendix Table IV.3.2/2
Hungary's imports from the countries of Southeastern Europe (Euro mn and growth rates)

Country	1995	2001	2003	2004	2005	Growth rates	
						2005 1995=100	2005 2001=100
Albania	0.6	0.3	0.1	0.1	1	.	.
Bosnia-Herzegovina	0.2	6	7	63	104	.	1,733
Bulgaria	16	47	54	73	76	475	162
Croatia	42	67	93	108	112	267	167
Macedonia	7	5	2	2	2	.	.
Romania	99	403	531	730	889	898	221
Serbia-Montenegro	1	62	62	87	108	.	174
Total	166	590	740	1,063	1,292	778	219
Share in total imports (%)	1.1	1.6	1.8	2.2	2.5		

Source: Central Statistical Office and Ministry of Economy and Transportation of Hungary and own calculations.

Appendix Table IV.3.2/3
Hungary's trade balance with the countries of Southeastern Europe (Euro mn and coverage ratio in %)

Country	1995	2001	2003	2004	2005	2003-2005 cumulative	Exports in % of imports 2003-2005 cumulative
Albania	3	10	11	16	25	52	5,300
Bosnia-Herzegovina	30	231	244	155	128	527	403
Bulgaria	13	71	87	150	249	486	339
Croatia	89	188	286	462	605	1,353	532
Macedonia	15	36	42	57	61	160	2,767
Romania	111	451	456	683	978	2,117	198
Serbia-Montenegro	29	156	219	322	391	932	463
Total	288	1,143	1,345	1,845	2,437	5,627	281
Share in total Hungarian trade balance	.	.	.	.	.	.	.

. – cannot be interpreted, since Hungary's overall trade balance registers large deficits, why trade balance with each of the Southeastern European countries shows continuous (and growing) surplus.

Source: own calculations based on figures provided by the Central Statistical Office and the Ministry of Economy and Transportation.

Appendix Table IV.3.2/4
Some key features of the Hungarian direct investments in the countries of Southeastern Europe

Country	FDI in Euro mn	Share in total FDI (%)	Ranking of foreign investors	Main sectors	Main companies
Bosnia-Herzegovina	.	.	.	Oil, Mining	MOL (a) Hungarian Aluminium Co.
Bulgaria	481	6.3	8.	Banking, Manufacturing, retail trade, real estate, hotels, telecommunications	OTP Hungarian Foreign Trade Bank, Dunapack Videoton, Matáv
Croatia	More than 1,000	About 9.0	4.	Oil, Financial services, Hotels, real estate, trade, manufacturing	MOL, OTP, Fornetti, Dalmácia Holiday Srl., Zalakerámia
Macedonia	618	48.3	1.	Telecommunications	Matáv
Montenegro	140	.	1.	Telecommunications, Hotels, real estate	Matáv, Hunguest Hotels Inc.
Romania	367(b)	2.8(b)	13(b)	Retail trade, manufacturing, banking, real estate, hotels, gasoline stations	MOL, OTP, TriGránit Richter, Dunapack Danubius, Zalakerámia
Serbia	.	.	.	Gasoline stations Banking, Real estate	MOL, OTP, TriGránit, Betonút

(a) together with the Croatian INA.

(b) Official Romanian figures. Hungarian estimates amount to approximately Euro 850 mn, substantially higher share in total FDI and ranking among the first ten foreign countries investing in Romania.

Source: own table and calculations based on OECD (2006), WIIW Database (2005) and company-related information published by Világgazdaság, August 18, 2006, p. 6.

Appendix Table V.2.7/1
Deka Converging Europe Indicator (DCEI) Scores for New Member Countries, Bulgaria, Romania, Croatia and Turkey(a)

Country	Total score	Monetary policy	Fiscal policy	Real economic convergence	Institutional adjustment
Czech Republic	80	100	75	85	80
Slovenia	83	75	85	95	80
Estonia	81	75	80	85	85
Slovakia	81	90	80	75	80
Poland	79	90	80	65	85
Latvia	77	65	85	75	85
Hungary	75	75	55	90	85
Lithuania	74	75	85	60	80
Bulgaria	65	75	85	35	80
Romania	63	40	90	55	80
Croatia	59	80	70	35	60
Turkey	47	45	70	40	40

(a) on a scoreboard from 0 to 100, being 100 the highest (best) score.

Source: Dr. Dietmar Hornung, BDeka Bank, as quoted by *Frankfurter Allgemeine Zeitung*, June 08, 2006.

Table VI.2.3/1. Selected examples of closing benchmarks in Croatia's accession negotiation

Chapter	Closing benchmarks
Chapter 3 Right of establishment and freedom to provide services	Croatia will have to comply with the *acquis* on the recognition of professional qualifications for EU citizens, As regards the right of establishment, Croatia will have to repeal any nationality requirements, Croatia has to align its legislation, in particular the Law Practice Act, in order to bring it fully in line with the requirements of the Stabilization and Association Agreement, Croatia has to align its legislation with the *acquis* on aliens, cross-border provision of services on a temporary basis and postal services
Chapter 6 Company Law	Croatia has to align the Companies Act, the Audit Act and its accounting legislation with the *acquis* and complete alignment with the directive on take-over bids
Chapter 9 Financial Services	Croatia has to transpose the relevant *acquis* into Croatian law, in particular on the insurance sector, investments services and securities markets, Croatia has to demonstrate continued progress in the enforcement of prudential requirements

Chapter 10 Information Society and Media	Croatia has to align with the *acquis* concerning electronic communications, electronic commerce, electronic signatures, information security and electronic media, and the Television without Frontiers Directive. Furthermore, Croatia has to complete the foreseen review of audiovisual media legislation Croatia has also to ensure sufficient administrative capacity to enforce the *acquis*
Chapter 18 Statistics	Croatia has to submit a detailed description of the foreseen methodology and of the organisational set up as well as relevant statistics, and key national account indicators with a detailed description of the methodology used
Chapter 32 Financial Control	Croatia has to adopt and implement Public Internal Financial Control (PIFC) legislation and inherent policies supported by adequate implementation capacity, Croatia has to safeguard the State Audit Institution's functional and financial independence, Croatia has to align the Criminal Code with the protection of the EU's financial interests (PIF) Convention and its protocols and its legislation for the protection of the Euro against counterfeiting, Croatia shall set up effective and efficient coordination

Source: Council of the European Union. Brussels, 26 June 2007 11232/07 (Presse 153), press.office@consilium.europa.eu and http://www.consilium.europa.eu/Newsroom.

Table VI.3.1/1
Mini-States in Europe

Country	Area (km²)	Population ('000)	GDP (USD mn)	GDP per head (USD)
Andorra	468	71	1,840	24,000
Cyprus	9,250	784	16,850	21,600
Iceland	103,000	299	10,340	34,900
Liechtenstein	160	34	825	25,000
Luxembourg	2,586	474	29,430	55,600
Malta	316	400	7,568	19,000
Monaco	2	33	870	27,000
San Marino	61	29	940	34,600
Vatican	0.44	1	.	.
For comparison				
Kosovo	10,912	2,100	3,287	1,565(a)
Montenegro	14,026	631	2,412(b)	3,800(b)

a) estimate.

b) at PPP.

Source: CIA World Factbook as quoted by Világgazdaság, May 24, 2006.

List of Abbreviations

ACP	African, Caribbean and Pacific (countries)
ATM	Autonomous Trade Measures
CAP	Common Agricultural Policy
CARDS	Community Assistance for Reconstruction, Development and Stabilization
CAS	Country Assistance Strategy (World Bank documents on individual countries)
CEE	Central and Eastern Europe
CEFTA	Central European Free Trade Area
CIA	Central Intelligence Agency
CMEA	Council on Mutual Economic Assistance
DCEI	Deca Converging Europe Indicator
DG	Directorate General (within the European Commission)
DM	Deutsche Mark (German Mark)
EAR	European Agency of Reconstruction
EBRD	European Bank for Reconstruction and Development
EC	European Commission
ECHO	European Community Humanitarian Office
EEC	European Economic Community
EIB	European Investment Bank
EIDHR	European Initiative for Democracy and Human Rights
EMU	Economic and Monetary Union
EU	European Union
FDI	Foreign Direct Investment
FRY	Federal Republic of Yugoslavia
FYROM	Former Yugoslav Republic of Macedonia
GCI	Growth and Competitiveness Index
GDP	Gross Domestic Product
GSP	General System of Preferences
HDI	Human Development Index
ICTY	International Criminal Tribunal on Yugoslavia
IMF	International Monetary Fund

IPA	Instrument of Pre-Accession Assistance
ISPA	Instrument for Structural Policies for Pre-Accession
KFOR	Kosovo Force
MIP	Multi-annual Indicative Programming
MoU	Memorandum of Understanding
NATO	North Atlantic Treaty Organization
OBNOVA	Committee for implementation of aid measures for Bosnia and Herzegovina, Croatia, the Federel Republic of Yugoslavia and the former Yugoslav Republic of Macedonia
OECD	Organization for Economic Cooperation and Development
OSCE	Organization for Security and Cooperation in Europe
PHARE	Pologne Hongrie Aide à la Reconstruction Économique (The EU's official technical and financial assistance program to Central and Eastern European countries from the very beginning of political and economic transformation)
PPP	Purchasing Power Parity
SAPARD	Special Accession Programme for Agriculture and Rural Development
SEE	Southeastern Europe
SEECP	South East European Cooperation Programme
SME	Small and Medium-sized Enterprise
SAA	Stabilization and Association Agreement
SAP	Stabilization and Association Process
SP	Stability Pact
TEMPUS	Trans European Mobility Programme for University Students
TINA	Transport Infrastructure Needs Assessment
UN	United Nations
UNCTAD	United Nations Conference on Trade and Development
UNMIK	United Nations Mission in Kosovo
USAID	United States Assistance for International Development
USD	United States Dollar
WB	Western Balkans
WEF	World Economic Forum
WIIW	Wiener Institut für Internationale Wirtschaftsvergleiche (Vienna Institute of Comparative Economic Studies)
WTO	World Trade Organization

Bibliography

Albanian Institute for International Studies (2004), *Albania and the European Union. The Stabilisation Association Agreement*, Report No. 3, Tirana, September, 35 pp.

Albanian Institute for International Studies (2005), *Albanian Brain Drain. Turning the Tide*, Tirana, 61 pp.

Altmann, Franz-Lothar (2005), "EU und Westlicher Balkan: Eine schwierige Verlobung", *Südosteuropa*, Vol. 53, No. 2, pp. 185-212.

Amato, Giuliano (ed.) (2005), "International Commission on the Balkans. The Balkans in Europe's Future", *Südosteuropa*, Vol. 53, No. 2, pp. 159-184.

Auswärtiges Amt – CAP – Bertelsmann Stiftung (2002), *Integrating the Balkans: Regional Ownership and European Responsibilities*, Balkan Forum, Discussion Paper, Berlin, July 15-16, 17 pp.

Balázs, Katalin and Szalóki, Katalin (2006), "Balkáni viszonyok – az EU és a nyugat-balkáni országok kapcsolata" (Balkan State of Affairs – Relations Between the EU and the Western Balkan Countries), *Európai Tükör*, Nos. 7 and 8, July-August, pp. 109-130.

BankAustria Creditanstalt (2005), *CEE Report No. 4*, Vienna, http://economic research-e.ba-ca-com.

Bartlett, William (2005), *Forms of Policy Transfer and Policy Convergence and Divergence in the Western Balkans*, SEERC Bulletin, No. 1, pp. 9-14.

Bassa, Zoltán (2005), "Bosnia-Herzegovina. Country study", Budapest, December 23, 23 pp. (manuscript).

Begovic, Boris and Mijatovic, Bosko (eds.) (2005), *Four Years of Transition in Serbia*, Center for Liberal Democratic Studies, Belgrade.

Biermann, Rafael (2002), "Stabilitaetspakt und EU-Balkanpolitik: Von der Stabilisierung zur Integration?", *Integration*, Vol. 25, No. 3, pp. 210-225.

Bildt, Carl (2006), *The EU needs a bolder Balkan strategy*, Center for European Reform, London, issue 46, February-March, p. 6.

Buchsteiner, Jochen (2006), "Bescheidenere Ziele", *Frankfurter Allgemeine Zeitung*, July 18, p. 1.

Buhigas Schubert, Carlos and Martens, Hans (2005), *The Nordic model: A recipe for European success?*, European Policy Center, Brussels, September, 114 pp.

Calic, Marie-Janine (2005), "Strategien zur Europaeisierung des Westlichen Balkan. Der Stabilisierungs- und Assoziierungsprozess auf dem Prüfstand", *Südosteuropa*, Vol. 53, No. 1, pp. 1-37.

Commission of the European Communities (2005), *Communication from the Commission. Comprehensive Monitoring Report on the State of Preparedness for EU Membership of Bulgaria and Romania*, Brussels, October 25, COM (2005) 534 final, 18 pp.

Crespo-Cuaresma, Jesús, Fidrmuc, Jarko and Silgoner, Maria Antoinette (2005), "On the Road: The Path of Bulgaria, Croatia and Romania to the EU and the Euro", *Europe-Asia Studies*, Vol. 57, No. 6, September, pp. 843-858.

Deutsche Bank (2005), *Key Economic Indicators (for the countries covered by the study)*, www.dbreasearch.de.

Djukanovic, Milo (2006), "Montenegro is No One's Junior Partner", *The Financial Times*, May 02, p. 13.

Economic Commission for Europe (2005a), *Economic Survey of Europe*, United Nations, New York and Geneva, No. 2.

Economic Commission for Europe (2005b), *Trends in Europe and North America 2005, The Statistical Yearbook of the Economic Commission for Europe*, United Nations, New York and Geneva, 126 pp.

Erdősi, Ferenc (2005), "A Balkán közlekedésének főbb földrajzi jellemzői" (Main geographic features of the Transportation in the Balkans), *Balkán Füzetek* (*Balkan Papers*), No. 3, Pécs, 124 pp.

Eurobarometer 62 (2004), *National Report. Executive Summary. Romania*, Autumn, 8 pp.

Eurobarometer 63.4 (2005), *National Report. Executive Summary. Bulgaria*, Spring, 8 pp.

European Bank for Reconstruction and Development (2005), *Transition Report*, London.

European Bank for Reconstruction and Development (2006a), *Transition Report update*, May, 82 pp.

European Bank for Reconstruction and Development (2006b), *Remittances as a source of finance in transition countries*, Transition Report update, May, pp. 2-8.

European Commission (2001), *Transport and Energy Infrastructure in South Eastern Europe*, Final Draft, Brussels, May 15, 25 pp.

European Commission (2002), DG Energy and Transport, *Status of the Pan-European Transport Corridors and Transport Areas. Developments and Activities in 2000 and 2001*, Final Report, Vienna, April, 17 pp.

European Commission (2003), *Regional Balkans Infrastructure Study – Transport*, Final Report, Brussels, July, 195 pp.

European Commission (2006), "Directorate General Economic and Financial Affairs", *Candidate Countries' Economies Quarterly*, January 06, 26 pp.

European Commission/World Bank (2005), *Regional Infrastructure Strategies and Projects in South East Europe. Working Table 2 of the Stability Pact*, Office for South East Europe, Sofia, May 17, 7 pp.

Falcetti, Eilsabetta, Sanfey, Peter and Taci, Anita (2003), *Bridging the Gaps? Private Sector Development, Capital Flows and the Investment Climate in South-Eastern Europe*, EBRD Working Paper No. 80, London, June, 28 pp.

Fullani, Ardian (2006), "Remittances: an Opportunity for Growth. The Albanian Migration to Italy as a Case Study", Bari, March 04 (manuscript) 4 pp.

Frattini, Franco (2005), *EU and the Western Balkans: Visa, Asylum and Immigration*, European Policy Center Conference, Brussels, November 30, Speech/05/754, 4 pp.

Gibson-Shaw, Richard (2006), "Revisiting, reevaluating and revising Balkan Free Trade Agreements", *Tirana Times*, March 10-17.

Gligorov, Vladimir (2002), *European Union Enlargement and the Balkans*, WIIW, Vienna (manuscript), 17 pp.

Gligorov, Vladimir (2005), "Balkan Transition", *European Balkan Observer*, Vol. 3, No. 2, October, pp. 10-23.

Grecic, Vladimir (2004), "Stable Population Movements as a Factor of Economic Stabilization and Integration of the Western Balkans into the European Union" (manuscript), 10 pp.

Hammermann, Felix and Schweickert, Rainer (2005), *EU Enlargement and Institutional Development: How Far Away Are the EU's Balkan and Black Sea Neighbors?*, Kiel Institute for World Economics, Kiel Working Papers, No. 1,263, November, 27 pp.

Hernádi, András (2006), *Serbia-Montenegro. Country study*, Budapest, January 9, 38 pp. (manuscript)

Holzner, Mario (2005), "Real Exchange Rate Distortions in Southeast Europe", *European Balkan Observer*, Vol. 3, No. 2, October, pp. 2-9.

Hunya, Gábor (2004), *Foreign Direct Investment in South East Europe in 2003-2004, A study commissioned by the Investment Compact for South East Europe, Stability Pact and OECD*, WIIW, Vienna, June, 36 pp.

Hunya, Gábor (2005), "Economic Assessment of Southeast Europe: Catching-Up Continues, But Accession Prospects Uncertain", *Romanian Journal of European Affairs*, Vol. 5, No. 3, October, pp. 55-73.

ICEG EC – Corvinus (2005a), *Balkán Monitor*, Budapest, No. 5.

ICEG EC – Corvinus (2005b), *SEE Monitor*, Budapest, No. 19.

ICEG European Center (2006), *Quarterly Forecast on South-Eastern Europe*, Summer, 27 pp.

Inotai, András (2005a), *The Employment Impact of FDI. The Experience of South East European Countries*. Discussion Paper. OECD Investment Compact for South East Europe, OECD, Paris, June.

Inotai, András (2005b), "Hungary as an Exporter of Capital", *The Analyst*, Vol. 1, No. 3, pp. 71-88.

Inotai, András (2005c), *A magyar tőkekivitel lehetőségei a környező országokba (Bulgária, Horvátország, Lengyelország, Románia, Szerbia-Montenegro, Szlovákia, Ukrajna). (Possibilities of Hungarian Capital Exports to the Neighbouring Countries – Bulgaria, Croatia, Poland, Romania, Serbia-Montenegro, Slovakia, Ukraine)*, Study prepared for the Ministry of Economy and Transportation, Budapest, October, 106 pp.

Inotai, András (2006), *The EU Point of View on Bulgarian and Romanian Process of Accession* (Document presented to the sixth regional meeting of T'Club, Sofia, January 31), 9 pp, http://tclub.epi-b.org.

International Monetary Fund (2005), *Direction of Trade Statistics Yearbook*, Washington D.C.

Kaminski, B. and De la Rocha, M. (2003), *Stabilization and Association Process in the Balkans. Integration Options and Their Assessment*, Washington D.C., August (Policy Research Working Paper No. 3,108.)

Kaufmann, D., Kraay, A. and Mastruzzi, M. (2005), "Governance Matters IV. Governance Indicators for 1996-2004", The World Bank, World Bank Institute, Washington D.C. Draft manuscript available via Internet www.worldbank.org/wbi/governance.

KOPINT (2005), *Konjunktúrajelentés (Report on the Economic Situation)*, Budapest, No. 3.

Jansson, Eric and MacDonald, Neil (2006), "Last fight will shape the future", *The Financial Times Supplement on Kosovo*, May 31, pp. 1-2.

Judah, Tim (2006), *The EU Must Keep Its Promise to the Western Balkans*, Centre for European Reform, London, July, 8 pp.

Kusic, Sinisa and Claudia Gruppe (2005), "Ohrfeige aus Brüssel – Kurzer Schall oder langer Schmerz? Die Verschiebung der EU-Beitrittsverhandlungen mit Kroatien", Südosteuropa, Vol. 53, No. 2, pp. 227-241.

Lakatos, Gábor (2005), *Croatia. Country study*, Budapest, December 14, 48 pp. (manuscript)

Lopandic, Dusko (2002), *Regional Initiatives in the Balkans – Autonomous Initiatives. Gutachten*, Balkan Forum, Planungsstab des Auswaertigen Amtes, Bertelsmann Stiftung, Centrum für angewandte Politikforschung, Berlin, May 13, 12 pp.

Martens, Michael (2005a), "Abschied von "Unmikistan", *Frankfurter Allgemeine Zeitung*, December 06.

Martens, Michael (2005b), "Unabhaengigkeit notfalls gegen Serbien und Russland", *Frankfurter Allgemeine Zeitung*, December 16.

Martens, Michael (2006a), "Der Praezedenzfall", *Frankfurter Allgemeine Zeitung*, May 03.

Martens, Michael (2006b), "Ein wohlfeiles Ammenmaerchen", *Frankfurter Allgemeine Zeitung*, May 29.

Martens, Michael (2006c), "Serbien und der Tag X", *Frankfurter Allgemeine Zeitung*, June 10, p. 5.

Martens, Michael (2006d), "Mladic in den Schulbüchern", *Frankfurter Allgemeine Zeitung*, February 23, p. 1.

Martens, Michael (2006e), "Der serbische Klempner", *Frankfurter Allgemeine Zeitung*, May 10.

Martens, Michael (2006f), "Für die Unabhaengigkeit, für den Aufschwung", *Frankfurter Allgemeine Zeitung*, May 19, p. 6.

Martens, Michael (2006g), "Prishtina, ein balkanischer Vorort von Utopia", *Frankfurter Allgemeine Zeitung*, June 14, p. 7.

Martens, Michael (2006h), "Wer soll es bezahlen? ", *Frankfurter Allgemeine Zeitung*, May 31, p. 10.

Martens, Michael (2006i), "Peitsche ohne Zuckerbrot", *Frankfurter Allgemeine Zeitung*, July 03.

Martens, Michael (2006j), "Balance der Machtlosigkeit", *Frankfurter Allgemeine Zeitung*, July 24.

Martens, Michael (2006k), "Kosovarische Seifenblasen", *Frankfurter Allgemeine Zeitung*, August 08, 2006, p. 5.

Michalopoulos, Constantine (2001), *The Western Balkans in World Trade. An Essay in Memoriam of Bela Balassa*, The World Bank, Washington D.C., October (draft), 23 pp.

Mintchev, Emil (2001), *South Eastern Europe at the Beginning of the 21st Century. New Dangers, New Strategies, New Perspectives*, Zentrum für Europaeische Integrationsforschung, Bonn, Discussion Paper C82. 30 pp.

Mladenova, Irena (2005), *Albania. Country study*, Sofia, December 29, 30 pp. (manuscript)

Novák, Tamás (2005), *The EU Accession Perspectives of the South East European Region*, Institute for World Economics, Budapest, July (manuscript), 79 pp.

Novák, Tamás (2006), *Romania. Country study*, Budapest, January 11, 24 pp. (manuscript)

OECD (2006), *Investment Compact Project Team Meeting*, (Rome, May 12), Official documents and handouts.

Petkova, Ivanka (2006), *Bulgaria. Country study*, Sofia, January 11, 34 pp. (manuscript)

Rehn, Olli (2006), *South East Europe in Transformation towards the European Union*, Speech/06/332, SEE Stability Pact Regional Table, Belgrade, May 30, 4 pp.

Reljic, Dusan (2003), "Reformstau in Serbien, Südosteuropa", Vol. 52, Nos. 1-3.

Reuter, Jens (2005a), "Organisierte Kriminalitaet in Südosteuropa", *Südosteuropa*, Vol. 53. No. 2, pp. 289-301.

Reuter, Jens (2005b), "Serbien und die EU – Wie weit ist der Weg nach Brüssel?", Südosteuropa, Vol. 53, No. 3, pp. 376-404.

RIINVEST (2005), "Patterns of the Foreign Aid Flows in the Post-Conflict Kosova", *European Balkan Observer*, Vol. 3, No. 3, December, pp. 2-14.

Rössler, Hans-Christian (2006), "Die grosse Wanderung", *Frankfurter Allgemeine Zeitung*, July 14, p. 5.

Schwarz, Karl-Peter (2006), "Die Balkan-Klausel", *Frankfurter Allgemeine Zeitung*, April 08, p. 1.

Spassova, Plamena (2004), *Regional Cooperation in the Balkans as an Essential Step towards EU Membership. Lessons of Visegrád*, Institute for World Economics Budapest, Working Papers No. 148, December, 28 pp.

Spassova, Plamena (2006), *Macedonia. Country study*, Sofia, January 20, 30 pp. (manuscript)

Stability Pact (2003), *Implementing Regional Transport Priorities in the Western Balkans*, A Report by the Chair of the Infrastructure Steering Group, Brussels, December 01, 14 pp.

Theofanis, Malkidis (2005), "The European Union, the Enlargement and the Southeastern Europe", *Romanian Journal of European Affairs*, Vol. 5. No. 2, pp. 51-63.

Török, Attila (2003), "Az Európai Unió és Délkelet-Európa (The European Union and Southeastern Europe)", PhD dissertation, Budapest.

Treaty establishing the Energy Community (2005), Brussels, 33 pp.

Tupy, Marian (2006), "Montenegro can seize its chance to be friendly to business", *The Financial Times*, May 27, p. 13.

UNCTAD (2005), *World Investment Report 2005. Transnational Corporations and the Internationalization of R+D*, United Nations, New York.

United Nations (2006), *International Migration and Development*, New York, May.

Van Meurs, Wim and Yannis, Alexandros (2002), *The European Union and the Balkans. From Stabilisation Process to Southeastern Enlargement. Strategy Recommendations. Bertelsmann Foundation*, Center for Applied Policy Research, Gütersloh-München, September, 30 pp.

Van Meurs, Wim and Weiss, Stefani (2005), *Qualifying (for) Sovereignty. Kosovo's Post-Status Status and the Status of EU Conditionality*, Bertelsmann Foundation, Discussion Paper. Gütersloh, December 06, 13 pp.

Vienna Institute for International Economic Studies (2005), *WIIW Database on 2005 Foreign Direct Investment in Central and Southeast Europe. Opportunities for Acquisition and Outsourcing*, Vienna, May, 87 pp.

Wiedemann, Erich, and Flottau, Renate (2006), "Absturz in die Hölle", *Der Spiegel*, No. 28, p. 99.

World Bank (2004), *Serbia-Montenegro: Republic of Serbia. An Agenda for Economic Growth and Employment. Poverty Reduction and Economic Management Unit, Europe and Central Asia Region*, Report No. 29,258-YU. Washington, D.C., December.

Further Readings

International, regional and Hungarian newspapers, journals

Informations available on the internet

Personal discussions, interviews

Unpublished materials and documents of international conferences and workshops.

College of Europe Studies

Europe is in a constant state of flux. European politics, economics, law and indeed European societies are changing rapidly. The European Union itself is in a continuous situation of adaptation. New challenges and new requirements arise continually, both internally and externally. The College of Europe Studies series exists to publish research on these issues done at the College of Europe, both at its Bruges and its Warsaw campus. Focused on the European Union and the European integration process, this research may be specialised in the areas of political science, law or economics, but much of it is of an interdisciplinary nature. The objective is to promote understanding of the issues concerned and to make a contribution to ongoing discussions.

Series Editors
Professors D. Hanf, D. Mahncke, I. Govaere and J. Pelkmans
for the College of Europe (Bruges and Warsaw)

Series Titles

No. 7 – András INOTAI, *The European Union and Southeastern Europe. Troubled Waters Ahead?*, 2007, 414 p., ISBN 978-90-5201-071-7

No. 6 – Inge GOVAERE & Hanns ULLRICH (eds.), *Intellectual Property, Public Policy and International Trade*, 2007, 234 p., ISBN 978-90-5201-064-9

No. 5 – Dominik HANF & Rodolphe MUÑOZ (dir.), *La libre circulation des personnes. États des lieux et perspectives*, 2007, 329 p., ISBN 978-90-5201-061-8

No. 3 – Dieter MAHNCKE & Jörg MONAR (eds.), *International Terrorism. A European Response to a Global Threat?*, 2006, 191 p., ISBN 978-90-5201-046-5

No. 2 – Paul DEMARET, Inge GOVAERE & Dominik HANF (eds.), *European Legal Dynamics – Revised and updated edition of* 30 Years of European Legal Studies at the College of Europe / *Dynamiques juridiques européennes – Édition revue et mise à jour de* 30 ans d'études juridiques européennes au Collège d'Europe, 2007, 571 p., ISBN 978-90-5201-067-0

No. 1 – Dieter MAHNCKE, Alicia AMBOS & Christopher REYNOLDS (eds.), *European Foreign Policy. From Rhetoric to Reality?*, 2004, 2nd printing/ 2e tirage 2006, 381 p., ISBN 978-90-5201-247-6